From Biography to History

From Biography to History

Best Books for Children's
Entertainment and Education

Edited by
Catherine Barr

Foreword by
James Cross Giblin

Contributors
Rebecca L. Thomas
Deanna McDaniel

R. R. Bowker®
New Providence, New Jersey

Published by R. R. Bowker,
a unit of Cahners Business Information
Copyright © 1998 by Reed Elsevier Inc.
All rights reserved
Printed and bound in the United States of America
Bowker® is a registered trademark of Reed Elsevier Inc.

From biography to history: best books for children's entertainment
    and education/edited by Catherine Barr.

    p. cm.
    Includes bibliographical references and indexes.
    ISBN 0-8352-4012-6
    1. Biography—Juvenile literature—Bibliography. 2. History—
Juvenile literature—Bibliography. I. Barr, Catherine, 1951-
Z5301.F76 1998
[CT104]   98-23147
016.92–dc21   CIP

ISBN 0-8352-4012-6

9 780835 240123

Contents

Foreword

by James Cross Giblin

When I was 11 and in the sixth grade, I was a voracious reader. One week it might be Eleanor Estes' family story, *The Moffats*, the next week *The Count of Monte Cristo*. And every week I looked forward to the new issues of *Time* and *Life* with their vivid accounts of the latest clashes in World War II, then in its final stages. However, I didn't often turn to an informational book—which may seem surprising, given the fact that I later became a writer of nonfiction for young people.

There were exceptions, though, and one of these stands out vividly in my memory. It was a biography of George Washington Goethals, chief engineer of the Panama Canal. I have no idea why I happened to choose the book, since I wasn't particularly interested in engineering. Maybe I had to read a biography for a book report in school, and Esther Abbott, the children's librarian at my hometown library in Ohio, recommended this book to me. However it happened, I know I was hooked from the very first page—hooked so strongly that I remembered the book all these years.

But I didn't remember the author's name. Finally, I decided to track the book down and find out who he or she was. I located a 1943 first edition in the Central Children's Room of The New York Public Library and discovered to my surprise that it was Howard Fast, the respected author of historical novels for adults as well as biographies for children. Among his best known adult titles were *Citizen Tom Paine* and *Spartacus*.

Sitting at a carrel in the library, I felt like a time traveler as I opened Fast's biography of Goethals and began to read. "The quiet, blue-eyed boy was not given to boasting. His inclination to sit and dream sometimes worried his parents and sometimes prompted other boys to poke fun at him. And then his answers, in a slow, liquid drawl, sent them into gales of laughter. There was no other drawl like that in Brooklyn."

Why had I responded so strongly to that opening as a boy of 11? Probably because, like all good writers of biography, Fast had focused on a situation with which many young readers could identify readily: the outsider who feels that his classmates don't understand him.

Reading on, I found myself caught up in the ongoing story of Goethals' life. After following George to West Point and recounting his early efforts as an engineer, Fast shifts the scene to Panama and explains the need for a canal across the isthmus. He describes the French effort to build a canal, which failed in large part because of a malaria epidemic that plagued the engineers and workers. At last France sold the rights and land for the future canal to the United States, and George Goethals was brought in to direct the vast project.

From that point, I felt I was right there on the building site with Goethals and his fellow workers. I suffered with them as they struggled against oppressive heat, yellow fever, and unexpected construction complications, and I shared in their triumph when they still managed to complete the canal ahead of schedule. All of which provides a marvelous example of the theme of this book—of how the story of one individual can lead the reader to a much broader and more informed view of history.

The boy who read and remembered Howard Fast's *Goethals and the Panama Canal* grew up to be an editor of books for children, as well as the author of juvenile histories and biographies. In the capacity of editor, I've learned to ask myself several basic questions when deciding whether I wanted to publish a particular biography. You've probably asked similar questions to your social studies classes.

First and foremost, does the author succeed in bringing the subject to life? And does he accomplish this without resorting to the sort of fictionalization that was once accepted in books like those in the Childhoods of Famous Americans series? Such books were filled with invented dialogue and made-up scenes, both of which are anathema to teachers and librarians today.

It should be pointed out, though, that there is a great difference between out-and-out fictionalization of the kind described above and the skillful use of fiction techniques to shape the story of the subject's life. For a story—a true one—lies at the heart of every well-written informational book, especially a well-written biography.

One of the most effective of these techniques is the inclusion of extracts from diaries, autobiographies, interviews, and news stories to convey the living voices of the subject and those around him. For example, when I was researching *Charles A. Lindbergh: A Human Hero*, I was delighted to find in a news story the following exchange of dialogue between a crowd of reporters and Lindbergh's mother when she visited the pilot shortly before his takeoff for Paris in 1927. Here is the passage from the book that incorporates this dialogue:

"Was your son a good boy?" one reporter asked.

"Just look at him," Mrs. Lindbergh replied.

"You had no trouble raising him?" another reporter asked.

"He raised himself," she said.

"Kiss him, so we can get a good-bye picture!" a reporter shouted.

"No," Mrs. Lindbergh said firmly. "I wouldn't mind if we were used to that," she added with a slight smile, "but we come of an undemonstrative Nordic race."

I doubt if any dialogue I might have invented would have done half as good a job of characterizing both Mrs. Lindbergh and her famous son.

Another technique many biographers use to evoke a particular scene is to weave in specific details of the actual setting. They often acquire these details by visiting the site in question. Russell Freedman made clear the value of such on-site research in his Newbery acceptance speech for *Lincoln: A Photobiography*:

"There's something magical about being able to lay your eyes on the real thing—something you can't get from your reading alone. As I sat at my desk in New York City and described Lincoln's arrival in New Salem, Illinois, at the age of 22, I could picture the scene in my mind's eye because I had walked down those same dusty lanes, where cattle still graze behind split-rail fences and geese flap about underfoot."

Lively, relevant anecdotes provide yet another means by which a biographer can add dimensions to his subject. If the anecdote injects a humorous note, so much the better. Jean Fritz is a master of this technique. For example, in her *And Then What Happened, Paul Revere?*, the reader learns that Revere was not only an ardent patriot and famous silversmith, but also a maker of false teeth. As Fritz herself has said, "I realized when I started doing research for my first biography that history wasn't what I'd been taught in school. History is full of gossip . . . I kept being surprised by the real people I met in the past. They all had their foibles and idiosyncrasies."

But the same foibles that make a subject seem human may create serious difficulties for the writer of children's biographies—particularly if they touch on controversial issues. A few decades ago, this wouldn't have presented a problem. Confronted by an anecdote, or even a basic fact, that suggested the subject had done something questionable or dishonorable, the biographer knew exactly what to do: ignore the matter because such things were not considered suitable for discussion in a children's book.

Not any more. With television beaming the dark side of every public figure and every major news event into their living rooms, there's no way that children today can be shielded from the unpleasant facts of life. Nor can writers for children ignore them in their books. But writers can strive for a balance between the positive and negative aspects that is often lacking in the mass media coverage that young people are exposed to.

This issue was brought home to me when I was writing the biography of Charles A. Lindbergh. Rarely in American history has there been such a sharp dichotomy between a person's accomplishments—in Lindbergh's case his almost incredible solo flight to Paris in 1927, along with his other contributions to aviation—and his errors, namely his flirtation with fascism in the 1930s and his open admiration of Nazi Germany.

If I'd been writing a biography for adults, I might have focused more intently on the part Lindbergh played in bringing about the appeasement of Adolf Hitler at Munich, and his subsequent speeches urging the United States to take an isolationist stand with regard to the war in Europe. But while I went into this phase of the flier's life in some detail, I decided it was my duty as a biographer for young people to offer a more even-handed interpretation. For I knew that my readers would probably have little or no prior knowledge of Lindbergh, and thus would be unable to make intelligent comparisons with other biographies.

Besides striving for balance in their portrayals, the best juvenile biographers also aim for an open-ended approach to the conclusions of their books. They realize that biography—like history itself—is an ongoing process, and new facts are constantly being discovered about even the most remote historical figures. Whether these facts concern the tomb of Alexander the Great or the personal life of John F. Kennedy, they're bound to affect the way future biographies are written. Why not help prepare the young readers of today's biographies to accept them?

Jean Fritz did an excellent job of summing up the connection between biography and history when she wrote, "As far as I am concerned, there can be no understanding of history without coming to terms with the makers and shakers, the oppressed and the oppressors, and seeing how they have been shaped by their times and in turn have shaped them."

Ralph Waldo Emerson put it even more succinctly: "There is properly no history; only biography."

So on to the pages that follow, which relate biography to history in myriad fresh and stimulating ways.

Preface

Sir Isaac Newton and gravity, Abraham Lincoln and the Civil War, Anne Frank and the Holocaust, Dr. Martin Luther King, Jr., and the civil rights movement, Boris Yeltsin and the collapse of the Soviet Union.

Many famous people are clearly connected to the events of their era. Students doing research on individuals often have an appreciation of the person's accomplishments but are less aware of the historical context. In order to fully understand the importance of achievements, students need supporting information about historical figures' eras, their childhoods and education, their professions, and the circumstances leading up to major world events during their lives.

From Biography to History: Best Books for Children's Entertainment and Education provides librarians and teachers with resources to meet this need, recommending up-to-date biographies and related books for nearly 300 men and women of historical interest to students in grades 3 to 9. The titles were selected to fit in with students' research needs and with the hope that they will find the information sufficiently entertaining to seek more details about the person and the era.

Titles included in this volume are selective, rather than inclusive. Biographies were selected using several criteria, including quality, currency, and audience. Standard selection sources were consulted, including *Best Books for Children*, 5th edition (R. R. Bowker, 1994), *Best Books for Young Adult Readers* (R. R. Bowker, 1996), *Best Books for Junior High Readers* (R. R. Bowker, 1991), and *Children's Catalog* (H. W. Wilson), as well as current reviewing sources including *School Library Journal* and *Booklist*. The contributors — both school librarians — examined potential books for inclusion and made selections based on organization, quality of writing, accessibility, special features, and interest, which are emphasized in the annotations. Related books were selected in a similar manner, focusing on issues, events, and accomplishments that would enhance understanding of the featured person.

The bibliographic information indicates whether each book is still in print. Most of the titles included were published in the 1990s. Those that are already out of print are generally available in public libraries. If a book is part of a publisher's series, this is noted at the end of the annotation.

Books have been designated for "Younger Readers," appropriate for grades 3 to 5, or "Older Readers," directed toward children in grades 6 to 9. These designations should be considered flexible, depending on the background knowledge of individual students. In some cases, a student reading a more advanced biography will appreciate the simplicity of a historical overview for a younger audience. Or a student reading an introductory biography may want the expanded presentation of a related book for an older audience. The variety of resources and levels will assist teachers and librarians in meeting the different needs of their students.

Author, title, and subject indexes expand the usefulness of *From Biography to History*. The Subject Index provides access to the accomplishments and professions of the featured individuals, linking scientists, politicians, activists, and so forth. It also connects biographees and their time periods. The Subject Index will be a useful aid in collection development.

In addition to the indexes we provide a Chronology, which makes it easy to pick out names relevant to a particular time period.

Librarians and teachers may want to share *From Biography to History* with their students, showing how it can expand opportunities for research and enjoyment. A student working on a biography report will find useful recommended selections about the individual. Related books will link the student to resources about the era, profession, or other events. For example, after reading about Elizabeth Cady Stanton, a student may want more information about voting, women's rights, and the Bill of Rights—all of which are covered in the related books for Stanton. The Subject Index then connects Elizabeth Cady Stanton to other activists, including Susan B. Anthony, Jane Addams, and Mary McLeod Bethune. It also takes the student to leaders in the women's movement—Betty Friedan and Gloria Steinem—and to leaders of other political movements, such as Cesar Chavez and Stokely Carmichael.

The Chronology will show that Harriet Beecher Stowe, Charles Dickens, and Henry David Thoreau were all close contemporaries of Elizabeth Cady Stanton, which may spur students to read about them and compare their works and beliefs.

This book would not have been possible without the work of many individuals and the availability of many excellent library resources. Deanna McDaniel used the library collections of the Shawnee Local Schools in Lima, Ohio, as well as the collection of the Lima Public Library. The staff and resources of the Logan County District Library in Bellefontaine, Ohio, were especially helpful to her. Rebecca Thomas used the library collections of the Shaker Heights (Ohio) City Schools. She is also appreciative of the people and materials at the Cleveland Heights-University Heights Public Library and the member libraries of CLEVNET. Both contributors found that the Internet library resources available through OPLIN saved them time and provided them with access to even more up-to-date resources.

We are especially grateful to Nan Hudes of R. R. Bowker for her support of this project, and to Nancy Bucenec of Bowker and the staff of Rock Hill Press for their contributions to the production of this book.

Adams, Abigail Smith (1744–1818), the wife of President John Adams, was the second First Lady of the United States, from 1797 through 1801. She painted a colorful picture of life in early Massachusetts in letters written to her husband both during and after the American Revolution.

Biographies for Younger Readers

Meeker, Clare Hodgson. *Partner in Revolution: Abigail Adams.* Illus. Benchmark Books 1998 (LB 0-7614-0523-2) 48pp.

The picture-book format of this biography makes it just right for younger readers. Photographs show the Adams home in Braintree and Peacefield along with furniture, china, portraits, and engravings of the era. Glossary, bibliography, and index. Part of the Benchmark Biographies series.

Biographies for Older Readers

Bober, Natalie S. *Abigail Adams: Witness to a Revolution.* Atheneum 1995 (cloth 0-689-31760-3) 248pp.

This book opens with a detailed chronology of the life of Abigail Adams, the wife of the second president of the United States and the mother of the sixth president. Chapters chronicle the life and era of this spirited woman and include many excerpts from her own writings. Reference notes, bibliography, and index.

Osborne, Angela. *Abigail Adams: Women's Rights Advocate.* Illus. Chelsea House 1989 (LB 1-55546-635-4) 112pp.

The emphasis in this book is on Abigail Adams as a political force behind her husband. She sought to improve the rights of women. The opening essay is entitled "Remember the Ladies" and is written by Matina S. Horner, a scholar of women's studies who has served as president of Radcliffe College. Index. Part of the American Women of Achievement series.

"Remember the Ladies. Be more generous and favorable to them than your ancestors. Do not put such unlimited power in the hands of the Husbands. If particular care and attention is not paid to the Ladies, we are determined to foment a Rebellion, and will not hold ourselves bound by any Laws in which we have no voice, or Representation."

(Osborne, p. 7)

Related Books for Younger Readers

Zeinert, Karen. *Those Remarkable Women of the American Revolution.* Illus. Millbrook Press 1996 (LB 1-56294-657-9) 96pp.

What was it like to be a woman during the Revolutionary War?
Besides meeting their regular responsibilities of managing their
homes and families, some women took an active role in the war.
Some served in the army (disguised as men), others acted as spies,
and still others met in groups to provide goods and services. Students will enjoy finding out about the differences between life now
and then and will be fascinated to find that, even then, individuals
challenged the roles expected for them. Timeline, chapter notes,
bibliography, and index.

Related Books for Older Readers

Mayo, Edith P., gen. ed. *The Smithsonian Book of the First
Ladies: Their Lives, Times and Issues.* Illus. Henry Holt 1996
(cloth 0-8050-1751-8) 352pp.

This lavish presentation describes the lives and eras of the first
ladies from Martha Washington through Hillary Rodham Clinton
(who wrote the Foreword). Throughout the book are essays about the
issues that were current for these women, such as: "Did the American Revolution Change Things for Women?" "Why Was It Hard for
Women to Get an Education?" and "How Have First Ladies Contributed to Campaigning?" The biographical sketches, although
brief, give wonderful insight into each woman's personality. This is
a fascinating look at a different perspective on the presidency. Bibliography, index, and a brief presentation of "The Smithsonian's
First Ladies Collection and the Exhibition."

Salmon, Marylynn. *The Limits of Independence: American
Women, 1760–1800.* Illus. Oxford University Press 1994 (LB 0-
19-508125-0) 144pp.

During the era of the Revolutionary War, women faced a variety of issues. Among the Iroquois, the arrival of settlers and soldiers
changed some women's responsibilities. In urban settings, women
became more involved in efforts related to the war with some even
taking part in the fighting (in disguise). This book looks at the way
changes in the political scene influenced the lives of women and
families. Chronology, detailed bibliography, and index. Part of the
Young Oxford History of Women in the United States series.

Adams, John

Adams, John (1735–1826), George Washington's vice president (1789–1797) and second president of the United States (1797–1801), was the father of John Quincy Adams. A key figure in the opposition to some of Britain's oppressive measures, he was a member of both Continental Congresses and a signer of the Declaration of Independence.

Biographies for Older Readers

Brill, Marlene Targ. *John Adams.* Illus. Children's Press 1986 (LB 0-516-01384-X) 100pp.

John Adams was considered an extremist by many of his contemporaries. Recognizing this feeling, Adams often avoided attention, leaving the limelight to others. A detailed chronology of American history is featured here with John Adams's life and accomplishments highlighted. Index. Part of the Encyclopedia of Presidents series.

Dwyer, Frank. *John Adams.* Illus. Chelsea House 1989 (o.p.)

The introductory chapters provide details about life in colonial America. John Adams was a contemporary of George Washington, Thomas Jefferson, and Benjamin Franklin. For more than a decade, he served overseas and negotiated agreements between European countries and our new country. Chronology, suggested readings, and index. Part of the World Leaders Past & Present series.

Stefoff, Rebecca. *John Adams: 2nd President of the United States.* Illus. Garrett Educational 1988 (LB 0-944483-10-0)

A chronology of John Adams's life opens this book and chapters feature his changing responsibilities. From "The Student" to "The Lawyer" to "The Patriot" to "The Ambassador," the author describes Adams's preparation to be vice president and, finally, president. Bibliography and index. Part of the Presidents of the United States series.

Related Books for Younger Readers

Young, Robert. *The Real Patriots of the American Revolution.*
Illus. Dillon Press 1997 (LB 0-87518-612-2) (cloth 0-382-39171-3)

The premise of this book (and series) is to consider alternative
points of view. Were the colonists patriots or guilty of treason? After
examining different events from the perspective of the colonists and
the Tories, the last chapter asks, "What Do You Think?" Students
could be encouraged to conduct a debate on the issues that led to the
Revolutionary War. Timeline, glossary, bibliography, and index. Part
of the Both Sides series.

Related Books for Older Readers

Hakim, Joy. *From Colonies to Country.* Illus. Oxford University
Press 1993 (LB 0-19-507749-0) (cloth 0-19-509508-1) 1993 (pap.
0-19-507750-4) 160pp.

Hakim recounts major events during the American Revolution.
Several "features" describe related topics, such as the condition of
roads and the "enlightened" ideas of Locke and Rousseau. The
detailed text is surrounded by captioned illustrations and fact boxes,
offering such information as the meaning of *magna* or an account of
a night when Benjamin Franklin and John Adams had to share a bed
at an inn. Chronology, bibliography, and index. Part of the History of
US series.

Kent, Deborah. *The American Revolution: "Give Me Liberty, or
Give Me Death!"* Illus. Enslow Publishers 1994 (LB 0-89490-521-
X) 128pp.

This is a well-done overview of the events leading up to the
American Revolution and of the country afterward. Chapter titles
include "The Shot Heard Round the World," "Taxation without Representation," "Beyond the Battlefield," "Shifting the Balance," "The
Final Act," and "Shaping the Peace." Included are some of Washington's letters to Martha Washington. Chronology, chapter notes,
and index. Part of the American War series.

The Revolutionaries. Illus. Time-Life Books 1996 (cloth 0-7835-
6256-X) 192pp.

The visually lush presentation of paintings, documents, and
artifacts is sure to appeal to students doing research or just looking
for an attractive presentation. The text describes the events of the
Revolutionary War, with inset essays on such topics as the work of a
Quaker housewife and the role of the Iroquois. An appended feature
describes what happened to key figures after the war. There is a page
of statistics of the era and a chronology of events of the war and of
politics, science, and the arts at the time. Bibliography and index.
Part of the American Story series.

Adams, John Quincy (1767–1848), the

eldest son of John and Abigail Adams, was the sixth president of the United States (from 1825 to 1829). He traveled widely as a young man and was known as a skilled diplomat. He served in the House of Representatives after his presidency, during which time he supported freedom of speech and debate on the issue of slavery.

Biographies for Younger Readers

Harness, Cheryl. *Young John Quincy.* Illus. by the author. Bradbury Press 1994 (cloth 0-02-742644-0) 48pp.

When John Quincy Adams was a boy, his father was involved in the Continental Congress. This book describes the events the young John Quincy would have experienced—encounters with soldiers and news of battles. The conversational style, colorful illustrations, and picture-book format make this a good introductory book.

Biographies for Older Readers

Greenblatt, Miriam. *John Quincy Adams: 6th President of the United States.* Illus. Garrett Educational 1990 (LB 0-944483-21-6) 128pp.

Before John Quincy Adams was president, he studied law, wrote essays defending the constitution, and served as an ambassador. After his presidency, he remained active in politics, serving as a member of the U.S. House of Representatives. Bibliography and index. Part of the Presidents of the United States series.

Kent, Zachary. *John Quincy Adams.* Illus. Children's Press 1987 (LB 0-516-01386-6) 100pp.

John Adams was often considered an extremist. His son, John Quincy Adams, was also criticized by his contemporaries, particularly for his outspoken efforts to continue debates over slavery in the House of Representatives. A timeline features events in American history and specifically during John Quincy Adams's era. Index. Part of the Encyclopedia of Presidents series.

Related Books for Younger Readers

Giblin, James Cross. *Fireworks, Picnics, and Flags: The Story of the Fourth of July Symbols.* Illus. by Ursula Arndt. Clarion 1983 (cloth 0-89919-146-0) (pap. 0-89919-174-6) 96pp.

In 1826, a celebration was organized for July 4 to mark the 50th anniversary of the Declaration of Independence. John Quincy Adams was president. Thomas Jefferson wrote a letter celebrating the 50 years since the Declaration. Sadly, he died at noon on that day. As it turned out, John Adams, John Quincy Adams's father, also died on that fourth of July. There are many fascinating anecdotes in this entertaining look at our national symbols. List of Important Events that occurred on July 4 and index.

Rubel, David. *Scholastic Encyclopedia of the Presidents and Their Times.* Illus. Scholastic 1994 (cloth 0-590-49366-3) 224pp.

During the presidency of John Quincy Adams, construction started on the Baltimore and Ohio Railroad line, many young women began to work in textile factories (earning $2.50 a week), and an antislavery newspaper, *Freedom's Journal,* was published. This book looks at each president, from Washington to Clinton, and describes events during their presidencies. List of election results and index.

Tunis, Edwin. *The Young United States, 1783 to 1830.* Illus. by the author. Crowell 1976 (LB 0-690-01065-6)

The subtitle calls this era "a time of change and growth, a time of learning democracy, a time of new ways of living, thinking, and doing," and the book captures this excitement. What was it like to live and work during the early years of our country? How did people travel? What was it like on farms, in cities, or in the wilderness? There is a wealth of information in the text accompanied by detailed illustrations. Originally published in 1969.

Related Books for Older Readers

Hakim, Joy. *The New Nation.* Illus. Oxford University Press 1993 (LB 0-19-507751-2) (cloth 0-19-509509-X) (pap. 0-19-507752-0) 160pp.

In the early years of our country, there were many challenges to the new government. Boxed sidebars with additional facts and anecdotes make for enjoyable reading, such as one describing an incident when the wife of John Quincy Adams wore rouge (a gift from the queen of Prussia). There is a feature about Alexander Hamilton and money, one on the "Star-Spangled Banner," and one on William Lloyd Garrison and the *Liberator.* Chronology, bibliography, and index. Part of the History of US series.

Addams, Jane (1860–1935), pioneer in American social reform and a leader of the women's suffrage movement, was a cofounder of Chicago's Hull House, which gave assistance to the poor. She was the author of several books, including two autobiographies, and was the recipient of the 1931 Nobel Peace Prize.

Biographies for Younger Readers

McPherson, Stephanie S. *Peace and Bread: The Story of Jane Addams.* Carolrhoda Books 1993 (LB 0-87614-792-9)

This book presents information in a clearly written text that is enhanced by numerous black-and-white photographs, including many of Jane Addams, her family, and the harsh conditions Addams worked to improve. Growing up in Cedarville, Illinois, Jane Addams experienced difficult times, yet her childhood was basically comfortable. On a trip to London, she observed poverty and destitution and became interested in helping the less fortunate. Index.

Simon, Charnan. *Jane Addams: Pioneer Social Worker.* Illus. Children's Press 1997 (LB 0-516-20391-6)

A wonderful book for students beginning research. The six brief chapters chronicle Jane Addams's life, emphasizing her efforts to improve the conditions for the immigrants in Chicago. Boxed sections address such issues as immigration and child labor. There is a section suggesting activities for students to do in their own communities. Index and list of resources, including addresses and online sites for community service organizations. Part of the Community Builders series.

Biographies for Older Readers

Kittredge, Mary. *Jane Addams: Social Worker.* Chelsea House (LB 1-55546-636-2)

This is a thorough and well-organized book. It describes her efforts to challenge social conventions—attending college during a time (the late 1800s) when few women had that opportunity. She later devoted her life to working to help the poor and change the atti-

"I am quite sure that women in politics thus far have been too conventional, too afraid to differ with the men, too unused to trust their own judgment, too skeptical of the wisdom of the humble to release the concern of simple women into ordering of political life, too inclined to narrow their historic perspective to experience the formal women's movement."

(Mitchard, p. 42)

tudes and treatment of the less fortunate. Students doing research will find this useful and informative. Chronology, bibliography, and index. Part of the American Women of Achievement series.

Mitchard, Jacquelyn. *Jane Addams: Pioneer in Social Reform and Activist for World Peace.* Illus. Gareth Stevens 1991 (LB 0-8368-0144-X)

Jane Addams founded Hull House, one of the first settlement houses for the poor in Chicago. Her pioneering spirit also led her to be involved in the Women's International League for Peace and Freedom. Chronology, glossary, and index. Part of the People Who Have Helped the World series.

Related Books for Younger Readers

Freedman, Russell. *Immigrant Kids.* Puffin 1995 (pap. 0-14-037594-5) 80pp.

The children of immigrants often worked long hours in factories and doing neighborhood jobs such as selling papers or making deliveries. This book describes their journey to America and their time at home, school, work, and play. Index. First published in 1980.

Leuzzi, Linda. *Urban Life.* Illus. Chelsea House 1995 (LB 0-7910-2841-0) 104pp.

One hundred years ago, urban life in America was very different. This was a time of growing industrialization. Cities became overcrowded; many people (including large numbers of immigrants) were looking for work; families often shared cramped tenements. Jane Addams is featured in this book for her work to improve miserable living conditions. Bibliography and index. Part of the Life in America 100 Years Ago series.

Related Books for Older Readers

Hakim, Joy. *An Age of Extremes.* Illus. Oxford University Press 1994 (LB 0-19-507759-8) (cloth 0-19-509513-8) (pap. 0-19-507760-1) 160pp.

The focus of this book is the end of the 19th century and the opening decades of the 20th century. Key figures from the early years include Andrew Carnegie, John D. Rockefeller, and J. P. Morgan, who became very wealthy in industry. Later years feature the conditions for workers, the rise of organized labor, and Jane Addams's efforts to reach out to the needy. The many illustrations and sidebars add to the interest of the presentation. Part of the History of US series.

Smith, Karen Manners. *New Paths to Power: American Women, 1890–1920.* Illus. Oxford University Press 1994 (LB 0-19-508111-0) 144pp.

The efforts of women in this era to change expectations about their role in society are the focus of this book. Chapters look at women at home, at work, in public life, in rebellion, and in war and peace. Women featured in this volume include Jane Addams (and Hull House) and Ida B. Wells (known in some books as Ida B. Wells-Barnett). Chronology, list of further readings, and index. Part of the Young Oxford History of Women in the United States series.

Alcott, Louisa May (1832–1888), an American writer, counted Emerson and Thoreau among her tutors and friends. She achieved recognition with *Hospital Sketches* (1863), which consisted of letters she wrote as a Civil War nurse, and went on to become famous with *Little Women* (1868–1869), a novel for and about young people.

Biographies for Younger Readers

Ryan, Cary, ed. *Louisa May Alcott: Her Girlhood Diary.* Illus. by Mark Graham. BridgeWater Books 1995 (pap. 0-8167-3139-X) 56pp.

Excerpts from Louisa May Alcott's diary capture her exuberant spirit and provide insight into her writing. Diary entries are expanded by descriptions of Alcott's experiences and era. Chronology, bibliography, and index.

Biographies for Older Readers

Greene, Carol. *Louisa May Alcott: Author, Nurse, Suffragette.* Illus. Children's Press 1984 (o.p.) 112pp.

Louisa May Alcott's best-known book, *Little Women*, was based on her own upbringing. This biography links her life to her writing and also tells of her other adult activities as a Civil War nurse and an advocate for women's rights. List of important dates and events, bibliography, and index. Part of the People of Distinction series.

Johnston, Norma. *Louisa May: The World and Works of Louisa May Alcott.* Illus. Simon & Schuster 1995 (pap. 0-688-12696-0) 256pp.

The narrative presentation of this very thorough biography reads like a novel. Louisa May Alcott was brought up in a home filled with the inventive ideas of her father, Bronson Alcott. She was encouraged to take risks but also saw the practical need to provide her family with an income. The annotated bibliography and extensive index make this useful for research.

Meigs, Cornelia. *Invincible Louisa.* Illus. Little, Brown 1968 (cloth 0-316-56590-3)

Winner of the 1934 Newbery Medal, this book is still a fine choice for learning about the author of *Little Women.* Included are black-and-white photographs of people and places—including Alcott's room at Orchard House and her sisters who were the models for the March sisters. Alcott's childhood experiences are clearly connected to her novels. Index.

Related Books for Younger Readers

Anderson, Gretchen, comp. *The Louisa May Alcott Cookbook.* Illus. by Karen Milone. Little, Brown 1985 (LB 0-316-03951-9)

Excerpts from *Little Women* and *Little Men* introduce recipes for foods mentioned in these books. There is a brief introduction giving information about Alcott's life and times. Many students would enjoy this book and become more involved in Alcott's novels. Bibliography and index.

Toynton, Evelyn. *Growing Up in America, 1830–1860.* Illus. Millbrook Press 1995 (LB 1-56294-453-3) 96pp.

What was it like to be a child during this time period? Read first about different regions and peoples: "Children in New England," "Children on the Plains," "Children of the Sioux," "Children on the Streets," and "Children in Bondage." Then the focus shifts to different activities: school, play, work, and reading. Children often worked—chopping trees, peeling apples, plowing; sometimes they were sold away from their families. Bibliography and index.

Related Books for Older Readers

Biel, Timothy Levi. *Life in the North During the Civil War.* Illus. Lucent 1997 (LB 1-56006-334-3) 112pp.

Those who were not part of the fighting still felt the impact of the Civil War. This book looks at army camps, rural life, urban life, and the war's impact on economics and politics. Chapter notes, two bibliographies (further reading and works consulted), and index. Part of the Way People Live series.

Alexander the Great (356 B.C.–323 B.C.), conqueror of the Persian Empire; succeeded his father, Philip II, as king of Macedon. Tutored as a youth by Aristotle, Alexander led campaigns against the Persians that earned him high marks as a military strategist.

Biographies for Younger Readers

Green, Robert. *Alexander the Great.* Illus. Franklin Watts 1996 (LB 0-531-20230-5) (pap. 0-531-15799-7) 64pp.

With short chapters divided by subheadings, this book provides clear, accessible information for research projects. Illustrations, often of sculpture or paintings, portray such dramatic events as the death of Philip II and the battle of Granicus. Timeline, list of additional readings, and index. Part of the Ancient Biography First Books series.

Biographies for Older Readers

Ash, Maureen. *Alexander the Great.* Illus. Children's Press 1991 (o.p.) 128pp.

From his childhood as crown prince to Philip II, king of Macedon, through his accomplishments as a soldier, ruler, and explorer, this thorough biography describes Alexander the Great. Illustrations include color photographs of the region today and of art and artifacts as well as maps and engravings. Timeline, glossary, bibliography, and index. Part of the World's Great Explorers series.

Wepman, Dennis. *Alexander the Great.* Illus. Chelsea House 1986 (LB 0-87754-594-4) 112pp.

This detailed biography makes excellent use of illustrations including engravings and black-and-white photographs of artifacts and statues. The accomplishments of Alexander the Great are described within the context of his vision of a unified empire. Chronology, bibliography, and index. Part of the World Leaders Past & Present series.

Related Books for Younger Readers

Dineen, Jacqueline. *The Greeks.* Illus. New Discovery Books 1991 (cloth 0-02-730650-X) 64pp.

Students will find background information in this colorful overview of the ancient Greek civilization. Presented in double-page spreads with many illustrations, the text offers information about everyday life (home, school, cooking, medicine) and politics (government, soldiers, Alexander the Great). Timeline, glossary, and index. Part of the Worlds of the Past series.

Pearson, Anne. *Ancient Greece.* Illus. Knopf 1992 (LB 0-679-91682-2) (cloth 0-679-81682-8) 64pp.

Titles in this series are a popular choice for students who like to browse for information. The format is appealing, especially the use of captioned illustrations surrounding the brief text. Art, architecture, politics, home life, work, and war are among the topics presented. Timeline and index. Part of the Eyewitness Books series.

Related Books for Older Readers

Nardo, Don. *Ancient Greece.* Illus. Lucent 1994 (LB 1-56006-229-0) 112pp.

Chapters examine "The Rise of City-States," "West Versus East: The Greek and Persian Wars," "Greek Versus Greek: The Peloponnesian War," and "Alexander's Conquests." Boxed sidebars provide such additional insights as a historian's account of a speech by Alexander the Great. Timeline, chapter notes, bibliographies (further reading and works consulted) and index. Part of the World History series.

Ali, Muhammad (1942–), an African American boxer and Olympic gold medal winner, was born Cassius Marcellus Clay, Jr. He changed his name when he became a Black Muslim. Ali won the heavyweight crown in 1964 but was stripped of it for his refusal to enter the military on religious grounds. The crown was later restored after a Supreme Court appeal and his defeat of George Foreman.

Biographies for Younger Readers

Lipsyte, Robert. *Free to Be Muhammad Ali.* HarperCollins 1978 (LB 0-06-023902-6)

Lipsyte, who has been a sports columnist for the *New York Times* and has written for *Sports Illustrated*, based this biography on his many interviews with and observations of Ali. Beginning with his triumph at the 1960 Olympics (as Cassius Clay), this book chronicles Ali's life through his fight with Leon Spinks in 1978. Index.

Sanford, William R., and Carl R. Green. *Muhammad Ali.* Illus. Crestwood House 1993 (LB 0-89686-739-0) 48pp.

This brief biography begins with a vignette of Ali's childhood in Louisville, Kentucky. After filing a report about his stolen bicycle, the policeman who took the report urged young Cassius Clay to begin training at a local boxing gym. Ali's successes made him a world-renowned figure. There are many black-and-white photographs and a trivia quiz (ten questions) spaced throughout the book. Index. Part of the Sports Immortals series.

Biographies for Older Readers

Conklin, Thomas. *Muhammad Ali: The Fight for Respect.* Illus. Millbrook Press 1992 (LB 1-56294-112-7) (pap. 1-56294-832-6) 104pp.

One of Ali's most famous moments did not take place in the boxing ring. It was when he refused to be inducted into the U.S. armed services. This book opens with that decision and examines the political, social, and religious issues that brought Ali to that point. Black-and-white photographs, chronology, source notes, bibliography, and index.

Diamond, Arthur. *Importance of Muhammad Ali.* Illus. Lucent 1995 (LB 1-56006-060-3) 112pp.

Opening with the list "Important Dates in the Life of Muhammad Ali," the text then offers a thorough biography of this famous fighter. Boxed inserts provide vignettes from other sources, for example, a *Sports Illustrated* article about Ali's boasting and comments from basketball star Bill Russell on Ali's refusal to go into the armed forces. Source notes for quotes, annotated bibliography, and index. Part of the Importance Of series.

Related Books for Younger Readers

Hills, Ken. *1960s.* Illus. Raintree Steck-Vaughn 1992 (LB 0-8114-3079-0) 47pp.

Students who do not have a clear understanding of the sequence of events in the 1960s will find this book very useful. Presented in chronological order are the civil rights movement (including the boxing and politics of Muhammad Ali); the deaths of John F. Kennedy, Robert Kennedy, and Dr. Martin Luther King; and the first moon landing. Conflicts in the Middle East, Vietnam, and Czechoslovakia are discussed. The format simulates a newspaper with headlines, columns, and supporting pictures, making an attractive overview. Glossary, bibliography, and index. Part of the Take Ten Years series.

Littlefield, Bill. *Champions: Stories of Ten Remarkable Athletes.* Illus. with paintings by Bernie Fuchs. Little, Brown 1993 (LB 0-316-52805-6) 144pp.

What does it take to be a champion? The ten successful athletes featured here are Satchel Paige, Julie Krone, Pelé, Joan Benoit Samuelson, Nate Archibald, Susan Butcher, Muhammad Ali, Billie Jean King, Diana Golden, and Roberto Clemente. Bibliography and index.

Rediger, Pat. *Great African Americans in Sports.* Illus. Crabtree 1996 (LB 0-86505-801-6) (pap. 0-86505-815-6) 64pp.

Seven athletes are presented in longer profiles and six others receive brief coverage. The training and achievements of Muhammad Ali, Arthur Ashe, Earvin Johnson, Michael Jordan, Jackie Joyner-Kersee, Carl Lewis, and Willie Mays are described with a focus on their efforts to overcome obstacles. The many color photographs and boxed facts and accomplishments are attractive and add interest for students. Part of the Outstanding African Americans series.

Related Books for Older Readers

Schulman, Arlene. *The Prizefighters: An Intimate Look at Champions and Contenders.* Illus. with photographs by the author. Lyons & Burford 1994 (cloth 1-55821-309-0) 176pp.

For more than ten years, Arlene Schulman photographed boxers. She visited gyms, observing fighters as they trained and sparred. She attended fights, meeting with the contenders, promoters, managers, and trainers. Champions past and present are profiled here along with many unknown fighters. In his introduction, boxing authority Budd Schulberg writes, "If you were scoring this book like a prizefight, you'd have to give Arlene Schulman every round." Index.

Weisbrot, Robert. *Marching Toward Freedom: From the Founding of the Southern Christian Leadership Conference to the*

Assassination of Malcolm X, 1957–1965. Illus. Chelsea House 1994 (pap. 0-7910-2256-0)

During the era presented in this book, black political and social activism grew and spread: Sit-ins, boycotts, the formation of organized groups such as the Southern Christian Leadership Conference, and the 1963 March on Washington. Cassius Clay (later Muhammad Ali) won a gold medal in the Olympics only to be refused service in a restaurant back home. This book concludes with the Watts riots and the death of Malcolm X. Chronology, bibliography and index. Part of the Milestones in Black American History series.

Amundsen, Roald (1872–1928), a Norwegian explorer, in 1911 became the first person to reach the South Pole. Earlier he was the commander of the first single ship to transit the Northwest Passage.

Biographies for Younger Readers

Langley, Andrew. *The Great Polar Adventure: The Journeys of Roald Amundsen.* Illus. by Kevin Barnes. Chelsea House 1994 (LB 0-7910-2820-8) 32pp.

The biographical information in this book is extended with boxed sections that ask "Did You Know?" Within the boxes is additional information about other explorers, arctic animals, the aurora borealis, crevasses, glaciers, and blizzards. The effect is very attractive. Glossary and index. Part of the Great Explorers series.

Biographies for Older Readers

Sipiera, Paul P. *Roald Amundsen and Robert Scott.* Illus. Children's Press 1990 (o.p.)

The first part of this book is devoted to Roald Amundsen, the next part to Robert Scott. The final chapters look at how their lives intertwined in their competition to reach the South Pole. In one of the appendices, there is a list of the daily rations for the men on the polar exploration. Timeline, glossary, bibliography, and index. Part of the World's Great Explorers series.

Daily rations for Amundsen's men: Biscuits (14 ounces); Dried milk (2.6 ounces); Chocolate (4.4 ounces); Pemmican (13 ounces); Total—about 2 pounds, 2 ounces; Total calories—4,560 per day
(Sipiera, p. 119)

Related Books for Younger Readers

Mason, Antony. *Peary and Amundsen: Race to the Poles.* Illus.
Raintree Steck-Vaughn 1995 (LB 0-8114-3977-1) 48pp.

Detailed information about polar expeditions is provided in
this well-illustrated book. The section "The Historical Background"
describes early expeditions, and later chapters look at the exploration of the North and South Poles. Robert Peary, Roald Amundsen,
and Robert Scott are among the explorers featured. List of further
readings, glossary, and index. Part of the Beyond the Horizons
series.

Ryan, Peter. *Explorers and Mapmakers.* Illus. by Christine Molan
and with photographs. Lodestar Books 1989 (o.p.) 48pp.

Early world travelers made maps to find their way back home
and to lead others. This book describes the journeys of explorers
including Columbus, Marco Polo, James Cook, and Roald Amundsen. Among the illustrations are artifacts of early maps and
sketches. Part of the Time Detectives series.

Sandak, Cass R. *The Arctic and Antarctic.* Illus. Franklin Watts
1987 (LB 0-531-10137-1)

Double-page spreads provide information about the exploration of these two polar regions. Chapters include "Peary and
After," "Racing South," and "An Antarctic Station." Students who
use this book will find general information about the conditions in
polar regions and brief mention of the accomplishments of explorers
such as Peary, Henson, and Amundsen. Timeline, glossary, and
index. Part of the New Frontiers Exploration in the 20th Century
series.

Related Books for Older Readers

Scheller, William. *The World's Great Explorers.* Illus. Oliver
Press 1992 (LB 1-881508-03-X) 160pp.

What does it take to be an explorer? After reading about the
exploits of the 12 explorers featured here, students will have an
understanding of the spirit, energy, and commitment that is needed.
Among those included are Muhammad ibn-Batuta, James Cook,
John Frémont, and Roald Amundsen. Chronology, bibliography, and
index. Part of the Profiles series.

A nderson, Marian (1897–1993) in 1955
was the first African American soloist to perform at
New York's Metropolitan Opera House. The famous
contralto had earlier been denied the right to
perform at a Daughters of the American Revolution
function in Washington, D.C., and sang instead to a
huge crowd on the steps of the Lincoln Memorial.

Marian, with Kosti at the piano, performed for 75,000 people at the Easter Sunday [1939] concert. Millions of listeners across America heard her on the radio.
(Ferris, p . 72)

Biographies for Younger Readers

McKissack, Patricia, and Fredrick McKissack. *Marian Anderson: A Great Singer.* Illus. with drawings by Ned Ostendorf and with photographs. Enslow Publishers 1991 (LB 0-89490-303-9) 32pp.

When Marian Anderson was a child in Philadelphia, she sang in the church choir. As she grew older, she studied music and practiced, becoming known around the world for her beautiful voice. She sang at the White House for President and Mrs. Franklin D. Roosevelt and later sang at the March on Washington in 1963. Index. Part of the Great African Americans series.

Biographies for Older Readers

Ferris, Jeri. *What I Had Was Singing: The Story of Marian Anderson.* Illus. Carolrhoda Books 1994 (LB 0-87614-818-6); First Avenue Editions (pap. 0-87614-634-5) 96pp.

As an African American growing up at the turn of the century, Marian Anderson faced discrimination. Despite the difficulties, she triumphed, using her wonderful voice to reach out to others. In the 1930s, when she was denied an opportunity to sing by the Daughters of the American Revolution, she was supported by Eleanor Roosevelt, who resigned from the DAR. This readable biography is enhanced by many photographs of Anderson and events of the era. Bibliography and index. Part of the Trailblazers Biographies series.

Related Books for Younger Readers

Medearis, Angela Shelf. *Come This Far to Freedom: A History of African Americans.* Illus. by Terea D. Shaffer. Atheneum 1993 (o.p.) 160pp.

Although the coverage is very brief, this book could be used to introduce students to the sequence of events in African American history. "From Homeland to Hardship," "Fighting for Freedom," "A Fresh Start," "A Movement for Equality," and "Breaking Down the Barriers" are the chapters in this book. The accomplishments of abolitionists, artists, scientists, singers, civil rights leaders, lawyers, soldiers, and others are briefly discussed. List of important dates, bibliography, and index.

Related Books for Older Readers

Haskins, Jim. *Black Music in America: A History Through Its People.* Illus. Crowell 1987 (cloth 0-690-04460-7) 80pp.

This book looks at the contributions of a variety of black artists including Marian Anderson, Louis Armstrong, Duke Ellington, Scott Joplin, Bessie Smith, and Stevie Wonder. "Early Slave Music," "Ragtime and the Blues," "Jazz," "Rhythm, Blues, and Arias," and "New Directions" are some of the topics covered. The wide range of material and eras makes this a good choice for background information for students. Bibliography and index.

Trotter, Joe William, Jr. *From a Raw Deal to a New Deal? African Americans, 1929–1945.* Illus. Oxford University Press 1996 (LB 0-19-508771-2) 128pp.

The Great Depression had a profound impact on all Americans, particularly African Americans. In the South, the collapse of the rural economy and the rise of the Ku Klux Klan created conditions of hardship and horror. In the North, there was widespread black unemployment and discrimination. Roosevelt's New Deal (which included the input of many black leaders), political diversity (including black participation in the Communist Party), and the influence of World War II are presented. Chronology, bibliography, and index. Part of the Young Oxford History of African Americans series.

Angelou, Maya (1928–), an African American author and activist, is well known for her autobiography *I Know Why the Caged Bird Sings.* Also a noted poet, she read "On the Pulse of Morning" at the inauguration of President Clinton.

"I speak to the black experience, but I am always talking about the human condition, about what we can endure, dream, fail, and still survive." (Pettit, p. 56, citing Jeffrey M. Elliot's *Conversations with Maya Angelou* [Jackson: University Press of Mississippi 1989])

Biographies for Older Readers

King, Sarah E. *Maya Angelou: Greeting the Morning.* Illus. Millbrook Press 1994 (LB 1-56294-431-2) (pap. 1-56294-725-7) 48pp.

Born in St. Louis, Missouri, Maya Angelou spent much of her childhood with her grandmother in Stamps, Arkansas. During a brief time with her mother in St. Louis, Angelou was abused—an event she struggled to deal with in her life and through her writing. Related readings, chronology, and index. Part of the Gateway Biographies series.

Lisandrelli, Elaine Silvinski. *Maya Angelou: More Than a Poet.* Illus. Enslow Publishers 1996 (LB 0-89490-684-4) 128pp.

Lisandrelli enhances this biography with quotations and clear source notes. She carefully connects events in Maya Angelou's life to her writing. Chronology, bibliography of books, audios, and videos, and index. Part of the African American Biographies series.

Pettit, Jayne. *Maya Angelou: Journey of the Heart.* Illus. Lodestar/Dutton 1996 (pap. 0-525-67518-3) 64pp.

This book opens with a description of Maya Angelou reading her inaugural poem, "On the Pulse of Morning," in January 1993. It was a triumphant moment for a woman who had known hardship, violence, discrimination, and injustice. Quotations from published interviews and from Angelou's books extend the descriptions. Chronology, endnotes, bibliography, and index. Part of the Rainbow Biography series.

Shapiro, Miles. *Maya Angelou: Author.* Illus. Chelsea House 1994 (LB 0-7910-1862-8) (pap. 0-7910-1891-1) 112pp.

Maya Angelou's life along with the different places she lived and how each influenced her development are fully examined. Abundant quotations are used throughout. Chronology, bibliography, and index. Part of the Black Americans of Achievement series.

Related Books for Younger Readers

Rediger, Pat. *Great African Americans in Literature.* Illus. Crabtree 1996 (LB 0-86505-802-4) (pap. 0-86505-816-4) 64pp.

Seven authors are featured in detailed portraits and six others are briefly featured. Included in the longer articles are Maya Angelou, James Baldwin, Ralph Ellison, Alex Haley, Zora Neale Hurston, Toni Morrison, and Alice Walker. For each author, there is information about growing up, overcoming obstacles, and special interests. The numerous photographs add to the appeal. Index. Part of the Outstanding African Americans series.

Related Books for Older Readers

Hakim, Joy. *All the People.* Illus. Oxford University Press 1995 (LB 0-19-507763-6) (cloth 0-19-509515-4) (pap. 0-19-507764-4) 160pp.

This is a great book for browsing through the second half of the 20th century. There is information on the iron curtain, Vietnam, the moon landing, and the end of the cold war. Both the civil rights movement and the women's rights movements are profiled and issues concerning Native Americans, farm workers, and immigrants are discussed. Chronology, bibliography, and index. Part of History of US series.

Trotter, Joe William, Jr. *From a Raw Deal to a New Deal? African Americans, 1929–1945.* Illus. Oxford University Press 1996 (LB 0-19-508771-2) 128pp.

Maya Angelou grew up during the Depression and her memories of this era are vividly portrayed in her work. This book presents the impact of this time of hardship on both the North and the South, with special focus on African Americans. There is also information on discrimination and political diversity. Chronology, bibliography, and index. Part of the Young Oxford History of African Americans series.

A̲nthony, Susan B. (1820–1906), an American women's rights leader, organized the Daughters of Temperance, which was the first U.S. temperance movement. She was instrumental in having laws passed in New York that gave women a say about their children and property. She was president of the National American Woman Suffrage Association (1881–1886).

Biographies for Younger Readers

Klingel, Cindy. *Susan B. Anthony: Crusader for Women's Rights (1820–1906).* Illus. by John Keely and Dick Brude. Creative Education 1987 (o.p.) 32pp.

Because her family followed the Quaker religion, which encouraged equal opportunities for education, Susan B. Anthony was allowed to attend school. Later, when she spoke out for temperance and women's rights, people were inspired by her eloquence. Part of the We the People series.

Biographies for Older Readers

Kendall, Martha E. *Susan B. Anthony: Voice for Women's Voting Rights.* Illus. Enslow Publishers 1997 (LB 0-89490-780-8) 128pp.

Susan B. Anthony is portrayed as an intelligent and courageous woman in this carefully researched book. In addition to voting rights for women, she was involved in such issues as equal educational opportunities for boys and girls, the antislavery movement, and property rights for women. Chronology, source notes, glossary, bibliography, and index. Part of the Historical American Biographies series.

Weisberg, Barbara. *Susan B. Anthony.* Illus. Chelsea House 1988 (cloth 1-55546-639-7)

This is a thorough biography that will be a good choice for any student doing research. It is well organized, making excellent use of quotations and photographs to extend the text. Susan B. Anthony's crusading spirit—against slavery and for temperance and equal rights, especially for women—is well portrayed. She was a tireless worker on behalf of those who were disenfranchised. Chronology, bibliography, and index. Part of the American Women of Achievement series.

Related Books for Younger Readers

Blumberg, Rhoda. *Bloomers!* Illus. by Mary Morgan. Bradbury Press 1993 (LB 0-02-711684-0); Aladdin 1996 (pap. 0-689-80455-5) 32pp.

The women's movement was led by the pioneering actions of Amelia Bloomer, Susan B. Anthony, and Elizabeth Cady Stanton. One of the early efforts of these women was to challenge the way women dressed. They stopped wearing the restricting corsets and heavy skirts and petticoats and began wearing loose-fitting trousers that came to be called "bloomers." This entertaining story could be a fun way to introduce this era.

Pascoe, Elaine. *The Right to Vote.* Illus. Millbrook Press 1997 (LB 0-7613-0066-X) 48pp.

While parts of this book look at contemporary issues such as the rights and responsibilities of citizens, there is information about the historical context of voting in America. There is information about voting in Colonial America and the fight for the rights of women and African Americans. There is an appendix on "Understanding the Bill of Rights." Glossary, bibliography, and index. Part of the Land of the Free series.

Related Books for Older Readers

Corbin, Carole Lynn. *The Right to Vote.* Illus. Franklin Watts 1985 (LB 0-531-04932-9)

One of the issues of the Revolutionary War was the right to vote on taxation. But that issue related only to men. It took many years, and the efforts of many people, to win voting rights for women and for other disenfranchised groups including blacks. Bibliography and index. Part of the Issues in American History series.

Sigerman, Harriet. *An Unfinished Battle: American Women, 1848–1865.* Illus. Oxford University Press 1994 (LB 0-19-508110-2) 144pp.

Women's rights and employment and their role in the Civil War are profiled. Key figures include Susan B. Anthony, Clara Barton, Elizabeth Cady Stanton, and Sojourner Truth. Chronology, bibliography, and index. Part of the Young Oxford History of Women in the United States series.

Appleseed, Johnny (1774–1845), gained fame for his propagation of apple trees through much of the American Midwest. Born John Chapman in north central Massachusetts, he left home in the early 1800s, moving southwest into Pennsylvania where he armed himself with apple seeds collected from a cider press. Heading west from Pennsylvania, he planted the seeds along the way as he traveled.

Biographies for Younger Readers

Aliki. *The Story of Johnny Appleseed.* Illus. by the author. Simon & Schuster 1971 (pap. 0-671-66746-7) 32pp.

This picture-book biography is a very readable introduction to the life of John Chapman. His love of nature and his willingness to help settlers, farmers, and native peoples are described in this brief book.

Kellogg, Steven, retel. *Johnny Appleseed: A Tall Tale.* Illus. by the author. William Morrow & Co. 1988 (LB 0-688-06418-3) (cloth 0-688-06417-5) 48pp.

Like Kellogg's other adaptations of tall tales, this one emphasizes the exaggerated exploits of John Chapman. Clearing land, planting apple trees, and helping settle the Ohio Valley are featured in this picture-book biography.

Lawlor, Laurie. *The Real Johnny Appleseed.* Illus. by Mary Thompson. Albert Whitman 1995 (LB 0-8075-6909-7) 63pp.

John Chapman was born at about the time that the Revolutionary War began. He grew up with the country. As the territory of America expanded, he began to travel into wilderness regions. Using the free seeds from the cider mills in eastern Pennsylvania, he began growing seedlings and selling them to settlers. This is a more detailed biography of John Chapman with an excellent bibliography and index.

Lindberg, Reeve. *Johnny Appleseed: A Poem.* Illus. by Kathy Jakobsen. Little, Brown 1990 (cloth 0-316-52618-5)

Written in verse, this biography is illustrated with folk art paintings that add details to the brief text. Endpapers show a map of the states visited by John Chapman, and there is a page of biographical text following the poem.

Related Books for Younger Readers

Perl, Lila. *Slumps, Grunts, and Snickerdoodles: What Colonial America Ate and Why.* Illus. by Richard Cuffari. Clarion 1975 (cloth 0-395-28923-8) 128pp.

During colonial times in New England, many colonists found the wild fruits too acidic and tart. They had apple trees sent from England and, as these matured, they began to expand their orchards. (Johnny Appleseed helped with this process.) Desserts with apples were very popular, and several are included here along with other favorite foods from the colonies and historical information about the region. Index.

Sherrow, Victoria. *Huskings, Quiltings, and Barn Raisings: Work-Play Parties in Early America.* Illus. by Laura LoTurco. Walker and Company 1992 (LB 0-8027-8188-8) (cloth 0-8027-8186-1) 78pp.

In the early days of America, neighboring colonists often got together to share work. Sometimes, the task was large, requiring many helpers. Other times, sharing the task provided camaraderie and entertainment. The harvest was an especially good time for shared work—husking corn, cooking apples, and collecting maple sugar. Bibliography and index.

Archimedes (287 B.C.–212 B.C.), a Greek mathematician and inventor, was the author of landmark works on geometry, arithmetic, and mechanics. He was a man of vision and practicality. He defined mathematical principles, worked out the laws of water displacement, and invented both new tools (the compound pulley and hydraulic screw) and new uses for old tools.

Biographies for Younger Readers

Lafferty, Peter. *Archimedes.* Illus. Franklin Watts 1991 (o.p.) 48pp.

Chapter 1 features "Archimedes' World," and the following chapters look at his contributions to mechanics and mathematics. The user-friendly format of this book includes colorful illustrations and boxed sections describing scientific principles. Chart of important dates, suggested readings, glossary, and index. Part of the Pioneers of Science series.

Biographies for Older Readers

Ipsen, D. C. *Archimedes: Greatest Scientist of the Ancient World.* Illus. Enslow Publishers 1988 (o.p.) 64pp.

The mathematical relations, physical laws, and mechanical equipment discovered by Archimedes are examined in detail. From simple machines, such as the water screw and the block and tackle, to the value of pi and the area of a circle, many basic principles were applied by this great scientist. Bibliography and index.

Related Books for Younger Readers

Endacott, Geoff. *Discovery and Inventions.* Illus. Viking Penguin 1991 (o.p.)

This colorful presentation has a brief text surrounded by captioned photographs and drawings. Many achievements are depicted—from Archimedes's theories about volume and levers and Leonardo da Vinci's work on flight and the body to nuclear power, lasers, and computers. After reading this overview, students will want to connect to more detailed books. Bibliography and index. Part of the Strange & Amazing Worlds series.

Pearson, Anne. *What Do We Know About the Greeks?* Illus. Peter Bedrick Books 1992 (LB 0-87226-356-8) 40pp.

Chapters pose questions: "Who Were the Greeks?" "What Did the Greeks Wear?" and "Were the Greeks Scientists?" Many colorful illustrations surround the text, adding interest and information. Timeline, glossary, and index. Part of the What Do We Know About? series.

Related Books for Older Readers

Baker, Rosalie F., and Charles F. Baker, III. *Ancient Greeks: Creating the Classical Tradition.* Illus. Oxford University Press 1997 (LB 0-19-509940-0) 280pp.

Arranged in chronological order, this book profiles the accomplishments of more than 30 Greek scientists, philosophers, military leaders, writers, and artists. Among those included are Homer, Aesop, Euripides, Socrates, Alexander the Great, Ptolemy I, and

Archimedes. There is a bibliography for each person profiled as well as a general bibliography for the book. Timeline, glossary, and index. Part of the Oxford Profiles series.

Armstrong, (Daniel) Louis "Satchmo" (1900–1971), was one of the most influential figures in the development and popularization of jazz. A cornet player, bandleader, and singer, his career spanned almost his entire life.

Biographies for Younger Readers

McKissack, Patricia, and Fredrick McKissack. *Louis Armstrong: Jazz Musician.* Illus. by Ned Ostendorf and with photographs. Enslow Publishers 1991 (LB 0-89490-307-1) 32pp.

This is a very simple biography that could be used to help young children do research. The chapters feature key events in Armstrong's life and include highlighted vocabulary words that are defined in the "Words to Know" section. In addition to black-and-white illustrations, photographs add to its appeal. Index. Part of the Great African Americans series.

Medearis, Angela Shelf. *Little Louis and the Jazz Band: The Story of Louis "Satchmo" Armstrong.* Illus. by Anna Rich. Lodestar/Dutton 1994 (pap. 0-525-67424-1)

For an introductory biography, this book is well researched and documented. The brief chapters tell the basic facts of Louis Armstrong's life—being sent to the Colored Waifs' Home for Boys, learning to love jazz, moving to Chicago, and becoming known worldwide for his music and his kindness. Chronology, endnotes, bibliography, and index. Part of the Rainbow Biography series.

Orgill, Roxane. *If Only I Had a Horn: Young Louis Armstrong.* Illus. by Leonard Jenkins. Houghton Mifflin 1997 (cloth 0-395-75919-6)

Vibrant illustrations with splashes of color add to this picture-book story of how Louis Armstrong acquired his horn; an author's note describes the many versions of this story and tells how he wrote this book. It would be a fine introduction to jazz and could easily be read aloud.

Biographies for Older Readers

Brown, Sandford. *Louis Armstrong: Swing Singing Satchmo.* Illus. Franklin Watts 1993 (LB 0-531-13028-2) (pap. 0-531-15680-X) 112pp.

This very detailed biography describes not only Armstrong's life but the roots of jazz and the unique environment of New Orleans. There are many quotations referenced in source notes, making this a fine choice for research projects. Glossary, bibliography, and index. Part of the Impact Biographies series.

Related Books for Younger Readers

Monceaux, Morgan. *Jazz: My Music, My People.* Illus. by the author. Knopf 1994 (cloth 0-679-85618-8) 64pp.

With an introduction by Wynton Marsalis and wonderful illustrations, this book describes key figures in jazz. From the early years through swing and onto bebop and modern jazz, students will enjoy this, an attractive and informative overview. Glossary and index.

Related Books for Older Readers

Collier, James Lincoln. *The Making of Jazz: A Comprehensive History.* Illus. Houghton Mifflin 1978 (o.p.)

No serious student of jazz should overlook this book. It is a comprehensive history, well documented with an extensive discography, bibliography, and index. From "The African Roots" to New Orleans to "The Swing Age" to bop, funk, and soul, this is a classic book for students in high school and beyond.

Friedwald, Will. *Jazz Singing: America's Great Voices from Bessie to Bebop and Beyond.* Illus. Scribner's 1990 (cloth 0-684-18522-9) 512pp.

This adult book would be a useful reference for high school students. Although some students may be overwhelmed by the details contained, this will teach all they need to know about Louis Armstrong, Bing Crosby, Ella Fitzgerald, Billie Holiday, and lesser personalities, as well as jazz styles including scat, crooning, torch singing, and swing.

Hakim, Joy. *War, Peace, and All That Jazz.* Illus. Oxford University Press 1995 (LB 0-19-507761-X) (cloth 0-19-509514-6) (pap. 0-19-507762-8) 192pp.

The social, political, and economic upheavals of World War I, Prohibition, the Roaring Twenties, the Depression, and World War II are presented in this book, which will help students understand the interrelationships between people and events. One chapter is devoted to "American Music," focusing on Louis Armstrong, Duke Ellington, and other jazz masters. Chronology, bibliography, and index. Part of the History of US series.

Seymour, Gene. *Jazz: The Great American Art.* Illus. Franklin Watts 1995 (LB 0-531-11218-7) 1996 (pap. 0-531-15793-8) 160pp.

This is an excellent overview of the roots, rhythm, and leaders of jazz music. Born in the musical traditions of Africa and linked to the spirituals of slavery, jazz merged many elements. Louis Armstrong and Duke Ellington are featured in chapters and their influence is felt throughout the book. More recent artists including Miles Davis, Cecil Taylor, and Wynton Marsalis are briefly profiled. Part of the African American Experience series.

Armstrong, **Neil Alden** (1930–) in 1969 was commander of the *Apollo 11* mission and the first man to set foot on the moon.

Statement by President Nixon to Armstrong— on the moon: "For one priceless moment in the whole history of man, all the people on this Earth are truly one; one in their pride in what you have done and one in our prayers that you will return safely to Earth."

(Kramer, p. 82)

Biographies for Younger Readers

Westman, Paul. *Neil Armstrong: Space Pioneer.* Illus. Lerner Publications 1980 (o.p.) 64pp.

From his childhood interest in aviation to his service in the Korean War to his years as a test pilot and, finally, to his first steps on the moon, this is a good introductory biography of Neil Armstrong. There is a list of the U.S. manned space flights from *Mercury 3* through *Apollo 17*. Part of the Lerner Achievers series.

Biographies for Older Readers

Kramer, Barbara. *Neil Armstrong: The First Man on the Moon.* Illus. Enslow Publishers 1997 (LB 0-89490-828-6) 112pp.

This is a well-researched book. There are numerous quotations (referenced in chapter notes). Since the landing on the moon, Armstrong has led a very private life, yet he remains a pioneering figure in space exploration. Bibliography and index. Part of the People to Know series.

Related Books for Younger Readers

Charleston, Gordon. *Armstrong Lands on the Moon.* Illus. Dillon Press 1994 (LB 0-87518-530-4) 32pp.

When Neil Armstrong became the first man on the moon, it was the culmination of the work of many people. This book describes the space program, focusing on the *Apollo* project, the moon landing, and subsequent trips to the moon. The double-page spreads should appeal to younger readers. Bibliography and index. Part of the Great 20th Century Expeditions series.

Cole, Michael D. *Apollo 11: First Moon Landing.* Illus. Enslow Publishers 1995 (o.p.) 48pp.

This is an especially well designed book for younger space enthusiasts. Short chapters, many quotations (with source notes), color photographs, a glossary, and a bibliography make this a good choice for students doing research. Index. Part of the Countdown to Space series.

Fraser, Mary Ann. *One Giant Leap.* Illus. by the author. Henry Holt 1993 (pap. 0-8050-5573-0) 88pp.

Detailed diagrams of the *Apollo 11* spacecraft and the *Saturn V* rocket complement the story of the first landing on the moon. Excerpts of the transcript of the mission are incorporated into the dramatic retelling of this event. The picture-book format captures the drama of the events.

Twist, Clint. *Gagarin and Armstrong: The First Steps in Space.* Illus. Raintree Steck-Vaughn 1995 (LB 0-8114-3978-X)

Beginning with "The Historical Background," this book describes the parallel efforts by Russia and the United States to explore space. The accomplishments of Yuri Gagarin and Neil Armstrong are described in detail. Later chapters discuss other space pioneers and related political events, including a brief look at the collapse of the Soviet system. Glossary, bibliography, and index. Part of the Beyond the Horizons series.

Related Books for Older Readers

Kennedy, Gregory P. *The First Men in Space.* Illus. Chelsea House 1991 (LB 0-7910-1324-3) 112pp.

Before there was an *Apollo* program and a moon landing, there was a race to put rockets, animals, and finally humans into space. This book provides a look at the history of the "space race," reflecting the tensions that existed between the Soviet Union and the United States. Bibliography and index. Part of the World Explorers series.

*Ashe talking about a
controversial South
African trip: "My own
case is complicated by
the fact that I'm the
only one. I am the
black tennis player, a
bloc by myself. . . .
The predicament I'm in
is that if I don't spread
out my assistance,
people become upset: I
become the bad guy
and I can't win."*
(Weissberg, p. 80)

Ashe, Arthur R. (1943–1993), an African American tennis player and human rights activist, was the first black man to win several major tennis tournaments, including Wimbledon, the Davis Cup, and the U.S. Open. He became an AIDS activist when he contracted the disease following heart surgery.

Biographies for Younger Readers

Kallen, Stuart A. *Arthur Ashe: Champion of Dreams and Motion.* Illus. Abdo & Daughters 1993 (LB 1-56239-255-7) 48pp.

Because his father worked as a special security officer for the Brookfield Playground, Arthur Ashe and his family lived in a home on the park grounds. This early opportunity to use athletic resources was important to Ashe, but he did not neglect his studies. The series emphasizes reaching goals through perseverance and effort. Index. Part of the I Have a Dream series.

Biographies for Older Readers

Collins, David R. *Arthur Ashe: Against the Wind.* Illus. Dillon Press 1994 (LB 0-87518-647-5) (pap. 0-382-24718-3) 128pp.

This book profiles Arthur Ashe as much more than a tennis player. He recovered from a heart attack only to be infected with the AIDS virus; yet he actively continued to oppose prejudice, discrimination, and apartheid. There are many quotations. Bibliography and index. Part of the People in Focus series.

Weissberg, Ted. *Arthur Ashe: Tennis Great.* Illus. Chelsea House 1991 (LB 0-7910-1115-1) 1992 (pap. 0-7910-1141-0) 112pp.

While this book describes Arthur Ashe's successful tennis career, it also focuses on his political activism. It took Ashe several years to receive a visa to travel to South Africa, and he was criticized for his visit. There were some who thought he should devote more energy to the condition of blacks in America. Despite this criticism, Ashe remained an outspoken champion for many causes. Chronology, bibliography, index, and appendix of tournament wins and Ashe's Davis Cup Record. Part of the Black Americans of Achievement series.

Wright, David. *Arthur Ashe: Breaking the Color Barrier in Tennis.* Illus. Enslow Publishers 1996 (LB 0-89490-689-5) 128pp.

This is a thoroughly researched book that makes excellent use of quotations and source notes. The book ends with Bud Collins's quotation about Arthur Ashe: "For the heroic Arthur Ashe, who showed us that sportsmanship even in a highly competitive game and world is a strength, not a weakness." Bibliography, chronology, and index. Part of the African American Biographies series.

Related Books for Younger Readers

Hammond, Tim. *Sports.* Illus. Knopf 1988 (LB 0-394-99616-X) (cloth 0-394-89616-5) 64pp.

A brief text accompanies double-page spreads on different sports, including basketball, rugby, baseball, cricket, tennis, golf, and martial arts. There are details about the history of each sport. For example, in tennis there are descriptions of changes in the rackets and the balls. Photographs with detailed captions surround the text and add visual appeal and information. Index. Part of the Eyewitness Books series.

Rediger, Pat. *Great African Americans in Sports.* Illus. Crabtree 1996 (LB 0-86505-801-6) (pap. 0-86505-815-6) 64pp.

Seven athletes are presented in longer profiles and six others receive brief coverage. The training and achievements of Muhammad Ali, Arthur Ashe, Earvin Johnson, Michael Jordan, Jackie Joyner-Kersee, Carl Lewis, and Willie Mays are described with a focus on their efforts to overcome obstacles. The many color photographs and boxed facts and accomplishments are attractive and add interest for students. Part of the Outstanding African Americans series.

Ritchie, David. *Sports and Recreation.* Illus. Chelsea House 1996 (LB 0-7910-2848-8) 104pp.

In the 19th century, many sports were popular that are still enjoyed today, such as golf, tennis, baseball, football, and basketball. But, as this book shows, the way these games were played was very different. The photographs are an important part of this book, showing differences in uniforms and locations. Bibliography and index. Part of the Life in America 100 Years Ago series.

Related Books for Older Readers

Collins, Bud, and Zander Hollander, eds. *Bud Collins' Modern Encyclopedia of Tennis.* Illus. Gale Research 1994 (cloth 0-8103-8988-6) 500pp.

This comprehensive reference book traces tennis from its roots through the Open era, following the careers of amateurs and professionals. There are numerous photographs, charts, and statistics. Bud Collins, a well-known journalist and tennis commentator, dedicated this book to Arthur Ashe. Index.

John J. Audubon

Audubon, John James (1785–1851), noted ornithologist and artist. Audubon's masterpiece, *The Birds of America,* included hand-colored life-size pictures of more than 1,000 birds.

Biographies for Younger Readers

Anderson, Peter. *John James Audubon: Wildlife Artist.* Illus. Franklin Watts 1995 (LB 0-531-20202-X) 1996 (pap. 0-531-15762-8) 64pp.

There are many features that make this book a fine choice for middle-grade students: information is presented in a logical, chronological order and there are sufficient illustrations (many reproductions of Audubon's work) to give readers a sense of the artist's work and to add variety to the presentation. Bibliography and index. Part of the First Book series.

Roop, Peter, and Connie Roop, eds. *Capturing Nature: The Writings and Art of John James Audubon.* Illus. by Rick Farley. Walker and Company 1993 (LB 0-8027-8205-1) (cloth 0-8027-8204-3) 48pp.

Using writings from Audubon's journals, letters, and books, the editors have assembled a collection of autobiographical vignettes to create this lovely book. Accompanying these are reproductions of Audubon's illustrations. A pleasure to read, this splendid account gives students a glimpse of Audubon's work and thoughts. Bibliography.

Biographies for Older Readers

Kastner, Joseph. *John James Audubon.* Illus. Harry N. Abrams 1992 (cloth 0-8109-1918-4) 92pp.

Born in France, Audubon came to America at age 18. His interest in nature, especially birds, led him to travel throughout America and to document nature and the frontier. There are numerous reproductions of Audubon's art, including a foldout section of paintings. List of illustrations and index. Part of the First Impressions series.

Related Books for Younger Readers

Smith-Baranzini, Marlene, and Howard Egger-Bovet. *US Kids History: Book of the New American Nation.* Illus. by T. Taylor Bruce. Little, Brown 1995 (cloth 0-316-96923-0) (pap. 0-316-22206-2) 96pp.

As the colonists created a new country, they had many decisions to make. This book gives historical information and personal accounts of the early years of America. Students will enjoy the detailed drawings as well as the stories, games, and activities. Learn about early expeditions and settlements. Do a project studying nature like John James Audubon. Bibliography and index. Part of the Brown Paper School series.

Toynton, Evelyn. *Growing Up in America, 1830–1860.* Illus. Millbrook Press 1995 (LB 1-56294-453-3) 96pp.

What was it like to be a child during this time period? There is information about children from different regions and peoples: "Children in New England," "Children on the Plains," "Children of the Sioux," "Children on the Streets," and "Children in Bondage." Then, the focus shifts to different activities: school, play, work, and reading. Children often worked—chopping trees, peeling apples, plowing—sometimes they were sold away from their families. Bibliography and index.

Related Books for Older Readers

Hakim, Joy. *Liberty for All?* Illus. Oxford University Press 1994 (LB 0-19-507753-9) (cloth 0-19-509510-3) (pap. 0-19-507754-7) 160pp.

This book covers the era before the Civil War. During this time, pioneers moved westward, displacing many native peoples. Sam Houston fought for Texas, Elizabeth Blackwell studied medicine, Sojourner Truth spoke against slavery, and John James Audubon painted the beauty of American wildlife. Students will be surprised by the many events in this era and how they shaped the nation's development. Chronology, bibliography, and index. Part of the History of US series.

Herb, Angela M. *Beyond the Mississippi: Early Westward Expansion of the United States.* Illus. Lodestar Books 1996 (pap. 0-525-67503-5) 128pp.

After the Louisiana Purchase, there were many opportunities for explorers, trappers, soldiers, and missionaries. Chapters focus on "Furs and Adventure," "Defending Their Homeland," and "From Texas to California." This book is filled with exciting adventures balanced by the impact on native peoples. Glossary, bibliography, and index. Part of the Young Readers' History of the West series.

Banneker, Benjamin (1731–1806), was an African American farmer and publisher. He was also a mathematician, astronomer, and surveyor, and was a member of the commission that planned Washington, D.C.

Biographies for Younger Readers

Ferris, Jeri. *What Are You Figuring Now? A Story About Benjamin Banneker.* Illus. by Amy Johnson. Carolrhoda Books 1988 (LB 0-87614-331-1) (pap. 0-685-19616-X) 56pp.

Six chapters present a readable and entertaining description of the life of Benjamin Banneker. In many ways, this reads like a novel, with conversation and dramatized events. Part of the Creative Minds series.

Pinkney, Andrea Davis. *Dear Benjamin Banneker.* Illus. by Brian Pinkney. Harcourt 1994 (cloth 0-15-200417-4) 32pp.

This picture-book biography focuses on Banneker's almanac—the first published almanac by a black man—and on his correspondence with Thomas Jefferson about equality and freedom.

Biographies for Older Readers

Conley, Kevin. *Benjamin Banneker: Scientist & Mathematician.* Illus. Chelsea House 1989 (LB 1-55546-573-0)

Students doing research will appreciate the organization and related features of this book. The detailed text includes quotations from Banneker's writings; the illustrations are reproductions from his almanac, astronomical drawings, and diary. Chronology and suggested further reading. Part of the Black Americans of Achievement series.

Related Books for Younger Readers

Kent, Deborah. *African-Americans in the Thirteen Colonies.* Illus. Children's Press 1996 (pap. 0-516-06631-5) 32pp.

The freedom sought by so many Europeans who came to America was not shared with many Africans and their descendants. The brief descriptions in this book tell of slavery as well as the limited freedoms of free blacks. Phillis Wheatley, Jean Baptiste Pointe du Sable, and Benjamin Banneker are among those briefly profiled. Index. Part of the Cornerstones of Freedom series.

Smith-Baranzini, Marlene, and Howard Egger-Bovet. *US Kids History: Book of the New American Nation.* Illus. by T. Taylor Bruce. Little, Brown 1995 (cloth 0-316-96923-0) (pap. 0-316-22206-2) 96pp.

Learn about Benjamin Banneker's work as a surveyor and on his almanac in this book covering the early years of America. Students will enjoy the detailed drawings as well as the stories, games, and activities. Bibliography and index. Part of the Brown Paper School series.

Related Books for Older Readers

Hoig, Stan. *A Capital for the Nation.* Illus. with photographs and old prints. Cobblehill Books 1990 (o.p.)

The location of the capital city was debated by politicians from the North and the South. The selection of an area of land along the Potomac River was a compromise to assure the southern leaders that the North would not dominate them. This book describes the construction of Washington, D.C., as well as some of the famous buildings. Bibliography and index.

Purvis, Thomas L. *Revolutionary America, 1763 to 1800.* Illus. Facts on File 1995 (cloth 0-8160-2528-2) 383pp.

Benjamin Banneker issued an almanac in the later years of the 18th century. Now, Thomas L. Purvis in turn has compiled detailed information on this era. Chapters include "Climate, Natural History, and Historical Geography," "Native American Life," "The Economy," "Population Statistics," "Diet and Health," "Religion," "Government," "The State and Territories," and "The Cities." This is a fascinating look at statistical data from the past. Part of the Almanacs of American Life series.

Barton, Clara (1821–1912), an American humanitarian, organized the American Red Cross in 1881 and headed the organization until 1904, presiding over relief work in the United States and overseas. During the Civil War, she worked in army camps and on the battlefield.

Biographies for Younger Readers

Sonneborn, Liz. *Clara Barton: Founder, American Red Cross.* Illus. Chelsea House 1991 (LB 0-7910-1565-3) 80pp.

Teacher, nurse, administrator, and organizer—Clara Barton performed many jobs in her lifetime. After her work in the Civil War, Barton provided relief services to the victims of the Johnstown flood and the Spanish-American War. Chronology and glossary. Part of the Junior World Biographies series.

Biographies for Older Readers

Dubowski, Cathy E. *Clara Barton: Healing the Wounds.* Illus. Silver Burdett 1990 (o.p.) 160pp.

Clara Barton grew up during an era when women were accepting more public responsibilities. She was a teacher, a nurse, and an administrator, serving as president of the American Red Cross and helping to establish the American Woman's Suffrage Association and the Woman's International Peace Association. This book describes those accomplishments in detail. Timelines (Barton's life and the Civil War), bibliography, and index. Part of the History of the Civil War series.

Hamilton, Leni. *Clara Barton: Founder, American Red Cross.* Illus. Chelsea House 1988 (LB 1-55546-641-9) 112pp.

In addition to founding the American Red Cross, Clara Barton was an educator who helped set up the first public school in New Jersey. During the Civil War, she nursed soldiers, organized the delivery of supplies, and created an agency to look for soldiers missing in action. Chronology, bibliography, and index. Part of the American Women of Achievement series.

Related Books for Younger Readers

Burger, Leslie, and Debra L. Rahm. *Red Cross / Red Crescent: When Help Can't Wait.* Lerner Publications 1996 (cloth 0-8225-2698-0) 80pp.

Around the world, a red cross on a white background is a symbol of help and neutrality. In Muslim countries, the symbol is a red crescent; in Israel, it is a red Star of David. Learn about the history of this service, as well as situations that have required this kind of help. A boxed section describes the formation of the American Red Cross. List of addresses and index. Part of the International Cooperation series.

Related Books for Older Readers

Brown, Pam. *Henry Dunant: Founder of the Red Cross, the Relief Organization Dedicated to Helping Suffering People All Over the World.* Illus. Gareth Stevens 1988 (o.p.) 68pp.

When Henry Dunant saw the neglect and poor treatment of the wounded at the battle of Solferino, Italy, he became committed to organizing efforts to help them and others in need. The result was the Red Cross. Most of this book is devoted to the early years of the Red Cross, but the last few sections look at the present-day activities of the Red Cross and the Red Crescent. There is an appended list of the principles of these organizations and addresses. Chronology, glossary, bibliography (including magazines related to health issues), and index. Part of the People Who Have Helped the World series.

Corrick, James A. *The Battle of Gettysburg.* Illus. Lucent 1996 (LB 1-56006-451-X) 112pp.

Gettysburg was a decisive battle of the Civil War. This book describes the events leading up to the battle as well as the horrible destruction that resulted. Several chapters focus on each day of the battle, and there are numerous sidebars—on field hospitals, Clara Barton and nursing, the role of black soldiers, and soldiers captured at Andersonville, for example. Chronology, bibliographies, and index. Part of the Battles of the Civil War series.

Beckwourth, James (1798–1867), an

American frontiersman, was born to a white man and a plantation slave. Beckwourth's father did not treat the boy like a slave. Instead, he was taken west to the Missouri wilderness and sent to school. Drawn to the mountains of the western United States, he served as a guide and fur trader and later discovered a route through the Sierra Nevada Mountains to the Sacramento Valley in California.

Biographies for Older Readers

Dolan, Sean. *James Beckwourth: Frontiersman.* Illus. Chelsea House 1992 (LB 0-7910-1120-8)

James Beckwourth lived in an era that encouraged his pioneering spirit. It was an era of trapping and trading, exploring and fighting, taking risks and telling stories about them. His love of the wilderness led him to become a "mountain man," blazing trails and roaming the frontier. Chronology, bibliography, and index. Part of the Black Americans of Achievement series.

Related Books for Younger Readers

Collins, James L. *The Mountain Men.* Illus. Franklin Watts 1996 (LB 0-531-20229-1) 64pp.

Mountain men were explorers, hunters, and fighters. They faced the challenges of the West, surviving hostile environments and people. This book profiles seven men, including Jim Bridger, James Beckwourth, and "Kit" Carson. The accounts in this book will provide students with information about the expansion into the West. Bibliography and index. Part of the First Books series.

Related Books for Older Readers

Herb, Angela M. *Beyond the Mississippi: Early Westward Expansion of the United States.* Illus. Lodestar Books 1996 (pap. 0-525-67503-5) 128pp.

After the Louisiana Purchase, there were many opportunities for explorers, trappers, soldiers, and missionaries. Chapters in this book focus on "Furs and Adventure," "Defending Their Homeland,"

and "From Texas to California." This book is filled with exciting adventures balanced by the impact on native peoples. Glossary, bibliography, and index. Part of the Young Readers' History of the West series.

Begin, Menachem (1913–1992), Israeli prime minister from 1977 to 1983, signed a landmark peace treaty (Camp David Accords) with Egypt in 1979. He shared the 1978 Nobel Peace Prize with Egyptian President Anwar al-Sadat.

Biographies for Older Readers

Amdur, Richard. *Menachim Begin.* Illus. Chelsea House 1988 (o.p.) 112pp.

Devoted to creating a Jewish state in Palestine, Begin was involved in radical, often violent, movements. He supported attacks and conflicts, yet he will be remembered for his participation in the historic Israeli-Egyptian peace treaty of 1979. Chronology, bibliography, and index. Part of the World Leaders Past & Present series.

Related Books for Older Readers

Carter, Jimmy. *Talking Peace: A Vision for the Next Generation.* Illus. Dutton 1993 (cloth 0-525-44959-0); NAL Dutton 1996 (pap. 0-525-45651-1) 168pp.

Former President Carter reflects on the importance of nonviolent conflict resolution and making a commitment to peacemaking techniques. Included are personal experiences and insights—from the Camp David Accords to his work with Habitat for Humanity to the efforts of the Carter Center in Atlanta. This is a powerful message from a man who has devoted his life to promoting peace and cooperation. Within his vision for the future are reflections on the past, providing a historical context for students. Notes on sources and index.

Messenger, Charles. *The Middle East.* Illus. Franklin Watts 1987 (LB 0-531-10539-3)

Chapters examine "The Sources of Conflict," "Arab versus Jew," "The Superpowers Step In," and "Holy War." There is information about the founding of Israel, the Six-Day War of 1967, the Yom Kippur War of 1973, the fall of the Shah, the growth of Islamic fundamentalism, and the activities of the PLO. There are several appendices, including one giving biographical information on important figures. Chronology and index. Part of the Conflict in the 20th Century series.

Ross, Stewart. *Arab-Israeli Conflict.* Illus. Raintree Steck-Vaughn 1996 (LB 0-8172-4051-9) 80pp.

Although the format of this book could make it accessible to younger students, the complexity of the issues might be better understood by an older audience. Issues include the formation of Israel, conflicts in the region, the Palestinians, and the peace process. There are many maps, making this a good overview for students who are just beginning to study this area. Timeline, glossary, bibliography, and index. Part of the Causes and Consequences series.

An inventor is "A man who looks upon the world and is not contented with things as they are. He wants to improve whatever he sees, he wants to benefit the world."

(Pasachoff, p. 131)

Bell, Alexander Graham (1847–1922),

an American scientist who emigrated from Scotland, is best known for the invention of the telephone, which was first demonstrated in 1865 with those famous words: "Watson, come here; I want you." He also developed a machine to record sound and worked on early planes and hydrofoil boats.

Biographies for Younger Readers

Joseph, Paul. *Alexander Graham Bell.* Illus. Abdo & Daughters 1997 (LB 1-56239-632-3)

Large print and wide line spacing make this a good biography for younger audiences. Chapters cover "The Early Years," "Aleck and His Animals," "The Telephone Is Born," and "Aleck Changes the World." Vocabulary words are highlighted and then defined in a glossary. Index. Part of the Checkerboard Biography Library: Inventors.

Lewis, Cynthia Copeland. *Hello, Alexander Graham Bell Speaking.* Illus. Dillon Press 1991 (LB 0-87518-461-8) 64pp.

As a child, Alexander Graham Bell learned Visible Speech, which was invented by his father, and was educated at home by his mother, who was deaf. This helped develop his interest in communication and invention. Index. Part of the Taking Part series.

Quiri, Patricia R. *Alexander Graham Bell.* Illus. Franklin Watts 1991 (o.p.) 64pp.

Besides giving information about Bell's life and inventions, this book includes some simple activities for young scientists. One project uses tuning forks; another is making a "telephone." Index. Part of the First Books series.

Biographies for Older Readers

Pasachoff, Naomi. *Alexander Graham Bell: Making Connections.* Illus. Oxford University Press 1996 (LB 0-19-509908-7) 144pp.

This is a thorough and well-researched book with excellent illustrations and sidebars that explain related topics—for example, "Electromagnetism: The Scientific Principle Underlying the Telephone" and "How a Telephone Works." Chronology, bibliography, and index. Part of the Oxford Portraits in Science series.

Pollard, Michael. *Alexander Graham Bell.* Illus. Exley 1991 (LB 1-85015-200-4)

The focus of this book is on the invention of the telephone and its impact on our lives. Details about improvements such as directories, exchanges, and dials are presented. Part of the Scientists Who Have Changed the World series.

Related Books for Younger Readers

Gan, Geraldine. *Communication.* Illus. Chelsea House 1997 (LB 0-7910-2845-3) 104pp.

How did people communicate in the 19th century? Newspapers and magazines were important for receiving information about news, politics, and fashion. The telegraph and telephone were being invented. Bibliography and index. Part of the Life in America 100 Years Ago series.

Holland, Gini, and Amy Stone. *Telephones.* Illus. Benchmark Books 1996 (LB 0-7614-0065-6) 64pp.

This book opens with a chapter on "Improving Communications" and goes on to talk about the improvements that have been made to the telephone. Important inventors and innovators are featured in boxed inserts. Alexander Graham Bell, Elisha Gray, Granville T. Woods, and Alfred Y. Cho are among those included. Timeline, bibliography, and index. Part of the Inventors and Inventions series.

Leuzzi, Linda. *Industry and Business.* Illus. Chelsea House 1997 (LB 0-7910-2846-1) 104pp.

After the Civil War, American industry began to thrive. This growth was aided by the efforts of innovators such as Thomas Edison and Alexander Graham Bell and of financiers and industrialists such as John D. Rockefeller and Andrew Carnegie. The role of workers and unions is also presented. Bibliography and index. Part of the Life in America 100 Years Ago series.

Related Books for Older Readers

Machines and Inventions. Illus. Time-Life Books 1990 (cloth 0-8094-9704-2)

This overview reference book looks at the impact of technology on industry and science, business, leisure time, the home, and medicine. The opening chapter, "Inventions That Changed History," discusses Bell's telephone, the box camera, television, and the printing press. Index. Part of the Understanding Science and Nature series.

"In Israel, in order to be a realist, you must believe in miracles."

(Vail, p. 13)

Ben-Gurion, David (1886–1973), born David Grün in Poland, served as Israel's first prime minister from 1948 to 1953. An active Zionist and organizer of resistance to British rule in Palestine, he was returned to the prime ministership in 1955, serving until 1963.

Biographies for Older Readers

Silverstein, Herma. *David Ben-Gurion.* Franklin Watts (LB 0-531-10509-1)

This very detailed biography traces the events that shaped the life of David Ben-Gurion. Throughout his life, he worked for the state of Israel. His leadership helped develop a strong Israeli economy and defense. The author discusses the influence of the Holocaust on his passionate commitment to creating a secure homeland in Palestine. Chapter notes, bibliography, and index. Part of the Impact Biographies series.

Vail, John. *David Ben-Gurion.* Valley of the Sun (LB 0-87754-509-X)

David Ben-Gurion dedicated his life to establishing a Jewish state in Palestine. He organized others to create a homeland, and, when they were successful, was elected the first prime minister of Israel. Bibliography and index. Part of the World Leaders Past & Present series.

Related Books for Younger Readers

Hills, Ken. *1940s.* Illus. Raintree Steck-Vaughn 1991 (o.p.) 47pp.

Students gain an understanding of the chronology of events in this decade. The main focus is on World War II and subsequent developments including the establishment of the United Nations and the creation of Israel. The format simulates a newspaper with headlines, columns, and supporting pictures, making an attractive overview. Glossary, bibliography, and index. Part of the Take Ten Years series.

Silverman, Maida. *Israel: The Founding of a Modern Nation.* Illus. by Susan Avishai. Dial 1998 (LB 0-8037-2136-6) (cloth 0-8037-2135-8) 112pp.

This book provides a historical foundation for understanding the struggles to create a Jewish homeland. Chapters focus on ancient times through British rule, ending with the birth of Israel in 1948. After this background information, there is a detailed timeline of Israel's history from 1948 to the present. Bibliography and index.

Related Books for Older Readers

Hiro, Dilip. *The Middle East.* Illus. Oryx Press 1996 (pap. 0-57356-004-9) 232pp.

The author gives an overview of the region followed by a focus on the individual countries. Each section of this very detailed book provides historical details as well as information about important issues and people. There is a chapter on the conflict between Arabs and Jews. There is information about the role of oil in the region, the crisis in Kuwait, the Gulf War, and the 1993 accord. Glossary, bibliography, and index. Part of the International Politics and Government series.

Messenger, Charles. *The Middle East.* Illus. Franklin Watts 1987 (LB 0-531-10539-3)

Chapters examine "The Sources of Conflict," "Arab versus Jew," "The Superpowers Step In," and "Holy War." There is information about the founding of Israel, the Six-Day War of 1967, the Yom Kippur War of 1973, the fall of the Shah, the growth of Islamic fundamentalism, and the activities of the PLO. There are several appendices, including one giving biographical information on important figures. Chronology and index. Part of the Conflict in the 20th Century series.

Bethune, Mary McLeod (1875–1955), a child of former slaves, founded the Daytona Normal and Industrial Institute for Negro Girls, which in 1904 became Bethune-Cookman College. In 1935 she organized the National Council of Negro Women.

Biographies for Younger Readers

Kelso, Richard. *Building a Dream: Mary Bethune's School.* Illus. by Debbe Heller. Raintree Steck-Vaughn 1992 (LB 0-8114-7217-5) 46pp.

Five brief chapters, an epilogue, and chapter notes help make this book a good choice for a beginning researcher. Focusing on Mary Bethune's efforts to open a school for black children in Florida, the author includes facts about segregation, racism, and perseverance. Part of the Stories of America series.

McKissack, Patricia, and Fredrick McKissack. *Mary McLeod Bethune: A Great Teacher.* Illus. by Ned Ostendorf and with photographs. Enslow Publishers 1991 (LB 0-89490-304-7) 32pp.

Mary Jane McLeod was born free. When she was a child, education was important to her, and her parents allowed her to go to school instead of helping in the fields. As an adult, she founded a school for African American children. To help young readers, key words are highlighted in bold print and defined in a glossary. Index. Part of the Great African Americans series.

Meltzer, Milton. *Mary McLeod Bethune: Voice of Black Hope.* Illus. by Stephen Marchesi. Puffin 1988 (pap. 0-14-032219-1) 64pp.

Mary McLeod Bethune founded several schools for African Americans. This book describes her efforts to educate young blacks and her encounter with a poet—Langston Hughes. Part of the Women of Our Time series.

Wolfe, Rinna E. *Mary McLeod Bethune.* Illus. Franklin Watts 1992 (LB 0-531-20103-1) 64pp.

The quotations in this book make the text lively and bring the commitment and character of Mary McLeod Bethune to life. Bethune was devoted to education. She dedicated her resources and energy to educating herself and then providing others with educational opportunities. Glossary, bibliography, and index. Part of the First Books series.

Biographies for Older Readers

Halasa, Malu. *Mary McLeod Bethune: Educator.* Illus. Chelsea House 1989 (LB 1-55546-574-9) 1993 (pap. 0-7910-0225-X) 112pp.

While best known for her efforts to promote educational opportunities for blacks, Mary McLeod Bethune was also a powerful political force. This book examines that power in such chapters as "The Politics of Persuasion" and "The Black Brain Trust." She served as the first president of the National Council of Negro Women and was a contemporary of Mary Church Terrell, Lady Nancy Astor (the first woman member of Parliament), and Eleanor Roosevelt. Chronology, bibliography, and index. Part of the Black Americans of Achievement series.

Related Books for Younger Readers

Leuzzi, Linda. *Education.* Illus. Chelsea House 1998 (LB 0-7910-2849-6) 104pp.

After examining the evolution of education in America, this book gives an overview of innovative educators and opportunities for different groups (including women and blacks). Reading this book will give students a foundation for understanding the efforts of Mary McLeod Bethune in the early 20th century. Bibliography and index. Part of the Life in America 100 Years Ago series.

Turner, Glennette Tilley. *Take a Walk in Their Shoes.* Illus. by
Elton C. Fax. Cobblehill Books 1989 (pap. 0-525-65006-7) 176pp.

One way to learn history is through dramatic interpretations.
This book profiles 14 African Americans whose courage and con-
victions helped change our world. Accompanying each profile is a
skit that encourages readers to perform an event related to the person's life. For Dr. Martin Luther King, Jr., the skit focuses on a
family discussing the impact of his life; for Charles Drew, the skit
involves schoolchildren learning about Dr. Drew, for whom their
school is named; for Mary McLeod Bethune, readers learn about the
school she founded. Garrett A. Morgan, Frederick Douglass, Maggie
Lena Walker, and Ida B. Wells are also included. Index.

Related Books for Older Readers

Katz, William L. *The New Freedom to the New Deal, 1913–1939.*
Illus. Raintree Steck-Vaughn 1993 (LB 0-8114-6279-X) 96pp.

The years covered in this book were filled with new opportunities. Blacks migrated to the North and participated in the cultural
and artistic celebration signified by the Harlem Renaissance. Educational opportunities were expanded. Women received the right to
vote and some, like Mary McLeod Bethune, were given political
responsibilities. This was also a time of hardship, particularly for
native peoples and Mexican-American workers. The Great Depression and the rise of fascism are also discussed. Sidebars focus on
specific people and events. Bibliography and index. Part of the History of Multicultural America series.

Levinson, Nancy Smiler. *Turn of the Century: Our Nation One
Hundred Years Ago.* Illus. Lodestar Books 1994 (pap. 0-525-
67433-0) 144pp.

At the beginning of the 1900s, America was becoming more
industrialized. Railroads allowed more people to go more places.
Inventions like the telephone, electricity, and the car were becoming a reality. The efforts of Mary McLeod Bethune and Booker T.
Washington led to improved educational opportunities for African
Americans. This is a readable book that will give students a context
for the events of this era. Bibliography and index.

Bhutto, Benazir

Bhutto, Benazir (1953–), served as prime minister of Pakistan from 1988 until 1990 and again from 1993 to 1996. The daughter of a former prime minister, she was the first woman to head an Islamic state in modern times. She was imprisoned several times for her earlier campaign for open elections and social change.

"We are determined to build a new Pakistan, a democratic Pakistan, committed to equality under the law for all people, men and women alike."
(Hughes, p. 124)

Biographies for Older Readers

Doherty, Katherine M., and Craig A. Doherty. *Benazir Bhutto.* Illus. Franklin Watts 1990 (o.p.) 144pp.

This is a thorough and thought-provoking biography that not only presents the life of Benazir Bhutto but also provides a look at the history and politics of Pakistan. The complexity of her opposition to the general who had overthrown, imprisoned, and later executed her father is described, as are the challenges she faced as the first woman to be elected prime minister of a Muslim nation. Bibliography and index. Part of the Impact Biographies series.

Hughes, Libby. *Benazir Bhutto: From Prison to Prime Minister.* Illus. Dillon Press 1990 (o.p.) 128pp.

In the bibliography are references to interviews with Benazir Bhutto and those who have known her. As a result, this book has a personal tone with quotations and insights into events in Bhutto's life. The Afterword by Bhutto stresses the challenges that she faces and her commitment to meeting them. Index. Part of the People in Focus series.

Related Books for Older Readers

Sheehan, Sean. *Pakistan.* Illus. Marshall Cavendish 1994 (LB 1-85435-583-X) 128pp.

While the focus of this book is on Pakistan today, there is a lot of historical information. One chapter describes early civilizations, the influence of the British, and the backdrop to the current political scene. Chapters on religion, the arts, and festivals also include historical details. Map, section with quick facts, glossary, bibliography, and index. Part of the Cultures of the World series.

Weston, Mark. *The Land and People of Pakistan.* Illus. Harper-Collins 1992 (o.p.) 224pp.

The format of this book makes it a good choice for students doing research. Five chapters are devoted to aspects of the history of Pakistan, from "Early History" (including the Indus civilization and the conversion to Islam) to "Pakistan Since 1971" (which discusses the execution of Zulfikar Ali Bhutto and the leadership of General Zia ul-Haq). There are boxed sections within each chapter that highlight specific events. "Mini Facts" section, filmography, discography, bibliography, and index. Part of the Portraits of the Nations series.

Blackwell, Elizabeth (1821–1910), born in Britain, was the first woman to be awarded a medical doctor's degree in the United States. Later, with her sister Emily, she set up an infirmary for women and children in New York City.

Biographies for Younger Readers

Schleichert, Elizabeth. *The Life of Elizabeth Blackwell.* Illus. by Antonio Castro. Twenty-First Century Books 1991 (o.p.) 89pp.

This is a very readable biography focusing on the accomplishments of Elizabeth Blackwell. She was the first credentialed female physician in the United States. She worked to improve health services to women and children and underprivileged groups. She encouraged women to study, opening a medical college for women. Bibliography and index. Part of the Pioneers in Health and Medicine series.

Biographies for Older Readers

Brown, Jordan. *Elizabeth Blackwell: Physician.* Illus. Chelsea House 1989 (LB 1-55546-642-7) 112pp.

Students writing reports will find this well-organized book useful. The black-and-white illustrations provide insight into Blackwell's life and her era, showing drawings and photos of contemporaries and of living conditions. The text emphasizes Blackwell as a pioneer not only for women, but also for improved health care and education. Chronology, bibliography, and index. Part of the American Women of Achievement series.

Kline, Nancy. *Elizabeth Blackwell: A Doctor's Triumph.* Illus. Conari Press 1997 (pap. 1-57324-057-5) 224pp.

In the Victorian era women were expected to work in the home, and people were particularly squeamish about allowing women to be educated about diseases or the body. Elizabeth Blackwell challenged these accepted restrictions; she stood alone. Today, women make up about half of the enrollment in medical schools. This book reads like a dramatic novel. Chronology, bibliography, and index. Part of the Barnard Biography series.

Related Books for Younger Readers

Miller, Brandon Marie. *Just What the Doctor Ordered: The History of American Medicine.* Illus. Lerner Publications 1997 (LB 0-8225-1737-X)

This is an amazing look at the history of medicine in America, from Native Americans through the present. Bloodletting with leeches, laxatives for purges, treating headaches with electricity, dissecting cadavers, the development of X-ray machines, pasteurization of milk, all give some perspective on our medical past and the amazing strides we have made. Bibliography and index.

Ritchie, David, and Fred Israel. *Health and Medicine.* Illus. Chelsea House 1995 (LB 0-7910-2839-9)

The first chapter examines "Medicine and the Civil War." Soldiers who survived the battles were unlikely to survive the treatment in a field hospital. Bibliography and index. Part of the Life in America 100 Years Ago series.

Related Books for Older Readers

Katz, William L. *The Westward Movement and Abolitionism, 1815–1850.* Illus. Raintree Steck-Vaughn 1993 (LB 0-8114-6276-5) 96pp.

During this era, many immigrants came to America, often joining in the westward expansion. Battles occurred in Texas and California and preparations were beginning for the Civil War. This book ends with the beginning of women's fight for equality, featuring the work of Dr. Elizabeth Blackwell, Lucretia Mott, and Elizabeth Cady Stanton. Part of the History of Multicultural America series.

Blériot, Louis (1872–1936), a French aviator, achieved fame in 1909 when he became the first person to fly across the English Channel. This self-taught pilot later formed a company that manufactured military aircraft used in World War I.

Biographies for Younger Readers

Provensen, Alice, and Martin Provensen. *The Glorious Flight: Across the Channel with Louis Blériot, July 25, 1909.* Illus. by the authors. Puffin 1987 (pap. 0-317-63651-0) 40pp.

Louis Blériot was a pioneer in the development of the airplane and won a contest when his plane was the first to cross the English Channel. This book received the 1984 Caldecott Award. It is a splendid read-aloud book and a wonderful way to connect readers to books about the history of aviation.

Related Books for Younger Readers

Moser, Barry. *Fly! A Brief History of Flight Illustrated.* Illus. by the author. HarperCollins 1993 (o.p.) 56pp.

Famous firsts in flight—the first ascent, the first flight, the first time past the sound barrier—are featured along with some of the people who helped pioneer developments in aviation. There are historical notes that provide more details about the inventions. Bibliography.

Weiss, Harvey. *Strange and Wonderful Aircraft.* Illus. by the author. Houghton Mifflin 1995 (cloth 0-395-68716-0) 64pp.

Before the first successful flight, there were many inventive attempts at flying. Did you know that the first passengers to make a hot air balloon flight were a sheep, a rooster, and a duck? This book describes some of the unusual experiments that led to the successful development of air transportation.

Related Books for Older Readers

Berliner, Don. *Aviation: Reaching for the Sky.* Illus. Oliver Press 1997 (LB 1-881508-33-1) 144pp.

Reading about the risks people took and the creativity of their efforts to fly is fascinating. In this book students will find information about the dirigible, glider, airplane, seaplane, helicopter, and more. List of "Important Events in Aviation History," glossary, bibliography, and index. Part of the Innovators series.

Bluford, Guion (1942–), an astronaut and aerospace engineer, was the first African American to fly into space (1983). He also flew aboard a Spacelab mission in 1985 and participated in two missions for the Department of Defense.

Biographies for Younger Readers

Haskins, Jim, and Kathleen Benson. *Space Challenger: The Story of Guion Bluford.* Illus. Lerner Publications 1984 (LB 0-87614-259-5) 64pp.

Guion Bluford has a Ph.D. in aerospace engineering and laser physics. He flew in the space shuttle *Challenger*, becoming the first African American in space. This authorized biography is filled with quotations from Bluford and photos of his life. Glossary and index. Part of the Trailblazers Biographies series.

Related Books for Younger Readers

Gold, Susan Dudley. *To Space and Back: The Story of the Shuttle.* Illus. Crestwood House 1992 (LB 0-89686-688-2) 48pp.

How was the space-shuttle program developed? How do astronauts prepare for space flight? This book provides historical information about the space shuttle and looks at specific flights, including the *Challenger* disaster. List of suggested readings, glossary, and index. Part of the Adventures in Space series.

"Many famous blacks went to Cape Canaveral, Florida, to watch the launching. . . . Bill Cosby [who was there] did not feel that Guy Bluford should be watched closely because he was black. 'Our race is one which has been qualified for a long time,' Cosby said. 'The people who have allowed Guy to make this mission are the ones who have passed the test.'"
(Haskins and Benson, p. 45)

Related Books for Older Readers

Burns, Khephra, and William Miles. *Black Stars in Orbit: NASA's African American Astronauts.* Illus. Harcourt 1995 (cloth 0-15-200432-7) (pap. 0-15-200276-6) 80pp.

Here is an overview of the involvement of African Americans in space flight, focusing on such well-known astronauts as Guion S. Bluford, Jr., and Mae C. Jemison. Much of the book looks at history, focusing on the importance of the flight training of the Black Eagles and Tuskegee airmen that opened opportunities to blacks to participate in NASA's space program. Index.

Haskins, Jim. *Black Eagles: African Americans in Aviation.* Illus. Scholastic 1995 (cloth 0-590-45912-0) 208pp.

Paving the way for Guy Bluford were many pioneers who overcame the limitations imposed by discrimination and found ways to succeed in aviation. Early African American pilots found that Europe was more open for opportunities. Later, the need for accomplished airmen in World War II allowed black pilots to demonstrate their abilities. From Eugene Bullard and Bessie Coleman through the Tuskegee airmen and the space age, this is a very thorough and readable book. Detailed chronology, bibliography, and index.

Bly, Nellie (1867–1922), born Elizabeth Cochrane Seaman, was a journalist known for her sensational stories in the *New York World,* particularly her account of a whirlwind round-the-world trip she made in 72 days. She also wrote articles exposing conditions in mental institutions.

Biographies for Younger Readers

Carlson, Judy. *"Nothing Is Impossible," Said Nellie Bly.* Illus. by Mike Eagle. Raintree Steck-Vaughn 1989 (LB 0-8172-3521-3) (pap. 0-8114-6721-X) 32pp.

Like many women in the 19th century, Nellie Bly challenged the accepted stereotyped roles. She became a newspaper reporter. One of her best-known stories involved her trip around the world in under 80 days. Part of the Real Readers series.

Quackenbush, Robert. *Stop the Presses, Nellie's Got a Scoop! A Story of Nellie Bly.* Illus. by the author. Simon & Schuster 1992 (o.p.)

This is a most enjoyable biography. Accompanying the information about Nellie Bly are humorous asides from two children who are learning about her. The endpapers extend the text, showing Nellie Bly's route and a day-by-day account of her trip around the world. Bibliography.

Biographies for Older Readers

Ehrlich, Elizabeth. *Nellie Bly.* Chelsea House 1989 (LB 1-55546-643-5) 111pp.

Nellie Bly's achievements as a journalist are clearly presented in this biography. The information is well organized with attractive illustrations. Students will find this book (and series) not only useful for research but interesting in itself. Chronology, bibliography, and index. Part of the American Women of Achievement series.

Emerson, Kathy Lynn. *Making Headlines: A Biography of Nellie Bly.* Illus. Silver Burdett 1989 (LB 0-87518-406-5) 112pp.

Nellie Bly was a reporter, but she was also a reformer who broke barriers for women by her intrepid adventures. This is a very readable biography, using many quotations. The illustrations are well placed to add information and interest. Bibliography and index. Part of the People in Focus series.

Related Books for Younger Readers

Burns, Peggy. *News.* Illus. Thomson Learning 1995 (LB 1-56947-342-7) 32pp.

From "The Invention of Printing" to "The News Media Today," this book looks at the history of gathering and reporting the news. There is information on news sheets—an illustration even shows one from the time of the Romans. Newspapers, telegraph services, radios, and television are also featured. There are addresses for the Museum of Broadcasting and for the Federal Communications Commission. Glossary, bibliography, and index. Part of the Stepping Through History series.

Fisher, Leonard Everett. *The Newspapers.* Illus. by the author. Holiday House 1981 (LB 0-8234-0387-4)

Students gain a chronological understanding of the growth of the newspaper industry in the 19th century, of the importance of the telegraph in spreading news rapidly, and of the role of the "penny press," which often featured scandals and crimes as well as political news. By the end of the century, there were newspaper chains controlled by men like Joseph Pulitzer and William Randolph Hearst. Index. Part of the Nineteenth Century America series.

Related Books for Older Readers

Fleming, Thomas. *Behind the Headlines: The Story of American Newspapers.* Illus. Walker and Company 1989 (LB 0-8027-6891-1) (cloth 0-8027-6890-3)

In America, newspapers have played an important role in politics and government. They have influenced opinions and promoted social change. Here is an overview of the history of American newspapers and such key people involved with them as Benjamin Franklin, Nellie Bly, Horace Greeley, and Joseph Pulitzer. Bibliography and index. Part of the Walker American History Series for Young People.

"Today Venezuela, Colombia, Ecuador, Peru, and Bolivia honor him as their liberator. Bolivia was named for him."

(Adler)

Bolívar, Simón (1783–1830), was a revolutionary leader best known for liberating much of South America from Spanish rule. He is today revered as the continent's greatest hero, although his ruthless pursuit of a united South America earned him many enemies, and he enjoyed little support in his later years.

Biographies for Younger Readers

Adler, David A. *A Picture Book of Simón Bolívar.* Illus. by Robert Casilla. Holiday House 1992 (LB 0-8234-0927-9) 32pp.

The picture-book format of this biography makes it a fine read-aloud book to introduce Simón Bolívar and the time in which he lived. Revolutions were taking place around the world, and many South American colonies began to seek independence from Spain. List of important dates. Part of the Picture Book Of series.

De Varona, Frank. *Simón Bolívar: Latin American Liberator.* Illus. Millbrook Press 1993 (LB 1-56294-278-6) (pap. 1-56294-812-1) 32pp.

Like many of the patriots of the American Revolution, Simón Bolívar was born into a wealthy family. He used his influence, education, and power to lead several South American countries to freedom from Spanish rule. This brief biography includes photographs of historic sites and reproductions of events. The design, with brief vignettes and bold-faced headings, makes this a useful book for a beginning researcher. Timeline, bibliography, and index. Part of the Hispanic Heritage series.

Biographies for Older Readers

Greene, Carol. *Simón Bolívar: South American Liberator.* Illus. Children's Press 1989 (o.p.)

In this detailed biography, there is information about the strategies and successes of Bolívar and the revolutionaries. This was a time of great upheaval: Napoleon spreading his influence in Europe; the beginnings of industry; independence in Mexico; and revolution throughout South America. Timeline and index. Part of the People of Distinction series.

Related Books for Younger Readers

Hinds, Kathryn. *The Incas.* Illus. Benchmark Books 1998 (LB 0-7614-0270-5) 80pp.

The Incas ruled the western coastal region of South America for more than 300 years. The arrival of the Spanish conquistadors led to the end of their empire. Chronology, glossary, bibliography, and index. Part of the Cultures of the Past series.

Hoobler, Dorothy, and Thomas Hoobler. *South American Portraits.* Illus. by Stephen Marchesi. Raintree Steck-Vaughn 1994 (LB 0-8114-6383-4) 96pp.

Information about South America and its peoples is hard for students to find. This book meets a need by focusing on accomplishments of important people of this continent including the liberators Simón Bolívar and José de San Martín, political figure Evita Perón, sports star Pelé, and writer Gabriel García Márquez. Source notes, glossary, bibliography, and index. Part of the Images Across the Ages series.

Related Books for Older Readers

Pateman, Robert. *Bolivia.* Illus. Marshall Cavendish 1995 (LB 0-7614-0178-4) 128pp.

Only one chapter is devoted to the history of Bolivia, but there is also history throughout this book, especially in the chapters dealing with religion, the arts, games, and festivals. The influence of the Incas and of Spanish adventurers is still very evident, as is the contribution of Simón Bolívar, who helped liberate several countries in South America (Bolivia is named for him). Maps, overview of facts, glossary, bibliography, and index. Part of the Cultures of the World series, which includes books on Venezuela, Colombia, and Peru.

Bonaparte, Napoleon (1769–1821), a brilliant military strategist and political and social reformer, declared himself emperor of France in 1804. He set out to conquer large areas of Europe with initial success. A coalition of European allies finally defeated him at Waterloo in 1815, and he was exiled to the British island of St. Helena.

Biographies for Younger Readers

Blackwood, Alan. *Napoleon.* Illus. by Richard Hook. Bookwright Press 1987 (LB 0-531-18094-8)

In this overview, information about Napoleon is presented on double-page spreads, often focusing on the battles and campaigns that he fought. List of important events, glossary, bibliography, and index. Part of the Great Lives series.

Biographies for Older Readers

Carroll, Bob. *The Importance of Napoleon Bonaparte.* Illus. Lucent 1994 (LB 1-56006-021-2) 112pp.

Students will appreciate this thorough presentation. Facts about Napoleon's life are documented with source notes. There is an annotated list of further readings along with an annotated bibliography of works consulted. Timeline and index. Part of the Importance Of series.

Related Books for Younger Readers

Giblin, James Cross. *The Riddle of the Rosetta Stone: Key to Ancient Egypt.* Illus. Crowell 1990 (LB 0-690-04799-1); Trophy 1993 (pap. 0-06-446137-8) 96pp.

When Napoleon occupied Egypt, he was accompanied by scientists and scholars. Near a town named Rosetta, Napoleon's soldiers discovered a black stone with writings on it. The deciphering of the Rosetta stone led to the understanding of Egyptian hieroglyphics. This book emphasizes the history of efforts to decode Egyptian writing. Bibliography and index.

Related Books for Older Readers

Jacobs, William J. *Great Lives: World Government.* Illus. Scribner's 1992 (cloth 0-684-19285-3) 320pp.

Political leaders of the 19th and 20th centuries are profiled, giving students a historical perspective on the people who have shaped our world. Among those included are Napoleon Bonaparte, Queen Victoria, Benito Mussolini, Winston Churchill, Gandhi, and Mikhail Gorbachev. Bibliography and index. Part of the Great Lives series.

Stefoff, Rebecca. *Scientific Explorers: Travels in Search of Knowledge.* Illus. Oxford University Press 1992 (LB 0-19-507689-3) 144pp.

For many explorers, the goals were discovery, conquest, and gold. For others, like those in this book, the focus was on mapping, research, and gathering information. James Cook, Charles Darwin, Lewis and Clark, and Jacques Cousteau are featured. There is a section on Napoleon's invasion of Egypt and the information that was gathered by his scientists. Chronology, bibliography, and index. Part of the Extraordinary Explorers series.

Walden, Ron W., and Joyce Milton. *The Enlightened Despots: Frederick the Great and Prussia/Napoleon and Europe.* Illus. Boston Publishing Co. 1987 (o.p.)

This is a lavishly illustrated book with portraits, reproductions, caricatures, and photographs of statues, furniture, and artifacts. The military accomplishments of Frederick and Napoleon are described, and the reader follows their careers from battles to palaces. Detailed index.

Boone, Daniel (1734–1820), born near Reading, Pennsylvania, was best known for his trailblazing activities on the American frontier.

Biographies for Younger Readers

Greene, Carol. *Daniel Boone: Man of the Forests.* Illus. by Steven Dobson. Children's Press 1990 (LB 0-516-04210-6) (pap. 0-516-44210-4) 48pp.

An introductory biography, this well-organized book provides basic information and glorifies Boone's pioneering spirit and the successful settlement of the frontier. There are numerous illustrations. List of important dates and index. Part of the Rookie Biographies series.

Biographies for Older Readers

Cavan, Seamus. *Daniel Boone and the Opening of the Ohio Country.* Illus. Chelsea House 1991 (LB 0-7910-1309-X) 112pp.

The focus of this book is the spirit behind the American pioneer. Daniel Boone's father emigrated from England seeking land, beginning a pattern of adventuring that would become the young Boone's heritage. An essay entitled "A Colorful Life" is illustrated with color reproductions of paintings of American pioneers and native peoples. Chronology, bibliography, and index. Part of the World Explorers series.

Lawlor, Laurie. *Daniel Boone.* Illus. Albert Whitman 1989 (LB 0-8075-1462-4) 160pp.

Well-researched selection for students doing research. Raised in a Quaker home, Daniel Boone faced an ongoing conflict between his philosophy of peace and his role as pioneer, hunter, and settler. Several chapters focus on the importance of Boonesborough to the success of the American Revolution. Chronology, footnotes, bibliography, and index.

Related Books for Younger Readers

Smith, Adam, and Katherine Snow Smith. *A Historical Album of Kentucky.* Illus. Millbrook Press 1995 (LB 1-56294-507-6) (pap. 1-56294-850-4) 64pp.

In "Opening the Frontier," the authors describe early settlements in Kentucky, including Harrodsburg, the first permanent settlement, and Boonesborough, settled by Daniel Boone and other frontiersmen. This book provides good information on the impact of these settlements on native peoples as well as on the development of Kentucky as a state. Addresses for more information on Kentucky are listed. Bibliography and index. Part of the Historical Albums series.

Steins, Richard. *A Nation Is Born: Rebellion and Independence in America (1700–1820).* Illus. Twenty-First Century Books 1993 (LB 0-8050-2582-0) 64pp.

Excerpts from letters, diaries, speeches, and other writings from this era introduce students to issues and concerns. Two chapters look at expansion and settlements: "Life in the New Country" and "The Nation Grows and Looks Westward." Timeline, bibliography, and index. Part of the First Person America series.

Related Books for Older Readers

Franck, Irene M., and David M. Brownstone. *The American Way West.* Illus. Facts on File 1991 (cloth 0-8160-1880-4) 128pp.

Focusing on different routes to the West, this book tells the story of the people who settled the American wilderness. Chapters describe "The Mohawk Trail," "The Wilderness Road and Other Trans-Appalachian Routes," "The Mississippi Route," "The Santa Fe Trail and the Chihuahua Trail," and "The Oregon Trail and the California Trail." Index. Part of the Trade and Travel Routes series.

Bourke-White, Margaret (1904–1971), an American photographer, is best known for her work for *Life* and *Time* magazines. Her photographs painted a vivid picture of the American landscape during the 1930s, 1940s, and 1950s. She also captured images from World War II, the South African mining industry, and the Korean War.

On photographing the Holocaust: "Correspondents are in a privileged and sometimes unhappy position. . . . They have an obligation to pass on what they see to others."
(Siegel, p. 95)

Biographies for Younger Readers

Welch, Catherine A. *Margaret Bourke-White.* Illus. by Jennifer Hagerman. Carolrhoda Books 1997 (cloth 0-87614-890-9); Lerner Publications 1996 (pap. 0-87614-956-5)

Reading like a novel, this book focuses on some of the exciting moments in Margaret Bourke-White's life—when she was on a ship that was torpedoed and when General James Doolittle allowed her to fly on a bombing mission. Timeline. Part of the On My Own Biographies series.

Biographies for Older Readers

Keller, Emily. *Margaret Bourke-White: A Photographer's Life.* Illus. with photographs of and by Bourke-White. Lerner Publications 1993 (o.p.) 128pp.

Margaret Bourke-White grew up loving nature, and she was encouraged by her father, who would answer her questions and introduce her to new ideas. His love of photography and machinery sparked her interest, allowing her to develop as an innovative, intrepid photographer. This is an excellent and readable biography. Source notes, bibliography, and index.

Siegel, Beatrice. *An Eye on the World: Margaret Bourke-White, Photographer.* Illus. Frederick Warne 1980 (o.p.)

As a photographer for *Life* magazine, Margaret Bourke-White illuminated the dramatic beauty of machinery and industry, the horror of war, and the tragedy of poverty. The author of this book used many photographs from the Bourke-White family's personal collection to add insight into her character, particularly as she battled Parkinsonism. Bibliography and index.

Related Books for Younger Readers

Czech, Kenneth P. *Snapshot: America Discovers the Camera.* Illus. Lerner Publications 1996 (cloth 0-8225-1736-1) 88pp.

Early photographs required the subject to remain immobile for many minutes. In the ensuing years photographs were used to document wars, to capture the beauty of the natural world, and to depict social conditions. From the early efforts of still photographers, moving pictures were developed. This historical presentation provides information on how images of America have been captured. Bibliography and index.

Wolf, Sylvia. *Focus: Five Women Photographers.* Illus. Albert Whitman 1994 (LB 0-8075-2531-6) 64pp.

Julia Margaret Cameron, Margaret Bourke-White, Flor Garduño, Sandy Skoglund, and Lorna Simpson are featured in this book. Like Bourke-White, Cameron and Garduño were trailblazers in their profession. Read about these contemporaries and the issues each faced. Skoglund and Simpson continue to challenge expectations today by creating innovative images. Bibliography.

Related Books for Older Readers

Steffens, Bradley. *Photography: Preserving the Past.* Illus. Lucent 1991 (LB 1-56006-212-6) 96pp.

After looking at early experiments in photography, chapters focus on the ways photography was first used, including Matthew Brady's work during the Civil War. The works of Alfred Stieglitz, Margaret Bourke-White, and Gordon Parks are mentioned. Timeline, glossary, bibliography, and index. Part of the Encyclopedia of Discovery and Invention series.

Braille, Louis (1809–1852), blind from the age of three, is renowned for his invention of the braille system of printing for the blind. His system, consisting of raised dots used in various combinations to denote letters and numbers, is also used for musical notation.

Biographies for Younger Readers

Freedman, Russell. *Out of Darkness: The Story of Louis Braille.* Illus. by Kate Kiesler. Clarion 1997 (LB 0-395-77516-7); Dutton (pap. 0-614-28670-0) 81pp.

This is a very readable biography that captures the emotions as Louis Braille tries to find a way for blind people to read. With his successful raised-dot system, "he opened the doors of knowledge to all those who cannot see" (from a plaque on the front of his home). Index.

Keeler, Stephen. *Louis Braille.* Illus. by Richard Hook. Bookwright Press 1986 (LB 0-531-18071-9)

Louis Braille became blind following a childhood accident. In the 1800s educational opportunities were limited for farming families like the Brailles. With the help of a priest, Louis was sent to school, where he excelled. Lists of dates and suggested readings, glossary, and index. Part of the Great Lives series.

Biographies for Older Readers

Birch, Beverley. *Louis Braille.* Illus. with photographs and drawings. Gareth Stevens 1989 (LB 0-8368-0097-4)

Louis Braille's printing system of raised dots has helped blind people around the world read and write. Today's computer technology makes it even more accessible as scanners can read print and change the text to braille. Photographs show a braille globe, Braille's family home, braille typewriters, and braille playing cards. Index. Part of the People Who Have Helped the World series.

Bryant, Jennifer Fisher. *Louis Braille: Teacher of the Blind.* Illus. Chelsea House 1994 (LB 0-7910-2077-0) 111pp.

At age 10, Louis Braille attended the Royal Institute for Blind Youth in Paris. There he invented his raised-dot alphabet. This detailed biography is well organized for students doing research. Chronology, bibliography, and index. Part of the Great Achievers: Lives of the Physically Challenged series.

Related Books for Older Readers

Kent, Deborah, and Kathryn A. Quinlan. *Extraordinary People with Disabilities.* Illus. Children's Press 1996 (LB 0-516-20021-6) 1997 (pap. 0-516-26074-X) 215pp.

This book profiles more than 50 people who have disabilities and describes their efforts to improve their own situations and to help others. From Louis Braille's reading system for the blind to I. King Jordan (the first deaf president of Gallaudet University) to baseball star Jim Abbott, there are a variety of accomplishments represented. List of resources (including a list of addresses and Internet sites), glossary, and index. Part of the Extraordinary People series.

Walters, Gregory J. *Equal Access: Safeguarding Disability Rights.* Illus. Rourke 1992 (LB 0-86593-174-7) 112pp.

Students researching disabilities will learn about the importance of equal access to resources and services. There is historical information about attitudes toward disabilities and the development of legislation, including the Rehabilitation Act of 1973 and the Americans With Disabilities Act of 1990. One chapter, "People Who Made a Difference," features Louis Braille, Helen Keller, Stephen Hawking, and others who have been active in the disability rights movement. Timeline, lists of media resources and addresses and phone numbers for organizations and hotlines, bibliography, and index. Part of the Human Rights series.

Brontë family, British poets and novelists, including **Charlotte** (1816–1855), **Emily** (1818–1848), and **Anne** (1820–1849). Their first poetry collection, *Poems by Currer, Ellis and Acton Bell*, was published in 1846; in 1847 Charlotte published *Jane Eyre*; Emily, *Wuthering Heights*; and Anne, *Agnes Gray*.

Biographies for Older Readers

Guzzetti, Paula. *A Family Called Brontë.* Illus. Silver Burdett 1994 (LB 0-87518-592-4) 128pp.

Reproductions of portraits and photographs of documents, rooms, and buildings add to this solid presentation. Being from the same home, Charlotte, Emily, and Anne Brontë had similar childhood experiences. In this biography, the sisters emerge as independent characters, and there is careful attention to individual personality details. Selected poems are also included. Chronology, bibliography and index. Part of the People in Focus series.

Martin, Christopher. *The Brontës.* Illus. Rourke 1989 (LB 0-86592-299-3) 112pp.

Chapters feature the childhood, education, and writings of the three Brontë sisters. Among the many illustrations are some from the film adaptation of *Wuthering Heights*. There are photographs of manuscript pages, portraits, and rooms at Haworth Parsonage, along with the address of the Brontë Parsonage Museum in West Yorkshire. Chronology, glossary, bibliography, and index. Part of the Life and Works series.

Related Books for Younger Readers

Ross, Stewart. *Charlotte Brontë and Jane Eyre.* Illus. by Robert Van Nutt. Viking Penguin 1997 (pap. 0-670-87486-8) 48pp.

Boxed inserts describe various aspects of Victorian life and extend this presentation, which examines the parallels between Charlotte Brontë's life and that of her fictional heroine. Black-and-white sketches and full-color paintings add to the appeal. Chronology of Charlotte Brontë's life and bibliography.

Related Books for Older Readers

Bentley, Phyllis. *The Brontës and Their World.* Illus. Scribner's 1969 (LB 0-684-16023-4)

Victorian England comes to life through the activities of the Brontë family and descriptions of events. The numerous black-and-white photographs and reproductions of manuscripts and letters provide additional details. Chronology and index.

Hill, Susan, ed., researched and compiled by Piers Dudgeon. *The Spirit of Britain: An Illustrated Guide to Literary Britain.* Illus. Headline Book Publishing 1997 (pap. 0-7472-7812-1) 224pp.

This is a travel guide to literary locations throughout Britain. Authors from Jane Austen through William Wordsworth are featured through the sites of their works. The West Yorkshire locations of the Brontës, Daphne du Maurier's Cornwall, and Charles Dickens's London are among the places included. Along the journey there are facts about the history and people of each region. This is a good choice for browsing and would be an especially useful resource for a study trip.

Brown, John (1800–1859), an American abolitionist, on October 16, 1859, led a group in the capture of the U.S. arsenal at Harpers Ferry, Virginia, which is now part of West Virginia. Robert E. Lee recaptured the arsenal and Brown was hanged on December 2.

Biographies for Younger Readers

Collins, James L. *John Brown and the Fight against Slavery.* Illus. Millbrook Press 1991 (LB 1-56294-043-0) (pap. 1-878841-72-6) 32pp.

Sidebar features on Harriet Tubman, Bleeding Kansas, and the Dred Scott case help link the story of John Brown's life to the events of his era. Timeline, bibliography, and index. Part of the Gateway Civil Rights series.

Everett, Gwen. *John Brown: One Man against Slavery.* Illus. with paintings by Jacob Lawrence. Rizzoli 1993 (cloth 0-8478-1702-4) 32pp.

This is a creative biographical retelling of John Brown's anti-slavery beliefs and the raid on Harpers Ferry. Told from the point of view of his daughter, Annie, the account is further enhanced by reproductions of gouache paintings (now in the Detroit Institute of Arts) by Jacob Lawrence, a renowned African American artist. Part of the Children's Library, Fine Arts for Young People series.

Biographies for Older Readers

Potter, Robert R. *John Brown: Militant Abolitionist.* Illus. by James P. Shenton. Raintree Steck-Vaughn 1995 (LB 0-8114-2378-6)

This is a good choice for students doing research. Chapters focus on John Brown's childhood, his almost missionary commitment to his beliefs, and his act of defiance at Harpers Ferry. There are maps and a list of places to visit. Key dates, list of recommended readings, glossary, bibliography, and index. Part of the American Troublemakers series.

Related Books for Younger Readers

Ray, Delia. *A Nation Torn: The Story of How the Civil War Began.* Illus. Lodestar Books 1990 (o.p.) 128pp.

Younger readers and researchers interested in the Civil War will find here a fascinating look at events that led to the war. Slavery was a key factor, but there were also other economic and political issues. Key figures include William Lloyd Garrison, John Brown, Abraham Lincoln, and Harriet Tubman. Glossary, bibliography, and index. Part of the Young Readers' History of the Civil War series.

Related Books for Older Readers

Lester, Julius. *From Slave Ship to Freedom Road.* Illus. with paintings by Rod Brown. Dial 1998 (pap. 0-8037-1893-4)

This is a merging of artistic interpretation and a narrative. Rod Brown's paintings about slavery—detailed, graphic works of art—are complemented by Julius Lester's equally intense text. From the cruelty of the Middle Passage to the humiliation of slavery to the joy of freedom, this is a record of horror and hope. List of paintings and their present locations.

Myers, Walter Dean. *Now Is Your Time! The African-American Struggle for Freedom.* Illus. HarperCollins 1991 (LB 0-06-024371-6) 1992 (pap. 0-06-446120-3) 304pp.

Chapters describe the experiences of Africans kidnapped for slavery, the Dred Scott case, the efforts of abolitionists, Reconstruction, such court decisions as *Brown* v. *Board of Education,* and later events in the civil rights movement. Bibliography (divided by topics, such as Plantation Life and John Brown) and index.

Ofosu-Appiah, L. H. *People in Bondage: African Slavery since the 15th Century.* Illus. Runestone Press 1993 (LB 0-8225-3150-X) 112pp.

After describing the existence of slavery in ancient societies, the author presents a detailed look at the enslavement of Africans in the 15th century and later. Descriptions of cruelty and physical abuse by the traders, on the journey, and on the plantations are given. The final chapter looks at "Slavery's Legacy." Index.

Bunche, Ralph J. (1904–1971), an African American statesman, launched a lengthy career with the United Nations, eventually becoming undersecretary-general in 1967. He initiated many peace initiatives and was a recipient of the Nobel Peace Prize.

Biographies for Younger Readers

McKissack, Patricia, and Fredrick McKissack. *Ralph J. Bunche: Peacemaker.* Illus. by Ned Ostendorf and with photographs. Enslow Publishers 1991 (LB 0-89490-300-4) 32pp.

Ralph Bunche studied at Harvard and was the first African American to earn a political science degree there. He traveled throughout Africa before working at the United Nations. For his efforts to bring world peace (particularly for resolving the Arab-Israeli war of 1948), Bunche received the Nobel Peace Prize in 1950, the first black man to do so. Index. Part of the Great African Americans series.

Related Books for Younger Readers

Blue, Rose, and Corinne J. Naden. *People of Peace.* Illus. Mill-brook Press 1994 (LB 1-56294-409-6) 80pp.

Eleven individuals who devoted their energy to the search for peace are profiled: philanthropist Andrew Carnegie; social worker Jane Addams; presidents Woodrow Wilson and Jimmy Carter; political leaders Mohandas Gandhi and Oscar Arias Sanchez; United Nations leaders Ralph Bunche and Dag Hammarskjöld; and activists Desmond Tutu, Betty Williams, and Mairead Corrigan Maguire. This is a great opportunity to see the characteristics of peacemakers and to recognize how their efforts have had an impact on the world's history. Glossary, bibliography, and index.

Related Books for Older Readers

Dornfeld, Margaret. *The Turning Tide: From the Desegregation of the Armed Forces to the Montgomery Bus Boycott (1948–1956).* Illus. Chelsea House 1995 (LB 0-7910-2255-2) (pap. 0-7910-2681-7) 144pp.

After serving America in World War II, many African Americans returned home to face discrimination and disillusionment. Ralph Ellison's *Invisible Man* captured these emotions. Yet there were great accomplishments, too—Ralph Bunche helped end the war in Palestine (and received the Nobel Peace Prize). Efforts to combat Jim Crow laws and attitudes led to the integration of the military, while the first steps of the civil rights movement were taken with the 1956 boycott in Montgomery. Bibliography and index. Part of the Milestones in Black American History series.

Bush, George Herbert Walker

(1924–), 41st president of the United States (1989–1993), struggled to maintain a balance between foreign policy and domestic concerns. His popularity was high after the successful end to the Gulf War, but the faltering economy cost him the 1993 general election.

Biographies for Younger Readers

Sandak, Cass R. *The Bushes.* Illus. Silver Burdett 1991 (o.p.)
48pp.

George Bush is the main focus of this book, although there is
some information about Barbara Bush and their children. Because
this account was written while Bush was still president, the book
concludes with some of his plans for the future. Students doing
research will need to find additional sources to update this information. List of suggested readings and index. Part of the First Families
series.

Biographies for Older Readers

Kent, Zachary. *George Bush.* Illus. Children's Press 1989 (LB 0-
516-01374-2) 100pp.

Published while Bush was president, this book focuses on his
expectations for the future. His family, service, and sharing are
stressed. These values influenced his leadership as a pilot in World
War II, a congressman from Texas, U.S. ambassador to the United
Nations, vice president, and, finally, president. Chronology and
index. Part of the Encyclopedia of Presidents series.

Pemberton, William E. *George Bush.* Illus. with photographs.
Rourke 1993 (cloth 0-86625-478-1)

This is a very accessible biography; liberally illustrated with
photographs, including a section in color. It includes a list of media
resources such as Bush's nomination acceptance speech and
"George Bush: An Intimate Portrait" from C-SPAN. Timeline, list of
achievements, glossary, bibliography, and index. Part of the World
Leaders series.

Related Books for Younger Readers

Twist, Clint. *1980s.* Illus. Raintree Steck-Vaughn 1994 (LB 0-
8114-3081-2) 47pp.

American politics in the 1980s were dominated by Ronald
Reagan and George Bush. World events included war in the Middle
East, U.S. accords with China, reforms in the USSR, political unrest
in China, and the opening of the Berlin Wall. The format simulates
a newspaper with headlines, columns, and supporting pictures,
making an attractive overview. Glossary, bibliography, and index.
Part of the Take Ten Years series.

Related Books for Older Readers

Hiro, Dilip. *The Middle East.* Illus. Oryx Press 1996 (pap. 0-57356-004-9) 232pp.

In this very detailed book, there is an overview of the region followed by a focus on the individual countries. In each section, there is historical information as well as information about important issues and people. For example, there is information about the discovery of oil and the important role it has come to play. There is a chapter on the conflict between Arabs and Jews. There is information about the crisis in Kuwait, the Gulf War, and the 1993 accord. Glossary, bibliography, and index. Part of the International Politics and Government series.

Kent, Zachary. *The Persian Gulf War: "The Mother of All Battles."* Illus. Enslow Publishers 1994 (LB 0-89490-528-7) 128pp.

Read about the quick world response to Iraq's invasion of Kuwait and the roles played by Bush, Saddam Hussein, Norman Schwarzkopf, and Colin Powell. Chronology, chapter notes, bibliography, and index. Part of the American War series.

Caesar, Augustus (63 B.C.–A.D. 14), born Gaius Octavius, is also know as Octavian. A grandnephew of Julius Caesar, he was the first Roman emperor. Credited with enacting many reforms in Rome and its territories, he tried to preserve the Roman borders established by Julius Caesar and established the concept of the Pax Romana.

Biographies for Older Readers

Walworth, Nancy Zinsser. *Augustus Caesar.* Illus. Chelsea House 1989 (LB 1-55546-804-7) 112pp.

The emphasis in this book is on Augustus Caesar's political skills as he instituted policies that would alter Western civilization. His plans included a stronger army, improved public services, and social legislation. Quotations in the margins give students insights into the thoughts of Caesar and his contemporaries, as well as what historians have said about this great leader. Chronology, list of suggested further readings, and index. Part of the World Leaders Past & Present series.

Related Books for Younger Readers

Macdonald, Fiona. *A Roman Fort.* Illus. by Gerald Wood. Peter Bedrick Books 1993 (cloth 0-87226-370-3) 48pp.

Detailed illustrations on double-page spreads will attract many readers. "The Roman Army," "Marching Camps," "Building the Fort," "A Soldier's Life," and "In Battle" are some of the chapters. Cut-away drawings illustrate additional features. Glossary and index. Part of the See Inside series.

Poulton, Michael. *Life in the Time of Augustus and the Ancient Romans.* Illus. by Christine Molan. Raintree Steck-Vaughn 1993 (o.p.) 63pp.

The many illustrations add to this book's appeal. There are descriptions of home life in Rome, life in the countryside, ships, and religion. Historical events and personalities of the time (Julius Caesar, Marc Antony, Cleopatra) are briefly presented. Glossary and index. Part of the Life in the Time Of series.

Related Books for Older Readers

Nardo, Don. *The Age of Augustus.* Illus. Lucent 1997 (LB 1-56006-306-8) 112pp.

From the rise of Octavian (who later became Augustus) through the death of Augustus and the succession of Tiberius, this is a well-organized, detailed book. Augustus proposed many improvements to Roman life—in services, transportation, family values, and policies. Boxed sidebars include excerpts from histories and literature. Chronology, suggestions for further readings, chapter notes, bibliography, and index. Part of the World History series.

Caesar, Julius (Gaius Julius Caesar)

(100 B.C.–44 B.C.), a Roman general and statesman, was given a mandate by the people of Rome in 45 B.C. to rule as dictator for life. He was assassinated by a group of republicans who feared he would install himself as monarch.

Biographies for Younger Readers

Green, Robert. *Julius Caesar.* Illus. Franklin Watts 1996 (LB 0-531-20241-0) 1997 (pap. 0-531-15812-8) 64pp.

During Caesar's rise to power, he expanded the influence of Rome. But he made many enemies, enemies who later assassinated him. The glossy paper and colorful illustrations are especially attractive. Timeline, list of suggested readings, and index. Part of the Ancient Biography First Books series.

Biographies for Older Readers

Bruns, Roger. *Julius Caesar.* Illus. Chelsea House 1988 (LB 0-87754-514-6) 112pp.

Julius Caesar was a statesman and military leader who brought glory to Rome and instituted major reforms in the government. For students doing research, this is a fine choice: the text is clearly written, and there are quotations in the margins from Caesar, his contemporaries, and historians. The illustrations extend the text and have detailed captions. Chronology, bibliography, and index. Part of the World Leaders Past & Present series.

Nardo, Don. *The Importance of Julius Caesar.* Illus. Lucent 1997 (LB 1-56006-083-2)

This very complete biography has reference aids and special features that make it a top choice for researchers. A chronology opens the book, and within the chapters, there are boxed excerpts from such famous writings as Plutarch's *Life of Caesar* and Suetonius's *Lives of the Twelve Caesars.* Chapter notes, list of suggested readings, bibliography, and index. Part of the Importance Of series.

Related Books for Younger Readers

Ganeri, Anita. *How Would You Survive as an Ancient Roman?* Illus. by John James. Franklin Watts 1995 (LB 0-531-14349-X) 1996 (pap. 0-531-15305-3) 48pp.

This colorful presentation is sure to attract younger readers and researchers. Each page has illustrations and informative captions that are grouped by such topics as home, family, food and drink, clothes, education, law and order, and army. Timelines from ancient history through today and of the Roman era, glossary and index. Part of the How Would You Survive? series.

"As Caesar loved me, I weep for him; as he was fortunate, I rejoice at it; as he was valiant, I honor him, but—as he was ambitious, I slew him."
(Brutus, in Act III, scene 2, of Shakespeare's *Julius Caesar*)

Related Books for Older Readers

Nardo, Don. *The Roman Republic.* Illus. Lucent 1994 (LB 1-56006-230-4) 100pp.

Before Julius Caesar, Marc Antony, and Cleopatra, there was the Roman Republic. Here are informative text, captioned illustrations, and sidebars such as excerpts from Shakespeare's *Julius Caesar* and a description of the exploits of Hannibal. Chronology, suggestions for further readings, chapter notes, bibliography, and index. Part of the World History series.

Steffens, Bradley. *The Fall of the Roman Empire.* Illus. Greenhaven 1994 (cloth 1-56510-098-0) 128pp.

What caused the end of the Roman empire? How did the decisions of the rulers influence the collapse of this great civilization? Presenting different theories and ideas, this book encourages students to think about the possibilities. Bibliography and index. Part of the Great Mysteries: Opposing Viewpoints series.

Sportscaster Vin Scully: "All of God's creatures have a purpose in life. Some seem to have a higher purpose. Roy Campanella was such a man. Roy's wheelchair was not a cross. It was much more like his throne. His presence provided inspiration for millions."

(Macht, p. 106)

Campanella, Roy (1921–1993), an

African American baseball star, played in the Mexican and black leagues and later with the Brooklyn Dodgers as a catcher. The National League named him most valuable player three times, and he was inducted into the Hall of Fame.

Biographies for Younger Readers

Greene, Carol. *Roy Campanella: Major-League Champion.* Illus. by Steven Dobson. Children's Press 1994 (LB 0-516-04261-0) (pap. 0-516-44261-9) 48pp.

Students who are just beginning to do research will appreciate these five brief chapters. The text, which is very easy to read, describes Campanella's success as a baseball player and his survival and triumph following the car accident that paralyzed him. Chronology and index. Part of the Rookie Biographies series.

Biographies for Older Readers

Macht, Norman L. *Roy Campanella: Baseball Star.* Illus. Chelsea House 1995 (LB 0-7910-2083-5) 128pp.

Part sports history and part a story of inspiration, this biography describes the life of Roy Campanella. After playing in the Negro Leagues, Campanella went on to the major leagues, becoming an All-Star with the Brooklyn Dodgers. Overcoming racial prejudice was just one challenge: Campanella later survived being paralyzed and became a source of motivation and admiration for his courageous spirit. Lists of suggested readings and Campanella's major-league statistics, chronology, and index. Part of the Great Achievers: Lives of the Physically Challenged series.

Related Books for Older Readers

Brashler, William. *The Story of Negro League Baseball.* Illus. Ticknor & Fields 1994 (cloth 0-395-67169-8) (pap. 0-395-69721-2) 144pp.

After discussing Jim Crow laws of this era, the author looks at teams and stars, including Roy Campanella, Satchel Paige, and Jackie Robinson. This is a great book for baseball fans and for students doing research. It is enjoyable to read, making good use of quotes and anecdotes. Bibliography and index.

Gardner, Robert, and Dennis Shortelle. *The Forgotten Players: The Story of Black Baseball in America.* Illus. Walker and Company 1993 (LB 0-8027-8249-3) (cloth 0-8027-8248-5) 128pp.

While acknowledging the lost opportunities for many black players, this book examines the experiences of players on segregated teams that led to the Negro Leagues. Information is given about "Life in the Negro Leagues" and there are personal observations from former players including Buck Leonard and Roy Campanella, as well as from others associated with the leagues. Chapter notes, bibliography, and index.

McKissack, Patricia, and Fredrick McKissack, Jr. *Black Diamond: The Story of the Negro Baseball Leagues.* Illus. Scholastic 1994 (cloth 0-590-45809-4) 1996 (pap. 0-590-45810-8) 192pp.

Baseball fans will enjoy looking through this book. Before Jackie Robinson entered the major league, the Negro Leagues offered black baseball players the opportunity to compete professionally. This book includes some "Player Profiles," a list of players in the Negro Leagues Hall of Fame, a timeline of black baseball set against the context of other civil rights events, and index.

Carmichael, Stokely (1941–), a radical civil rights activist born in Trinidad, led the Student Nonviolent Coordinating Committee, changing the group's goal of ending segregation to "black liberation." He later joined the Black Panther movement.

Biographies for Younger Readers

Cwiklik, Robert. *Stokely Carmichael and Black Power.* Illus. Millbrook Press 1993 (LB 1-56294-276-X) (pap. 1-56294-839-3) 32pp.

Within the civil rights movement there were diverse beliefs—from the nonviolence of Martin Luther King, Jr., to the anger and hostility of Stokely Carmichael and Eldridge Cleaver. There is a boxed section that describes the Black Panthers. This is a good introduction to a controversial era. Chronology, bibliography, and index. Part of the Gateway Civil Rights series.

Related Books for Younger Readers

Lucas, Eileen. *Civil Rights: The Long Struggle.* Illus. with photographs. Enslow Publishers 1996 (LB 0-89490-729-8) 112pp.

The focus of this book is not just on the civil rights movement; it is on the history of freedom, government, and the First Amendment. The changes of the 1960s are highlighted not only in the nonviolence of Martin Luther King, Jr., but in the confrontational efforts of such other leaders as Stokely Carmichael. Chronology, chapter notes (documenting quotes), glossary, bibliography, and index. Part of the Issues in Focus series.

Related Books for Older Readers

Katz, William L. *The Great Society to the Reagan Era.* Illus. Raintree Steck-Vaughn 1993 (LB 0-8114-6282-X) 96pp.

In the years covered by this volume there were many issues that faced America. "Black Power" and "The Black Panthers" challenged the nonviolent efforts of Dr. King and his followers. There was an emphasis on "Multicultural and Bilingual Education" as well as "Opening the Political Process," with the elections of Julian Bond, Shirley Chisholm, Barbara Jordan, and others. Issues facing immigrants from Mexico and Arab countries as well at those for native peoples and women are presented. Bibliography and index. Part of the History of Multicultural America series.

Carnegie, Andrew (1835–1919), born in Scotland, was a philanthropist who donated more than $350 million to libraries, universities, and other institutions after making his fortune in the United States in iron and steel production.

Biographies for Older Readers

Bowman, John. *Andrew Carnegie: Steel Tycoon.* Illus. Silver Burdett 1989 (o.p.) 128pp.

From "Scottish Origins" through "The Gospel of Wealth" and "A Full Life," this book gives a solid portrayal of the noted businessman and philanthropist. When Andrew Carnegie emigrated to Pittsburgh from Scotland, he entered a city where industrial growth was just beginning. He became a part of that growth, channeling his energy and enthusiasm into a variety of endeavors that would bring him a great fortune—which he later chose to share to benefit others. Bibliography and index. Part of the American Dream: Business Leaders of the 20th Century series.

Meltzer, Milton. *The Many Lives of Andrew Carnegie.* Franklin Watts 1997 (cloth 0-531-11427-9)

Meltzer uses well-researched information and amusing anecdotes to make Andrew Carnegie come to life. There are details about the hardships of Carnegie's early years and the energy he put into achieving success. Carnegie's interest in education and learning is especially fascinating. With limited formal schooling, Carnegie always worked to acquire knowledge and improve his skills. His philanthropy to libraries encouraged others to do the same. The source notes in this book feature primary and secondary sources. Index.

Related Books for Younger Readers

Brown, Gene. *The Struggle to Grow: Expansionism and Industrialization (1880–1913).* Illus. Twenty-First Century Books 1993 (LB 0-8050-2584-7) 64pp.

This is an attractive overview from frontier days to immigrants to industry to politics. Vignettes feature such key people and issues as women pioneers, Ellis Island, the success of Andrew Carnegie, and child labor. Younger readers will find this an accessible book. Timeline, bibliography, and index. Part of the First Person America series.

Related Books for Older Readers

Hakim, Joy. *An Age of Extremes.* Illus. Oxford University Press 1994 (LB 0-19-507759-8) (cloth 0-19-509513-8) (pap. 0-19-507760-1) 160pp.

The focus of this book is the end of the 19th century and the opening decades of the 20th century. In the early years, very wealthy key figures include Andrew Carnegie, John D. Rockefeller, and J. P. Morgan. Later years cover the conditions of workers, the rise of organized labor, and Jane Addams's efforts to reach out to the needy. Sidebars add to the interest. Part of the History of US series.

Carson, Rachel Louise (1907–1964),

American marine biologist and writer, called attention to the dangers of insecticides in her 1962 book, *Silent Spring.* Her other noted works include *The Sea Around Us* (1951) and *The Edge of the Sea* (1954).

U.S. Secretary of the Interior, Stewart L. Udall: "She made us realize that we had allowed our fascination with chemicals to override our wisdom in their use."

(Harlan, p. 113)

Biographies for Younger Readers

Kudlinski, Kathleen V. *Rachel Carson: Pioneer of Ecology.* Illus. by Ted Lewin. Puffin 1988 (pap. 0-14-032242-6) 64pp.

Here is a readable introduction to the life of Rachel Carson. Chapters feature important influences in Carson's life, including her decision to become a scientist in an era when women were not encouraged in that study and her lifelong fascination with the sea. Part of the Women of Our Time series.

Stwertka, Eve. *Rachel Carson.* Illus. Franklin Watts 1991 (o.p.)

Today environmental concerns are important issues, but in the 1960s, these concerns were just beginning to emerge. This biography is a fine introduction for beginning researchers. Included is an address for the Rachel Carson Council, Inc. List of suggested readings, glossary, and index. Part of the Biographies First Book series.

Biographies for Older Readers

Harlan, Judith. *Sounding the Alarm: A Biography of Rachel Carson.* Illus. Silver Burdett 1989 (LB 0-87518-407-3) 128pp.

While Rachel Carson was finishing *Silent Spring,* she learned she had cancer. She showed great courage as she faced criticism about her book and dealt with her terminal illness. Bibliography and index. Part of the People in Focus series.

Wadsworth, Ginger. *Rachel Carson: Voice for the Earth.* Illus. Lerner Publications 1992 (LB 0-8225-4907-7) 128pp.

The chapters in this book are arranged to present information in chronological order (Chapter One: 1907–1919, Chapter Two: 1919–1929, etc.). This could be useful to students who are researching just one aspect of Rachel Carson's life. The text is well written, making excellent use of quotations, and there is a list of conservation organizations and their addresses. Bibliography and index.

Related Books for Younger Readers

Law, Kevin J. *The Environmental Protection Agency.* Illus. Chelsea House 1988 (o.p.) 96pp.

The Environmental Protection Agency was created in 1970 in response to the concerns of naturalists, scientists, and other ecology-minded people. This book describes the history of the environmental movement, the responsibilities of the EPA, and the problems that exist today. Glossary, bibliography, and index. Part of the Know Your Government series.

Whitman, Sylvia. *This Land Is Your Land: The American Conservation Movement.* Illus. Lerner Publications 1994 (LB 0-8225-1729-9) 88pp.

Many students will be able to use this book to get an overview of environmental issues. Efforts to preserve wilderness areas, to control pollution, and to establish recycling routines are discussed. Theodore Roosevelt, Rachel Carson, John Wesley Powell, and John Muir are included as is information about government agencies and environmental organization. Bibliography and index.

Related Books for Older Readers

McGowen, Tom. *1960–1969.* Illus. Twenty-First Century Books 1995 (LB 0-8050-3436-6) 80pp.

Research from earlier eras influenced the discoveries in this decade. In physics, there was research in holography and quarks. In geology, the Leakeys researched early humans. Rachel Carson wrote *Silent Spring,* alerting us to the dangers of pesticides. In space exploration, there was the first man in space (Yuri Gagarin), the first walk in space (Aleksei Arkhipovich Leonov), and the first man on the moon (Neil Armstrong). Bibliography and index. Part of the Yearbooks in Science series.

Stefoff, Rebecca. *The American Environmental Movement.* Illus. Facts on File 1995 (cloth 0-8160-3046-4) 160pp.

After examining the settlement of the American wilderness, this book looks at efforts to preserve wilderness areas. There are details about the environmentalists, scientists, and political activists who have championed the cause of protecting the natural world. Chronology, list of agencies and organizations, bibliography, and index. Part of the Social Reform Movements series.

Carter, James Earl, Jr. (1924–), the 39th U.S. President (1977–1981), negotiated the Camp David Accords between Israel and Egypt in 1979. He put energy conservation policies into effect, concluded the Panama Canal treaties in 1978, and founded the U.S. Habitat for Humanity program that provides housing to the needy.

Biographies for Younger Readers

Carrigan, Mellonee. *Jimmy Carter: Beyond the Presidency.* Illus. Children's Press 1995 (LB 0-516-04193-2) (pap. 0-516-44193-0) 32pp.

While the focus of this book is on Jimmy Carter's service to his country and the world since he left the presidency, the beginning of the book looks at his early life and time in office. There is a description of the foundation of the Carter Center of Emory University in

1982 and the Atlanta Project in 1991 and of his work for Habitat for Humanity. No chapter or subject divisions. Timeline and index. Part of the Picture-Story Biographies series.

Sandak, Cass R. *The Carters.* Illus. Silver Burdett 1993 (o.p.) 48pp.

This book profiles Jimmy Carter and Rosalynn Smith Carter as they moved from the navy to the governor's office in Georgia to the White House. The final section features "The Carter Legacy," calling him "enigmatic," "well-read," and "honest," stressing how he respected tradition and stood by his principles. List of further readings and index. Part of the First Families series.

Biographies for Older Readers

Lazo, Caroline. *Jimmy Carter on the Road to Peace.* Illus. Dillon Press 1996 (LB 0-382-30262-0) (pap. 0-382-39263-9) 160pp.

After examining Jimmy Carter's early life and presidency, this book focuses on his service to our country and the world as a former president. Lazo states: "With the possible exception of John Quincy Adams, who served 17 years in Congress after leaving the White House, Jimmy Carter is the most effective former president in American history" (p. 8). Chapters document his ongoing efforts to promote world peace and on behalf of Habitat for Humanity. The thorough bibliography includes books, periodicals, and television programs. Index. Part of the People in Focus series.

Wade, Linda R. *James Carter.* Illus. Children's Press 1989 (LB 0-516-01372-6) 100pp.

Black-and-white photographs document the life of Jimmy Carter, who went from being virtually unknown in national politics to becoming president of the United States. Chapters feature stages of his life: "In the Navy," "The Businessman and Civic Leader," "The Politician," "The Candidate," and "The President." A chronology highlights Carter's contributions within the context of U.S. political and social growth. Index. Part of the Encyclopedia of Presidents series.

Related Books for Younger Readers

Blue, Rose, and Corinne J. Naden. *People of Peace.* Illus. Millbrook Press 1994 (LB 1-56294-409-6) 80pp.

Eleven individuals who have devoted their energy to the search for peace are profiled. Philanthropist Andrew Carnegie; social worker Jane Addams; presidents Woodrow Wilson and Jimmy Carter; political leaders Gandhi and Oscar Arias Sanchez; United Nations leaders Ralph Bunche and Dag Hammarskjöld; and activists Desmond Tutu, Betty Williams, and Mairead Corrigan

Maguire. This is a great opportunity to see the characteristics of peacemakers and their impact on world history. Glossary, bibliography, and index.

Twist, Clint. *1970s.* Illus. Raintree Steck-Vaughn 1994 (LB 0-8114-3080-4) 47pp.

Students will learn about protests of the Vietnam War, the Watergate scandal, and the presidencies of Richard Nixon, Gerald Ford, and Jimmy Carter. Hot spots in this decade included the Middle East, South Africa, Nicaragua, Pakistan, and India. The format simulates a newspaper with headlines, columns, and supporting pictures, making an attractive overview. Glossary, bibliography, and index. Part of the Take Ten Years series.

Related Books for Older Readers

Carter, Jimmy. *Talking Peace: A Vision for the Next Generation.* Illus. Dutton 1993 (cloth 0-525-44959-0); NAL Dutton 1996 (pap. 0-525-45651-1) 168pp.

Former President Carter reflects on the importance of nonviolent conflict resolution and a commitment to peacemaking techniques. Included are personal experiences and insights—from the Camp David Accords to his work with Habitat for Humanity to the efforts of the Carter Center in Atlanta. This is a powerful message from a man who has devoted his life to promoting peace and cooperation. Within his vision for the future are reflections on the past, providing a historical context for students. Notes on sources and index.

Cooney, James A. *Think About Foreign Policy: The U.S. and the World.* rev. ed. Illus. Walker and Company 1993 (LB 0-8027-8116-0) (pap. 0-8027-7368-0) 160pp.

The opening chapter asks "What Is American Foreign Policy?" Chapters then examine issues related to such events as the Spanish-American War, the cold war era, the Cuban Missile Crisis, and the Vietnam War. After reading this book, students will have a better understanding of decisions that are being made today. At the end of each broad chapter, there are review questions. Appendices include information and addresses for such organizations as the Foreign Policy Association and SANE (a peace movement group) and documents including Federalist Paper No. 51, the Truman Doctrine, and the Marshall Plan. Glossary, bibliography, and detailed index. Part of the Think series.

Carver, George Washington

(1864?–1943), born into slavery, was for nearly 50 years the agricultural research director at Alabama's Tuskegee Institute. He is credited with discovering hundreds of uses for the sweet potato, soybean, and peanut.

Biographies for Younger Readers

McLoone, Margo. *George Washington Carver: A Photo-Illustrated Biography.* Illus. Bridgestone Books 1997 (cloth 1-56065-516-X)

This is just the kind of book younger researchers need—well organized with double-page spreads covering such topics as "Plant Wizard," "Teacher at Tuskegee," and "International Fame." There is a section of "Words from George Washington Carver" and even lists of addresses (for example, the George Washington Carver Museum) and Internet sites. Timeline, glossary, bibliography, and index. Part of the Read and Discover Photo-Illustrated Biographies series.

Nicholson, Lois P. *George Washington Carver: Scientist.* Illus. Chelsea House 1994 (LB 0-7910-1763-X) (pap. 0-7910-2114-9) 80pp.

George Washington Carver's accomplishments as a scientist are clearly presented in this book. It also emphasizes the ecological ideas he applied to farming, including crop rotation and the use of organic fertilizers. The format will meet the needs of middle-grade students—it is well organized and makes good use of captioned illustrations. Chronology, glossary, bibliography, and index. Part of the Junior Black Americans of Achievement series.

Biographies for Older Readers

Adair, Gene. *George Washington Carver: Botanist.* Illus. Chelsea House 1989 (LB 1-55546-577-3) (pap. 0-7910-0234-9) 112pp.

Junior high and high school students will appreciate this thorough presentation that opens with a fascinating account of George Washington Carver's testimony before the House Ways and Means Committee in 1921. Originally it was to be given in 10 minutes, but Carver spoke for more than an hour, engaging the congressmen with his knowledge, humor, and dignity. There is also information about the impact of the racial attitudes of the era on Carver's recognition. Chronology, bibliography, and index. Part of the Black Americans of Achievement series.

Kremer, Gary R. *George Washington Carver: In His Own Words.* Illus. University of Missouri Press 1990 (pap. 0-8262-0785-5) 224pp.

The author uses documents from the George Washington Carver National Monument in Diamond, Missouri, and from the Tuskegee Institute Archives in Alabama to compile a unique portrait of this scientist and educator. Kremer's comments extend the text, providing additional insights. This is fine original-source material. Chronology, notes, and index.

Related Books for Younger Readers

Voices From America's Past. Illus. Raintree Steck-Vaughn 1991 (LB 0-8114-2770-6) 128pp.

Included here are first-person accounts of experiences throughout American history. There are voices from the Puritan colonies, the Revolutionary War, and the Civil War, from the Oregon Trail, from cowboys, and Native Americans, from Eleanor Roosevelt and from Dr. Martin Luther King, Jr. George Washington Carver writes about his life, and Cesar Chavez reflects on organizing farm workers. Students will appreciate the many illustrations and text. Timelines and index. Part of the Voices series.

Related Books for Older Readers

Stanley, Phyllis M. *American Environmental Heroes.* Illus. Enslow Publishers 1996 (LB 0-89490-630-5) 128pp.

This detailed presentation provides a chronological look at people who brought attention to environmental issues. The writings of Henry David Thoreau reflected concerns about the natural world as did the work of Rachel Carson. George Washington Carver proposed agricultural changes to protect the soil. John Muir founded the Sierra Club to promote wilderness preservation. Guide to national parks, chapter notes, bibliography, and index. Part of the Collective Biographies series.

Yount, Lisa. *Black Scientists.* Illus. Facts on File 1991 (LB 0-8160-2549-5) 128pp.

George Washington Carver, Daniel Hale Lewis, Charles Richard Drew, and John P. Moon are among the scientists included. Reading about their accomplishments gives an insight into their eras and experiences. Most of the individuals profiled were active in the first half of the 20th century, so reading about them develops an awareness for the conditions of this time period. For each person there is a chronology and bibliography. Index. Part of the American Profiles series.

Cassatt, Mary (1844–1926), an American painter, left the United States in 1866 to study and paint abroad. After she settled in Paris and joined the Impressionist movement, her simple paintings drew the attention of French painter Edgar Degas.

Biographies for Younger Readers

Brooks, Philip. *Mary Cassatt: An American in Paris.* Illus. Franklin Watts 1995 (cloth 0-531-20183-X) 64pp.

In the mid-19th century, art was not considered an acceptable career for a woman. Mary Cassatt defied these conventions, and her father, to study painting in Europe. There are many reproductions in this book, which reports her struggles and successes as an artist. Younger readers will find the brief chapters very accessible. Bibliography and index. Part of the First Book series.

Turner, Robyn Montana. *Mary Cassatt.* Illus. Little, Brown 1992 (o.p.)

Many paintings and sketches by Mary Cassatt illustrate this very readable, brief biography, which is written as a narrative and organized chronologically. Part of the Portraits of Women Artists for Children series.

Biographies for Older Readers

Plain, Nancy. *Mary Cassatt: An Artist's Life.* Silver Burdett 1994 (LB 0-87518-597-5) 168pp.

Mary Cassatt's devotion to her art challenged the accepted role for a woman of her time. Her association with the Impressionist school further challenged accepted attitudes. This biography is both thorough and readable. Timeline, bibliography, and index. Part of the People in Focus series.

Related Books for Younger Readers

Welton, Jude. *Impressionism.* Illus. Dorling Kindersley 1993
(cloth 1-56458-173-X) 64pp.

Social changes in the 19th century that influenced artists and
their techniques brought about the Impressionist movement. Featured in this book are issues that inspired such artists as Monet,
Pissarro, Degas, and Cassatt. Extensive illustrations include sketches, paintings, and photographs. Lists of biographical dates for
important artists (including Manet, Degas, Renoir, and Cassatt) and
of the galleries that exhibit the paintings reproduced in this book,
glossary, and index. Part of the Eyewitness Art series.

Related Books for Older Readers

Janson, H. W., and Anthony F. Janson. *History of Art for Young
People.* 5th ed. Illus. Abrams 1997 (cloth 0-8109-4150-3) 632pp.

In this classic art history book covering prehistory through the
1990s, students can examine wonderful works of art and read a
detailed account of the era and the artists. There are numerous illustrations, many in color. Chronological charts examine different
aspects of each era; for example, politics, religion, science, architecture, sculpture, and painting. Glossary, bibliography, and index.

*"What bothers the
United States the most
is that we have made a
socialist revolution
right under their noses.
Workers and peasants,
comrades, this is a
socialist and
democratic revolution
of the poor, by the
poor, and for the
poor."*
(Vail, p. 82)

Castro, Fidel (1926–), a Cuban
revolutionary, toppled the country's government in
1959 and established a communist regime. He has
ruled as a dictator ever since.

Biographies for Older Readers

Brown, Warren. *Fidel Castro: Cuban Revolutionary.* Illus. Millbrook Press 1994 (o.p.) 128pp.

Born into an aristocratic family, Fidel Castro became a radical
and a revolutionary, influenced by the writings of José Martí, a
Cuban poet who wrote of justice and equality. This biography pro-

vides an in-depth look at how Castro has led a communist regime for more than 30 years. Quotations are documented with source notes. Chronology, bibliography, and index.

Vail, John. *Fidel Castro.* Illus. Chelsea House 1988 (o.p.) 112pp.

An appealing feature of this biography (and series) is the use of quotations in the margins and well-captioned photographs to expand the text. List of suggestions for further readings, chronology, and index. Part of the World Leaders Past & Present series.

Related Books for Older Readers

Dolan, Edward F., Jr., and Margaret M. Scariano. *Cuba and the United States: Troubled Neighbors.* Illus. Franklin Watts 1987 (o.p.) 128pp.

After discussing the arrival of early explorers and the issues of the Spanish-American War, chapters in this book look at "From Suspicions to Missiles," "Castro's Failed Dream," and "Cuba and the United States Today." Published before the changes in the Soviet bloc, students will get a perspective on the historical issues related to this island neighbor. Part of the Impact Book series.

Rice, Earle, Jr. *The Cuban Revolution.* Illus. Lucent 1995 (o.p.) 112pp.

This is a very thorough book with a format that provides students with a lot of information. The basic text is well organized, there are numerous illustrations with informative captions, and there are sidebars and many quotations. Students will learn about the Spanish conquest of Cuba and the revolution and the rule of Castro. Chapter notes, glossary, bibliography, and index. Part of the World History series.

Cather, Willa Sibert (1873–1947), an American novelist, centered many of her works in Nebraska, vividly portraying the pioneering spirit on the Great Plains and the challenges women faced during that period.

Biographies for Younger Readers

Streissguth, Tom. *Writer of the Plains: A Story about Willa Cather.* Illus. by Karen Ritz. Carolrhoda Books 1997 (LB 1-57505-015-3)

Willa Cather and her family moved when she was a child from Virginia to Nebraska. Her experiences shaped her writing, filling it with details about the harsh life on the plains and the strength of many of the people who settled there. List of selected works by Willa Cather, bibliography, and index. Part of the Creative Minds Biographies series.

Biographies for Older Readers

Gerber, Philip. *Willa Cather.* rev. ed. Twayne Publishers 1995 (cloth 0-8057-4035-X) 192pp.

This serious critical biography will provide older students (and even adults) with excellent information. The book begins with biographical information and then examines Cather's writing. There are chapters and notes on Cather biographies and her scholarship. Detailed bibliography (with primary and secondary sources) and index. Part of the Twayne's United States Authors series.

Keene, Ann T. *Willa Cather.* Silver Burdett 1994 (LB 0-671-86760-1) 155pp.

From her birth in Virginia to her early years in Nebraska to her work in Pittsburgh and New York, there is a wealth of information in this readable biography. Junior high and older students will find it a valuable resource with its fine selection of quotations from Cather's writing that connects to her experiences. Chronology, chapter notes, bibliography, and index. Part of the Classic American Writers series.

Slote, Bernice. *Willa Cather: A Pictorial Memoir.* Illus. with photographs by Lucia Woods and others. University of Nebraska Press 1973 (cloth 0-8032-0828-6) 134pp.

This book combines biographical information on Willa Cather with photographs of her family, homes, life, and work, with excerpts from her writing along with photographs of the region to expand the reader's understanding of this author's inspiration. This attractive, well-documented book gives a unique perspective on Willa Cather. Index.

Related Books for Younger Readers

Rounds, Glen. *Sod Houses of the Great Plains.* Illus. by the author. Holiday House 1995 (LB 0-8234-1162-1) 1996 (pap. 0-8234-1263-6)

Early settlers to the plains states found land but limited building materials. Being resourceful, they made use of the most plentiful building material—sod. In this entertaining book, lively illustrations complement the simple text.

Thompson, Kathleen. *Nebraska.* Illus. Raintree Steck-Vaughn 1996 (LB 0-8114-7347-3) (pap. 0-8114-7453-4) 48pp.

Describing the history and geography of Nebraska, this book has a chapter called "Art from the Endless Prairie." Willa Cather, Susette La Flesche, Henry Fonda, Johnny Carson, and other artists and performers are featured. Timeline of historical events, facts about Nebraska, and index. Part of the Portrait of America series.

Related Books for Older Readers

Gombar, Christina. *Great Women Writers, 1900–1950.* Illus. Facts on File 1996 (cloth 0-8160-3060-X) 128pp.

In the early years of this century, women had to challenge expectations to achieve success. Reading about their efforts gives an insight into this era. Included here are Edith Wharton, Willa Cather, Gertrude Stein, Katherine Anne Porter, Zora Neale Hurston, Pearl Buck, Eudora Welty, and Flannery O'Connor. Index. Part of the American Profiles series.

Hargrove, Jim. *Nebraska.* Illus. Children's Press 1989 (LB 0-516-00473-5) 144pp.

Several chapters describe the history of Nebraska. Included are "The First Nebraskans," "The Explorers," "On the Road to Statehood," and "A Land Transformed." This would be a good choice for students looking for background information. "Facts at a Glance," maps, and index. Part of the America the Beautiful series.

Peavy, Linda, and Ursula Smith. *Pioneer Women: The Lives of Women on the Frontier.* Illus. Smithmark 1996 (cloth 0-8317-7220-4) 144pp.

Historical photographs show the faces, hardships, and accomplishments of women who helped settle the American frontier. Chapters describe the journey, homes, families, and communities. Source notes, bibliography, and index.

*"I am convinced that
the truest act of
courage, the strongest
act of manliness is to
sacrifice ourselves for
others in a totally
nonviolent struggle for
justice."*

(Gonzales, p. 118)

Chavez, Cesar (1927–1993), a Hispanic-American labor leader, in 1962 formed the National Farm Workers Association, which later was renamed the United Farm Workers of America. He led a series of boycotts against California grape growers.

Biographies for Younger Readers

Cedeño, Maria E. *Cesar Chavez: Labor Leader.* Illus. Millbrook Press 1993 (LB 1-56294-280-8) (pap. 1-56294-808-3) 32pp.

Like Martin Luther King, Jr., Cesar Chavez admired the writings of Mahatma Gandhi. Chavez applied Gandhi's nonviolent teachings to his efforts to unionize migrant workers. Written before Chavez's death, this book is a good source for information about his early life and beliefs. Timeline, list of suggested readings, and index. Part of the Hispanic Heritage series.

Conord, Bruce W. *Cesar Chavez: Union Leader.* Illus. Chelsea House 1993 (pap. 0-7910-1999-3) 80pp.

Cesar Chavez used fasting, boycotts, and other nonviolent actions to bring attention to the needs of migrant workers. He organized workers, forming the National Farm Workers Association, and helped them achieve such benefits as insurance and a buyers cooperative. Chronology (which ends in 1991, two years before Chavez's death), glossary, bibliography, and index. Part of the Junior World Biographies series.

Biographies for Older Readers

Gonzales, Doreen. *Cesar Chavez: Leader for Migrant Farm Workers.* Illus. Enslow Publishers 1996 (LB 0-89490-760-3) 128pp.

This is a very complete biography with features that will assist students doing research. Quotations are referenced with source notes. The final chapter, "There Is More Time Than Life," describes Chavez's death. Chronology, bibliography, and index. Part of the Hispanic Biographies series.

Related Books for Younger Readers

DeRuiz, Dana Catharine, and Richard Larios. *La Causa: The Migrant Farmworkers' Story.* Illus. by Rudy Gutierrez. Raintree Steck-Vaughn 1993 (LB 0-8114-7231-0) 92pp.

Written like a narrative, this book describes the development of the United Farm Workers and the efforts to improve working conditions and pay. Picketing and boycotts are described as the UFW sought to gain public attention and support for their cause. Part of the Stories of America series.

Voices From America's Past. Illus. Raintree Steck-Vaughn 1991 (LB 0-8114-2770-6) 128pp.

First-person accounts tell of experiences throughout American history from the Puritan colonies to the civil rights movement. Cesar Chavez reflects on organizing farm workers. Students will appreciate the many illustrations and the text that describes the significance of the writings. Timelines with each inclusion and index. Part of the Voices series.

Related Books for Older Readers

Altman, Linda Jacobs. *Migrant Farm Workers: The Temporary People.* Illus. Franklin Watts 1994 (LB 0-531-13033-9) 128pp.

Altman provides a strong foundation of knowledge on the history of migrant workers in America, looking at the early treatment of native peoples and immigrants from Ireland and China. The focus then shifts to migrant labor in California and the efforts of Cesar Chavez, Dolores Huerta, and others to organize these workers. There are details about union efforts for migrant workers in Texas, Ohio, and Florida as well. This is a thorough book with a well-organized presentation of information. There are many quotations that add personal insights to these events. Source notes, bibliography, and index. Part of the Impact Book series.

Chisholm, Shirley (1924–), a teacher and public official, became the first African American woman elected to the U.S. House of Representatives, in which she served from 1969 until 1983. After leaving Congress, she taught at Mount Holyoke College.

"Success comes from doing to the best of your ability what you know in your heart are the right things to do."

(Pollack, p. 59)

Biographies for Younger Readers

Jackson, Garnet N. *Shirley Chisholm: Congresswoman.* Illus.
Modern Curriculum Press 1994 (LB 0-8136-5241-3) (pap. 0-8136-
5247-2)

As a narrative, this book could be read aloud to introduce students to the life of Shirley Chisholm and to discuss finding facts and doing research. Glossary. Part of the Beginning Biographies series.

Pollack, Jill S. *Shirley Chisholm.* Illus. Chelsea House 1994 (LB
0-531-20168-6) 64pp.

Shirley Chisholm's family stressed the importance of education. As an African American and a woman in the 1940s, she met many obstacles. This book describes how she overcame them to break barriers, becoming a New York assemblywoman and the first black woman in the U.S. House of Representatives. Part of the First Book series.

Related Books for Younger Readers

Kosof, Anna. *The Civil Rights Movement and Its Legacy.* Illus.
Franklin Watts 1989 (o.p.) 112pp.

Key moments in history—*Brown* v. *Board of Education*, the Montgomery bus boycott, integration in Little Rock, and protest marches—capture the milestones of the civil rights movement. Excerpts from interviews and speeches add to the picture of this era of America's history. Bibliography and index.

Related Books for Older Readers

Kelley, Robin D. G. *Into the Fire: African Americans Since 1970.*
Illus. Oxford University Press 1996 (LB 0-19-508701-1) 144pp.

One chapter, "It's Nation Time! From Black Feminism to Black Caucus," examines the growing political power among blacks, citing the elections of Carl Stokes, Shirley Chisholm, and Barbara Jordan. Other chapters look at urban poverty, the black middle class, and the ongoing efforts of African Americans to be represented and recognized. Chronology, bibliography, and index. Part of the Young Oxford History of African Americans series.

Morin, Isobel V. *Women of the U.S. Congress.* Illus. Oliver Press
1994 (LB 1-881508-12-9) 160pp.

From Jeannette Rankin, the first woman elected to the U.S. Congress, through Dianne Feinstein, Patty Murray, and Carol Moseley Braun—who were elected in 1993—this book profiles the accomplishments of 11 women. Margaret Chase Smith, Shirley Chisholm, Barbara Jordan, and Nancy Landon Kassebaum are also included. List of women who served in the U.S. Congress, bibliography, and index. Part of the Profiles series.

Churchill, Sir Winston Leonard Spencer

(1874–1965), a British statesman and author, became prime minister in 1940 and led Britain through the rest of World War II. Despite his popularity during the war, his government was defeated in 1945. He served again from 1951 to 1955. Churchill won the Nobel Prize for literature in 1955.

"It was the nation and the race dwelling around the globe that had the lion's heart. I had the luck to be called upon to give the roar."
(Severance, p. 109)

Biographies for Older Readers

Lace, William W. *The Importance of Winston Churchill.* Illus. Lucent 1995 (LB 1-56006-067-0) 112pp.

After presenting a chronology of Churchill's life, this book presents information in a varied and interesting format. The chapter text provides basic information organized chronologically and divided by subheadings. There are captioned photographs and boxed sidebars that feature quotations and related topics. In one sidebar, Churchill reflects on the bravery of British troops; in another, his private secretary discusses his 1945 election defeat. Part of the Importance Of series.

Severance, John B. *Winston Churchill: Soldier, Statesman, Artist.* Illus. Clarion 1996 (cloth 0-395-69853-7) 144pp.

This elegant biography will be very helpful to students. The writing is superb, especially the descriptions of the impact of the two world wars on the people of Britain and the different roles Churchill played. The section "Winston's Wit" features comments by Churchill, and quotations are used throughout the book. Detailed bibliography and index

Related Books for Younger Readers

Steins, Richard. *The Allies Against the Axis: World War II (1940–1950).* Illus. Twenty-First Century Books 1993 (LB 0-8050-2586-3)

The numerous excerpts from documents make this a great source for students researching this period in history. Included are letters between FDR and Churchill as well as passages from speeches and books by Truman, MacArthur, Churchill, and Eisenhower.

Pearl Harbor, the bombing of Tokyo, the role of women, rationing, and the iron curtain are among the topics presented. Timeline, bibliography, and index. Part of the First Person America series.

Related Books for Older Readers

Corbishley, Mike, et al. *The Young Oxford History of Britain & Ireland.* Illus. Oxford University Press 1996 (cloth 0-19-910035-7) 416pp.

From the ancient peoples through medieval kingdoms to the British empire and modern Britain, this book give a great overview of these countries. There is information about the Magna Carta, the impact of the Industrial Revolution, and the role of England in World Wars I and II. The many illustrations make this a very informative book, both in text and visually. Charts of the Succession and of prime ministers and index.

Jacobs, William J. *Great Lives: World Government.* Illus. Scribner's 1992 (cloth 0-684-19285-3) 320pp.

Political leaders of the 19th and 20th centuries are profiled, giving students a historical perspective on the figures who have shaped our world. Among those included are Napoleon Bonaparte, Queen Victoria, Gandhi, Golda Meir, Fidel Castro, Ho Chi Minh, and Mikhail Gorbachev. Reading about Mussolini, Stalin, Hitler, and Churchill will help students see different points of view of World War II and the decisions made during the war. Bibliography and index. Part of the Great Lives series.

Clemente, Roberto Walker

(1934–1972), a Puerto Rican baseball player, was a defensive outfielder for the Pittsburgh Pirates for 18 years. He was the first Hispanic player elected to the Baseball Hall of Fame. He died in a plane crash while on a mission to aid earthquake victims in Nicaragua.

Biographies for Younger Readers

Greene, Carol. *Roberto Clemente: Baseball Superstar.* Illus. by Steven Dobson. Children's Press 1991 (LB 0-516-04222-X) (pap. 0-516-44222-8) 48pp.

When students are learning to do research, they often need easier books with a clear text, supportive illustrations, and such reference aids as an index. This book meets that need. Roberto Clemente's baseball career and efforts to help others are stressed. Baseball statistics, chronology, and index. Part of the Rookie Biographies series.

West, Alan. *Roberto Clemente: Baseball Legend.* Illus. Millbrook Press 1993 (LB 1-56294-367-0) (pap. 1-56294-811-3) 32pp.

Roberto Clemente was signed by the Pirates in 1954. He faced prejudice and racial slurs, yet met them with dignity and pride. His humanitarian efforts inspired people as much as his success as a baseball player. Sidebars cover "Puerto Ricans and *Jibaros*" and "Latin Players in the Big Leagues." Chronology, bibliography, and index. Part of the Hispanic Heritage series.

Biographies for Older Readers

Walker, Paul Robert. *Pride of Puerto Rico: The Life of Roberto Clemente.* Illus. Gulliver Books 1988 (cloth 0-15-200562-5) 1991 (pap. 0-15-263420-7) 144pp.

A detailed table of contents will provide access to facts about Roberto Clemente, but there is no index. The text highlights Clemente's greatness as a player and a person. His death, on a humanitarian mission to take supplies to earthquake victims in Nicaragua, is described, as are his widow's successful efforts to create a sports complex in Puerto Rico. Baseball statistics and bibliography.

Related Books for Younger Readers

Krull, Kathleen. *Lives of the Athletes: Thrills, Spills (And What the Neighbors Thought).* Illus. by Kathryn Hewitt. Harcourt 1997 (cloth 0-15-200806-3) 96pp.

Biographical vignettes and anecdotes introduce readers to 20 athletes, including Jim Thorpe, Johnny Weissmuller, Babe Didrikson Zaharias, Jesse Owens, Jackie Robinson, Sir Edmund Hillary, Roberto Clemente, Arthur Ashe, and Wilma Rudolph. A surfer, a soccer star, a volleyball player, and an expert in the martial arts are among the less well-known athletes featured. Bibliography.

Littlefield, Bill. *Champions: Stories of Ten Remarkable Athletes.*
Illus. with paintings by Bernie Fuchs. Little, Brown 1993 (LB 0-
316-52805-6) 144pp.

What does it take to be a champion? Roberto Clemente is one
of the successful athletes portrayed here. Students can compare his
story with the careers of Satchel Paige, Julie Krone, Pelé, Joan
Benoit Samuelson, Nate Archibald, Susan Butcher, Muhammad Ali,
Billie Jean King, and Diana Golden. Bibliography and index.

Related Books for Older Readers

Press, David P. *A Multicultural Portrait of Professional Sports.*
Illus. Marshall Cavendish 1994 (LB 1-85435-661-5) 80pp.

Focusing on the role of minorities and women, this book covers a wide range of sports. Roberto Clemente's contribution to Latin
American baseball is profiled in a boxed section. Chronology, glossary, bibliography, and index. Part of the Perspectives series.

Cleopatra (69 B.C.–30 B.C.), queen of
Egypt, won the throne after she rebelled against her
brother and husband, Ptolemy XII, with the help of
Julius Caesar. She later married Marc Antony, a
Roman statesman, and they committed suicide when
defeated by Roman forces.

Biographies for Younger Readers

Stanley, Diane, and Peter Vennema. *Cleopatra.* Illus. by Diane
Stanley. William Morrow & Co. 1994 (LB 0-688-10414-2) (cloth 0-
688-10413-4) 48pp.

In the note on sources, the authors indicate that much of the
information about Cleopatra has been based on legend and that
many documents from her lifetime were destroyed after her death.
Even Plutarch's histories were written a hundred years after her
death. The large picture-book presentation lacks reference aids and
would be challenging for researchers, but it is smoothly written and
fascinating to read. The gouache illustrations for this book add to the
narrative presentation.

Biographies for Older Readers

Brooks, Polly Schoyer. *Cleopatra: Goddess of Egypt, Enemy of Rome.* Illus. HarperCollins 1995 (LB 0-06-023608-6) (cloth 0-06-023607-8) 160pp.

This biography opens with a look at "Cleopatra's World" and proceeds to examine her childhood, her relationships with Caesar and Marc Antony, and her death. An author's note discusses the limited resources about Cleopatra as well as the Roman propaganda that was created about her. This is well organized for research and well written for informational reading; chapter notes expand the presentation. Chronology, bibliography, and index.

Hoobler, Dorothy, and Thomas Hoobler. *Cleopatra.* Illus. Chelsea House 1987 (LB 0-87754-589-8) 112pp.

Cleopatra's liaisons with Julius Caesar and Marc Antony linked her with two of the most powerful men of her era. In the margins of this book there are highlighted quotations from such historians as Suetonius and Plutarch, and the opening chapter provides background on Egypt before Cleopatra. Chronology, bibliography, and index. Part of the World Leaders Past & Present series.

Related Books for Younger Readers

The Roman World: Hannibal, Julius Caesar, Cleopatra. Illus. Marshall Cavendish 1988 (o.p.)

Featuring three key figures in Roman history, this book has many illustrations and format features that will appeal to younger readers. A timeline for each character shows "Their Place in History" and there is a boxed profile of each leader. The main text is surrounded by sidebars of information, such as one on "City Life" and one on "The Games." An expanded chronology features developments in politics and war, religion and learning, art and literature, and science and society. Glossary, bibliography, and index. Part of the Exploring the Past series.

Related Books for Older Readers

Meltzer, Milton. *Ten Queens: Portraits of Women in Power.* Illus. by Bethanne Andersen. Dutton 1998 (cloth 0-525-45643-0)

Women rulers have often lived in the shadow of their husbands. These queens, including Cleopatra, Isabel of Spain, Elizabeth I, and Catherine the Great, ruled in their own right. Each profile describes the personalities and the events of their era. Bibliography and index.

Steffens, Bradley. *The Fall of the Roman Empire.* Illus. Greenhaven 1994 (cloth 1-56510-098-0) 128pp.

What caused the end of the Roman empire? How did the decisions of the rulers influence the collapse of this great civilization? Presenting different theories and ideas, this book encourages students to think about the possibilities. Bibliography and index. Part of the Great Mysteries: Opposing Viewpoints series.

What Life Was Like on the Banks of the Nile, Egypt, 3050–30 B.C. Illus. Time-Life Books 1996 (cloth 0-8094-9378-0) 192pp.

Pharaohs, pyramids, and great treasures are part of the history of the early years of ancient Egypt. A timeline shows students many landmarks, from the predynastic period to the times of Tuthmosis I, Tutankhamun, and Ramses the Great to the Greek and Roman periods. This is an attractive book for researchers and browsers. Glossary, bibliography, and index.

Cleveland, Stephen Grover

(1837–1908), the 22nd president (1885–1889) and 24th president (1893–1897) of the United States, was respected for his independence and integrity. Refusing to bow to party politics and to the spoils system, he often angered his party.

Biographies for Older Readers

Collins, David R. *Grover Cleveland: 22nd and 24th President of the United States.* Illus. Garrett Educational 1988 (LB 0-944483-01-1)

An opening chronology shows that Grover Cleveland followed a well-organized path to politics—studying law then serving as assistant district attorney, sheriff, mayor (of Buffalo), governor (of New York), and president. Within the chapters, there are subheadings that help readers focus on key events and sidebars on such topics as cartoonist Thomas Nast and the Populist movement. Part of the Presidents of the United States series.

Kent, Zachary. *Grover Cleveland.* Illus. Children's Press 1988 (LB 0-516-01360-2) 100pp.

Chapters feature "The Minister's Son," "The Veto President," "The Second Term," and "Princeton Retirement." Grover Cleveland was a fiscally cautious president who was elected to a second term to halt the free spending of the administration of Benjamin Harrison. There is a fascinating account of Cleveland's battle with cancer and his efforts to keep his illness confidential. Chronology and index. Part of the Encyclopedia of Presidents series.

Related Books for Younger Readers

Havens, John C. *Government and Politics.* Illus. Chelsea House 1997 (LB 0-7910-2847-X) 104pp.

From "The Gilded Age" to Teddy Roosevelt's "A Square Deal," students learn about the end of the 19th century. If you think politicians use negative tactics now, read about the mudslinging politics during the campaign of Grover Cleveland. There are newspaper cartoons and photographs of campaign memorabilia to add to this lively presentation. Bibliography and index. Part of the Life in America 100 Years Ago series.

Related Books for Older Readers

Judson, Karen. *The Presidency of the United States.* Illus. Enslow Publishers 1996 (LB 0-89490-585-6) 128pp.

This book describes the responsibilities of the president and how they have changed. There is a list of "strong" presidents: George Washington, Thomas Jefferson, Andrew Jackson, Abraham Lincoln, Theodore Roosevelt, Woodrow Wilson, Franklin D. Roosevelt, and Harry Truman. And there is a list of those who "strengthened" the presidency, including John Adams, James K. Polk, Andrew Johnson, Rutherford B. Hayes, Grover Cleveland, and Dwight Eisenhower. Students will be fascinated by the rationale for these selections. There are many anecdotal details about the men who have held this office. Chapter notes, glossary, bibliography, and index. Part of the American Government in Action series.

Pious, Richard M. *The Young Oxford Companion to the Presidency of the United States.* Illus. Oxford University Press 1994 (cloth 0-19-507799-7) 368pp.

There are so many details in this book that students will read it for research and for enjoyment. The overall arrangement is alphabetical. There are biographical sketches of all the presidents and vice presidents. Some of the wives are featured, too. Amnesty and executive privilege are discussed, as are presidential advisers, policies, decisions, and perks. Chronology, lists of further readings and presidential historic sites and libraries, bibliography, and index. This is part of the Young Oxford Companion series.

The White House home page is http://www.whitehouse. gov/. The president's e-mail address is president@whitehouse. gov.

Clinton, William Jefferson (1946–), the 42nd president of the United States (1993–), was the nation's youngest governor when he won election in Arkansas in 1978.

Biographies for Younger Readers

Cwiklik, Robert. ***Bill Clinton: Our Forty-Second President.*** Illus. Millbrook Press 1993 (o.p.) 48pp.

This is a brief biography that concludes with the 1992 election. There are no chapter divisions, but its chronological order will make it accessible for specific research requests. A special feature is a map showing the distribution of the electoral votes in the 1992 election. Index. Part of the Gateway Biographies series.

Landau, Elaine. ***Bill Clinton and His Presidency.*** Illus. Franklin Watts 1997 (LB 0-531-20295-X) (pap. 0-531-15841-1)

Students will find this a good resource for reports and projects. It includes Clinton's re-election and has well-planned chapters with many quotations (with sources) and excellent photographs. List of suggestions for further readings and Internet resources, glossary, and index. Part of the First Book series.

Biographies for Older Readers

Kent, Zachary. ***William Jefferson Clinton.*** Illus. Children's Press 1993 (o.p.) 100pp.

Readers follow the life of Bill Clinton from his childhood ("A Place Called Hope") to his re-election to a non-consecutive term as governor of Arkansas ("The Comeback Kid") to his current service as president. Numerous photographs and a clearly organized text make this appealing for students doing research. Timeline and index. Part of the Encyclopedia of Presidents series.

Martin, Gene L., and Aaron Boyd. *Bill Clinton: President from Arkansas.* Illus. Tudor Publishers 1993 (LB 0-936389-31-1) 104pp.

This is a solid presentation with chapters featuring Bill Clinton's childhood, education, governorship, national political efforts, and presidency. Students doing research will find the information readable and organized but will miss reference aids like a bibliography or an index.

Related Books for Younger Readers

Rubel, David. *Scholastic Encyclopedia of the Presidents and Their Times.* Illus. Scholastic 1994 (cloth 0-590-49366-3) 224pp.

This book looks at each president, from Washington to Clinton, and describes events during his presidency. Featured under Clinton are his status as a "baby boomer," the budget deficit, the role of Hillary Rodham Clinton, and advances in computer technology. List of election results and index.

Related Books for Older Readers

Corzine, Phyllis. *The Palestinian-Israeli Accord.* Illus. Lucent 1997 (LB 1-56006-181-2)

Readers learn about the political, social, and religious issues in the Middle East. There are chapters on "Israel and Its Enemies," "Arafat and the PLO," and "Voices of the Opposition." The Camp David agreement is discussed along with the 1993 accord, which was signed near the beginning of Bill Clinton's presidency. Current concerns in the Middle East are profiled, including ongoing problems with Saddam Hussein. This is a well-organized book. The chapters are further divided into subheadings, which help students browsing for information. Glossary, bibliography, and index. Part of the Lucent Overview series.

Pious, Richard M. *The Young Oxford Companion to the Presidency of the United States.* Illus. Oxford University Press 1994 (cloth 0-19-507799-7) 368pp.

Students researching the role of the president will find this volume useful and enjoyable. In addition to biographical sketches, it examines the privileges and responsibilities of the office. Chronology, list of presidential historic sites and libraries, bibliography, and index. Part of the Young Oxford Companion series.

Cody, William F. "Buffalo Bill"

(1846–1917), American Pony Express rider, hunter, and frontiersman, best known for his role as a performer in Wild West shows.

Biographies for Younger Readers

Robison, Nancy. *Buffalo Bill.* Illus. Franklin Watts 1991 (LB 10-531-20007-8) 64pp.

Chapters feature the many roles of "Buffalo Bill" Cody: "Buffalo Hunter," "Soldier, Scout, and Justice of the Peace," and "The Actor Receives the Medal of Honor." Cody lived during the era of western expansion, and his colorful life capitalized on his skills as a frontiersman and a showman. Bibliography and index. Part of the First Books Biographies series.

Sanford, William R., and Carl R. Green. *Buffalo Bill Cody: Showman of the Wild West.* Illus. Enslow Publishers 1996 (LB 0-89490-646-1) 48pp.

Bill Cody's exploits often read like a dime novel. (In fact, he was the featured character in hundreds of dime novels.) With short chapters, this is an easy book for students to read and use for research. Chapter notes, glossary, bibliography, and index. Part of the Legendary Heroes of the Wild West series.

Related Books for Younger Readers

Morley, Jacqueline. *How Would You Survive in the American West?* Illus. by David Antram. Franklin Watts 1996 (LB 0-531-14382-1) 1997 (pap. 0-531-15308-8) 48pp.

The focus of this book is the pioneer settler on a journey to the West. A time spiral relates this era to other historical events. Double-page spreads look at such topics as planning the journey, finding supplies, coping with storms, meeting Indians, helping others, and treating illnesses. The text is surrounded by numerous illustrations with informative captions. Timeline, glossary, and index. Part of the How Would You Survive? series.

Ritchie, David. *Frontier Life.* Illus. Chelsea House 1996 (cloth 0-7910-2942-9) 104pp.

One appealing feature of this book is the inclusion of color illustrations that depict such items as the cover of a dime novel, a poster from Buffalo Bill's Wild West Show, and a lithograph of a Conestoga wagon. The chapters describe life on the frontier and are well illustrated with black-and-white photographs, reproductions, and drawings. Bibliography and index. Part of the Life in America 100 Years Ago series.

Van Der Linde, Laurel. *The Pony Express.* Illus. New Discovery Books 1993 (LB 0-02-759056-9) 72pp.

Delivering messages to the frontier of America was slow and unreliable until the Pony Express was established. From "Early Mail Routes" and "Opening Day" to "Riders and Famous Rides" and "The End of the Line," this book presents a brief history of the Pony Express. Bibliography and index.

Coleman, Bessie (1893–1926), African American aviator, was the first black woman to earn a pilot's license. Because of discrimination in the United States, she traveled to France to learn to fly. She was killed in 1926 during a flying exhibition.

Biographies for Younger Readers

Fisher, Lillian M. *Brave Bessie: Flying Free.* Illus. Hendrick-Long Publishing 1995 (cloth 0-937460-94-X) 88pp.

Bessie Coleman began her life in a small town in Texas. She traveled to France to learn to be a pilot and then crossed America as a barnstormer at airshows. A postscript features the Bessie Coleman stamp that was issued by the U.S. Postal Service in April 1995. Glossary, bibliography of books about airplanes and aviators, and index.

Johnson, Dolores. *She Dared to Fly: Bessie Coleman.* Illus. Benchmark Books 1997 (LB 0-7614-0487-2) 48pp.

To overcome prejudices at home, Bessie Coleman went to France to take flying lessons. She then worked as a stunt pilot, a dangerous career that resulted in many injuries and, eventually, her death. Glossary, bibliography, and index. Part of the Benchmark Biographies series.

Biographies for Older Readers

Hart, Philip S. *Up in the Air: The Story of Bessie Coleman.* Illus. Carolrhoda Books 1996 (LB 0-87614-949-2)

Students doing research will find this book an excellent choice. Chapters are well organized, and there are many photographs to document events. The Afterword describes how Bessie Coleman's achievements inspired other African Americans to enter the field of aviation. Mentioned in the bibliography is a film, *Flyers in Search of a Dream.* Explanatory notes, bibliography, and a detailed index.

Related Books for Younger Readers

Boyne, Walter J. *The Smithsonian Book of Flight for Young People.* Illus. Atheneum 1988 (LB 0-689-31422-1); Aladdin (pap. 0-689-71212-X) 128pp.

This attractive book is a good choice for research and browsing. Arranged chronologically, there are many archival photographs that show the development of flight. Information is organized into three parts: "From Dream to Reality," "Two Wars and Between," and "Jets, Rockets, and Realism." This presentation could be used by many levels of students, all of whom will appreciate the wonderful photographs. Bibliography and index.

Related Books for Older Readers

Moolman, Valerie, and the editors of Time-Life Books. *Women Aloft.* Illus. Time-Life Books 1981 (LB 0-8094-3288-9)

Beginning with "The First Hurdle: Proving They Were Fit to Fly," this book looks at women pioneers of flight. Amelia Earhart is a major focus, but there is information about other women who took risks, particularly during the war years. Bessie Coleman is included with a boxed section, "A Quest for Equality in the Air." Excellent photographs make this a good book for browsers. Bibliography and index. Part of the Epic of Flight series.

Tessendorf, K. C. *Barnstormers and Daredevils.* Illus. Atheneum 1988 (LB 0-689-31346-2) 96pp.

After the success of the Wright brothers, planes became important for transportation, entertainment, and war. At the end of World War I, many pilots wanted to continue to work in the air, becoming barnstormers and putting on airshows. This book features these daredevils and their stunts. Chapter notes, bibliography, and index.

Columbus, Christopher (1451–1506), a Spanish explorer and discoverer of America when he landed in the Bahamas in 1492, later set sail for Puerto Rico and other Caribbean islands, where he founded a colony in Hispaniola. He then traveled to South America, exploring Venezuela, and in 1502 he sailed to Central America on his last voyage.

Biographies for Younger Readers

Adler, David A. *Christopher Columbus: Great Explorer.* Illus. by Lyle Miller. Holiday House 1991 (LB 0-8234-0895-7) 48pp.

Beginning with a list of important dates, the five brief chapters then expand the chronological details. Some information is provided about the cruelty shown to the native peoples by the explorers. Index. Part of the First Biographies series.

Adler, David A. *A Picture Book of Christopher Columbus.* Illus. by John Wallner and Alexandra Wallner. Holiday House 1991 (LB 0-8234-0857-4) 1992 (pap. 0-8234-0949-X) 32pp.

This simple biography describes several voyages of Columbus. It would be a good book to read aloud to introduce his life and era. Timeline. Part of the Picture Book Of series.

Fritz, Jean. *The Great Adventure of Christopher Columbus: A Pop-up Book.* Illus. by Tomie dePaola. Putnam's 1992 (cloth 0-399-22113-1)

This is fun to share! On one page, Columbus visits the king and queen. When a tab is moved, he bows down to them. On another page, Columbus's ship pops up from the page. Pull a tab and a ship moves through the water. This has a surprisingly detailed text and would complement more traditional resource books.

Fritz, Jean. *Where Do You Think You're Going, Christopher Columbus?* Illus. by Margot Tomes. Putnam's 1980 (cloth 0-399-20723-6); Paperstar 1997 (pap. 0-698-11580-5) 80pp.

This biography is written as a sustained narrative but the detailed index will allow readers to find specific details. As with other biographies by Fritz, this is very enjoyable reading with information about Columbus's motivation to find riches and personal glory.

Sis, Peter. *Follow the Dream: The Story of Christopher Columbus.* Illus. by the author. Knopf 1991 (LB 0-679-90628-2) (cloth 0-679-80628-8); Random House 1996 (pap. 0-679-88088-7) 40pp.

When Columbus journeyed west across the Atlantic, he hoped to find a new route to the Orient. Instead, he was one of the first Europeans to reach the Americas. The picture-book format makes this a good introductory resource; the focus is only on Columbus's childhood and the voyage of 1492, ending with his arrival in the Americas. The illustrations are detailed and intriguing.

Biographies for Older Readers

Meltzer, Milton. *Columbus and the World Around Him.* Illus. Franklin Watts 1990 (LB 0-531-10899-6) 160pp.

What was it like in Europe at the time of Columbus? How did the expectations and beliefs of Europeans influence the treatment of the people whose lands were "discovered"? This book looks at Columbus's life within the context of the culture, information, and thinking of his era. In his time, the resources of the New World were considered open opportunities for wealth and fame—and the people of the New World were considered part of the resources to be exploited. This is a critical biography, well written and well organized. Meltzer makes excellent use of sources. Index.

West, Delno C., and Jean M. West. *Christopher Columbus: The Great Adventure and How We Know about It.* Illus. Atheneum 1991 (o.p.) 144pp.

This book is not just a biography; it provides insight into the work of historians and the documents and resources they use. There is information about the maps, ships, and equipment that Columbus used. Chapter titles, sidebar features, pictures, and maps are listed in the contents, providing quick access to topics. The illustrations include facsimile maps, artifacts (like a compass and astrolabe), and documents (for example, a book that has marginal notes by Columbus). This book would be excellent for students doing in-depth research. It does provide insight into the tragic impact of the arrival of Europeans on the native inhabitants. Bibliography and index.

Related Books for Younger Readers

Brenner, Barbara. *If You Were There in 1492.* Illus. Bradbury Press 1991 (LB 0-02-712321-9) 112pp.

As the title suggests, this book looks beyond exploration and explorers in 1492 and gives a picture of everyday life. Focusing primarily on life in Spain, chapters include "Food and Clothing," "Sickness and Health," "Education," "Arts and Entertainment," and "Crime and Punishment." Printing, monarchs, maps, and ships are additional topics. Chapter notes, bibliography, and index.

Dyson, John. *Westward with Columbus.* Illus. with photographs by Peter Christopher. Scholastic 1991 (cloth 0-590-43846-8) (pap. 0-590-43847-6) 64pp.

John Dyson and Luís Coin recreated the voyage of Columbus on a replica of the *Niña.* Some chapters in this book flash back to the time of Columbus and imagine the role of a young boy on the ship. There are numerous illustrations and boxed sidebars featuring such information as "Building a Caravel," "The Admiral's Fleet," "How Columbus Found His Way," and "Gifts from the New World." List of recommended reading and glossary. This is a fun book for browsing. Part of the Time Quest Book series.

Fritz, Jean, et al. *The World in 1492.* Illus. Henry Holt 1992 (o.p.) 89pp.

Insightful essays by award-winning authors provide information about the many civilizations and accomplishments in the world in 1492. Arranged by continents, information about history, customs, and beliefs is presented. This book provides an important model for a multicultural perspective of history.

Related Books for Older Readers

Dor-Ner, Zvi. *Columbus and the Age of Discovery.* Illus. William Morrow & Co. 1991 (o.p.) 372pp.

As a companion volume to the PBS series of the same name, this large, heavily illustrated book looks at the social, political, and intellectual activities of the late 15th century. The greed of the European explorers and their exploitation of the people in the New World are presented along with the heroic bravery of their adventures. Students doing research will find this a thorough and challenging resource. The bibliography is not just annotated, the sources are discussed in detail. Excellent chapter notes and index. Zvi Dor-Ner served as the executive producer of the television series, which should also be considered a resource for students.

Pelta, Kathy. *Discovering Christopher Columbus: How History Is Invented.* Illus. Lerner Publications 1991 (LB 0-8225-4899-2) 96pp.

Students will be fascinated by this book, which discusses how history is often changed. The voyages of Columbus, the support of the Spanish royalty, the stories Columbus told to keep their support, and the changing views of explorers are examined. List of sources and index. Part of the How History Is Invented series.

Yue, Charlotte, and David Yue. *Christopher Columbus: How He Did It.* Illus. by the authors. Houghton Mifflin 1992 (cloth 0-395-52100-9) 144pp.

While this book does provide information about Columbus's voyages, the main focus is on the tools and materials that were essential to his accomplishment. One chapter, "The Means," includes information about financing, ships, crews, and supplies. There are detailed descriptions of the compass, sandglass, sounding lead, quadrant, astrolabe, and maps and charts. This is a great source of historical support information for understanding the complexities and challenges of exploration. List of additional readings, bibliography, and fine index.

Cook, James (1728–1779), British explorer and navigator, is best known for his round-the-world voyages. "Captain" Cook's major explorations included expeditions to the South Pacific, where he led a group of astronomers to Tahiti to track the transit of the planet Venus across the Sun, a circumnavigation of New Zealand, and charting of Australia.

Biographies for Older Readers

Kent, Zachary. *James Cook.* Illus. Children's Press 1991 (o.p.)

Captain James Cook explored and mapped large areas of the South Pacific, opening these areas to the rest of the world. The illustrations enhance this straightforward account, combining reproductions and portraits with color photographs of the vegetation and geography of Australia, New Zealand, Hawaii, and other islands. Timeline, glossary, bibliography, and index. Part of the World's Great Explorers series.

Related Books for Younger Readers

Johnstone, Michael, ed. *Explorers.* Illus. Candlewick Press 1997 (cloth 0-7636-0314-7) 32pp.

Read all about it! This book uses the format of a newspaper (with sensational headlines and columns of text) to present information about explorers. The Phoenicians, Columbus, Captain Cook, Sacagawea, Peary, Scott, and Livingstone are among those featured. The illustrations are very appealing—colorful and fun. The pages on Captain Cook include a cutaway illustration of the *Endeavour.* The information is brief and the tone is irreverent, which may interest reluctant researchers. Timeline and index. Part of the History News series.

Ryan, Peter. *Explorers and Mapmakers.* Illus. by Christine Molan and with photographs. Lodestar Books 1989 (o.p.) 48pp.

As people traveled around the world, they made maps to find their way back home and to lead others. Focusing on such explorers as Columbus, Marco Polo, James Cook, and Roald Amundsen, this book describes their journeys. Included in the illustrations are artifacts of early maps and sketches. Part of the Time Detectives series.

Waterlow, Julia. *The Explorer Through History.* Illus. by Tony Smith. Thomson Learning 1994 (cloth 1-56847-101-7)

From the Phoenicians to the Vikings to explorers in Africa and to space, this gives students a basic overview of exploration. James Cook's journeys to the Pacific are given several pages of coverage as are the expeditions of Lewis and Clark and Dr. David Livingston. Illustrations and fact boxes add to the appeal. Timeline, glossary, bibliography, and index. Part of the Journey Through History series.

Related Books for Older Readers

Scheller, William. *The World's Great Explorers.* Illus. Oliver Press 1992 (LB 1-881508-03-X) 160pp.

What does it take to be an explorer? After reading about the 12 explorers featured here, students will have an understanding of the necessary spirit, energy, and commitment. Among those included are Muhammad ibn-Batuta, James Cook, John Frémont, and Roald Amundsen. Chronology, bibliography, and index. Part of the Profiles series.

Stefoff, Rebecca. *Scientific Explorers: Travels in Search of Knowledge.* Illus. Oxford University Press 1992 (LB 0-19-507689-3) 144pp.

    Many explorers set out to conquer new territories or to find new wealth. For others, like those in this book, the focus was on mapping, research, and gathering information. James Cook, Charles Darwin, Lewis and Clark, and Jacques Cousteau are featured. There is a section on Napoleon's invasion of Egypt and the information that was gathered by his scientists. Chronology, bibliography, and index. Part of the Extraordinary Explorers series.

Cortés, Hernán (1485–1547), also known as Hernando Cortez, was a Spanish explorer and the conqueror of Mexico. Under commission from the Spanish governor of Cuba, Cortés took Aztec ruler Montezuma hostage and governed the Aztecs through him.

Biographies for Younger Readers

Jacobs, William J. *Cortés: Conqueror of Mexico.* Illus. Franklin Watts 1994 (LB 0-531-20138-4) 64pp.

    Two chapter titles in this book capture the essence of Cortés and many of his contemporaries: "A Dream of Fame and Fortune" and "In Search of Gold." Other chapters use the words "conquest" and "conqueror," but they are balanced with some regard for Cortés's success at accomplishing his mission. Chronology, bibliography, and index. Part of the First Book Explorer series.

Biographies for Older Readers

Stein, R. Conrad. *Hernando Cortés: Conquerer of Mexico.* Illus. Children's Press 1991 (o.p.) 128pp.

    Like many European explorers, Cortés had a mission to acquire wealth by taking it, with force if necessary, from the people he encountered on his journeys. His cruelty and his accomplishments are discussed in this book. Appendices describe sources of information from the era and reproduce some historical maps. Timeline, glossary, and index. Part of the World's Great Explorers series.

Related Books for Younger Readers

Chrisp, Peter. *The Spanish Conquests in the New World.* Illus. Thomson Learning 1993 (cloth 1-56847-123-8)

More than half of this book describes Cortés and the Aztecs, while the rest of the book looks at Pizarro and the Incas and the efforts of Christian missionaries. Numerous illustrations and boxed sections with quotations and commentaries will appeal to students. List of books to read, glossary, and index. Part of the Exploration and Encounters series.

Maestro, Betsy, and Giulio Maestro. *Exploration and Conquest: The Americas After Columbus: 1500–1620.* Illus. by Giulio Maestro. Lothrop, Lee & Shepard 1994 (LB 0-688-09268-3) (cloth 0-688-09267-5)

This beautifully illustrated book is fascinating to read. The narrative text is arranged chronologically and features the explorations of Cortés, Pizarro, de Soto, Cartier, Drake, John Smith, Champlain, and others. Part of the text describes the slave trade and there is information not only about exploration but about conquest and the impact of these "explorers" on the native inhabitants. This is a companion volume to *The Discovery of the Americas.*

Related Books for Older Readers

Marrin, Albert. *Empires Lost and Won: The Spanish Heritage in the Southwest.* Illus. Atheneum 1997 (cloth 0-689-80414-8)

This is a very detailed and well-documented book that examines the impact of the Spanish conquistadors on Mexico and the border states. Cabeza de Vaca, Cortés, and Coronado are among those who brought European greed, religion, and diseases to this region. After describing the conquest, the author examines the settlement of American pioneers, mountain men, and the war that resulted. Detailed notes, bibliography, and index.

Cousteau, Jacques Yves (1910–1997), a French oceanographer, is best known for his efforts to explain the wonders of the sea to the general public through documentary films and books. He is credited with the invention in 1943 of the self-contained underwater breathing apparatus (scuba), in which he collaborated with Emil Gagnan.

Biographies for Younger Readers

Reef, Catherine. *Jacques Cousteau: Champion of the Sea.* Illus. by Larry Raymond. Twenty-First Century Books 1992 (LB 0-8050-2114-0) 72pp.

Jacques Cousteau was well known for his interest in the sea. This book describes his inventions and focuses on his environmental efforts. It is well organized and readable, making it a fine choice for students beginning the research process. Glossary and index. Part of the Earth Keepers series.

Biographies for Older Readers

Markham, Lois. *Jacques-Yves Cousteau: Exploring the Wonders of the Deep.* Raintree Steck-Vaughn 1997 (LB 0-8172-4404-2)

Jacques Cousteau was an inventor and explorer. His television programs brought the wonders of the underwater world into the homes of people around the world. A special feature of this book are essays on such related topics as "Diving Dangers" and "Anatomy of a Cousteau Television Show." The book ends with Cousteau celebrating his 85th birthday in 1995. Glossary, bibliography, and index. Part of the Innovative Minds series.

Sinnott, Susan. *Jacques-Yves Cousteau.* Illus. Children's Press 1992 (o.p.) 128pp.

Published in 1992, prior to Cousteau's death, this thorough biography will be a great choice for information about his early life, inventions, and devotion to the sea. There are many photographs of Cousteau and his family, but there are also beautiful color photographs of underwater life. Timeline, chapter notes, glossary, bibliography, and index. Part of the World's Great Explorers series.

Related Books for Younger Readers

Hoff, Mary K., and Mary M. Rodgers. *Oceans.* Illus. Lerner Publications 1991 (LB 0-8225-2505-4) 72pp.

Students will learn a lot about activities that threaten the oceans and the damage that has already been done. Overfishing, discarding toxins, oil spills, and trash on the beaches are discussed. List of organizations, glossary, and index. Part of the Our Endangered Planet series.

Related Books for Older Readers

Sedge, Michael H. *Commercialization of the Oceans.* Illus. Franklin Watts 1987 (o.p.) 128pp.

The oceans have been a source of transportation, food, recreation, and other resources. This book looks at ways to use the sea to provide more materials; however, it also examines negative effects such as pollution and depletion of resources. Bibliography and index. Part of the Impact Book series.

Stefoff, Rebecca. *Extinction.* Illus. Chelsea House 1992 (LB 0-7910-1578-5) 128pp.

Examining the history of extinct species, the author discusses prehistoric creatures, Darwin's theories, and today's endangered and threatened species. Addresses of conservation organizations and government agencies, glossary, bibliography, and index. Part of the Earth at Risk series.

Crazy Horse (1842?–1877), a chief of the Oglala Sioux, joined with Chief Sitting Bull to defeat Gen. George A. Custer at Montana's Little Bighorn in 1876. He persistently fought against white settlement in the Black Hills of South Dakota, the homeland of the Sioux.

Biographies for Younger Readers

Schomp, Virginia. *Heroic Sioux Warrior: Crazy Horse.* Illus.
Benchmark Books 1997 (LB 0-7614-0522-4) 48pp.

This biography in picture-book format gives a brief overview of
Crazy Horse and his era. Well illustrated with art and photographs,
this is a fine choice as an introduction or for beginning research. The
bibliography includes books on Crazy Horse and on the Sioux as
well as videos and a list of places to visit (with addresses). Glossary
and index. Part of the Benchmark Biographies series.

Biographies for Older Readers

Freedman, Russell. *The Life and Death of Crazy Horse.* Illus.
with drawings by Amos Bad Heart Bull. Holiday House 1996
(cloth 0-8234-1219-9) 144pp.

This is an excellent biography. The writing is elegant and full
of drama. The research is meticulous. There is a selective bibliography that discusses sources such as interviews from the 1930s with
the surviving relatives of Crazy Horse and resources on Custer and
Little Big Horn. Even the illustrations are fascinating. Done by a
cousin of Crazy Horse, they are a picture history that was acciden-
tally discovered in 1926 by a graduate student. Chronology and
detailed index.

St. George, Judith. *Crazy Horse.* Illus. Putnam's 1994 (cloth 0-
399-22667-2) 189pp.

The story of Crazy Horse is both heroic and tragic. As a warrior during the time of the settlement of the West, Crazy Horse tried
to protect the interests of his people, often fighting the soldiers who
came into his territory. In this exceptional biography, students will
gain an insight into the perspective of Crazy Horse and the Sioux.
Extensive bibliography and index.

Related Books for Younger Readers

Dolan, Terrance. *The Teton Sioux Indians.* Illus. Chelsea House
1995 (cloth 0-7910-1680-3) (pap. 0-7910-2032-0)

Six chapters describe the circumstances of the Teton Sioux
during the settlement of their lands by white pioneers. Led by Red
Cloud, Sitting Bull, and Crazy Horse, the Teton Sioux resisted the
U.S. Army, yet were forced onto settlements. Color photographs
show the artistry of these people. Chronology, glossary, and index.
Part of the Junior Library of American Indians series.

Sneve, Virginia Driving Hawk. *The Sioux: A First Americans Book.* Illus. by Ronald Himler. Holiday House 1993 (LB 0-8234-1017-X) 32pp.

The author spent her childhood on the Rosebud Sioux Reservation. She opens the book with a creation myth, then describes the Sioux territory and peoples of the 19th century, the encroachment of settlers, and important Sioux leaders including Sitting Bull and Crazy Horse. Appended are a list of the Sioux tribes and a verse from the Lakota Pipe Ceremony. The index will help younger students with research questions. Part of the First Americans series.

Related Books for Older Readers

Bonvillain, Nancy. *The Teton Sioux.* Illus. Chelsea House 1994 (pap. 0-7910-1688-9)

After describing the life of the Teton Sioux, the text focuses on the encroaching settlers and the army, including a detailed explanation of the events at Wounded Knee. This is a well-organized presentation that is accessible to students doing research. A section of color photographs shows clothing, shoes, bags, and other items. Glossary, bibliography, and index. Part of the Indians of North America series.

Brown, Dee. *Wounded Knee: An Indian History of the American West.* Illus. Adapted by Amy Ehrlich from Dee Brown's *Bury My Heart at Wounded Knee.* Henry Holt 1994 (pap. 0-8050-2700-9) 224pp.

Readers who want a detailed critical account of the struggle of the Indians against the encroachment from white settlers will want to read this adaptation of the original adult book. This is a story of invasion, of conquerors who used their own laws and armies to take away homes and destroy civilizations. It will be useful for students in middle school and high school. Sources are clearly documented in notes. Bibliography and index.

Ferrell, Nancy Warren. *The Battle of the Little Bighorn in American History.* Illus. Enslow Publishers 1996 (LB 0-89490-768-9) 128pp.

For years there was fighting among settlers, Native Americans, and the U.S. Army. The Battle of Little Bighorn was fought over many of the issues that faced different native peoples—loss of tribal lands, broken promises and treaties, and mistreatment from soldiers and settlers. This book examines those issues and puts them into perspective for students doing research. Timeline, list of further readings, chapter notes, and index. Part of the In American History series.

Crockett, Davy (1786–1836), an

American frontiersman, died defending the Alamo from Mexican assault. He was born near Greenville, Tennessee, and served as a representative from his home state in the U.S. House of Representatives (1827–1831 and 1833–1835).

Biographies for Younger Readers

Adler, David A. *A Picture Book of Davy Crockett.* Illus. by John Wallner and Alexandra Wallner. Holiday House 1996 (LB 0-8234-1212-1) 1998 (pap. 0-8234-1343-8) 32pp.

Davy Crockett's life is often confused with the legends and tall tales that have been told about him. Some of these evolved from his own story-telling skills. This is a well-written introductory biography that could be read aloud. List of important dates. Part of the Picture Book Of series.

Sanford, William R., and Carl R. Green. ***Davy Crockett: Defender of the Alamo.*** Illus. Enslow Publishers 1996 (LB 0-89490-648-8) 48pp.

The reference aids in this book make it a good choice for students doing research. Hunter, congressman, frontiersman, and author, Davy Crockett led a life filled with adventure. Chapter notes, glossary, bibliography, and index. Part of the Legendary Heroes of the Wild West series.

Related Books for Younger Readers

Bredeson, Carmen. ***The Battle of the Alamo: The Fight for Texas Territory.*** Illus. Millbrook Press 1996 (LB 0-7613-0019-8) 64pp.

At the Battle of the Alamo, a small group of defenders (including Jim Bowie and Davy Crockett) lost their lives and were defeated by Santa Anna. The violence of this battle, and the loss of these heroic figures, became a focal point for the efforts to liberate Texas. An epilogue describes the later accomplishments of key figures. Chronology, list of further readings, source notes, and index. Part of the Spotlight on American History series.

Wood, Tim. *The Wild West.* Illus. Viking Penguin 1998 (pap. 0-670-87528-7)

Double-page spreads feature such topics as "The Wild West," "Frontiersmen," "Native Americans," Homesteaders," and "End of the Frontier." Students will be attracted to the numerous illustrations that surround the columns of text and by the four "see-through" pages that lift up to reveal more details about the places and people who settled the American frontier. List of key dates, glossary, and index. Part of the See Through History series.

Curie, Marie (1867–1934), born Marja Sklodowska in Poland, shared the 1903 Nobel Prize for chemistry with her husband, Pierre, and Henri Becquerel for their research on radioactivity. She later won a second Nobel Prize for her work on radium and radium compounds.

Biographies for Younger Readers

Fisher, Leonard Everett. *Marie Curie.* Illus. by the author. Macmillan 1994 (cloth 0-02-735375-3) 32pp.

The scientific explorations of Marie Curie resulted in the discovery of radium. She continued her research even after learning of the hazards of working with radioactive materials. The book opens with a chronology. Written as a narrative, it is enhanced by dramatic black-and-white paintings. The picture-book format makes this a good springboard to further research.

Parker, Steve. *Marie Curie and Radium.* Illus. by the author. Chelsea House 1992 (LB 0-7910-3011-3) 32pp.

In addition to describing the life and accomplishments of Marie Curie, this book also explains the scientific properties of radium and the impact this discovery had on other research. There are numerous illustrations and sidebars, such as one featuring other great thinkers of this era (Charles Darwin and Auguste Comte). There is an excellent timeline that describes what was occurring in science, exploration, politics, and arts in Marie Curie's time. Glossary and index. Part of the Science Discoveries series.

Biographies for Older Readers

Greene, Carol. *Marie Curie: Pioneer Physicist.* Illus. Children's Press 1984 (o.p.) 112pp.

This straightforward biography will be a solid source for research. The text, accompanied by black-and-white photographs, is readable and presents information chronologically. Timeline and index. Part of the People of Distinction series.

Pflaum, Rosalynd. *Marie Curie and Her Daughter Irene.* Illus. Lerner Publications 1993 (LB 0-8225-4915-8) 144pp.

Between the two of them, Marie Curie and her daughter Irene received three Nobel Prizes. This book gives an in-depth look at the lives of these women and their devotion to scientific inquiry. There are many photographs and a map of Paris. Students doing research will find this a wonderful example of a well-organized biography. Source notes, detailed bibliography (listing books, articles, manuscript sources, and interviews), and index.

Related Books for Younger Readers

Sharman, Margaret. *1900s: The First Decade.* Illus. Raintree Steck-Vaughn 1991 (LB 0-8114-3073-1) 47pp.

Events of the first decade of the 20th century included the death of Queen Victoria, the success of the Wright brothers, the discoveries of Marie and Pierre Curie, and the production of the Model T. The format simulates a newspaper with headlines, columns, and supporting pictures, making an attractive overview that gives students a feeling of time and place. Glossary, bibliography, and index. Part of the Take Ten Years series.

Related Books for Older Readers

McGowen, Tom. *1900–1919.* Illus. Twenty-First Century Books 1995 (LB 0-8050-3431-5) 80pp.

In the early 1900s, Albert Einstein published his work on radioactivity. Pierre and Marie Curie worked with radioactive materials, leading to the discovery of polonium and radium. Walter Reed researched yellow fever. In this book (and series), students can connect advances in physics, chemistry, astronomy, biology, geology, and aeronautics. It is fascinating to see how many events occurred simultaneously. Bibliography and index. Part of the Yearbooks in Science series.

Mulcahy, Robert. *Medical Technology: Inventing the Instruments.* Illus. Oliver Press 1997 (LB 1-881508-34-X) 144pp.

In the 17th century, medical treatment included bleeding (to balance the humors) and the use of herbs and medicines from apothecaries. Mulcahy describes the development of scientific instruments that improved medical treatment. Included are the thermometer, stethoscope, radiation therapy, and electrocardiograph. The work of Antonie van Leeuwenhoek, Wilhelm Roentgen, and Marie Curie is described. Medical timeline, glossary, bibliography, and index. Part of the Innovators series.

Da Vinci, Leonardo (1452–1519), an Italian painter, architect, sculptor, engineer, and scientist, was perhaps the first true Renaissance man. Among his most famous paintings are *The Last Supper*, painted about 1495, and *Mona Lisa*, dating from around 1503.

Biographies for Younger Readers

Lafferty, Peter. *Leonardo da Vinci.* Illus. Bookwright Press 1990 (LB 0-531-18348-3)

Beginning with a look at "Leonardo's World," this book describes the accomplishments of this great inventor and thinker. The illustrations include many reproductions of Leonardo's drawings. There are sidebar features describing "Early Inventions" and "Research into Anatomy." Timeline, glossary, bibliography, and index. Part of the Pioneers of Science series.

Provensen, Alice. *Leonardo da Vinci: The Artist, Inventor, Scientist in Three-Dimensional Movable Pictures.* Illus. Viking Penguin 1984 (pap. 0-670-42384-X) 12pp.

Leonardo is acknowledged as a master artist, yet he was also a remarkable inventor, architect, and engineer. This pop-up book brings his creativity to life. One flying machine lifts up when a tab is pulled. Pull down on a flap for another page and the bright colors of a painting go dull as they are absorbed into the porous wall. This is a wonderful book for sparking interest.

Skira-Venturi, Rosabianca. *A Weekend with Leonardo da Vinci.* Illus. Trans. by Ann Keay Beneduce. Rizzoli 1992 (cloth 0-8478-1440-8) 64pp.

The text is written as if by Leonardo himself, and the reader is invited to spend a weekend with him. Along the way, there is information about his life and work. Photographs of sketches, paintings, and locations are accompanied by informative captions. There is a guide to several museum collections, including the Louvre and Uffizi. Timeline and list of the works reproduced in this book. Part of the Weekend With series.

Stanley, Diane. *Leonardo da Vinci.* Illus. by the author. William Morrow & Co. 1996 (LB 0-688-10438-X) (cloth 0-688-10437-1) 48pp.

Leonardo da Vinci was born in 1452. He was an artist, inventor, researcher, designer, and dreamer. This beautiful book captures the essence of Leonardo and his era. Bibliography.

Venezia, Mike. *Da Vinci.* Illus. by the author. Children's Press 1989 (LB 0-516-02275-X) (pap. 0-516-42275-8) 32pp.

Reproductions of Leonardo's works are presented along with cartoon-style illustrations from the author that depict characters, often in humorous activities. The text is very simple and entertaining. Along with learning about Leonardo's life, readers are encouraged to look at details in his paintings. Part of the Getting to Know the World's Greatest Artists series.

Related Books for Younger Readers

Caselli, Giovanni. *The Renaissance and the New World.* Illus. by the author. Peter Bedrick Books 1985 (o.p.) 48pp.

This is a very inviting book with numerous detailed illustrations. It covers many locations—Italy, Germany, England, Spain, France, and more. This book will give students a lot of background information for reports. Bibliography. Part of the History of Everyday Things series.

Cole, Alison. *The Renaissance.* Illus. Dorling Kindersley 1994 (cloth 1-56458-493-3) 64pp.

Opening with "What is the Renaissance?" Cole looks at different locations and artists including Leonardo da Vinci, Albrecht Dürer, Titian, Raphael, and Michelangelo. Like other books in this series, this book makes great use of illustrations, which surround the text. Chronology, list of featured works, glossary, and index. Part of the Eyewitness Art series.

Howarth, Sarah. *Renaissance Places.* Illus. Millbrook Press 1992 (o.p.) 48pp.

Background information about such locations as the city, theater, palace, library, and home of the Renaissance era are presented here. This book will give students a context for their studies of this time. There are many drawings and paintings. Glossary, bibliography, and index. Part of the People and Places series.

Wood, Tim. *The Renaissance.* Illus. Viking Penguin 1993 (pap. 0-670-85149-3) 48pp.

Readers will enjoy learning about this fascinating time. Topics are presented on double-page spreads and feature exploration, painting and sculpture, architecture, printing, and astronomy. There are four "see-through" scenes that allow readers to look inside buildings and a ship. List of key dates, glossary, and index. Part of the See Through History series.

Dalai Lama (1935–), born Lhamo Thondup, is the 14th Dalai Lama, the title given to the spiritual leader of Tibetan Buddhism. After the Chinese took over Tibet, he cooperated briefly with his country's new overseers but fled into exile in 1959. The Dalai Lama was awarded the Nobel Peace Prize in 1989.

"I believe that the Buddhist emphasis on love and patience has helped us considerably in coming through this difficult period of our history."
(Stewart, p. 115)

Biographies for Younger Readers

Stewart, Whitney. *To the Lion Throne: The Story of the Fourteenth Dalai Lama.* Illus. Snow Lion Publications 1990 (pap. 0-937938-75-0) 165pp.

The Dalai Lama left Tibet in 1959 and has lived in exile in India since then. This brief biography is illustrated with numerous black-and-white photographs. The chapters are only two to three pages long and can be accessed through the table of contents. Family tree, suggested reading lists (one for adults, one for children), and glossary.

Biographies for Older Readers

Perez, Louis G. *The Dalai Lama.* Illus. Rourke 1993 (cloth 0-86625-480-3) 112pp.

From his installation as the Dalai Lama through his training and exile, this book provides detailed information for researchers. Timeline, annotated list of books by the Dalai Lama, list of media resources, glossary, annotated bibliography, and index. Part of the World Leaders series.

Stewart, Whitney. *The 14th Dalai Lama: Spiritual Leader of Tibet.* Lerner Publications 1996 (LB 0-8225-4926-3) 128pp.

The Dalai Lama was born in 1935 and named Lhamo Thondup, which means "Wish-Fulfilling Goddess." There is a fascinating discussion of how he was discovered to be the 14th Dalai Lama, a process that involved visits from religious officials who gave the young Lhamo Thondup tests to pass. He is now in exile, and the text describes his efforts to promote nonviolence. This is a very fine biography. Source notes, bibliography (including books by the Dalai Lama), and index. Part of the Newsmakers Biographies series.

Related Books for Older Readers

Levi, Patricia. *Tibet.* Illus. Marshall Cavendish 1996 (LB 0-7614-0277-2) 128pp.

There are many historical references throughout this book. In the "History" chapter, topics include "The Reigns of the Dalai Lamas" and "The Chinese Liberation." Chapters on "Religion," "Language," "Arts," and "Festivals" all include historical and cultural details that would give students useful background information. "Quick Notes" section, glossary, bibliography, and index. Part of the Cultures of the World series.

Normanton, Simon. *Tibet: The Lost Civilisation.* Illus. Viking Penguin 1988 (o.p.) 192pp.

Until the 20th century, little was known about the people or culture of this isolated country. Normanton describes expeditions to Tibet, ceremonies and customs, political upheaval, and the Chinese invasion that led to the exile of the Dalai Lama. This is a thorough book with many archival photographs.

Darwin, Charles Robert (1809–1882), English naturalist, is best known for formulating the theories of organic evolution and natural selection. He explored these theories in *On the Origin of Species* (1859) and *The Descent of Man* (1871).

Biographies for Younger Readers

Anderson, Margaret J. *Charles Darwin: Naturalist.* Illus. Enslow Publishers 1994 (LB 0-89490-476-0) 128pp.

This book is well organized for research. The chapters are clearly written and are enhanced by black-and-white photographs and drawings. Chronology, suggestions for further readings, chapter notes, glossary, and index. Part of the Great Minds of Science series.

Parker, Steve. *Charles Darwin and Evolution.* Illus. by the author. Chelsea House 1995 (LB 0-7910-3007-5) 32pp.

The format of this book is visually appealing. There are brief chapters with the text surrounded by clearly captioned illustrations (photographs, maps, reproductions). Boxed sidebars feature information such as Darwin's findings on the Galapagos finches. Timeline ("The World in Darwin's Time," connecting activities in science with events in exploration, politics, and arts), glossary, and index. Part of the Science Discoveries series.

Biographies for Older Readers

Evans, J. Edward. *Charles Darwin: Revolutionary Biologist.* Illus. Lerner Publications 1993 (LB 0-8225-4914-X)

Charles Darwin's family included scientists and manufacturers (his father was a physician; his mother's family, the Wedgwoods, were famous for pottery). The detailed text in this book is accompanied by many black-and-white illustrations. Bibliography and index.

Nardo, Don. *Charles Darwin.* Illus. Chelsea House 1993 (LB 0-7910-1729-X) 112pp.

Quotations from letters and writings by Darwin and his contemporaries make this a great resource for students working on projects. There is a beautiful description of the rain forest and a map of the five-year voyage of the *Beagle*. Several chapters discuss the political and religious controversy arising from *On the Origin of Species*. Chronology, bibliography, and index. Part of the Chelsea House Library of Biography series.

Stefoff, Rebecca. *Charles Darwin and the Evolution Revolution.* Illus. Oxford University Press 1996 (LB 0-19-508996-0) 128pp.

Charles Darwin's scientific theories involved him in controversy and debate. In addition to describing Darwin's life and work, this book has sidebars that examine related topics, such as "What is a Species?" and "Mendelian Genetics." This is an advanced presentation for in-depth research. Chronology, glossary, bibliography, and index. Part of the Oxford Portraits in Science series.

Related Books for Younger Readers

Blake, Arthur. *The Scopes Trial: Defending the Right to Teach.* Illus. Millbrook Press 1994 (LB 1-56294-407-X) 64pp.

Chapters describe the background to the Scopes trial—including Darwin's theory and the fundamentalists' efforts to keep it from being taught—the law in Tennessee, and the people involved. Chronology, bibliography, and index. Part of the Spotlight on American History series.

Related Books for Older Readers

Aaseng, Nathan. *Genetics: Unlocking the Secrets of Life.* Illus. Oliver Press 1996 (LB 1-881508-27-7) 144pp.

Genetic research has led to information about natural selection, dominant and recessive traits, the double helix, DNA, and synthetic genes. Focusing on specific researchers and scientists, this book describes these discoveries and more. There is a list of Nobel Prize winners in physiology and medicine (through 1995). Glossary, detailed bibliography, and index. Part of the Innovators series.

Nardo, Don. *The Scopes Trial.* Illus. Lucent 1997 (LB 1-56006-268-1)

In *Origin of Species*, Charles Darwin outlined the idea of natural selection and the theory of evolution. Many people found his writings controversial and challenged the teaching of his theories. This book examines one of the more famous challenges, spotlighting the people, strategies, results, and implications. Bibliography and index. Part of the Famous Trials series.

Davis, Jefferson (1808–1889), born near Elkton, Kentucky, served as a U.S. senator from Mississippi (1847–1851 and 1857–1861) and as U.S. secretary of war (1853–1857) before being named president of the Confederacy (1861–1865). He was seized by Union forces in 1865 and spent two years in prison.

Biographies for Younger Readers

Kent, Zachary. *Jefferson Davis.* Illus. Children's Press 1993 (pap. 0-516-46664-X) 32pp.

This presentation is brief, but it does capture the highlights of the life of Jefferson Davis. Best known as the president of the Confederacy, Davis was trained at West Point and served in the army and in Congress. Index. Part of the Cornerstones of Freedom series.

Biographies for Older Readers

King, Perry Scott. *Jefferson Davis.* Illus. Chelsea House 1990 (LB 1-55546-806-3) 112pp.

The format of this book makes it a fine choice for students doing research. In addition to the text, there are numerous illustrations whose captions provide additional insights into the people and way of life of Davis's era. The text is well organized and thorough, and in the margins there are many quotations from Jefferson Davis and his contemporaries. Bibliography, chronology, and index. Part of the World Leaders Past & Present series.

Related Books for Younger Readers

Smith, Carter, ed. *Prelude to War.* Illus. Millbrook Press 1993 (LB 1-56294-261-1) 96pp.

Describing the events that led to the Civil War, this book provides students with an understanding of the divided agendas of the North and the South. Features include "The Industrial North," "The South: The Cotton Kingdom," "Uncle Tom's Cabin," "Free Blacks," "Abraham Lincoln," "Jefferson Davis," and "The Birth of the Confederacy." Timeline, brief bibliography, and index. Part of the Sourcebook on the Civil War series.

Related Books for Older Readers

Reger, James P. *Life in the South during the Civil War.* Illus. Lucent 1997 (LB 1-56006-333-5) 112pp.

With many quotations in the text and boxed sidebars adding such vignettes as "A Little Belle's Ball" and "Free at Last . . . Or Were They?" students will find useful background information about the way of life in the South. The lives of plantation owners, slaves, and "crackers" are described, and two chapters look at the war and its impact. Chapter notes, annotated bibliographies, and index. Part of the Way People Live series.

De Soto, Hernando

De Soto, Hernando (1500?–1542), a Spanish explorer who served as governor of Cuba, led a 16th-century expedition through a large area of the southeastern and south central United States. Members of that expedition are believed to be the first Europeans to have seen the Mississippi River.

Biographies for Older Readers

Carson, Robert. *Hernando De Soto: Expedition to the Mississippi River.* Children's Press 1991 (o.p.) 128pp.

This book describes Hernando de Soto as a man of honor. While de Soto searched for new lands and new treasures, he did not use his conquests as an opportunity for violence and destruction. Students who read this biography will learn about the exploits of other, more ruthless conquerors, along with the accomplishments of de Soto. Timeline, bibliography, and index. Part of the World's Great Explorers series.

Whitman, Sylvia. *Hernando de Soto and the Explorers of the American South.* Illus. Chelsea House 1991 (LB 0-7910-1301-4) 112pp.

Europeans explorers wanted gold and glory. Hernando de Soto went on expeditions with Cordóba and Pizarro before leading an expedition to Florida and into the eastern mountains of North America. There is a color photoessay in the middle of the book showing paintings of John White, who journeyed to the East Coast of America in the 1580s and documented the region. Chronology, bibliography, and index. Part of the World Explorers series.

Related Books for Older Readers

Franck, Irene M., and David M. Brownstone. *The American Way West.* Illus. Facts on File 1991 (cloth 0-8160-1880-4) 128pp.

Focusing on different routes to the West, this book describes the people who settled the American wilderness. Chapters cover "The Mohawk Trail," "The Wilderness Road and Other Trans-Appalachian Routes," "The Mississippi Route," "The Santa Fe Trail and the Chihuahua Trail," and "The Oregon Trail and the California Trail." Index. Part of the Trade and Travel Routes series.

Hakim, Joy. *The First Americans.* Illus. Oxford University Press 1993 (LB 0-19-507745-8) (cloth 0-19-509506-5) 1993 (pap. 0-19-507746-6) 160pp.

When the European explorers "discovered" the Americas, native peoples were already established. This book looks at Indian societies from the earliest peoples to the first settlements. Columbus, Ponce de León, Pizarro, and the conquistadors are profiled. Chronology, bibliography, and index. Part of the History of US series.

Dickens, Charles (1812–1870), a British author, is considered one of the greatest novelists in the English language. His novels, which include *Oliver Twist, Great Expectations,* and *A Tale of Two Cities,* are noted for the richness of their characters and their portrayal of all layers of English society.

Biographies for Younger Readers

Collins, David R. *Tales for Hard Times: A Story About Charles Dickens.* Illus. by David Mataya. Carolrhoda Books 1990 (LB 0-87614-433-4) 64pp.

Six easy-to-read chapters chronicle the life of Charles Dickens. The hardships of his childhood influenced his writing, giving him experiences and people that made his novels so popular and so real. List of books by Dickens and bibliography. Part of the Creative Minds Biographies series.

Stanley, Diane, and Peter Vennema. *Charles Dickens: The Man Who Had Great Expectations.* Illus. by Diane Stanley. William Morrow & Co. 1993 (LB 0-688-09111-3) (cloth 0-688-09110-5) 48pp.

Once you start reading this book, you will not want to put it down. The writing is superb and the full-color gouache illustrations are outstanding. Dickens's life mirrored some of the events in his novels, and that connection is made by the authors. The sustained narrative of this book is very readable. Bibliography.

Related Books for Younger Readers

Giblin, James Cross. *Chimney Sweeps: Yesterday and Today.*
Illus. by Margot Tomes and with photographs. Crowell 1982 (o.p.)
64pp.

Much of this book focuses on chimney sweeps of the past—particularly those in 19th-century England. Chapters describe "Climbing Boys," "A Climbing Boy's Day," and "Help for Climbing Boys." This would be a good background book for students ready to read Dickens. Bibliography and index.

Langley, Andrew. *The Industrial Revolution.* Illus. Viking Penguin 1994 (pap. 0-670-85835-8) 48pp.

Many students will be attracted by the four "see-through" pages in this book. Readers can lift the roof or side from a coal miner's cottage, a railroad station, a factory, and a ship. The factory scene includes a quotation from Charles Dickens on the horrible working conditions of this era. There is information about health, disease, social reforms, and immigration. List of key dates, glossary, and index. Part of the See Through History series.

Related Books for Older Readers

Hill, Susan, ed., researched and compiled by Piers Dudgeon. *The Spirit of Britain: An Illustrated Guide to Literary Britain.* Illus. Headline Book Publishing 1997 (pap. 0-7472-7812-1) 224pp.

This is a travel guide featuring literary locations throughout Britain that are tied to authors from Jane Austen through William Wordsworth. The West Yorkshire settings of the Brontës, Daphne du Maurier's Cornwall, and Charles Dickens's London are included. Along the journey there are facts about the history and people of each region. This is a good choice for browsing and would be an especially useful resource for a study trip.

Disney, Walt (1901–1966), an American film producer, is best known as a pioneer in the production of full-length animated cartoons. In the 1950s his company began developing amusement parks built around some of the themes and characters from his films.

Biographies for Older Readers

Cole, Michael D. *Walt Disney: Creator of Mickey Mouse.* Illus. Enslow Publishers 1996 (LB 0-89490-694-1) 112pp.

Walt Disney was a pioneer in animation and movies. The thorough presentation in this book looks at his well-known accomplishments (Mickey Mouse, the Seven Dwarfs, Disneyland) and also describes "The Disney Tradition." There are well-selected quotations (with chapter notes). This will meet both the interest and informational needs of readers. Chronology, bibliography, and index. Part of the People to Know series.

Ford, Barbara. *Walt Disney: A Biography.* Illus. Walker and Company 1989 (LB 0-8027-6865-2) (cloth 0-8027-6864-4) 160pp.

This book begins with Walt Disney's vision for animated features and family entertainment and ends with a brief look at the changes at the Disney Studios under Michael Eisner. It is a fascinating story of dreams, hard work, and success. Index.

Related Books for Younger Readers

The History of Moviemaking: Animation and Live-Action—from Silent to Sound, Black and White to Color. Illus. with photographs and drawings. Scholastic 1994 (cloth 0-590-47645-9) 47pp.

Lights, camera, action! Learn about magic lantern shows, motion pictures, animation, and special effects. Plastic overlay pages and stickers involve the reader. Part of the Voyages of Discovery series.

Italia, Bob. *Mickey Mouse.* Illus. Abdo & Daughters 1991 (LB 1-56239-053-8) 202pp.

Before he was Mickey Mouse, did you know his name was Mortimer? This book describes the development of one of the world's most popular cartoon characters. There are many color photographs of Mickey Mouse, and there is a discussion of the Disney theme parks and the Mickey Mouse Club. Although this is very brief, it provides useful background information. Part of the Behind the Creation Of series.

Related Books for Older Readers

Finch, Christopher. *The Art of Walt Disney: From Mickey Mouse to the Magic Kingdoms.* New Concise Edition. Illus. Portland House 1988 (cloth 0-517-66474-7)

There are many illustrations in this book that make it especially attractive and entertaining. An early cartoon featuring "Oswald the Lucky Rabbit" shows how Mickey Mouse developed. There are sketches from *Steamboat Willie* and other classic cartoon

(From obituary in **New York Times***): "He had a genius for innovation; his production was enormous; he was able to keep sure and personal control over his increasingly far-flung enterprise; his hand was ever on the public pulse. He was, in short, a legend in his own lifetime—and so honored many times over. Yet none of this sums up Walt Disney."*

(Cole, p. 96)

features, such as *Snow White, Fantasia,* and *Bambi.* Walt Disney's interest in television is also described, along with the development of Disneyland and Disney World.

Nardo, Don. *Animation: Drawings Spring to Life.* Illus. Lucent 1992 (o.p.) 96pp.

What were the first animated films? How were new techniques developed? Besides Walt Disney, what other animators were part of the Golden Age of animation? This book gives a strong presentation of the history of animation. There are great illustrations from animated classics including *Fantasia* and the *Looney Tunes* cartoons. This is fun to read, providing information about a very interesting topic. Glossary, bibliographies (further reading and works consulted), and index. Part of the Encyclopedia of Discovery and Invention series.

Douglass, Frederick (1817?–1895), an African American author and abolitionist, escaped from slavery in 1838, fleeing to New Bedford, Massachusetts, and adopting the name Douglass. He urged other slaves to flee their captors both before and during the Civil War.

Biographies for Younger Readers

Adler, David A. *A Picture Book of Frederick Douglass.* Illus. by Samuel Byrd. Holiday House 1993 (LB 0-8234-1002-1) 1995 (pap. 0-8234-1205-9) 32pp.

Because this has a picture-book format, it is a good choice to use for an overview of Frederick Douglass's life. From his childhood as a slave in Maryland to his work on his own antislavery newspaper in New York to his meeting President Lincoln at the White House, this is a dramatic presentation. Timeline. Part of the Picture Book Of series.

McLoone, Margo. *Frederick Douglass.* Illus. Bridgestone Books 1997 (cloth 1-56065-517-8)

Did you know there is a Frederick Douglass Museum and Cultural Center? The Internet site for this center is given in this book, along with mail addresses for other useful sites. Information is presented in double-page spreads. This is a fine choice for a student beginning to learn research skills. Timeline, glossary, bibliography, and index. Part of the Read and Discover Photo-Illustrated Biographies series.

Biographies for Older Readers

Douglass, Frederick. Ed. by Michael McCurdy. *Escape from Slavery: The Boyhood of Frederick Douglass in His Own Words.* Illus. by Michael McCurdy. Knopf 1994 (cloth 0-679-84652-2) (pap. 0-679-84651-4) 64pp.

Frederick Douglass's own words are compelling, especially since we know that he learned to read and write in defiance of the laws of his time. Excerpts in this book tell of Douglass's life from childhood through his marriage to Anna Murray. The text provides students with a wonderful opportunity to access an original source. Bibliography.

Russell, Sharman Apt. *Frederick Douglass: Abolitionist Editor.* Illus. Chelsea House 1988 (LB 1-55546-580-3) (pap. 0-7910-0204-7) 112pp.

This comprehensive biography will be very useful for reports. It is well organized and has supportive illustrations, for example, a reproduction from the *Liberator*, William Lloyd Garrison's abolitionist newspaper, and a handbill advertising the sale of slaves. There are many pictures of Douglass and his contemporaries. Chronology, bibliography, and index. Part of the Black Americans of Achievement series.

Related Books for Younger Readers

Hamilton, Virginia. *Many Thousand Gone: African Americans from Slavery to Freedom.* Illus. by Leo Dillon and Diane Dillon. Knopf 1993 (LB 0-394-92873-3) (cloth 0-394-82873-9) 1995 (pap. 0-679-87936-6) 160pp.

Organized in three parts, this book provides an insight into the lives and feelings of slaves: Part One, "Slavery in America"; Part Two, "Running-Aways"; and Part Three, "Exodus to Freedom." Topics include "Advertisements," "The Nat Turner Rebellion," "The Brave Conductor," and "The Tide of Freedom." Bibliography and index.

Related Books for Older Readers

Henry, Christopher. *Forever Free: From the Emancipation Proclamation to the Civil Rights Bill of 1875 (1863–1875).* Illus. Chelsea House 1995 (LB 0-7910-2253-6) (pap. 0-7910-2679-5)

From the Civil War (and the efforts of blacks to be soldiers) to Reconstruction to the beginning of political power, this book describes key issues in the history of African Americans. Many of the illustrations are reproductions of historical scenes, including battles, lynchings, and the activities of the Ku Klux Klan. Bibliography and index. Part of the Milestones in Black American History series.

Meltzer, Milton, ed. *Frederick Douglass: In His Own Words.* Illus. by Stephen Alcorn. Harcourt 1991 (cloth 0-15-229492-9) 240pp.

After reading about Frederick Douglass, students will find it valuable to read his own words. The three parts of this book are "Before the War," "The War Years," and "After the War." Within those sections are topic groupings of speeches and writings, such as "For Mr. Lincoln," "Men of Color, to Arms!," "The Ballot for Women," and "Stamp Out the Klan!" There is an appended group of biographical portraits on such political and social leaders as Susan B. Anthony and William Lloyd Garrison. Source notes and index.

Paulson, Timothy J. *Days of Sorrow, Years of Glory, 1831–1850: From the Nat Turner Revolt to the Fugitive Slave Law.* Illus. Chelsea House 1994 (LB 0-7910-2263-3) (pap. 0-7910-2689-2) 112pp.

Among the milestone events for this era that open this book are the efforts of abolitionists, the Seminole wars, the slave revolt on the *Amistad,* the publication of the *North Star* by Frederick Douglass, and the efforts of Harriet Tubman on the Underground Railroad. These events and others are expanded in the following chapters. Bibliography and index. Part of the Milestones in Black American History series.

Drake, Sir Francis (1540–1596), an

English naval hero, became the first of his countrymen to circle the globe on a voyage that stretched from 1577 to 1580. Drake was an admiral in the English fleet that defeated the Spanish Armada.

Biographies for Older Readers

Bard, Roberta. *Francis Drake: First Englishman to Circle the Globe.* Illus. Children's Press 1992 (o.p.) 128pp.

From "Early Life" to "The World Encompassed" to "The Armada" and "The Last Voyage," this is a thorough biography. Information about the politics of this era (Henry VIII and Elizabeth I) is incorporated. There is an appendix featuring a map, "Great Voyages from 1492 to 1580." Timeline, glossary, bibliography, and index. Part of the World's Great Explorers series.

Duncan, Alice Smith. *Sir Francis Drake and the Struggle for an Ocean Empire.* Illus. Chelsea House 1993 (LB 0-7910-1302-2) 112pp.

Pirate or protector—Sir Francis Drake raided Spanish outposts, enriched the treasury of Queen Elizabeth I, and organized the defeat of the Spanish Armada. The detailed text is accompanied by many black-and-white photographs and there is a section of color illustrations of people and moments related to the Armada (such as a portrait of Queen Elizabeth and of ships of the English fleet). Chronology, bibliography, and index. Part of the World Explorers series.

Marrin, Albert. *Sea King: Sir Francis Drake and His Times.* Illus. Atheneum 1995 (cloth 0-689-31887-1) 168pp.

In this comprehensive biography, there is information about the social, political, and economic issues that influenced the adventures of Sir Francis Drake and other explorers. The acquisition of wealth was one of the driving forces for expeditions, and Drake's skill as a mariner allowed him to acquire great treasures. Excellent bibliography, detailed chapter notes, and fine index. Students will appreciate the scholarship of this book.

Related Books for Younger Readers

Shakespeare's England: Henry VIII, Elizabeth I, William Shakespeare. Illus. Marshall Cavendish 1989 (LB 0-86307-999-7)

For each person featured, there is an opening portrait, insights into important events, and a description of everyday life. A chronology is divided into subject areas: politics and war, science and exploration, religion and society, art and literature. The many colorful illustrations and boxed sidebars add to this attractive presentation. Glossary, bibliography, and index. Part of the Exploring the Past series.

Related Books for Older Readers

Lace, William W. *Defeat of the Spanish Armada.* Illus. Lucent 1997 (LB 1-56006-458-7)

Using many quotations and boxed sidebars, this book adds extra details to the basic description of the issues of the conflict between England and Spain in the 16th century. Information about the personalities of the era, eating on the ships, how guns were fired, and strategies for the battles are included. Chronology, bibliographies, and index. Part of the Battles of the Middle Ages series.

Lace, William W. *Elizabethan England.* Illus. Lucent 1995 (LB 1-56006-278-9) 128pp.

The reign of Elizabeth I spanned the second half of the 16th century. During this era, there were challenges to religious and astronomical beliefs. Explorations led to the establishment of new colonies. Shakespeare's plays were written and performed and the Globe Theater was opened. Chronology, chapter notes, bibliographies, and index. Part of the World History series.

Drew, Charles Richard (1904–1950),

an African American physician and surgeon, developed a method for preserving blood plasma for transfusion. During World War II, he was named director of the first American Red Cross blood bank.

Biographies for Younger Readers

Talmadge, Katherine S. *The Life of Charles Drew.* Illus. by Antonio Castro. Twenty-First Century Books 1991 (o.p.) 89pp.

After Charles Drew became one of the first African Americans to be certified as a surgeon, he assisted with the medical education of African American students. He was a pioneer in blood research. Using many quotations, this book chronicles his accomplishments in medicine and in promoting social change. List of suggestions for further readings and index. Part of the Pioneers in Health and Medicine series.

Wolfe, Rinna E. *Charles Richard Drew, M.D.* Illus. Franklin Watts 1991 (LB 0-531-20021-3) 64pp.

A well-respected doctor, researcher, and teacher, Charles Drew was not a member of the American Medical Association because the Washington, D.C., chapter was segregated. The seven brief chapters in this book describe the social and political issues that Dr. Drew faced and overcame. Glossary, bibliography, and index. Part of the First Books Biographies series.

Related Books for Younger Readers

Fisher, Leonard Everett. *The Doctors.* 2nd ed. Illus. by the author. Marshall Cavendish 1996 (LB 0-7614-0481-3) 48pp.

Students who read this book will be fascinated by the descriptions of medical treatment, training, and service during the early years in America. One medicine for plague was "black powder from toads." Formal training for doctors was just beginning and was very inconsistent. Part of the Colonial American Craftsman series.

Hayden, Robert C. *11 African American Doctors.* rev. and expanded. Illus. Twenty-First Century Books 1992 (LB 0-8050-2135-3) 208pp.

Hayden writes about the accomplishments of 11 African Americans who contributed to medical advancements through teaching and research. They all faced discrimination, economic hardships, and even hostility, yet they achieved success. Included are Arthur C. Logan, Jane C. Wright, Charles R. Drew, Daniel Hale Williams, and others. Students who read these accounts will gain insight into the history of those who faced limits and went beyond them. Part of the Achievers: African Americans in Science and Technology series.

Miller, Brandon Marie. ***Just What the Doctor Ordered: The History of American Medicine.*** Illus. Lerner Publications 1997 (LB 0-8225-1737-X)

This is an amazing look at the history of medicine in America, from Native Americans through the present. Bloodletting with leeches, laxatives for purges, treating headaches with electricity, dissecting cadavers, the development of X-ray machines, pasteurization of milk—all give some perspective on our medical past and the amazing strides we have made. Bibliography and index.

Related Books for Older Readers

Yount, Lisa. ***Black Scientists.*** Illus. Facts on File 1991 (LB 0-8160-2549-5) 128pp.

George Washington Carver, Daniel Hale Lewis, Charles Richard Drew, and John P. Moon are among the scientists included. Reading about their accomplishments gives an insight into their eras and experiences. For each person, there is a chronology and bibliography. Index. Part of the American Profiles series.

In Up from Slavery: *"My own belief is, although I have never before said so in so many words, that the time will come when the Negro in the South will be accorded all the political rights which his ability, character and material possessions entitle him to."* (Hamilton, p. 83)

Du Bois, W. E. B. (1868–1963), an African American educator and author, in 1909 cofounded the National Negro Committee, which a year later became the National Association for the Advancement of Colored People. He was an early crusader for racial equality.

Biographies for Younger Readers

Cavan, Seamus. ***W. E. B. Du Bois and Racial Relations.*** Illus. Millbrook Press 1993 (LB 1-56294-288-3) (pap. 1-56294-794-X) 32pp.

This brief book deals with many difficult topics: racism, violence, lynching, the Ku Klux Klan, and discrimination. Boxed sections discuss the Klan and Du Bois's conflict with Booker T. Washington. Bibliography and index. Part of the Gateway Civil Rights series.

Moss, Nathaniel. *W. E. B. Du Bois: Civil Rights Leader.* Illus.
Chelsea House 1995 (o.p.)

W. E. B. Du Bois lived for nearly a century. Born just after the
Civil War, he confronted discrimination and racism yet he went on
to receive a Ph.D. from Harvard. He cofounded the NAACP and
worked for Pan-Africanism—unity for people of African descent.
This biography is clearly written and illustrated with many photographs. Chronology, suggestions for further readings, glossary, and
index. Part of the Junior World Biographies series.

Biographies for Older Readers

Hamilton, Virginia. *W. E. B. Du Bois: A Biography.* Illus. Crowell
1992 (o.p.) 192pp.

As an early leader of the civil rights movement, W. E. B. Du
Bois was outspoken in his efforts to assure equality for blacks. This
book is filled with encounters with such key figures as Marcus Garvey, Booker T. Washington, and Mary McLeod Bethune. Several
chapters deal with Du Bois's indictment, trial, and acquittal for "failure to register as agents of a foreign principal." This is a
comprehensive and well-written book, documented with source
notes. Bibliography and index.

McKissack, Patricia, and Fredrick McKissack. *W. E. B. Du Bois.*
Illus. Franklin Watts 1990 (LB 0-531-10939-9) 112pp.

Du Bois believed that intellectual pursuits—education, writing, research—were the paths that would lead to improved
conditions for African Americans. Read about his involvement in
the Harlem Renaissance, a time that celebrated black talent and
accomplishments. This is a great choice for students doing in-depth
research. Appendix of the writings of W. E. B. Du Bois, source notes,
bibliography, and index. Part of the Impact Biographies series.

Related Books for Older Readers

Grossman, James R. *A Chance to Make Good: African Americans, 1900–1929.* Illus. Oxford University Press 1997 (LB
0-19-508770-4)

The early years of the 20th century were full of dramatic
changes for African Americans. Many blacks left the rural South,
hoping for better opportunities in the North. African Americans were
establishing social and political organizations, including the National Association for the Advancement of Colored People. Booker T.
Washington, Mary Church Terrell, and W. E. B. Du Bois were key
figures in these efforts. Chronology, bibliography, and index. Part of
the Young Oxford History of African Americans series.

Hauser, Pierre. *Great Ambitions: From the "Separate but Equal" Doctrine to the Birth of the NAACP (1896–1909)*. Illus. Chelsea House 1995 (cloth 0-7910-2264-1) (pap. 0-7910-2690-6)

In the late 1800s, opportunities for blacks were often separate and unequal. Through the early years of the new century, many people spoke out for equality. This book looks at Jim Crow laws, the Niagara Movement, and the founding of the NAACP. Key figures in this era include W. E. B. Du Bois, Paul Laurence Dunbar, Booker T. Washington, Ida Wells-Barnett, and William Monroe Trotter. Bibliography and index. Part of the Milestones in Black American History series.

McKissack, Patricia, and Fredrick McKissack. *The Civil Rights Movement in America: From 1865 to the Present.* 2nd ed. Illus. Children's Press 1991 (LB 0-516-00579-0) 352pp.

This thorough book will be very useful to students doing research. From the years after the Civil War through the early years of the civil rights movement and ending with a discussion of the women's movement and children's rights, there is a wealth of information here. The organization of the book is inviting: it is divided into chronological eras, each opening with a timeline; there are topic subdivisions; and there are "Cameos" on key people and issues. Bibliography and index.

Dunbar, Paul Laurence (1872–1906), an African American poet and author, drew on African American dialects and folklore for his poetry, of which *Lyrics of Lowly Life* is a prime example. Dunbar also produced short stories and novels of African American life in the southern United States.

Biographies for Older Readers

Gentry, Tony. *Paul Laurence Dunbar.* Illus. Chelsea House 1989 (LB 1-55546-583-8) (pap. 0-7910-0223-3) 112pp.

Paul Laurence Dunbar published his first poem when he was just 16. He continued writing, receiving worldwide attention. The photographs in this book show many contemporaries of Dunbar, including Frederick Douglass, the Wright brothers, William Dean Howells, and Claude McKay, providing a visual connection with this era and the accomplishments of others. Appendix of books by Paul Laurence Dunbar, chronology, bibliography, and index. Part of the Black Americans of Achievement series.

McKissack, Patricia. *Paul Laurence Dunbar: A Poet to Remember.* Illus. Children's Press 1984 (o.p.) 112pp.

During his life, Paul Laurence Dunbar was often criticized for his dialect poems, yet they provided a connection to the language, rhythm, and culture of African Americans. This is a readable book with helpful research aids. Timeline and index. Part of the People of Distinction series.

Related Books for Older Readers

Bair, Barbara. *Though Justice Sleeps: African Americans, 1880–1900.* Illus. Oxford University Press 1997 (cloth 0-614-25378-0)

The 20 years featured in this book should have been a time of accomplishment for many former slaves and their children. Instead, injustices continued, leading black citizens to become more politically active and seek opportunities. Key figures include Booker T. Washington, Paul Laurence Dunbar, Ida B. Wells, and Frances E. Harper. Chronology, bibliography, and index. Part of the Young Oxford History of African Americans series.

Katz, William L. *The Great Migrations, 1880s–1912.* Illus. Raintree Steck-Vaughn 1993 (LB 0-8114-6278-1) 1995 (pap. 0-8114-2915-6) 96pp.

During the years covered in this book, there was a large movement of people to and within America. Immigrants arrived from European and Asian countries. African Americans relocated from the rural South to the cities in the North. Boxed sections feature related issues (child labor) and people (Dr. Daniel Hale Williams, Madam C. J. Walker, and Paul Laurence Dunbar). Bibliography and index. Part of the History of Multicultural America series.

Earhart, Amelia (1897–1937), an American aviator, in 1928 became the first female to cross the Atlantic in a plane. She repeated the crossing as a solo pilot in 1932. She disappeared on a flight with Frederick Noonan over the Pacific in 1937.

Biographies for Younger Readers

Chadwick, Roxane. *Amelia Earhart: Aviation Pioneer.* Illus. Lerner Publications 1987 (LB 0-8225-0484-7); First Avenue Editions (pap. 0-8225-9515-X) 56pp.

Amelia Earhart was the first woman to fly across the Atlantic Ocean. Her pioneering spirit led her to attempt to fly around the world. This brief book is written as a narrative with no chapter divisions and no index. List of "Records and Firsts of Amelia Earhart" and list of three books by her. Part of the Achievers Biographies series.

Lauber, Patricia. *Lost Star: The Story of Amelia Earhart.* Illus. Scholastic 1990 (pap. 0-590-41159-4) 96pp.

This well-written biography features details about the early life of this pioneering pilot. Her last flight ended with her mysterious disappearance, which is still questioned today. List of suggested readings and index.

Wood, Leigh Hope. *Amelia Earhart.* Illus. Chelsea House 1997 (LB 0-7910-2294-3) 80pp.

Charles Lindbergh was the first person to fly solo across the Atlantic. Amelia Earhart was the second. This book has many features to recommend it to students. It has an appealing format with a good balance of photographs and text. The text is readable and well organized. Chronology, list of further readings, glossary, and index. Part of the Junior World Biographies series.

Biographies for Older Readers

Randolph, Blythe. *Amelia Earhart.* Illus. Franklin Watts 1987 (o.p.) 144pp.

Growing up in Kansas, Amelia Earhart was considered intelligent and adventurous. Those characteristics continued into her adulthood as she accomplished many aviation firsts. In this detailed biography, there are many quotations (often from Earhart's writings). List of records set, bibliography, and index. Part of the Impact Biographies series.

Woog, Adam. *Amelia Earhart.* Illus. Lucent 1997 (LB 1-56006-261-4)

After focusing on Amelia Earhart's life, the text offers several chapters posing questions about her death: "How Did Earhart Die?" "Was Earhart a Spy?" and "Was There a Government Cover-Up?" This should provide a different perspective for research projects. Within each chapter there are boxed sections that provide additional information. Bibliography and index. Part of the Mysterious Deaths series.

Related Books for Younger Readers

Boyne, Walter J. *The Smithsonian Book of Flight for Young People.* Illus. Atheneum 1988 (LB 0-689-31422-1); Aladdin (pap. 0-689-71212-X) 128pp.

This attractive book is a good choice for research and browsing. Arranged chronologically, there are many archival photographs that show man's fascination for flight. Information is organized into three parts: "From Dream to Reality," "Two Wars and Between," and "Jets, Rockets, and Realism." This presentation could be used by many levels of students, all of whom will appreciate the wonderful photographs. Bibliography and index.

Spangenburg, Ray, and Diane K. Moser. *The Story of Air Transport in America.* Illus. Facts on File 1992 (LB 0-8160-2260-7) 96pp.

From the early attempts at flight to the influence of the world wars to the aircraft of the 1990s, this book provides a well-organized overview of the history of aircraft. Each chapter has a boxed timeline of "Historical Headlines" and there are sidebars on key people and events, including Amelia Earhart, Jacqueline Cochran, and the flight of the *Voyager.* Appendix on "Major Events in U.S. Air Transport," glossary, bibliography, and index. Part of the Connecting a Continent series.

Related Books for Older Readers

Moolman, Valerie, and the editors of Time-Life Books. *Women Aloft.* Illus. Time-Life Books 1981 (LB 0-8094-3288-9)

Beginning with "The First Hurdle: Proving They Were Fit to Fly," this book looks at women pioneers of flight. Amelia Earhart is a focal point of the book, but there is information about other women who took risks, particularly during the war years. Excellent photographs make this a good book for browsers, too. Bibliography and index. Part of the Epic of Flight series.

Stacey, Tom. *Airplanes: The Lure of Flight.* Illus. Lucent 1990 (LB 1-56006-203-7) 96pp.

Many people have dreamed of flying. The ancient Greek myth of Daedalus focuses on flight as do drawings of Leonardo da Vinci. Balloons and gliders led to experiments with powered flight, including the efforts of the Wright brothers. The author provides a chronological look at aircraft, including the rockets of the space age. Glossary, bibliography, and index. Part of the Encyclopedia of Discovery and Invention series.

Eastman, Charles (1858–1939), a Santee Sioux physician and author, worked to help young people and the ill on reservations. He was a lecturer and author of several books on Native Americans' rights.

Biographies for Older Readers

Anderson, Peter. *Charles Eastman: Physician, Reformer, and Native American Leader.* Illus. Children's Press 1992 (o.p.) 152pp.

After receiving his medical training at Boston University, Charles Eastman (born Ohiyesa of the Santee Sioux) returned to provide medical treatment on the Sioux reservation. He helped treat survivors of Wounded Knee. A timeline includes information about Eastman's life as well as other historical events. Index. Part of the People of Distinction series.

Related Books for Older Readers

Katz, Jane B., comp. and ed. *We Rode the Wind: Recollections of Native American Life.* Illus. Runestone Press 1995 (LB 0-8225-3154-2) 128pp.

The Introduction gives an overview of the way of life of the native peoples of the Great Plains. Eight personal accounts follow, including passages from Charles Eastman, Waheenee, and Black Elk. The result is a description of the changing conditions for these peoples. Source notes, glossary, and index.

McCormick, Anita Louise. *Native Americans and the Reservation in American History.* Illus. Enslow Publishers 1996 (LB 0-89490-769-7) 128pp.

Government legislation took tribal lands from native people, forcing them to live on restricted reservations. This book describes that process and includes chapters on "Early Relations with European Settlers," "Native American Removal Policy," and "Life on Reservations." Timeline, suggestions for further readings, chapter notes, and index. Part of the In American History series.

Eastman, George (1854–1932), an American inventor and industrialist, invented the Kodak camera, as well as the first practical roll film and a developing process.

Biographies for Younger Readers

Joseph, Paul. *George Eastman.* Illus. Abdo & Daughters 1997 (LB 1-56239-635-8)

This book has features that make it a good choice for younger researchers. The brief text contains bold-faced words that appear in the glossary. Photographs are used to add information and sustain interest. Timeline, glossary, and index. Part of the Checkerboard Biography Library: Inventors series.

Mitchell, Barbara. *Click! A Story about George Eastman.* Illus.
by Jan Hosking Smith. Carolrhoda Books 1986 (LB 0-87614-289-
7); Lerner Publications (pap. 0-87614-472-5) 64pp.

Taking pictures wasn't always a simple process. George Eastman created "a strip of paper coated with collodion and a sensitized
gelatine emulsion" (p. 31), which came to be called "film." He came
up with many more innovations to make picture-taking easy. Part of
the Creative Minds Biographies series.

Biographies for Older Readers

Holmes, Burnham. *George Eastman.* Illus. Silver Burdett 1992
(LB 0-382-24170-3) (pap. 0-382-24176-2) 144pp.

It is fitting that there are fascinating photographs accompanying this biography. One shows a man having his picture taken. A
metal ring is designed to hold his head still. Other photographs show
early advertisements for the Eastman Dry Plate and Film Company.
Chapters describe the arrival of motion pictures and Eastman's contributions to educational programs. Chronology, bibliography, and
index. Part of the Pioneers in Change series.

Related Books for Younger Readers

Holland, Gini. *Photography.* Illus. Benchmark Books 1996 (LB 0-
7614-0066-4) 64pp.

Three chapters—"The Fathers of Photography," "A Revolution in Film," and "Cameras Hide, Seek, and Tell All"—examine
the history of photography and cameras. Boxed sidebars feature photography pioneers including Julia Margaret Cameron, George
Eastman, and Ansel Adams. A final chapter looks at cameras and
computers. Timeline, bibliography, glossary, and index. Part of the
Inventors and Inventions series.

Jeffries, Michael, and Gary A. Lewis. *Inventors and Inventions.*
Illus. Smithmark 1992 (o.p.) 64pp.

Six subject groupings present accomplishments in "Industry
and Commerce," "Around the Home," "On the Move," "Weapons
and Warfare," "Communications," and "Electronics and Science."
There is information about Elias Howe and the sewing machine;
George Eastman and the Kodak camera; Robert Fulton and the
steamboat; and Robert Goddard and Wernher von Braun and rocketry. These brief reports will spur students to learn more. Bibliography
and index. Part of the Facts America series.

Related Books for Older Readers

Steffens, Bradley. *Photography: Preserving the Past.* Illus. Lucent 1991 (LB 1-56006-212-6) 96pp.

After looking at early experiments in photography, chapters focus on the ways photography was first used, such as Matthew Brady's work during the Civil War. Later developments, such as George Eastman's Kodak camera are also profiled. Timeline, glossary, bibliography, and index. Part of the Encyclopedia of Discovery and Invention series.

Edelman, Marian Wright (1939–), an

African American social activist and attorney, served as counsel to the National Association for the Advancement of Colored People from 1963 to 1968. A strong advocate of children's rights to education and health care, she began the Children's Defense Fund in 1973.

> *"Don't be afraid of taking risks or of being criticized. It's the way you learn to do things right."*
> (Otfinoski, p. 53)

> *"Never think life is not worth living or that you cannot make a difference. Never give up."*
> (Otfinoski, p. 57)

Biographies for Younger Readers

Burch, Joann J. *Marian Wright Edelman: Children's Champion.* Illus. Millbrook Press 1994 (LB 1-56294-457-6) (pap. 1-56294-742-7) 48pp.

While working as a lawyer during early years of the civil rights movement, Marian Wright Edelman often provided bail money and legal services to those who were arrested. Her involvement in that movement provided her with skills and political connections to work on behalf of children. Chronology, bibliography, and index. Part of the Gateway Biographies series.

Otfinoski, Steven. *Marian Wright Edelman: Defender of Children's Rights.* Illus. Blackbirch Press 1991 (LB 1-56711-029-0) (pap. 1-56711-060-6) 64pp.

One chapter in this book is "The 101st Senator," referring to Marian Wright Edelman's knowledge and effectiveness in working with politicians. This book is well illustrated with photographs that document the era of the civil rights movement and the needs of young people. Glossary, bibliography, and index. Part of the Library of Famous Women series.

Biographies for Older Readers

Siegel, Beatrice. *Marian Wright Edelman: The Making of a Crusader.* Illus. Simon & Schuster 1995 (cloth 0-02-782629-5) 157pp.

This is an excellent biography that is especially well suited for students working on research projects. The text is well written and uses many quotations by and about Edelman. The book concludes with a poem/prayer by Edelman, "O God of All Children." The index is very detailed and leads to related topics and people. Selected bibliography with comments by the author about the usefulness of each source.

Related Books for Younger Readers

Fry, Annette R. *The Orphan Trains.* Illus. New Discovery Books 1994 (LB 0-02-735721-X) 96pp.

Fry examines how the Reverend Charles Loring Brace founded the Children's Aid Society and organized hundreds of "orphan trains" in the late 1800s. There is also information about other societies and hospitals that helped orphans and unwanted children. Addresses for organizations, chapter notes, bibliography, and index. Part of the American Events series.

Related Books for Older Readers

Landau, Elaine. *Your Legal Rights: From Custody Battles to School Searches, the Headline-Making Cases That Affect Your Life.* Walker and Company 1995 (LB 0-8027-8360-0) (cloth 0-8027-8359-7) 128pp.

In one chapter, "A Shameful History Continues," the author profiles abusive treatment of children throughout history, focusing on the absence of rights for children. Later chapters look at more recent efforts to protect children and provide them with advocates. Source notes, bibliography, and index.

Meltzer, Milton. *Cheap Raw Material: How Our Youngest Workers Are Exploited and Abused.* Illus. Viking Penguin 1994 (pap. 0-670-83128-X) 192pp.

This is a very detailed historical account of the use of children as workers. Meltzer profiles child labor during the time of slavery, in mills and mines, children as migrant workers, and efforts to deal with abuses. The focus is on America, but there is some information about conditions in other countries. Source notes, bibliography, and index.

Edison, Thomas Alva (1847–1931), an
American inventor best known for his development
of the incandescent lamp in 1879, also invented the
record player and the microphone. Another major
contribution was the first electric power plant, in
New York.

Biographies for Younger Readers

Adler, David A. *A Picture Book of Thomas Alva Edison.* Illus. by
John Wallner and Alexandra Wallner. Holiday House 1996 (o.p.)
32pp.

    Even as a child, Thomas Edison was curious about the world
and created experiments to try to understand how things worked. He
eventually received 1,093 patents. Timeline. Part of the Picture
Book Of series.

Adler, David A. *Thomas Alva Edison: Great Inventor.* Illus. by
Lyle Miller. Holiday House 1990 (LB 0-8234-0820-5) 48pp.

    There are seven chapters in this book. Students who have been
introduced to Edison through Adler's *A Picture Book of Thomas Alva
Edison* could use this book to find information for their own reports.
Timeline and index. Part of the First Biographies series.

Parker, Steve. *Thomas Edison and Electricity.* Illus. Harper-
Collins 1992 (LB 0-7910-3012-1) 32pp.

    Extensive illustrations add to the appeal of this brief biogra-
phy. The final chapter looks at the impact of Edison's accomplishments
on the world today. There is an appended section titled "The World
in Edison's Time." Glossary and index. Part of the Science Discoveries series.

Biographies for Older Readers

Adair, Gene. *Thomas Alva Edison: Inventing the Electric Age.*
Illus. Oxford University Press 1996 (LB 0-19-508799-2) 1997
(pap. 0-19-511981-9) 144pp.

    There are features in this biography that take it beyond the
basic "life story." Inserted among the chapters are sidebars on such
topics as "Electricity: A Few Key Facts" and "The Electric Light

Then and Now." Chronology, lists of "Museums and Historic Sites Related to Thomas Edison" and further readings, and index. Part of the Oxford Portraits in Science series.

Anderson, Kelly C. *The Importance of Thomas Edison.* Lucent 1994 (LB 1-56006-041-7) 112pp.

Opening with a detailed timeline, this book provides brief information on Edison's early life but focuses most of the text on his accomplishments. There are many boxed sections that provide additional information, such as Edison's conflicts with other scientists and his explanation of recording sound waves. Source notes for quotes, annotated bibliography, and index. Part of the Importance Of series.

Related Books for Younger Readers

Anderson, Carol D., and Robert Sheely. *Techno Lab: How Science Is Changing Entertainment.* Illus. Silver Moon Press 1995 (cloth 1-881889-63-7) 58pp.

Students learn about history and innovations in five entertainment areas: movies, sound recordings, television, video games, and virtual reality games. From Edison's phonograph to the laser and digital technology of CDs, this book looks at the past, present, and future. Suggested activities, glossary, and index. Part of the Science Lab series.

Cosner, Shaaron. *The Light Bulb.* Illus. Walker and Company 1984 (LB 0-8027-6257-0) 64pp.

Look around your house. How many light bulbs do you see? Look outside. There are light bulbs in the streetlights and in the traffic signals. This book describes the development, enhancement, and production of the light bulb, from the work of Edison through the bulbs used today. Index. Part of the Inventions That Changed Our Lives series.

Platt, Richard. *Smithsonian Visual Timeline of Inventions.* Illus. Dorling Kindersley 1994 (cloth 1-56458-675-8) 64pp.

More than 400 inventions are presented in this book—from prehistoric tools to virtual reality. Inventors are also presented, including Galileo, Jacques Cousteau, the Wright brothers, Karl Benz, and Edison. As students study inventors, they may want to create their own timeline, using this book as a model. Index of inventions and index of inventors.

Pollard, Michael. *The Light Bulb and How It Changed the World.* Illus. Facts on File 1993 (cloth 0-8160-3145-2) 48pp.

Students will enjoy the format of this book. There are lots of illustrations surrounding the text and many accomplishments are cited, including the work of Michael Faraday, Samuel Morse, Alexander Graham Bell, and Edison. One entertaining spread features "The Electric Home" and describes innovations including vacuum cleaners, washing machines, and toasters. Glossary, bibliography, and index. Part of the History and Invention series.

Related Books for Older Readers

Gutnik, Martin J. *Electricity: From Faraday to Solar Generators.* Illus. Franklin Watts 1986 (o.p.) 96pp.

Scientific details accompany drawings of electronic devices such as a simple galvanometer, Faraday's generator, and an AC generator. Key figures include Edison, Michael Faraday, Hans Christian Oersted, and Alexander Graham Bell. Detailed chronology, glossary, and index. Part of the History of Science series.

Edmonds, Emma (1841–1898) was born and raised in Canada. She wrote a book, *Nurse and Spy*, in 1865 detailing her service as a Union spy named "Frank Thompson."

Biographies for Older Readers

Reit, Seymour. *Behind Rebel Lines: The Incredible Story of Emma Edmonds, Civil War Spy.* Harcourt 1988 (pap. 0-15-200424-6) 144pp.

Could a woman disguise herself as a man and serve during the Civil War? This book describes how Emma Edmonds did just that. In between missions as a spy, she worked as a nurse on battlefields and in hospitals (still disguised as a man). This book gives several descriptions of her aiding injured and dying soldiers. List of further readings. Part of the Odyssey series.

"It was not my intention, or desire, to seek my own personal ease and comfort while so much sorrow and distress filled the land. But the great question to be decided was, what can I do? What part can I myself play in this great drama?"
(quoted in Reit, p. 98)

147

Stevens, Bryna. *Frank Thompson: Her Civil War Story.* Illus. Macmillan 1992 (LB 0-02-788185-7) 144pp.

Bryna Stevens has used excerpts from *Nurse and Spy* and from other Civil War documents to tell this fascinating tale. There are many details of battle conditions and strategies. The illustrations for this book are engravings from Edmonds's autobiography. List of sources and index.

Related Books for Younger Readers

Blashfield, Jean F. *Women at the Front: Their Changing Roles in the Civil War.* Illus. Franklin Watts 1997 (LB 0-531-20275-5)

Blashfield describes women's role in society during this era as well as the contributions that many made to the Civil War. Clara Barton's efforts are featured and there is information about women who served in the military, including Emma Edmonds. List of "Major Events of the Civil War," bibliography (including books, videos, CD-ROMs, and Internet sites), and index. Part of the First Book series.

Related Books for Older Readers

Ray, Delia. *Behind the Blue and Gray: The Soldier's Life in the Civil War.* Illus. Lodestar Books 1991 (pap. 0-525-67333-4) 112pp.

This fascinating book full of photographs describes the daily life of soldiers for the North and South. What did they eat and how did they get their food? How did they pass the time before or after battles? What medical treatment did they receive? Students will gain a more personal understanding of soldiers' experiences during this war. Glossary, bibliography, and index. Part of the Young Readers' History of the Civil War series.

War Between Brothers. Illus. Time-Life Books 1996 (cloth 0-7835-6251-9) 192pp.

Chapters feature "The Country at War," "Gibraltar of the West," "High-Water Mark of the Confederacy," and "Showdown." Within each chapter are essays that provide more personal insights, such as one on "The Soldier's Life." There is also information about the experiences of women in the war. Sidebar features and numerous photographs and quotations make this a user-friendly volume. It is extremely well documented and an excellent choice for research projects. Chronology, bibliography, and index. Part of the American Story series.

Einstein, Albert (1879–1955), a German-born physicist who fled to the United States after Adolf Hitler's National Socialists took power, is best known for his formulation of the special and general theories of relativity. Although he was a pacifist, he encouraged the U.S. government to explore the possibility of an atomic bomb.

"Nothing truly valuable arises from ambition or from a mere sense of duty; it stems rather from love and devotion towards men and towards objective things."
(Goldenstern, p. 105)

Biographies for Younger Readers

Goldenstern, Joyce. *Albert Einstein: Physicist and Genius.* Illus. Enslow Publishers 1995 (LB 0-89490-480-9) 128pp.

In addition to the standard biographical information, Goldenstern provides additional activities. After reading about scientific principles, students are encouraged to perform simple experiments. One activity uses balloon space to illustrate Einstein's theory of relativity and curved space. The text is straightforward with quotations that are referenced in chapter notes. Chronology, glossary, bibliography, and index. Part of the Great Minds of Science series.

Parker, Steve. *Albert Einstein and the Laws of Relativity.* Illus. Chelsea House 1994 (LB 0-7910-3003-2) 32pp.

The format is very appealing. There are brief chapters with a clearly written text (words in boldface are in the glossary). Surrounding the text are illustrations with captions and sidebars on related topics such as a description of electromagnetic waves and Einstein's support of the establishment of a Jewish homeland. A feature called "The World in Einstein's Time" describes developments in science, exploration, politics, and art during his lifetime. Glossary and index. Part of the Science Discoveries series.

Reef, Catherine. *Albert Einstein: Scientist of the 20th Century.* Illus. Silver Burdett 1991 (LB 0-87518-462-6) 64pp.

Five brief chapters describe Einstein's life. There are many black-and-white photographs. Students may relate to Einstein's struggles to perform in school and his later success as a scientist, describing the theory of relativity. Glossary and index. Part of the Taking Part series.

Biographies for Older Readers

Bernstein, Jeremy. *Albert Einstein and the Frontiers of Physics.*
Illus. Oxford University Press 1996 (LB 0-19-509275-9) 192pp.

This is a very detailed biography for the serious student, especially one who has some knowledge of physics and advanced math (although it is certainly readable without that knowledge). Sidebars lighten the format—for example, "Einstein's Proof of the Pythagorean Theorem" and "How to Detect Crank Physics." Chronology, bibliography, and index. Part of the Oxford Portraits in Science series.

McPherson, Stephanie S. *Ordinary Genius: The Story of Albert Einstein.* Carolrhoda Books 1995 (LB 0-87614-788-0) 96pp.

Albert Einstein is best known for his scientific theories, yet he also promoted the creation of a Jewish homeland (he was even considered for the presidency of Israel). Throughout his life, he pursued creative concepts in physics while advocating world peace. Extensive bibliography and index. Part of the Trailblazers Biographies series.

Related Books for Older Readers

Biel, Timothy Levi. *Atoms: Building Blocks of Matter.* Illus.
Lucent 1990 (o.p.) 96pp.

From the beginnings of the atomic theory to potential uses of the atom, this book describes the past, present, and future of atomic power and radioactivity. The work of J. J. Thornson, Ernest Rutherford, Niels Bohr, and Albert Einstein are featured. Numerous drawings greatly aid the understanding of the concepts. Glossary, bibliography, and index. Part of the Encyclopedia of Discovery and Invention series.

McGowen, Tom. *1900–1919.* Illus. Twenty-First Century Books 1995 (LB 0-8050-3431-5) 80pp.

In the early 1900s, Albert Einstein published his work on radioactivity. Pierre and Marie Curie worked with radioactive materials, leading to the discovery of polonium and radium. Walter Reed researched yellow fever. In this book, students can connect the advances in physics, chemistry, astronomy, biology, geology, and aeronautics. It is fascinating to see how many events occurred simultaneously. Bibliography and index. Part of the Yearbooks in Science series.

Stwertka, Albert. *The World of Atoms and Quarks.* Illus. Twenty-First Century Books 1995 (LB 0-8050-3533-8) 96pp.

Research on the atom has spanned many years. John Dalton's observations led to early theories. Robert Brown researched the motion of atoms, which was refined by Albert Einstein. This is a brief but technical presentation on atoms, quantum mechanics, and particles. There is a chart of the periodic elements and a "particle guide." Bibliography, glossary, and index. Part of the Scientific American Sourcebooks series.

Eisenhower, Dwight David

(1890–1969), the 34th president of the United States, gained prominence as a military commander during World War II when he led the Allied invasion of Europe (D-Day) in 1944. "Ike," as he was popularly known, cut off ties with Cuba shortly after Fidel Castro came into power.

Biographies for Older Readers

Hargrove, Jim. *Dwight D. Eisenhower.* Illus. Children's Press 1987 (LB 0-516-01389-0) 100pp.

Most of this book is devoted to Eisenhower's service during World War II with the final two chapters describing his presidency. There are numerous black-and-white photographs. The chronology features events throughout American history, with Eisenhower's era highlighted. Index. Part of the Encyclopedia of Presidents series.

Sandberg, Peter Lars. *Dwight D. Eisenhower.* Illus. Chelsea House 1986 (LB 0-87754-521-9) 112pp.

This book has an interesting format that presents information through the basic text, detailed captions to pictures, and bold-faced quotations from Eisenhower, his contemporaries, and historians. It will meet the needs of students who like to browse for information and those who like to read a straightforward text. Chronology, bibliography, and index. Part of the World Leaders Past & Present series.

Van Steenwyk, Elizabeth. *Dwight D. Eisenhower, President.*
Walker and Company 1987 (LB 0-8027-6671-4) (cloth 0-8027-
6670-6) 128pp.

From Abilene to West Point to World War II to the presidency
and finally to retirement, this book gives a straightforward account
of the life of Dwight D. Eisenhower. Bibliography and index. Part of
the Presidential Biography series.

Related Books for Younger Readers

Sharman, Margaret. *1950s.* Illus. Raintree Steck-Vaughn 1992 (LB
0-8114-3078-2) 47pp.

Students researching events of the 1950s will learn about the
war in Korea, the conquest of Mount Everest, the beginning of the
space race, and the presidency of Dwight Eisenhower. During this
decade, Castro came to power in Cuba, the Dalai Lama left Tibet,
and Queen Elizabeth II was crowned. The format simulates a newspaper with headlines, columns, and supporting pictures, making an
attractive overview that helps students put events into perspective.
Glossary, bibliography, and index. Part of the Take Ten Years series.

Steins, Richard. *The Postwar Years: The Cold War and the
Atomic Age (1950–1959).* Illus. Twenty-First Century Books 1993
(LB 0-8050-2587-1) 64pp.

What is unique about this book (and series) is the inclusion of
documentary accounts of events. For example, there is an excerpt
from remarks by Sen. Joseph McCarthy in the *Congressional Record,*
"Elvis Hysteria" is taken from *Life* magazine, and Dr. Martin Luther
King, Jr., writes about the Montgomery bus boycott. These and other
first-person accounts are linked by a clearly written text that adds to
the understanding of this era. Timeline, bibliography, and index.
Part of the First Person America series.

Related Books for Older Readers

Cohen, Daniel. *Joseph McCarthy: The Misuse of Political Power.*
Illus. Millbrook Press 1996 (LB 1-56294-017-0) 128pp.

This is a fascinating book. How was Joseph McCarthy able to
influence so many people? Why didn't his opponents, including
President Eisenhower, take stronger measures against him? The
1954 Army-McCarthy hearings transfixed the American public just
as the cold war was gaining intensity. This book provides insights
into the political, economic, and social issues of this era. Chronology, notes, bibliography, and index.

Stein, R. Conrad. *World War II in Europe: "America Goes to War."* Illus. Enslow Publishers 1994 (LB 0-89490-525-2) 128pp.

With the German invasion of Poland, the Second World War began. The organization of this book makes it useful for students doing research into such generals as Eisenhower and George Patton and key battles including the D-Day invasion. The chapters cover broad topics and are subdivided for easier access to related topics. Chronology, chapter notes (documenting quotations), bibliography, and index. Part of the American War series.

Elizabeth I (1533–1603), queen of England (1558–1603) during a period of great prosperity, was the daughter of Henry VIII and Ann Boleyn. Taking the throne during troubled times, she restored confidence to the country, and almost every facet of the economy blossomed, as did the arts and maritime exploration.

Biographies for Younger Readers

Greene, Carol. *Elizabeth the First: Queen of England.* Illus. by Steven Dobson. Children's Press 1990 (pap. 0-516-44214-7) 48pp.

The text is very brief with large, easy-to-read print. Younger students will find this a simple introduction to research. There are numerous reproductions of famous paintings that make the era come to life. List of important dates and index. Part of the Rookie Biographies series.

Stanley, Diane, and Peter Vennema. *Good Queen Bess: The Story of Elizabeth I of England.* Illus. by Diane Stanley. Simon & Schuster 1990 (LB 0-02-786810-9) 40pp.

This excellent biography combines outstanding writing with wonderful illustrations. Written as a narrative, it is very readable and focuses on exciting events of the era. Elizabeth's uncertain position in childhood and her successes as queen are dramatically presented. Bibliography.

Related Books for Younger Readers

Shakespeare's England: Henry VIII, Elizabeth I, William Shakespeare. Illus. Marshall Cavendish 1989 (LB 0-86307-999-7)

For each person featured, there is an opening portrait, insights into important events, and a description of everyday life. A chronology is divided into subject areas: politics and war, science and exploration, religion and society, art and literature. The many colorful illustrations and boxed sidebars add to this attractive book. Glossary, bibliography, and index. Part of the Exploring the Past series.

Related Books for Older Readers

Lace, William W. *Elizabethan England.* Illus. Lucent 1995 (LB 1-56006-278-9) 128pp.

The reign of Elizabeth I spanned the second half of the 16th century. During this era there were challenges to religious and astronomical beliefs. Explorations led to the establishment of new colonies. Shakespeare's plays were written and performed and the Globe Theater was opened. Chronology, chapter notes, bibliographies, and index. Part of the World History series.

Yancey, Diane. *Life in the Elizabethan Theater.* Illus. Lucent 1996 (LB 1-56006-343-2) 112pp.

Although Shakespeare, is, of course, a large part of this book, it also covers the theater, other playwrights of the time, the audience, and Queen Elizabeth's sponsorship. Lists of further readings and works consulted, chapter notes, and index. Part of the Way People Live series.

"Jazz is like the automobile and airplane. It is modern and it is American. . . . Jazz is the freedom to play anything, whether it has been done before or not. It gives you freedom."

(Woog, p. 79)

Ellington, Duke (1899–1974), an African American jazz composer, band leader, and pianist, gained national recognition after he formed a band that played at Harlem nightclubs in the 1920s and 1930s. His works include "Mood Indigo" and "Solitude."

Biographies for Older Readers

Frankl, Ron. *Duke Ellington.* Illus. Chelsea House 1988 (LB 1-55546-584-6) (pap. 0-7910-0208-X) 112pp.

From "Stomp, Look, Listen" through "Drop Me Off in Harlem" to "Duke's Place," this book provides students doing research with clear, well-organized information. Numerous black-and-white photographs add interest and information. "Selected Discography," chronology, further readings, and index. Part of the Black Americans of Achievement series.

Stwertka, Eve. *Duke Ellington: A Life of Music.* Illus. Franklin Watts 1994 (LB 0-531-13035-5) 112pp.

Duke Ellington's life and impact spanned most of this century. Arriving in Harlem during the Harlem Renaissance, he connected with other musicians who challenged musical traditions and who achieved great success playing at clubs like the Cotton Club. Later, as musical tastes changed, Ellington became a revered figure, touring with his band as "Ambassadors of Good Will" for the U.S. State Department (p. 98). The well-documented text with source notes will be very useful for students doing research and for those who want to know more about a fascinating man and era. Detailed bibliography (including Ellington's appearances in films and video). Part of the Impact Biographies series.

Woog, Adam. *The Importance of Duke Ellington.* Illus. Lucent 1996 (LB 1-56006-073-5) 112pp.

This biography supports both research and browsing. There is a chronology at the beginning of the book, followed by the text, which expands the chronological information. Black-and-white photographs with detailed captions appear on almost every page and extend the text. Sidebars feature comments and quotes from authors, musicians, contemporaries, and Ellington himself. Annotated list of further readings, chapter notes, annotated bibliography, and index. Part of the Importance Of series.

Related Books for Older Readers

Collier, James Lincoln. *The Making of Jazz: A Comprehensive History.* Illus. Houghton Mifflin 1978 (o.p.)

No serious student of jazz and jazz musicians should overlook this book. It is a comprehensive history, well-documented with an extensive discography, bibliography, and index. This is a classic book for students in high school and beyond.

Grossman, James R. *A Chance to Make Good: African Americans, 1900–1929.* Illus. Oxford University Press 1997 (LB 0-19-508770-4)

The early years of the 20th century were full of dramatic changes for many African Americans. Louis Armstrong and Duke Ellington were among those whose lives and work were influenced by these changes. Chronology, bibliography, and index. Part of the Young Oxford History of African Americans series.

Seymour, Gene. *Jazz: The Great American Art.* Illus. Franklin Watts 1995 (LB 0-531-11218-7) 1996 (pap. 0-531-15793-8) 160pp.

This is an excellent overview of the roots, rhythm, and leaders of jazz music. Born in the musical traditions of Africa and linked to the spirituals of slavery, jazz merged many elements. Louis Armstrong and Duke Ellington are featured in chapters and their influence is felt throughout the book. More recent artists, including Miles Davis, Cecil Taylor, and Wynton Marsalis, are briefly profiled. Part of the African American Experience series.

Quotation about Invisible Man *"It's a novel about innocence and human error, a struggle through illusion to reality."* (Bishop, p. 82)

Ellison, Ralph (1914–1994), African American author, wrote about the black experience in America. His best-known work is *Invisible Man* (1952).

Biographies for Older Readers

Bishop, Jack. *Ralph Ellison: Author.* Illus. Chelsea House 1988 (LB 1-55546-585-4) (pap. 0-7910-0202-0) 112pp.

Ralph Ellison came to Harlem during the era called the Harlem Renaissance and met innovators and intellectuals including Alain Locke (an African American educator and philosopher), Langston Hughes, and Richard Wright, who mentored and encouraged Ellison. There are many excerpts from Ellison's *Invisible Man* and quotations from Ellison. Chronology, list of further readings, and index. Part of the Black Americans of Achievement series.

Related Books for Younger Readers

Rediger, Pat. *Great African Americans in Literature.* Illus. Crabtree 1996 (LB 0-86505-802-4) (pap. 0-86505-816-4) 64pp.

Among the authors featured in detailed portraits are Maya Angelou, James Baldwin, Ralph Ellison, Alex Haley, Zora Neale Hurston, Toni Morrison, and Alice Walker. For each, information is given about their childhoods, obstacles they overcame, and their special interests. Numerous photographs add to the appeal. Index. Part of the Outstanding African Americans series.

Related Books for Older Readers

Dornfeld, Margaret. *The Turning Tide: From the Desegregation of the Armed Forces to the Montgomery Bus Boycott (1948–1956).* Illus. Chelsea House 1995 (LB 0-7910-2255-2) (pap. 0-7910-2681-7) 144pp.

After serving America in World War II, many African Americans returned home to face discrimination and disillusionment. Ralph Ellison's *Invisible Man* captured some of the emotions felt by many blacks. Efforts to combat Jim Crow laws and attitudes led to the integration of the military, while the first steps of the civil rights movement were taken with the 1956 boycott in Montgomery. Bibliography and index. Part of the Milestones in Black American History series.

Eriksson, Leif (c. 975–1020), an Icelandic explorer, is said to have been the first European to land in North America. He was the son of Erik the Red, an explorer, who founded a colony on Greenland from which Leif made his many voyages.

Biographies for Younger Readers

Humble, Richard. *The Age of Leif Eriksson.* Illus. by Richard Hook. Franklin Watts 1989 (o.p.) 32pp.

The visual presentation of this book will attract many students. In addition to describing the accomplishments of Leif Eriksson and his father, Erik the Red, this book gives details about Viking exploration. There is a cutaway drawing of a Viking longship, information about the hardships the sailors faced, and descriptions of Viking settlements. This is part of the Exploration through the Ages series.

Biographies for Older Readers

Simon, Charnan. *Leif Eriksson and the Vikings.* Illus. Children's Press 1991 (LB 0-516-03060-4)

Leif Eriksson reached North America nearly 500 years before Columbus. This book describes his journeys and also discusses the work of archaeologists and other scholars trying to document the location of settlements. Timeline of Viking explorations, glossary, bibliography, and index. Part of the World's Great Explorers series.

Related Books for Younger Readers

Hinds, Kathryn. *The Vikings.* Illus. Benchmark Books 1998 (LB 0-7614-0271-3) 80pp.

This book would be a good choice for all students. The accessible text and inviting format make it accessible for younger readers, while the depth of the presentation provides a good base for understanding the Vikings for older readers. Chapters focus on the history, culture, belief system, and the legacy of this fascinating people. Chronology, glossary, bibliographies, and index. Part of the Cultures of the Past series.

Margeson, Susan M. *Viking.* Illus. with photographs by Peter Anderson. Knopf 1994 (LB 0-679-96002-3) (cloth 0-679-86002-9) 64pp.

"Who Were the Vikings?" "Discovering New Lands," "At Home," and "Runes and Picture Stones" are among the chapters in this book. The format is appealing, with many captioned illustrations surrounding the text. The sections on Viking ships, warriors, weapons, and explorations will serve as good background information for reports. Index. Part of the Eyewitness series.

Martell, Hazel Mary. *What Do We Know About the Vikings?* Illus. Peter Bedrick Books 1992 (LB 0-87226-355-X) 40pp.

Readers are introduced to Viking clothes, food, families, homes, holidays, travel, and more. Each double-page spread focuses on one topic and there are numerous subtopics and illustrations. Timeline, glossary, and index. Part of the What Do We Know About? series.

Related Books for Older Readers

Stefoff, Rebecca. *The Viking Explorers.* Illus. Chelsea House 1993 (LB 0-7910-1295-6) 112pp.

The naval power of the Vikings allowed them to attack many North Sea neighbors and then to explore and conquer areas on the continent of Europe, in the Middle East, and in North America. A picture essay shows tapestries and other artifacts of "The Fury of the Northmen." Chronology, bibliography, and index. Part of the World Explorers series.

Faraday, Michael (1791–1867), an English scientist, discovered electromagnetic induction, which led to major developments in industrial electrical machinery. With little formal education, Faraday worked at the laboratory of the Royal Institution in London, where he became director and received many scientific honors.

Biographies for Older Readers

Gutnik, Martin J. *Michael Faraday: Creative Scientist.* Illus. Children's Press 1986 (LB 0-516-03224-0)

In addition to his experiments with electromagnetism, Michael Faraday was committed to a scientific philosophy that valued inquiry and that encouraged lecturing and teaching. The strength of his beliefs led him to leave his career as a bookbinder and achieve success as a scientist and philosopher. Timeline, glossary, and index. Part of the People of Distinction series.

Related Books for Younger Readers

Lafferty, Peter, and Julian Rowe. *The Inventor Through History.* Illus. by Tony Smith and Steve Wheele. Thomson Learning 1993 (LB 1-56947-013-4) 48pp.

Topics range from "The First Books" to "The Age of Electricity," "Into the Air," and "The Electronic Age." The basic text is surrounded by informative illustrations and boxed sidebars featuring such figures as Johannes Gutenberg, James Watt, Faraday, Thomas

Alva Edison, and the Wright Brothers. Students will be interested to learn how the works of individuals combine to create final products. Part of the Journey Through History series.

Pollard, Michael. *The Light Bulb and How It Changed the World.* Illus. Facts on File 1993 (cloth 0-8160-3145-2) 48pp.

Students will enjoy the format of this book. Illustrations surround the text and many accomplishments are cited, including the work of Faraday, Samuel Morse, Alexander Graham Bell, and Thomas Edison. One entertaining spread features "The Electric Home" and describes such innovations as vacuum cleaners, washing machines, and toasters. Glossary, bibliography, and index. Part of the History and Invention series.

Related Books for Older Readers

Dale, Henry, and Rodney Dale. *The Industrial Revolution.* Illus. Oxford University Press 1992 (cloth 0-19-520967-2) 64pp.

Chapters feature "Power," "Iron and Steel," "Mining," "Transport," "Textile Machinery," "Industrial Chemistry," and "Agriculture." Students will be fascinated by the many archival illustrations and the accomplishments of scientists including James Watt, Antoine Lavoisier, and Faraday. Chronology, bibliography, and index. Part of the Discoveries and Inventions series.

Gutnik, Martin J. *Electricity: From Faraday to Solar Generators.* Illus. Franklin Watts 1986 (o.p.) 96pp.

The author combines scientific details with drawings of electronic devices including a simple galvanometer and Faraday's generator. In addition to Faraday, there is information on Thomas Alva Edison, Hans Christian Oersted, and Alexander Graham Bell. Detailed chronology, glossary, and index. Part of the History of Science series.

Farnsworth, Philo Taylor (1906–1971), American inventor, was a farm boy fascinated by technology. At the age of 13, he conceived how television would operate.

Biographies for Younger Readers

McPherson, Stephanie S. *TV's Forgotten Hero: The Story of Philo Farnsworth.* Illus. Carolrhoda Books 1996 (LB 1-57505-017-X) 96pp.

Although Philo Farnsworth is responsible for the development of the basic components of the television, his accomplishments are not well known. In 1927, his experiments led to success when he completed the first electronic television. The Afterword describes how, in 1985, school children in Utah began work for a statue of Farnsworth to be placed in the U.S. Capitol Rotunda, which was unveiled in 1990. Students reading this book may be inspired to find projects of their own. Chapter notes, bibliography (books, periodicals and documents, video, interview with the author), and index.

Related Books for Younger Readers

Gano, Lila. *Television: Electronic Pictures.* Illus. Lucent 1990 (o.p.) 96pp.

Students will learn about the technical development of television and about the growth of networks, programs, and advertising. The impact of television on politics and social issues is also profiled. Glossary, bibliography, and index. Part of the Encyclopedia of Discovery and Invention series.

Related Books for Older Readers

Wakin, Edward. *How TV Changed America's Mind.* Illus. Lothrop, Lee & Shepard 1996 (cloth 0-688-13482-3) 240pp.

Each of the five parts of this book features a different decade—from the 1950s through the 1990s. Within each section, chapters focus on key issues in the history and development of television. Included are chapters on Joseph R. McCarthy, the Checkers speech, the civil rights movement, the Vietnam War, Watergate, Christa McAuliffe, the Gulf War, Rodney King, and the O. J. Simpson trial. Detailed bibliography and index.

Farragut, David Glasgow (1801–1870), a bold American admiral, became a hero during the Civil War when he defeated a Confederate fleet at Mobile, Alabama.

Biographies for Older Readers

Foster, Leila M. *David Glasgow Farragut: Courageous Navy Commander.* Illus. Children's Press 1991 (o.p.) 152pp.

Before he was a teenager, David Glasgow Farragut served as a midshipman on a ship during the War of 1812. Later, he commanded ships in the Civil War. Students will find the accounts of battles very dramatic. Timeline, glossary, and index. Part of the People of Distinction series.

Shorto, Russell. *David Farragut and the Great Naval Blockade.* Illus. Silver Burdett 1990 (pap. 0-382-24050-2) 160pp.

A four-page "Civil War Time Line" opens this book, which also includes a timeline of David Farragut's life and accomplishments. As a child, James Glasgow Farragut was befriended by naval Commander David Porter. Farragut (who changed his name to David) was a midshipman at age nine and won important battles for the North during the Civil War. The reference aids in this book will lead students to many other sources. There are sources on Farragut, the War of 1812, naval history, and the Civil War. Index. Part of the History of the Civil War series.

Related Books for Younger Readers

Black, Wallace B. *Blockade Runners and Ironclads: Naval Action in the Civil War.* Illus. Franklin Watts 1997 (cloth 0-531-20272-0)

Chapters describe "The War Begins," "The Mississippi Campaign," and "Confederate Deep-Sea Raiders." Admiral Farragut is featured and there is information about blockades, attacks, and battles. List of "Major Events of the Civil War," bibliography (with books, videos, CD-ROMs, and Internet sites), and index. Part of the First Book series.

Smith, Carter, ed. *The First Battles.* Illus. Millbrook Press 1993
(LB 1-56294-262-X)

Early events of the Civil War include the preparations of both
sides, the battles of Bull Run and Shiloh, the naval war, and the battle of New Orleans. Following a detailed timeline, information is
presented on double-page spreads, making this a good introduction
for students. Bibliography and index. Part of the Sourcebook on the
Civil War series.

Related Books for Older Readers

Golay, Michael. *The Civil War.* Illus. Facts on File 1992 (LB 0-
8160-2514-2) 192pp.

This very detailed history analyzes the issues that led to the
Civil War before describing specific events in such chapters as "The
Uses of Sea Power," "Battles Lost and Won," and "Grant and Lee."
There are many quotations. Bibliography and index. Part of the
America at War series.

Farrakhan, Louis (1933–), born Louis Eugene Wolcott, was a supporter of Malcolm X, founded the Nation of Islam in the U.S., and promotes black separatism.

Biographies for Older Readers

Haskins, Jim. *Louis Farrakhan and the Nation of Islam.* Illus.
Walker and Company 1996 (LB 0-8027-8423-2) (cloth 0-8027-
8422-4)

After an opening chapter on the Million Man March, this biography describes other key events in the life of this controversial
figure. Included are his relationship with Malcolm X as well as his
connection with other African American leaders. Students doing
research will find this an excellent resource. List of suggestions for
further readings, source notes, and index.

Related Books for Younger Readers

Andryszewski, Tricia. *The March on Washington 1963: Gathering to Be Heard.* Illus. Millbrook Press 1996 (LB 0-7613-0009-0) 64pp.

One of the defining moments of the civil rights movement was Martin Luther King, Jr.'s "I Have a Dream" speech on August 28, 1963. This book describes the events that led up to the march and features excerpts from some of the other speeches, including those of Whitney Young and A. Philip Randolph. The text of the "I Have a Dream" speech is included. The book ends with a brief look at the Million Man March and the different ideas behind it and the 1963 march on Washington. Bibliography and index. Part of the Spotlight on American History series.

Related Books for Older Readers

Banks, William H., Jr. *The Black Muslims.* Illus. Chelsea House 1996 (LB 0-7910-2593-4) (pap. 0-7910-2594-2)

From the Million Man March to the economic efforts of many Muslims to the life and assassination of Malcolm X, here is an overview of the role of Black Muslims in the civil rights movement. Louis Farrakhan is profiled in a chapter called "The Charmer." The many black-and-white photographs add interest. Students doing research will find this very useful. Chronology, bibliography, and index. Part of the African American Achievers series.

Cottman, Michael H. *Million Man March.* Illus. Crown 1995 (pap. 0-517-88763-0)

Wonderful black-and-white photographs capture the many moods and emotions of the participants in the Million Man March on October 16, 1995. There is background information on the organization of the march and the agenda of Louis Farrakhan. One chapter features excerpts from Farrakhan's speech. List of milestones and bibliography.

Fleming, Sir Alexander (1881–1955), a

Scottish bacteriologist, discovered penicillin by accident in 1928 and shared the 1945 Nobel Peace Prize with Ernst Chain and Sir Howard Florey for their contributions in this area. Earlier he discovered lysozyme, an antibacterial substance found in tears and other body secretions.

Biographies for Younger Readers

Kaye, Judith. *The Life of Alexander Fleming.* Illus. Twenty-First Century Books 1993 (o.p.) 88pp.

Alexander Fleming first noticed the blue mold that was to become penicillin in 1928, yet it was years before that became reality. This book describes Fleming's scientific training and the dedication that turned this seemingly small discovery into a major, lifesaving event. Bibliography and index. Part of the Pioneers in Health and Medicine series.

Tames, Richard. *Alexander Fleming.* Illus. Franklin Watts 1990 (o.p.) 32pp.

The pleasant format is visually appealing and informative. Two columns of text provide the basic information, while sidebars enclosed in colorful boxes give additional information—for example, on such scientists as Sir Almroth Wright and Howard Florey. There are several illustrations or photographs on every page, which also provide variety and information. Chronology, glossary, bibliography, and index. Part of the Lifetimes series.

Biographies for Older Readers

Gottfried, Ted. *Alexander Fleming: Discoverer of Penicillin.* Illus. Franklin Watts 1997 (cloth 0-531-11370-1)

Although this is a fairly brief biography, the concepts and vocabulary make it appropriate for middle-school students. Quotations are used effectively. There is information about the scientific process and the impact of Fleming's discoveries on epidemics and World War I injuries. Chronology, suggestions for further readings, glossary, and index. Part of the Book Report Biography series.

"For the birth of something new, there has to be a happening. Newton saw an apple fall; James Watt watched a kettle boil; Roentgen fogged some photographic plates. And these people knew enough to translate ordinary happenings into something new."
(Otfinoski, p. 1)

"If I might offer advice to the young laboratory worker, it would be this—never neglect an extraordinary appearance or happening. It may be—usually is, in fact—a false alarm which leads to nothing, but it may on the other hand be the clue provided by fate to lead you to some important advance."
(Otfinoski, p. 76)

Otfinoski, Steven. *Alexander Fleming: Conquering Disease with Penicillin.* Illus. Facts on File 1992 (LB 0-8610-2752-8) 128pp.

Each of the 12 chapters in this book opens with a quotation from Alexander Fleming or a contemporary commenting on his work. Additional quotations are used in the text to provide insight into his work and accomplishments. This is a fine choice for students doing research. It is detailed and readable. Chapter notes, glossary, annotated bibliography, and index. Part of the Makers of Modern Science series.

Related Books for Older Readers

Jacobs, Francine. *Breakthrough: The True Story of Penicillin.* Illus. Dodd, Mead 1985 (o.p.) 128pp.

Reading this is like reading a thriller—who will put the clues together and finally make the discovery? There are insights into the personalities of the scientists researching penicillin, specifically Alexander Fleming and Howard Florey, and there is information about the experimental process. The first chapter gives background information on such earlier researchers as Edward Jenner, Joseph Lister, Louis Pasteur, and Robert Koch. Chapter notes, bibliography, and index.

Nardo, Don. *Germs: Mysterious Microorganisms.* Illus. Lucent 1991 (LB 1-56006-214-2) 96pp.

What are germs? In this book, students will learn about the benefits and hazards of germs. From plagues, epidemics, and biological warfare to the use of germs to clean up oil spills and treat waste materials, this book is a good source of scientific information. Timeline, glossary, bibliography, and index. Part of the Encyclopedia of Discovery and Invention series.

Ford, Henry (1863–1947), an American industrialist, built his first automobile in 1892. In 1903 he formed the Ford Motor Company and introduced standard interchangeable parts and assembly-line production.

Biographies for Younger Readers

Joseph, Paul. *Henry Ford.* Abdo & Daughters 1997 (LB 1-56239-636-6)

Beginning researchers will find this a good choice for introductory information about Henry Ford. Most of the chapters are on double-page spreads and cover topics from "The Early Years" to "The Model T" to "The Assembly Line" to "Making a Difference." New words appear in bold-faced type and are included in a glossary. Timeline and index. Part of the Checkerboard Biography Library: Inventors series.

Kent, Zachary. *The Story of Henry Ford and the Automobile.* Illus. Children's Press 1990 (o.p.) 32pp.

The focus is on Henry Ford's efforts to establish his company and successfully mass-produce automobiles. Brief facts about his childhood are presented before the text and illustrations describe assembly lines, the Model T, and the success of the Ford Motor Company. There are no chapter divisions; students will have to use the index to find specific facts. Part of the Cornerstones of Freedom series.

Mitchell, Barbara. *We'll Race You, Henry: A Story About Henry Ford.* Illus. by Kathy Haubrich. Carolrhoda Books 1986 (LB 0-87614-291-9); First Avenue Editions 1987 (pap. 0-87614-471-7) 64pp.

This is an entertaining presentation, written in a narrative style that reads like a novel. It will be especially useful to students who want to *read* about Henry Ford; students doing research may find it difficult to find specific facts. The emphasis is on Henry Ford's creative spirit and enthusiasm for experimentation. Part of the Carolrhoda Creative Minds series.

Biographies for Older Readers

Harris, Jacqueline L. *Henry Ford.* F. Watts 1984 (LB 0-531-04754-7) 116pp.

Spanning the Tin Lizzie to the Model T to the Ford Motor Company, this is a detailed biography. One chapter describes the impact of unions on the auto industry and an epilogue looks at the future of mass production of automobiles. There is an excellent chronology that includes information about the development of the internal combustion engine and other car-related inventions as well as Henry Ford's accomplishments. List of suggestions for further readings and index. Part of the Impact Biographies series.

Related Books for Younger Readers

Leuzzi, Linda. *Transportation.* Illus. Chelsea House 1995 (LB 0-7910-2840-2)

Leuzzi covers steam transportation, railroads, motor vehicles, and air transportation. Among developments featured are Henry Ford and the assembly line and the Wright brothers turning their knowledge of bicycles into powered flight. Bibliography and index. Part of the Life in America 100 Years Ago series.

Oxlade, Chris, and Steve Parker and Nigel Hawkes. *The Book of Great Inventions.* Illus. by David Russell and Ian Thompson. Shooting Star Press 1995 (LB 1-57335-147-4)

Four areas of interest to many readers are featured in this book: "Ships and Boats," "The Car," "Flying Machines," and "Into Space." In the section on the car, there is information about the pioneers of car design as well as later mass production. The section on space examines early research into rocketry and reaching the moon. This is an attractive book with many color illustrations.

Sharman, Margaret. *1900s: The First Decade.* Illus. Raintree Steck-Vaughn 1991 (LB 0-8114-3073-1) 47pp.

Students will be able to place the production of early automobiles into a global context with this volume. Other events in the first decade of the 20th century included the death of Queen Victoria, the success of the Wright brothers, and the discoveries of Marie and Pierre Curie. The format simulates a newspaper with headlines, columns, and supporting pictures, making an attractive overview. Glossary, bibliography, and index. Part of the Take Ten Years series.

Related Books for Older Readers

Dale, Rodney, ed. *Early Cars.* Illus. Oxford University Press 1994 (LB 0-19-521002-6) 64pp.

An informative text is combined with excellent illustrations. Many ideas led to the successful development of the car. Look at Snowden's carriage, which was propelled by horses walking in a circle. Chronology, bibliography, and index. Part of the Discoveries and Inventions series.

Wilkinson, Philip, and Michael Pollard. *Transportation.* Illus. by Robert Ingpen. Chelsea House 1994 (LB 0-7910-2768-6) 96pp.

From the wheel to boats and ships to engines and rockets, this is a great book for browsing. It features many vehicles and gives an overview of the history of transportation. James Watt, Henry Ford, the Wright brothers, and Robert Goddard are among the individuals featured. Bibliography and index. Part of the Ideas That Changed the World series.

Forten, Charlotte L. (1837–1914), an African American educator and author, was a volunteer teacher of illiterate slaves abandoned by their owners on coastal islands off the southeastern United States during the Civil War. She later wrote articles and a book about her Sea Islands experience.

Biographies for Older Readers

Burchard, Peter. *Charlotte Forten: A Black Teacher in the Civil War.* Illus. Crown 1995 (cloth 0-517-59242-8) 96pp.

Born in 1837, Charlotte Forten grew up in an educated family that supported the abolition of slavery and worked for improved opportunities for blacks and women. She wrote about her life and era in her journals. There are many excerpts from Charlotte Forten's journals that will give students access to original source material. Bibliography and index.

Related Books for Older Readers

Katz, William L. *The Civil War to the Last Frontier, 1850–1880.* Illus. Raintree Steck-Vaughn 1993 (LB 0-8114-6277-3) (pap. 0-8114-2914-8) 96pp.

The focus here is the Civil War era, with an emphasis on the contributions of African Americans. However, the plan of this series is to look at multicultural experiences, so there is information on the role of Native Americans, Mexican Americans, and immigrants, such as the Chinese. Numerous photographs add to the presentation. Students will find the boxed sidebars fascinating. Bibliography and index. Part of the History of Multicultural America series.

Meltzer, Milton, ed. *The Black Americans: A History in Their Own Words, 1619–1983.* Illus. Crowell 1984 (LB 0-690-04418-6); Trophy 1987 (pap. 0-06-446055-X) 320pp.

This is a collection of personal accounts of the experiences of African Americans. There are excerpts from the memoirs of slaves, from educator Charlotte Forten while observing a regiment of young freedmen, from Fannie Lou Hamer during unofficial hearings on brutality in Mississippi, and from Maya Angelou on being a black female artist. Issues from slavery to the Ku Klux Klan, to marches, boycotts, and political power, are presented. Source note and index.

Frank, Anne (1929–1945) and her family went into hiding in Amsterdam during the Nazi occupation of the Netherlands. Her diary, discovered after her death in a concentration camp, describes with humor their difficult years in seclusion.

Biographies for Younger Readers

Adler, David A. *A Picture Book of Anne Frank.* Illus. by Karen Ritz. Holiday House 1993 (LB 0-8234-1003-X) 1994 (pap. 0-8234-1078-1) 32pp.

Long before younger students are able to read and understand Anne Frank's diary, many are interested in her story. This picture-book presentation is a solid introduction to her life. An author's note provides insight into his research. Chronology. Part of the Picture Book Of series.

Tames, Richard. *Anne Frank.* Illus. Franklin Watts 1989 (o.p.) 32pp.

Within chapters that chronicle the experiences of the Frank family, there are sidebars about related issues. One features "Nazis and Jews," another describes "The Conquest of Holland," still another discusses "Concentration Camps." This presentation will help students relate Anne Frank's life to the events in the world around her. Addresses for the Anne Frank Foundation and the Anne Frank Museum are provided. Glossary, bibliography, and index. Part of the Lifetimes series.

Biographies for Older Readers

Frank, Anne, with an introduction by Eleanor Roosevelt. *Anne Frank: The Diary of a Young Girl.* Illus. Trans. from Dutch by B. M. Mooyaart-Doubleday. Doubleday 1967 (cloth 0-385-04019-9); Pocket Books 1985 (pap. 0-685-05466-7) 312pp.

Anne Frank's diary is not a story of war, deprivation, and horror. It is a testament to the hope and dreams of a young girl and to the courage of the many people who endured, aided, and experienced incredible hardships. The endpapers show photographs of Anne and the "Secret Annexe."

van der Rol, Ruud, and Rian Verhoeven (in association with the Anne Frank House). *Anne Frank: Beyond the Diary: A Photographic Remembrance.* Illus. Trans. by Tony Langham and Plym Peters. Viking Penguin 1993 (pap. 0-670-84932-4) 112pp.

Many of the early photographs in this book were taken by Otto Frank, Anne's father, and are published here for the first time. Later photographs document the horrors of the Holocaust and include scenes in the concentration camps and even the transportation list that includes the names of the Frank family. They are accompanied by thorough captions, explanatory text, and excerpts from Anne's diary. This is a compelling presentation that provides students with additional source materials for research. Chronology, source notes, and index.

Related Books for Younger Readers

Auerbacher, Inge. *I Am a Star: Child of the Holocaust.* Illus. by Israel Bernbaum and with photographs. Prentice-Hall 1986 (o.p.) 96pp.

Like Anne Frank's *Diary*, this is a book about hope and horror. The author describes her childhood experiences in Terezin, a concentration camp north of Prague. She tells of terrible conditions, interspersed with moments of kindness and compassion. This is a book for many audiences. Timetable of the war years and bibliography.

Ayer, Eleanor H. *The United States Holocaust Museum: America Keeps the Memory Alive.* Illus. Dillon Press 1994 (o.p.)

Written like a tour of the United States Holocaust Museum, this book takes readers on a walk through history. Beginning with the Hall of Witness, where visitors receive an "Identity Card" remembering a victim of the Holocaust, readers visit displays covering the war from the early years to the end. The final chapter describes the Hall of Remembrance, with a vault filled with ashes taken from each of the death camps. Timeline of the Holocaust, bibliography, and index.

Related Books for Older Readers

Holocaust Series. Illus. Blackbirch Press 1998

This eight-volume series provides so much information on the Holocaust that to focus on one volume would leave readers with an incomplete understanding of the roots, events, people, and impact of the Holocaust. Each volume has an introduction by Michael Berenbaum, Survivors of Shoah, Visual History Foundation in Los Angeles. There are numerous photographs. Each volume also has a chronology, list of further readings, source notes, bibliography, and index. The format would be accessible to many students; those in middle school and older would find this a valuable resource. Individual titles in the series are *Forever Outsiders: Jews and History from Ancient Times to August 1935*, by Linda Jacobs Altman (1-56711-200-5); *Smoke to Flame: September 1935 to December 1938*, by Victoria Sherrow (1-56711-201-3); *The Blaze Engulfs: January 1939 to December 1941*, by Victoria Sherrow (1-56711-202-1); *A Firestorm Unleashed: January 1942 to June 1943*, by Eleanor H. Ayer (1-56711-204-8); *Inferno: July 1943 to April 1945*, by Eleanor H. Ayer (1-56711-205-6); *From the Ashes: May 1945 and After*, by Eleanor H. Ayer and Stephen D. Chicoine (1-56711-206-4); *Voices and Visions: A Collection of Primary Sources*, compiled by Dr. William L. Shulman (1-56711-207-2); *Resource Guide: A Comprehensive Listing of Media for Further Study*, compiled by Dr. William L. Shulman (1-56711-208-0).

Rabinovici, Schoschana. *Thanks to My Mother.* Illus. Trans. from German by James Skofield. Dial 1998 (cloth 0-8037-2235-4)

When the author was eight, her life became filled with fear, horror, and death. She and her mother survived the arrival of the German army in Vilnius, Lithuania, by living in the Vilnius ghetto. When that was destroyed, they were moved to concentration camps. This memoir serves as another testament to the strength of the human spirit.

Franklin, Benjamin (1706–1790), American statesman, writer, and scientist, is famous for his contributions to the creation of the United States of America and to the understanding of electricity. He wrote *Poor Richard's Almanac* (1732).

Biographies for Younger Readers

Adler, David A. *Benjamin Franklin: Printer, Inventor, Statesman.* Illus. by Lyle Miller. Holiday House 1992 (LB 0-8234-0929-5) 48pp.

Looking at the chronology that opens this book, it is striking to realize that Benjamin Franklin lived to be 84 years old. Even into his 70s and 80s, he negotiated treaties and served at the Constitutional Convention. The six chapters in this book are easy to read. Index. Part of the First Biographies series.

Adler, David A. *A Picture Book of Benjamin Franklin.* Illus. by John Wallner and Alexandra Wallner. Holiday House 1990 (LB 0-8234-0792-6) 1991 (pap. 0-8234-0882-5) 32pp.

The picture-book format of this biography makes it a good choice for reading aloud. Children can be shown how facts are woven into the narrative and they can begin to learn research skills. List of important dates. Part of the Picture Book Of series.

Aliki. *The Many Lives of Benjamin Franklin.* Illus. by the author. Simon & Schuster 1988 (pap. 0-671-66491-3) 32pp.

The full-color illustrations are very appealing and there are captions along with cartoon-style balloons for character speech. One clever page illustrates sayings from *Poor Richard's Almanac.* In this attractive presentation, the combination of humor and information encourages students to enjoy learning about Benjamin Franklin.

Fritz, Jean. *What's the Big Idea, Ben Franklin?* Illus. by Margot Tomes. Coward-McCann 1976 (cloth 0-698-20365-8); Paperstar 1996 (pap. 0-698-11372-1) 48pp.

Written as a narrative, this is just the right book to give to students who enjoy being entertained as they learn new information. The author weaves facts and many humorous moments together in the text. The illustrations add to the fun. Jean Fritz has written several biographies with questioning titles. Source notes.

Biographies for Older Readers

Meltzer, Milton. *Benjamin Franklin: The New American.* Illus. Franklin Watts 1988 (o.p.) 288pp.

This is a noteworthy book. It is clearly written, yet very detailed. There are quotations from Franklin's writings along with reproductions of documents and official portraits. This should be a first choice for students doing research. Source notes and index.

Osborne, Mary Pope. *The Many Lives of Benjamin Franklin.* Illus. Dial 1990 (o.p.) 144pp.

One fascinating chapter in this book looks at Franklin's work as a scientist and inventor. The illustrations include his sketches for designs as well as pictures of the Franklin stove, a library chair (with hidden steps), and an armonica. Using this book for research, students will be fascinated by his diverse accomplishments. Timeline, bibliography, and index.

Related Books for Younger Readers

Stein, R. Conrad. *The Declaration of Independence.* Illus. Children's Press 1995 (LB 0-516-06693-5) (pap. 0-516-46693-3)

Although Thomas Jefferson is known as the primary author of the Declaration of Independence, Benjamin Franklin also served on the committee of writers (with John Adams, Roger Sherman, and Robert Livingston). This book describes the initial events of the American Revolution and the work of the Second Continental Congress. Facsimile of the Declaration of Independence, timeline, glossary, and index. Part of the Cornerstones of Freedom series.

Related Books for Older Readers

Hakim, Joy. *Making Thirteen Colonies.* Illus. Oxford University Press 1993 (LB 0-19-507747-4) (cloth 0-19-509507-3) 1993 (pap. 0-19-507748-2) 160pp.

Information is presented through the text, in captioned illustrations, in boxed sidebars, in quotations in the margins, even in jokes. From the founding of the colonies, through their development as 13 entities, to the issues that led to the war, this is an entertaining and informative book. Chronology, bibliography, and index. Part of the History of US series.

Jaffe, Steve H. *Who Were the Founding Fathers? Two Hundred Years of Reinventing American History.* Illus. Henry Holt 1996 (cloth 0-8050-3102-2) 160pp.

In answering the title question, the author suggests that, depending on your point of view and your time in history, the founding fathers were traitors, hypocrites, or patriots. This book examines a variety of views of history, showing how it is reshaped to meet different political and social needs. Benjamin Franklin is presented as an accomplished diplomat, businessman, and inventor but also as manipulative and self-serving. This is a challenging, informative, and thought-provoking look at history and how it is presented. Source notes, bibliography and index.

Frémont, John Charles (1813–1890),

American explorer, took part in expeditions to the Pacific Coast and mapped the Oregon Trail. He also served in the Senate and was governor of Arizona.

Biographies for Younger Readers

Sanford, William R., and Carl R. Green. *John C. Frémont: Soldier and Pathfinder.* Illus. Enslow Publishers 1996 (LB 0-89490-649-6) 48pp.

Nicknamed "the Pathfinder," John Charles Frémont was committed to help America reach "from sea to shining sea." This book looks at Frémont's successes as an explorer and mapmaker and his failures as a candidate for president, a Civil War soldier, and a businessman. Chapter notes, glossary, bibliography, and index. Part of the Legendary Heroes of the Wild West series.

Biographies for Older Readers

Harris, Edward D. *John Charles Frémont and the Great Western Reconnaissance.* Illus. Chelsea House 1990 (LB 0-7910-1312-X) 112pp.

John Charles Frémont led five expeditions into the western frontier of America, exploring and mapping an area that would later contain 13 states. In this detailed account, students learn about the belief that colonization and settlement were the right of the pioneers of the1800s. One special feature is a picture essay called "Visions of the West," which shows the paintings of several artists, including Charles M. Russell and Emanuel Leutze. Chronology, list of further readings, and index. Part of the World Explorers series.

Related Books for Older Readers

Bentley, Judith. *Explorers, Trappers, and Guides.* Illus. Henry Holt 1995 (LB 0-8050-2995-8) 96pp.

As explorers and settlers moved West, they encountered hardships and hostile conditions. Chapters focus on "The Journey," "Exploring the Interior," and "The Fur-Trapping Life." There is information about conflict and emigration. Featured figures include Jim Beckwourth, James Clyman, Frémont, and Lewis and Clark. Source notes, bibliography, and index. Part of the Settling the West series.

Spangenburg, Ray, and Diane K. Moser. *The Story of America's Railroads.* Illus. Facts on File 1991 (LB 0-8160-2257-7) 96pp.

Access to the American West was improved by the development of the transcontinental railroad. From the explorations of John Frémont and Lewis and Clark, the "Railroad Robber Barons" won and lost great fortunes. There are many maps and illustrations along with boxed sections on such topics as the role of the railroads in the Civil War and the employment of Chinese immigrants. Glossary, bibliography, and index. Part of the Connecting a Continent series.

Friedan, Betty Naomi (1921–), an American feminist and writer, founded the National Organization for Women (NOW) in 1966. Taking a moderate position in the women's movement, she wrote *The Feminine Mystique* (1963) and *The Fountain of Age* (1993).

Biographies for Older Readers

Blau, Justine. *Betty Friedan: Feminist.* Illus. Chelsea House 1990 (LB 1-55546-653-2) 112pp.

Here is a well-organized look at this pioneering feminist. Her key accomplishments are featured, from her book *The Feminine Mystique* to her founding and presidency of the National Organization for Women to her political and social activism. There are many quotations from her books, which students may then consider for additional information. Chronology, list of further readings, and index. Part of the American Women of Achievement series.

Related Books for Younger Readers

Brill, Marlene Targ. *Let Women Vote!* Illus. Millbrook Press 1996 (LB 1-56294-589-0) 64pp.

To understand the women's movement of the 1960s, students will want to read about earlier experiences of women in America. Chapters look at "The Rights of Women and Slaves," "Small Steps Toward Suffrage," and "From Jail to Victory." In "The Dream Continues" there is information about more-recent steps forward. Part of the Spotlight on American History series.

Related Books for Older Readers

Chafe, William H. *The Road to Equality: American Women Since 1962.* Illus. Oxford University Press 1994 (LB 0-19-508325-3) 144pp.

During World War II women took on new roles, roles they did not want to relinquish at the end of the war. The dilemma faced by many women was described in Betty Friedan's *The Feminine Mystique,* which describes the frustrations, opportunities, and possibilities that many women faced during this era and today. Chronology, bibliography, and index. Part of the Young Oxford History of Women in the United States series.

May, Elaine Tyler. *Pushing the Limits: American Women, 1940–1961.* Illus. Oxford University Press 1994 (LB 0-19-508084-X) 144pp.

Readers learn about the women's rights and civil rights movements and about the role of women in wartime and as society changed with the move toward suburbia. Chronology, bibliography, and index. Part of the Young Oxford History of Women in the United States series.

Fulton, Robert (1765–1815), an American engineer and inventor, in 1807 launched his steamboat *Clermont* on the Hudson River. It became the first such American vessel to achieve commercial success. He was a jack-of-all-trades, including gun making and portrait painting.

Biographies for Younger Readers

Bowen, Andy Russell. *A Head Full of Notions: A Story about Robert Fulton.* Illus. by Lisa Harvey. Carolrhoda Books 1996 (cloth 0-87614-876-3)

   Robert Fulton had many ideas. As a youngster, he made a paddle wheel to make it easier to move his friend's boat for fishing. He designed a machine that spun flax and another that twisted hemp into rope. He worked on designs for a submarine before designing and running several successful steamboats. The brief chapters are very readable. Bibliography and index. Part of the Carolrhoda Creative Minds series.

Landau, Elaine. *Robert Fulton.* Illus. Franklin Watts 1991 (LB 0-531-20016-7) 64pp.

   Reading this book introduces students to a fascinating inventor and businessman. Although there are no chapter divisions, the index will help those who want specific facts. The information in the narrative follows a generally chronological order and there are many illustrations (photographs, paintings, documents) that expand the text. This is a fine presentation for students just beginning to learn research skills. List of suggestions for further readings and glossary. Part of the First Books Biographies series.

Related Books for Younger Readers

Siegel, Beatrice. *The Steam Engine.* Illus. Walker and Company 1986 (LB 0-8027-6656-0) (cloth 0-8027-6655-2) 64pp.

   Throughout history, people have tried to harness power sources to make work easier. Waterwheels and windmills were used in ancient times, but it took many years and many inventors for the technology to be developed to use the power of steam. Many drawings add to understanding the process. Index. Part of the Inventions That Changed Our Lives series.

Related Books for Older Readers

Wilkinson, Philip, and Michael Pollard. *Transportation.* Illus. by
Robert Ingpen. Chelsea House 1994 (LB 0-7910-2768-6) 96pp.

Featuring many vehicles, this is in essence an overview of the
history of transportation. From the wheel to boats and ships to
engines and rockets, this is a great book for browsing. James Watt,
Henry Ford, the Wright brothers, and Robert Goddard are among
those featured. Bibliography and index. Part of the Ideas That
Changed the World series.

Galileo (1564–1642), an Italian
astronomer and physicist, was interested in the
science of measurement. He invented the hydrostatic
balance. He is also credited with the construction in
1609 of the first astronomical telescope, which he
used to discover Jupiter's four largest moons. Galileo
was tried for his belief that the earth revolved
around the sun.

Biographies for Younger Readers

Fisher, Leonard Everett. *Galileo.* Illus. by the author. Macmillan
1992 (LB 0-02-735235-8) 32pp.

Galileo's inventions, including the microscope and a telescope,
and his discoveries, like the law of the pendulum, have influenced
modern science. His conclusions often put him in conflict with the
political and religious leaders of his time. The text is very readable
and the black-and-white paintings add drama to the presentation.
Chronology.

Hightower, Paul W. *Galileo: Astronomer and Physicist.* Illus.
Enslow Publishers 1997 (LB 0-89490-785) 128pp.

Following information about Galileo, there are four activities
in this book that encourage students to apply scientific principles.
For example, one activity focuses on using a pendulum. Chronology,
list of further readings, chapter notes, and index. Part of the Great
Minds of Science series.

Parker, Steve. *Galileo and the Universe.* Illus. Chelsea House
1995 (LB 0-7910-3008-3) 32pp.

A very useful feature of this book (and series) is a timeline that
shows the relationship between the events of the scientist (in this
case, Galileo) and other worldwide milestones in exploration, politics, and the arts. The text is surrounded by illustrations, often with
sidebar details such as a description of a proportional compass or
different views of the solar system. Glossary and index. Part of the
Science Discoveries series.

Sis, Peter. *Starry Messenger: A Book Depicting the Life of a
Famous Scientist, Mathematician, Astronomer, Philosopher,
Physicist—Galileo Galilei.* Illus. by the author. Farrar, Straus &
Giroux 1996 (cloth 0-374-37191-1) 40pp.

Galileo's book, *The Starry Messenger,* shared his vision of the sky
and of the earth. His support of the Copernican belief that the earth
moved around the sun brought him before the pope's court, where he
was found guilty of heresy in 1633. In 1992, he was pardoned. The
picture-book format of this book incorporates information into the
illustrations. This book received a Caldecott Honor award in 1997.

Related Books for Younger Readers

Asimov, Isaac, with revisions and updating by Francis Reddy.
Astronomy in Ancient Times. Illus. Gareth Stevens 1995 (LB 0-
8368-1191-7) 32pp.

Students will enjoy this attractive presentation on ancient
astronomy and the discoveries of Copernicus, Tycho Brahe, and
Galileo. A brief text is enhanced by many drawings and historical
illustrations. Fact file, lists of places to visit and addresses of places
to write, glossary, bibliography (including videos), and index. Part of
the Isaac Asimov's New Library of the Universe series.

Hawkes, Nigel. *Mysteries of the Universe.* Illus. Copper Beech
Books 1995 (LB 1-56294-939-X) 40pp.

Historical details are woven throughout the information on the
work of Galileo and Copernicus and theories about the universe.
Past beliefs are contrasted with more contemporary views. Many colorful illustrations make this an appealing book for browsing.
Timeline and index. Part of the Mysteries Of series.

Related Books for Older Readers

Hitzeroth, Deborah. *Telescopes: Searching the Heavens.* Illus.
Lucent 1991 (LB 1-56006-209-6) 96pp.

This book provides excellent background information on telescopes and those who study the heavens. Chapters discuss the
invention of the telescope, radio telescopes, satellite-borne tele-

scopes, and the Hubble Space telescope. Copernicus, Brahe, and Galileo are among the historical figures covered. Glossary, bibliography, and index. Part of the Encyclopedia of Discovery and Invention series.

Mammana, Dennis. *Star Hunters: The Quest to Discover the Secrets of the Universe.* Illus. Running Press 1990 (o.p.) 160pp.

This oversized book combines excellent information with an attractive format. Historical details are presented from the explorations of the ancient Greeks to the mathematical ideas of Johannes Kepler to the work of Galileo. More-recent history, such as the work of Edwin Hubble and Albert Einstein, is included. The final chapters look at the space program and plans for the future. The illustrations include photographs, prints, and even historical notes, drawings, and instruments. Index.

Gallaudet, Thomas H. (1787–1851),
educator of the deaf, opened the first free U.S. school for the deaf. His sons followed in his footsteps, with Thomas starting a church in New York City for deaf mutes and Edward opening what is now Gallaudet College in Washington, D.C.

"All the children of silence must be taught to sing their own song."
(Neimark, p. 72)

Biographies for Younger Readers

Bowen, Andy Russell. *A World of Knowing: A Story about Thomas Hopkins Gallaudet.* Illus. by Elaine Wadsworth. Carolrhoda Books 1995 (LB 0-87614-871-2) (pap. 0-87614-954-9) 64pp.

This biography focuses on Thomas Gallaudet's early efforts to teach deaf children and to find the funding, support, and understanding to establish a school for them. There is a page showing the letters of the American Manual Alphabet. Bibliography and index. Part of the Carolrhoda Creative Minds series.

Biographies for Older Readers

Neimark, Anne E. *A Deaf Child Listened: Thomas Gallaudet, Pioneer in American Education.* William Morrow & Co. 1983 (cloth 0-688-01719-3) 160pp.

When Thomas Gallaudet began to teach deaf students, there was a continuing debate about the oral or silent system. Gallaudet founded the American School for the Deaf. List of "National Service Organizations and Centers for the Deaf," bibliography, and index.

Related Books for Older Readers

Kent, Deborah, and Kathryn A. Quinlan. *Extraordinary People with Disabilities.* Illus. Children's Press 1996 (LB 0-516-20021-6) 1997 (pap. 0-516-26074-X) 215pp.

The authors profile more than 50 people who have disabilities and describe their efforts to improve their own situations and to help others. From Louis Braille's reading system for the blind to I. King Jordan (the first deaf president of Gallaudet University) to baseball star Jim Abbott, there are a variety of accomplishments represented. List of resources (including a list of addresses and Internet sites), glossary, and index. Part of the Extraordinary People series.

Walker, Lou Ann. *Hand, Heart, and Mind: The Story of the Education of America's Deaf People.* Illus. Dial 1994 (pap. 0-8037-1225-1) 144pp.

A great source for historical information. The first chapter looks at the education and treatment of deaf people in ancient times through the Middle Ages. Issues such as "The Duel Between Words and Signs" and "Mainstreaming or Residential School?" are presented along with information about educational programs. List of "Twentieth-Century Deaf People of Achievement," bibliography, and index.

Gandhi, Mohandas Karamchand
(1869–1948), an Indian political and spiritual leader, worked for India's independence from Great Britain. "Mahatma," as he was known, promoted religious tolerance and practiced passive resistance.

Biographies for Younger Readers

Fisher, Leonard Everett. *Gandhi.* Illus. by the author. Atheneum 1995 (cloth 0-689-80337-0) 32pp.

Dramatic black-and-white paintings capture the emotions and energy of the life of Mohandas Gandhi. The picture-book format makes it a good choice to introduce this leader, perhaps even reading it aloud. Chronology and map.

Lazo, Caroline. *Mahatma Gandhi.* Illus. Dillon Press 1993 (LB 0-87518-526-6) 64pp.

The biographical information is intertwined with details about Hindu customs, British rule of India, and nonviolent protests. With many quotations and black-and-white photographs, this is an accessible choice for students doing research. Bibliography and index. Part of the Peacemakers series.

Biographies for Older Readers

Severance, John B. *Gandhi: Great Soul.* Illus. Clarion 1997 (cloth 0-395-77179-X) 144pp.

With clear writing and a fine selection of black-and-white photographs, this book is an excellent choice for reading and research. Chapters describe Gandhi's childhood, his commitment to peaceful resistance, his political career, and his death. The opening chapter stresses Gandhi's influence on such activists as Nelson Mandela and Dr. Martin Luther King, Jr. Bibliography and index.

Related Books for Younger Readers

Blue, Rose, and Corinne J. Naden. *People of Peace.* Illus. Millbrook Press 1994 (LB 1-56294-409-6) 80pp.

Eleven individuals who have devoted their energy to the search for peace are profiled: philanthropist Andrew Carnegie; social worker Jane Addams, presidents Woodrow Wilson and Jimmy Carter; political leaders Mohandas Gandhi and Oscar Arias Sanchez; United Nations leaders Ralph Bunche and Dag Hammarskjöld; and activists Desmond Tutu, Betty Williams, and Mairead Corrigan Maguire. This is a great opportunity for students to assess the characteristics of peacemakers and their impact on world history. Glossary, bibliography, and index.

Cumming, David. *India.* Illus. Thomson Learning 1995 (cloth 1568473842)

The format of this book is very appealing for students, presenting facts about modern India in the context of colonialism and the history of India. Glossary, bibliography, and index. Part of the Economically Developing Countries series.

Ganeri, Anita. *Exploration Into India.* Illus. New Discovery Books 1994 (LB 0-02-718082-4) (pap. 0-382-24733-7) 48pp.

This would be a useful book for students doing research. There are many colorful illustrations and boxed sections with additional information. Chapters are arranged chronologically, from "India to A.D. 1001" through "Modern India." There is information about Muslim invaders, the Mogul Empire, and the British Raj. Time chart, glossary, and index. Part of the Exploration Into series.

Related Books for Older Readers

Jacobs, William J. *Great Lives: World Government.* Illus. Scribner's 1992 (cloth 0-684-19285-3) 320pp.

Political leaders of the 19th and 20th centuries are profiled in this book, giving students a historical perspective on the people who have shaped our world. Among those included are Napoleon Bonaparte, Queen Victoria, Gandhi, Golda Meir, Fidel Castro, Ho Chi Minh, and Mikhail Gorbachev. Bibliography and index. Part of the Great Lives series.

McNair, Sylvia. *India.* Illus. Children's Press 1991 (LB 0-516-02719-0) 128pp.

Much of this book is devoted to the history of India. From "Ancient India" to "The East India Company" and "The Long Road to Swaraj," this is well-organized for research. There is a section of mini-facts and an index. Part of the Enchantment of the World series.

Gates, William (1955–), an American business entrepreneur, cofounded Microsoft Corporation, which has become the dominant manufacturer of software for the personal computer. Microsoft also produces personal computer operating systems.

Biographies for Younger Readers

Simon, Charnan. *Bill Gates: Helping People Use Computers.*
Illus. Children's Press 1997 (LB 0-516-20290-1)

With an appealing format and a focus on helping others, this is
a great book to share with younger students. It provides an overview
of Bill Gates's life with related information in boxed sections. For
example, the concept of an "Operating System" is presented, as is
information about Paul Allen. The "In Your Community" page suggests activities for students. Timeline, brief bibliography (including
organizations and online sites), and index. Part of the Community
Builders series.

Zickgraf, Ralph. *William Gates: From Whiz Kid to Software
King.* Illus. Garrett Educational 1992 (LB 1-56074-016-7) 64pp.

This book focuses on the business knowledge that Bill Gates
and Paul Allen needed to achieve their great success with Microsoft
Corporation. Such terms as "corporate culture," "venture capital,"
and "going public" are explained along with the technology of the
software produced by Microsoft. Glossary and index. Part of the Wiz-
ards of Business series.

Biographies for Older Readers

Boyd, Aaron. *Smart Money: The Story of Bill Gates.* Illus. Morgan Reynolds 1995 (LB 1-883846-09-9) 112pp.

Bill Gates developed Microsoft Corporation, the largest computer software company in the world. This book describes his
childhood and education, and the personality that has been important in his great success. Chronology, source notes, glossary, and
index. Part of the Notable Americans series.

Related Books for Younger Readers

Wilkinson, Philip, and Jacqueline Dineen. *Art and Technology
Through the Ages.* Illus. by Robert Ingpen. Chelsea House 1994
(LB 0-7910-2769-4) 93pp.

From the development of pottery and glass to the creation of
"thinking machines," this book shows how innovators have
improved the quality of life. The book and the important contribution of Gutenberg are discussed. The phonograph, telephone, radio,
kinetoscope, and computer are also presented. This is a good choice
for students who enjoy browsing. The format, with many colorful
illustrations, is appealing. Part of the Ideas That Changed the World
series.

Wright, David. *Computers.* Illus. Benchmark Books 1996 (LB 0-7614-0064-8) 64pp.

Early devices related to computers include the abacus in China and an adding wheel invented by Pascal. The Jacquard loom used punched cards to communicate design instructions. This is an appealing book that makes fine use of illustrations and photographs to depict developments. Individuals featured in boxed sidebars include Charles Babbage, John von Neumann, Grace Murray Hopper, William Gates, and Steve Chen. Timeline, glossary, bibliography, and index. Part of the Inventors and Inventions series.

Related Books for Older Readers

Nardo, Don. *Computers: Mechanical Minds.* Illus. Lucent 1990 (LB 1-56006-206-1) 96pp.

Beginning with "The Development of Computers," Nardo describes computer generations from vacuum tubes to microchips. Applications are also discussed. Although some details are dated, students will get some useful background information from this book. Part of the Encyclopedia of Discovery and Invention series.

Gehrig, Lou (1903–1941), a baseball player with the New York Yankees, boasted a lifetime batting average of .340 with nearly 500 home runs during his major league career. He was named the American League's Most Valuable Player in 1927 and 1936, but his career ended shortly after he was diagnosed with amyotrophic lateral sclerosis, an incurable disease.

Biographies for Younger Readers

Adler, David A. *Lou Gehrig: The Luckiest Man Alive.* Illus. by Terry Widener. Harcourt 1997 (cloth 0-15-200523-4) 32pp.

The picture-book format of this biography makes it a good choice to read aloud. The stylized acrylic illustrations are dramatic. Gehrig's dignity, courage, and perseverance are emphasized and add to the heroic tale.

Rambeck, Richard. *Lou Gehrig.* Illus. Child's World 1994 (LB 1-56766-073-8) 32pp.

Younger sports fans are often attracted to informational books with photos, and this presentation will meet that need. Pages in this book feature sections of text with photographs on facing pages. The brief text is readable and focuses on the highlights of Gehrig's career (although it does refer to his consecutive game streak as still standing). Part of the Sports Superstars series.

Related Books for Younger Readers

Ritter, Lawrence S. *The Story of Baseball.* rev. and expanded. Illus. William Morrow & Co. 1990 (cloth 0-688-09056-7) (pap. 0-688-09057-5) 224pp.

In Part One, read about baseball history and key figures, including Ty Cobb, Honus Wagner, Babe Ruth, and Lou Gehrig. There is a chapter on Jackie Robinson and the color barrier. Part Two looks at strategies for playing the game and ends with "Why Is Baseball So Popular?" Index.

Ward, Geoffrey C., and Ken Burns. *25 Great Moments.* Illus. Knopf 1994 (cloth 0-679-86751-1) (pap. 0-679-96751-6) 64pp.

Could you name 25 great moments of baseball? The authors' choices include Babe Ruth predicting his home run, Lou Gehrig Day at Yankee Stadium, Jackie Robinson breaking the color barrier, Roger Maris getting 61 home runs, and many more wonderful events. Hank Aaron, Joe DiMaggio, the Griffeys, and Bob Feller are some of the great names in this book. Index. Part of the Baseball: The American Epic series of books, which is excerpted from the longer book *Baseball: An Illustrated History* (from the PBS television series).

Ward, Geoffrey C., and Ken Burns with Robert Walker. *Who Invented the Game?* Illus. with photographs. Knopf 1994 (LB 0-679-96750-8) (cloth 0-679-86750-3) 64pp.

Based on the PBS documentary, this book uses archival photographs to capture important moments from the history of baseball. From "The Game Begins" to "Free Agents and Million-Dollar Men," students will enjoy this well-written overview. Index. Part of the Baseball: The American Epic series of books, which is excerpted from the longer book *Baseball: An Illustrated History* (from the PBS television series).

Related Books for Older Readers

Ward, Geoffrey C., and Ken Burns. *Baseball: An Illustrated History.* Illus. Knopf 1994 (cloth 0-679-40459-7) 1996 (pap. 0-614-20476-3) 512pp.

This is an incredible book for both the baseball fan and for anyone interested in the social history of America as reflected in a sport. Students will want to browse through the memorabilia of baseball and read about the evolution of the game. For the most part, the chapters focus on decades and look at every aspect of the game, including the rules, the players, the owners, the facilities, and the fans. Filled with wonderful photographs. This is the companion book to the PBS television series. Bibliography and index.

Geronimo (1829?–1909), Native American leader of the Chiricahua Apache, led resistance against government efforts to relocate his people. He was captured and escaped several times. He eventually became a very successful farmer and also participated in the inaugural procession of President Theodore Roosevelt.

Biographies for Younger Readers

Sanford, William R. *Geronimo: Apache Warrior.* Illus. Enslow Publishers 1994 (LB 0-89490-510-4) 48pp.

From "Massacre in Mexico," when Geronimo's wife, mother, and children were killed, to "Geronimo's Later Years," this book gives a well-organized introduction to the Apache leader. Chapter notes, glossary, bibliography, and index. Part of the Native American Leaders of the Wild West series.

Biographies for Older Readers

Hermann, Spring. *Geronimo: Apache Freedom Fighter.* Illus. Enslow Publishers 1997 (LB 0-89490-864-2) 128pp.

The struggle of Geronimo and his people against the encroachment of soldiers and settlers was violent. There were raids, scalp hunters, and imprisonment. Students who want a critical look at the westward expansion in America will find this very useful. Chronology, chapter notes, glossary, bibliography, and index. Part of the Native American Biographies series.

Shorto, Russell. *Geronimo and the Struggle for Apache Freedom.* Illus. Silver Burdett 1989 (LB 0-382-09571-5) (pap. 0-382-09760-2) 144pp.

In the introduction by Alvin M. Josephy, Jr., the issue of "discovery" is raised, focusing on the arrival of Europeans and the impact on native peoples. Geronimo's life chronicles the struggle of the Apache to maintain their freedom and land. Because there is no index, students doing research will have to use the table of contents to access general topics. Bibliography. Part of the Alvin Josephy's Biography of the American Indians series.

Related Books for Younger Readers

Claro, Nicole. *The Apache Indians.* Illus. Chelsea House 1992 (LB 0-7910-1656-0) 1993 (pap. 0-7910-1946-2) 80pp.

Chapter titles include "A Mighty People," "Spanish Strangers," "Fighting Americans," and "On the Reservation." Students who are just beginning to research this period will appreciate the brief chapters and clear organization. The final chapter looks at the lives of surviving Apaches today. A section of color photographs depicts Apache artistry. Chronology, glossary, and index. Part of the Junior Library of American Indians series.

Related Books for Older Readers

Cox, Clinton. *The Forgotten Heroes: The Story of the Buffalo Soldiers.* Illus. Scholastic 1996 (pap. 0-590-45122-7) 192pp.

After the Civil War, many black men enlisted in the U.S. Army and were assigned duty on the frontier. This put the soldiers in conflict with native peoples trying to keep their homelands. Encounters with Crazy Horse, Quanah Parker, Sitting Bull, and Geronimo are among those described. Students will find the irony of this situation as compelling as the writing. Detailed bibliography and index.

Melody, Michael E. *The Apache.* Illus. Chelsea House 1989 (LB 1-55546-689-3) (pap. 0-7910-0352-3) 112pp.

Well-organized chapters trace the Apache from their origins to reservation life. There are descriptions of broken promises and the loss of Apache lands. The unsuccessful efforts of Cochise, Geronimo, and other leaders to keep their lands are described. A picture essay in the middle of the book has color photographs of Apache art. Glossary, bibliography, and index. Part of the Indians of North America series.

Ginsburg, Ruth Bader (1933–),
confirmed as a Supreme Court Justice in 1993, was the second woman to sit on the nation's highest court, after Sandra Day O'Connor. She earlier taught at Columbia University's School of Law and served for 13 years as a circuit judge on the U.S. Court of Appeals in Washington, D.C.

Biographies for Younger Readers

Henry, Christopher. *Ruth Bader Ginsburg.* Illus. Franklin Watts 1994 (LB 0-531-20174-0) 64pp.

This is a very inviting book for beginning researchers. The chapters follow a well-organized, chronological approach and there are photographs, often in color, on almost every page. The photographs provide variety for the reader and the captions expand the text. Glossary, bibliography, and index. Part of the First Book series.

Italia, Bob. *Ruth Bader Ginsburg.* Illus. Abdo & Daughters 1994 (LB 1-56239-098-8)

This is a good introductory biography of the second female Supreme Court Justice. Readers who are aided by larger print and brief, focused chapters will find this accessible. Glossary and index. Part of the Supreme Court Library series.

Biographies for Older Readers

Ayer, Eleanor H. *Ruth Bader Ginsburg: Fire and Steel on the Supreme Court.* Illus. Silver Burdett 1994 (LB 0-87518-651-3) (pap. 0-382-24721-3)

This detailed biography uses many quotations (referenced in chapter notes). Chapters focus on Ruth Bader Ginsburg's work on the Women's Rights Project and as a judge on the U.S. Court of Appeals. Specific cases and issues are discussed. Timeline, bibliography, and index. Part of the People in Focus series.

Bredeson, Carmen. ***Ruth Bader Ginsburg: Supreme Court Justice.*** Illus. Enslow Publishers 1995 (LB 0-89490-621-6) 128pp.

Born in 1933, Ruth Bader grew up in an era that discriminated against women and Jews. Her appointment to the Supreme Court in 1993 capped a career of intellectual and judicial successes. There are many quotations that provide insights into Ginsburg's character and beliefs. Chronology, chapter notes, bibliography, and index. Part of the People to Know series.

Related Books for Younger Readers

Friedman, Leon. ***The Supreme Court.*** Illus. Chelsea House 1987 (o.p.) 96pp.

This book examines the creation, scope, and activities of the Supreme Court. Key cases that established the powers of the court are described as are specific cases that have influenced life in America, such as school desegregation, *Miranda* v. *Arizona*, and abortion rights. This book is well organized for research. Glossary, bibliography, and index. Part of the Know Your Government series.

Related Books for Older Readers

Kronenwetter, Michael. ***The Supreme Court in the United States.*** Illus. Enslow Publishers 1996 (LB 0-89490-536-8) 112pp.

Chapters describe "The U.S. Judicial System," "How the Court Works," and "Historic Decisions." One fascinating chapter looks at "Politics and the Court," describing the nomination process and issues involved in the confirmation hearings. Chapter notes, glossary, bibliography, and index. Part of the American Government in Action series.

Riley, Gail Blasser. ***Miranda v. Arizona: Rights of the Accused.*** Illus. Enslow Publishers 1994 (LB 0-89490-504-X) 128pp.

On every police program on television, the arresting officers say "You have the right to remain silent." How did we get that right? This book examines the Supreme Court case that led to that ruling. There is a "You Be the Judge" activity. Students could learn more about important cases of the past by reading other books in this series, including *Brown* v. *Board of Education,* and *Gideon* v. *Wainwright.* Chapter notes, glossary, bibliography, and index. Part of the Landmark Supreme Court Cases series.

Goddard, Robert Hutchings

(1882–1945), an American physicist who designed and fired the first liquid fuel rocket, helped to develop the theory of rocket action, and built many rocket devices, including a steering mechanism.

Biographies for Older Readers

Coil, Suzanne M. *Robert Hutchings Goddard: Pioneer of Rocketry and Space Flight.* Illus. Facts on File 1992 (LB 0-8610-2491-6) 144pp.

This authoritative biography uses many quotations from Goddard's own writings (referenced in chapter notes). They provide insight into Goddard's quest to create a successful rocket. List of Goddard's milestones, glossary, bibliography, and index. Part of the Makers of Modern Science series.

Streissguth, Tom. *Rocket Man: The Story of Robert Goddard.* Illus. Carolrhoda Books 1995 (LB 0-87614-863-1) 96pp.

Goddard's research into propulsion and rocketry provided the foundation for the American space program. He considered his failures to be opportunities to experiment and refine his theories. This biography reads like a scientific thriller with many dramatic moments, yet it is well researched. Notes, glossary, bibliography, and index.

Related Books for Younger Readers

Fox, Mary Virginia. *Rockets.* Illus. Benchmark Books 1996 (LB 0-7614-0063-X) 64pp.

This is a good choice for introductory information about rockets. The chapters are well organized and easy to read. Boxed sidebars introduce such key people as Robert Goddard, Wernher von Braun, Ernst Stuhlinger, and other pioneers as well as more recent innovators including Saverio Morea (who was project manager for the Lunar Roving Vehicle) and Lonnie Reid (who works with propulsion systems). Timeline, glossary, bibliography, and index. Part of the Inventors and Inventions series.

Related Books for Older Readers

Aaseng, Nathan. *1930–1939.* Illus. Twenty-First Century Books 1995 (LB 0-8050-3433-1) 80pp.

Many scientific milestones took place in the 1930s. This book presents these in eight groupings: Chemistry, Transportation, Communication and Information, Measurement and Detection, Construction, Outer Space, Medicine, and Physics. Robert Goddard and rocketry, Vannevar Bush and the Differential Analyzer (an early computer-related machine), and Ernest Lawrence and the cyclotron (a device to fire particles at atoms) are discussed. Bibliography and index. Part of the Yearbooks in Science series.

DeWaard, E. John, and Nancy DeWaard. *History of NASA: America's Voyage to the Stars.* Illus. Exeter Books 1984 (cloth 0-671-06983-7)

This oversized book is filled with wonderful illustrations—photographs and early drawings by Leonardo da Vinci. It shows how the work of Robert Goddard and Dr. Wernher von Braun led to the flights of Alan Shepard and John Glenn. The photographs on the moon are sure to captivate readers of all ages. From the first orbit to walks in space to the *Challenger* disaster, this is a dramatic and informative book. Index.

Smith, Howard E., Jr. *Daring the Unknown: A History of NASA.* Illus. Gulliver Books 1987 (cloth 0-15-200435-1) 128pp.

This book begins with "The Dawn of the Space Age," featuring the experiments of Robert Goddard. The launch of *Sputnik* was also the debut of the space race, leading to the founding of the National Aeronautics and Space Administration. Projects from *Mercury* to *Apollo-Soyuz* are presented along with *Skylab* and the space shuttle. Bibliography and index.

Goodall, Jane (1934–), a British ethnologist, became an expert on chimpanzees after living among and studying them for several years in Africa. She wrote several popular books on the subject and founded the Jane Goodall Institute for Wildlife Research, Education, and Conservatory.

Biographies for Younger Readers

Ferber, Elizabeth. *A Life With Animals: Jane Goodall.* Illus. Benchmark Books 1997 (LB 0-7614-0489-9) 48pp.

Students will be captivated by the wonderful photographs in this book. The picture-book format makes it accessible to younger readers, who will learn about Jane Goodall's love of animals, research in Africa, and interest in providing "A Better Life for Animals." The bibliography connects readers to books about Goodall and about chimpanzees. Index. Part of the Benchmark Biographies series.

Fromer, Julie. *Jane Goodall: Living With the Chimps.* Illus. by Antonio Castro. Twenty-First Century Books 1992 (o.p.) 88pp.

To study chimpanzees, Jane Goodall entered their world, observing them in their natural habitat. This book describes Goodall's childhood and education as well as her efforts to study and protect chimpanzees and other wildlife. Glossary and index. Part of the Earth Keepers series.

Biographies for Older Readers

Pratt, Paula Bryant. *The Importance of Jane Goodall.* Illus. Lucent 1997 (LB 1-56006-082-4) 112pp.

Jane Goodall is known for her research and her crusade for conservation and protection in Africa. The text of this book is very informative and it is extended by boxed sidebars that include additional insights—excerpts from Goodall's books and from the work of other researchers. Chapter notes, bibliographies, and index. Part of the Importance Of series.

Related Books for Older Readers

Claggett, Hilary D., ed. *Wildlife Conservation.* H. W. Wilson 1997 (cloth 0-8242-0915-X)

The essays in this book are organized into five sections: Why Conserve Wildlife? Endangered Species and Their Enemies, Legislation and Politics, Managing Ecosystems, and New Directions in Wildlife Conservation. List of addresses of conservation organizations, facts about endangered species, details of major legislation, and index. Part of the Reference Shelf series.

Gutfreund, Geraldine Marshall. *1970–1979.* Illus. Twenty-First Century Books 1995 (LB 0-8050-3437-4) 80pp.

During the 1970s, paleoanthropologists found the skeleton of an early human; Jane Goodall was observing more aggressive behaviors in chimpanzees; information about AIDS was just emerging; Stephen Hawking's theories were being advanced; space probes revealed fascinating new information; and the *Apollo* space missions continued. Bibliography and index. Part of the Yearbooks in Science series.

Stefoff, Rebecca. ***Extinction.*** Illus. Chelsea House 1992 (LB 0-7910-1578-5) 128pp.

Examining the history of extinct species, the author discusses prehistoric creatures, Darwin's theories, and today's endangered and threatened species. List of addresses of conservation organizations and government agencies, glossary, bibliography, and index. Part of the Earth at Risk series.

Gorbachev, Mikhail Sergeyevich

(1931–), a Soviet statesman and political leader, was the last leader of the Soviet Union. He implemented precedent-setting policies to democratize Soviet politics and society. His reformist philosophy greatly improved relations with the United States. He won the Nobel Peace Prize in 1990.

Andrei Gromyko said of Gorbachev: "Comrades, this man has a nice smile, but he's got iron teeth."
(Butson, p. 95)

Biographics for Older Readers

Butson, Thomas. ***Mikhail Gorbachev.*** Illus. Chelsea House 1989 (pap. 0-7910-0571-2) 112pp.

In the margins surrounding the text, there are many quotations from historians and world leaders past and present. Lenin, Gromyko, Marx, Trotsky, and "Tip" O'Neill are among those whose insights extend this text. This was written while Gorbachev was still in power, so students will need to use other books or periodicals to update this information. Chronology, bibliography, and index. Part of the World Leaders Past & Present series.

Oleksy, Walter. ***Mikhail Gorbachev: A Leader for Soviet Change.*** Illus. Children's Press 1989 (o.p.) 152pp.

This book incorporates many quotations into the narrative (and references them in chapter notes). Chapter titles include "Openness and Change," "A Call for Reform," and "A Thaw in the Cold War."

The thorough timeline looks at Gorbachev's life within the context of Soviet politics and includes a detailed account of the reforms of the 1980s. Index. Part of the People of Distinction series.

Related Books for Younger Readers

Kallen, Stuart A. *Gorbachev/Yeltsin: The Fall of Communism.* Illus. Abdo & Daughters 1992 (LB 1-56239-105-4)

The format of this book makes the information accessible to students in upper elementary and middle schools. The circumstances leading to the collapse of the Soviet Union are briefly presented. Glossary and index. Part of the Rise & Fall of the Soviet Union series.

Related Books for Older Readers

Pietrusza, David. *The End of the Cold War.* Illus. Lucent 1995 (LB 1-56006-280-0) 112pp.

Opening with a detailed chronology of the cold war, Pietrusza goes on to describe the growth of communism, solidarity in Poland, and the rise of Gorbachev. There are many quotations as well as boxed features on related topics. Chapter notes, glossary, two annotated bibliographies (further reading and works consulted), and index. Part of the World History series.

Warren, James A. *Cold War: The American Crusade Against World Communism, 1945–1991.* Illus. Lothrop, Lee & Shepard 1996 (cloth 0-688-10596-3) 288pp.

After World War II, the United States and the Soviet Union were locked in an antagonistic relationship that influenced world politics and policies. This book profiles the rivalry between these two countries and includes information about Berlin, Korea, and Vietnam. This is a detailed analysis of a complex era. Two appendices look at budgetary issues, including defense spending, during these years. Chronology, notes, bibliography, and index.

Grant, Ulysses Simpson (1822–1885),

18th president of the United States, was the Civil War commander in chief of the Union Army and a key figure in bringing about the Union victory. His presidential administration was said to be one of the most corrupt in the nation's history.

Biographies for Older Readers

Kent, Zachary. *Ulysses S. Grant: Eighteenth President of the United States.* Illus. Children's Press 1989 (LB 0-516-01364-5) 100pp.

   As a general, Ulysses S. Grant led the Union soldiers to victory in the Civil War. As president, Grant was inexperienced in politics and was considered weak even by members of his own party. Chronology of American History and index. Part of the Encyclopedia of Presidents series.

Marrin, Albert. *Unconditional Surrender: U. S. Grant and the Civil War.* Illus. Atheneum 1994 (cloth 0-689-31837-5) 208pp.

   This is a wonderful book for both the researcher and the reader. Brief biographical data about Grant's early life and his presidency are included; the focus is on his years as a military leader in the Civil War. Shiloh, Vicksburg, and Appomattox are featured along with Sherman, Sheridan, and Lee. This is very readable and makes excellent use of quotations (referenced in chapter notes). Bibliography and index.

Rickarby, Laura A. *Ulysses S. Grant and the Strategy of Victory.* Illus. Silver Burdett 1991 (pap. 0-382-24053-7) 160pp.

   Focusing mainly on Grant's military accomplishments, this biography describes his training at West Point, participation in the war with Mexico, and leadership in the Civil War. Grant's political career, including the troubles he faced as president, is briefly featured. Timeline of the Civil War as well as one for Grant, sources, bibliography, and index. Part of the History of the Civil War series.

"It was my fortune or misfortune to be called to the office of Chief Executive without any previous political training . . . Mistakes have been made . . . I never wanted to get out of a place as much as I did to get out of the Presidency."
(Kent, p. 810)

Quotation from Robert E. Lee: "Now, I have carefully searched the military records of both ancient and modern history, and have never found Grant's superior as a general. I doubt if his superior can be found in all history."
(Marrin, p. v)

Related Books for Younger Readers

Smith, Carter, ed. *One Nation Again: A Sourcebook on the Civil War.* Illus. Millbrook Press 1993 (LB 1-56294-266-2) 96pp.

Following the Civil War was the time of Reconstruction. This book opens with a detailed timeline that links the events in America to those around the world. The book covers the period from the death of Lincoln to the presidencies of Andrew Johnson and Ulysses S. Grant, and ends with the election of Rutherford B. Hayes and the increased industrialization of America. Bibliography and index. Part of A Sourcebook on the Civil War series.

Related Books for Older Readers

Hakim, Joy. *War, Terrible War.* Illus. Oxford University Press 1994 (LB 0-19-507755-5) (cloth 0-19-509511-1) (pap. 0-19-507756-3) 160pp.

Chapters feature many of the major figures related to the Civil War: Harriet Tubman, Abraham Lincoln, Jefferson Davis, and John Brown. Lee, Grant, McClellan, and other military leaders are also highlighted. Students will find insights into important issues and there are boxed features on such topics as slavery, the navy, and songs of the Civil War. Illustrations surround the text and there are many quotations and observations in the margins. Chronology, bibliography, and index. Part of the History of US series.

Shiloh. Illus. Time-Life Books 1996 (cloth 0-7835-4707-2) 167pp.

For researchers as well as those interested in the Civil War, this is an excellent selection. The actual text is fairly brief, providing connecting details about the fighting at Shiloh. Most of the book consists of selections from diaries and letters, which are accompanied by photographs and memorabilia. The result is a compelling look at the people involved in this deadly battle (a chart shows that the casualties at Shiloh, including killed, wounded, and missing, were more than 13,000 for the Federal troops and more than 10,000 for the Confederates). Bibliography and index. Part of the Voices of the Civil War series.

Gutenberg, Johann (1397?–1468), an

early printer in Germany, is believed by many to have been the first European to use movable type. His invention of printing is said to have taken place in Strasbourg as early as 1436.

Biographies for Younger Readers

Burch, Joann J. *Fine Print: A Story about Johann Gutenberg.* Illus. by Kent Alan Aldrich. Carolrhoda Books 1991 (LB 0-87614-682-5); First Avenue Editions 1992 (pap. 0-87614-565-9) 64pp.

The six chapters in this book take the few facts that are known about Gutenberg's life and weave them into an interesting, readable story. The book opens with a glossary of new terms. List of sources and suggestions for further reading. Part of the Carolrhoda Creative Minds series.

Fisher, Leonard Everett. *Gutenberg.* Illus. by the author. Macmillan 1992 (LB 0-02-735238-2) 32pp.

Dramatic black-and-white paintings depict the events of Gutenberg's life and era. While there are not many known facts about Gutenberg's life, Fisher expands what is known into a fascinating overview. Chronology.

Pollard, Michael. *Johann Gutenberg.* Illus. Exley 1992 (LB 1-85015-255-1)

The long subtitle for this book is "The story of the invention of movable type and how printing led to a knowledge explosion." The many illustrations, including a reproduction of Gutenberg's "forty-two line Bible," add to the visual appeal of this brief presentation. Chronology, glossary of printing terms, and index. Part of the Scientists Who Have Changed the World series.

Related Books for Younger Readers

Brookfield, Karen. *Book.* Illus. with photographs by Laurence
Pordes. Knopf 1993 (LB 0-679-94012-X) (cloth 0-679-84012-5)
64pp.

    Covering the development of writing and the growth of the pub-
lishing industry and of libraries, this book is both entertaining and
informative. The text is surrounded by numerous illustrations showing manuscript books and the work of Gutenberg and other pioneers
of printing. Index. Part of the Eyewitness Books series.

Krensky, Stephen. *Breaking into Print: Before and After the
Invention of the Printing Press.* Illus. by Bonnie Christensen. Little, Brown 1996 (cloth 0-316-50376-2) 32pp.

    This is a lovely book. The illustrations capture the look of an
illuminated manuscript. Krensky gives details about the early work
of the Chinese and Koreans before the focus shifts to Johann Gutenberg. The large picture-book format makes it an appealing choice for
sharing with groups, although many readers will enjoy it on their
own. Chronology.

Wilkinson, Philip, and Jacqueline Dineen. *Art and Technology
Through the Ages.* Illus. by Robert Ingpen. Chelsea House 1994
(LB 0-7910-2769-4) 93pp.

    From the development of pottery and glass to the creation of
"thinking machines," this book shows how innovators have
improved the quality of life. The book and the important contribution of Gutenberg are discussed, as is Edison's phonograph. The
telephone, radio, kinetoscope, and computer are also presented.
This is a good choice for students who enjoy browsing. The presentation, with many colorful illustrations, is attractive. Part of the Ideas
That Changed the World series.

Related Books for Older Readers

Steffens, Bradley. *Printing Press: Ideas into Type.* Illus. Lucent
1990 (LB 1-56006-205-3) 96pp.

    Early chapters look at "The Origin of Printing" and "Guten-
berg's World." Later chapters examine such issues as "Freedom of
the Press" and "Printing in the Computer Age." Glossary, bibliographies, and index. Part of the Encyclopedia of Discovery and
Invention series.

Hall, Daniel Weston (1841–?), served

on a whaling ship in his teens, keeping a journal of his adventures entitled *Arctic Rovings or, the Adventures of a New Bedford Boy on Sea and Land.*

Biographies for Younger Readers

Stanley, Diane. *The True Adventure of Daniel Hall.* Illus. by the author. Dial 1995 (pap. 0-8037-1468-8) 40pp.

When he was 14, Daniel Hall left Massachusetts on a Yankee whaling ship. This book describes his dramatic adventure, including mistreatment by the captain and survival in Siberia. This biography is based on the journal written by Daniel Hall. Diane Stanley's retelling and color paintings add to the drama.

Related Books for Younger Readers

Carrick, Carol. *Whaling Days.* Illus. by David Frampton. Clarion 1993 (cloth 0-395-50948-3) 40pp.

The woodcuts in this book capture the drama of life on a whaling ship and the text describes the hard conditions. One picture shows a cutaway of a ship. Students will learn about the impact of uncontrolled hunting on the whale population—a problem that continues today. This is an attractive and readable book.

Chrisp, Peter. *The Whalers.* Illus. Thomson Learning 1995 (LB 1-56847-421-0) 48pp.

Chapters feature "The First Whalers," "Life on a Whaling Ship," and "The Survival of the Whale." There are many details about hunting, killing, and the use of whale meat. Many illustrations surround the text and there are boxed features on such topics as "An American Whaler" and "Medicine, Margarine, and Meat." Timeline, glossary, bibliography, and index. Part of the Remarkable World series.

Gourley, Catherine, in association with Mystic Seaport Museum. *Hunting Neptune's Giants: True Stories of American Whaling.* Illus. Millbrook Press 1995 (LB 1-56294-534-3) 96pp.

Gourley presents information about the crew, daily life, and the dangers and business of whaling. Archival prints and photographs give a visual reference for the era and excerpts from logs, diaries, journals, and other documents provide personal insights. Lists of sources and places to visit or call, and index.

Halley, Edmund, or Edmond

(1656–1742), an English astronomer, was the first to accurately calculate the orbit of a comet, using Isaac Newton's theory of gravitational pull. The major comet on which he made his calculations was subsequently named for Halley, who in 1720 was appointed the royal astronomer.

Biographies for Older Readers

Heckart, Barbara Hooper. *Edmond Halley: The Man and His Comet.* Children's Press 1984 (o.p.) 112pp.

Halley's astronomical studies continued the work of Tycho Brahe and Johannes Kepler. He worked with Isaac Newton to find the mathematical formula for the motion of the planets. This book was published just before the 1985–1986 return of Halley's comet; it features suggested activities for comet-watching and a timeline of the appearance of the comet. Chronology, glossary, thorough bibliography, and index. Part of the People of Distinction series.

Related Books for Younger Readers

Snedden, Robert. *Space.* Illus. Chelsea House 1995 (LB 0-7910-3029-6) 48pp.

Throughout history, people have been fascinated by the heavens. This book provides a chronological overview of theories about planets, comets, gravity, relativity, and more. The studies of Copernicus, Galileo, Halley, Hubble, Einstein, and Newton are featured. Part of the Science Horizons series.

Related Books for Older Readers

Vogt, Gregory. *Halley's Comet: What We've Learned.* Illus.
Franklin Watts 1987 (o.p.) 96pp.

This is a very detailed presentation about the discovery and study of Halley's comet. There is information about Edmund Halley's original observations as well as details gathered from the 1986 visit of the comet. (The comet is expected again in 2061.) Numerous drawings explain scientific principles. Glossary, bibliography, and index. Part of the First Books series.

Hamer, Fannie Lou (1917–1977), an African American civil rights activist, was born into a Mississippi sharecropper family, the granddaughter of a slave. She was a member of the Mississippi Freedom Party's delegation to the 1964 Democratic Convention in Atlantic City, New Jersey.

Biographies for Younger Readers

Colman, Penny. *Fannie Lou Hamer and the Fight for the Vote.*
Illus. Millbrook Press 1993 (LB 1-56294-323-5) (pap. 1-56294-789-3) 32pp.

It is inspiring to read about the courage of civil rights leaders such as Fannie Lou Hamer. This biography links Hamer's work to the events of her era. There are references to the Ku Klux Klan, poll taxes, freedom songs, protests, and arrests. Timeline, list of additional resources (including videos and recordings), and index. Part of the Gateway Civil Rights series.

Biographies for Older Readers

Mills, Kay. *This Little Light of Mine: The Life of Fannie Lou Hamer.* Illus. Dutton 1993 (o.p.)

This very thorough biography is for serious students in high school (even adults). The text is detailed and often intense, particularly in descriptions of the mistreatment and injustices endured by Fannie Lou Hamer and others who sought increased rights. Chronology, notes, and index.

Rubel, David. *Fannie Lou Hamer: From Sharecropping to Politics.* Illus. Silver Burdett 1990 (LB 0-382-09923-0) (pap. 0-382-24061-8) 128pp.

Rubel starts off with a timeline running from *Brown* v. *Board of Education* (1954) to the death of Martin Luther King, Jr., the Civil Rights Act, and the Poor People's March (1968). Each chapter opens with a quotation, and more are woven into the text, giving students access to many important thoughts from this time. This is a thorough presentation that deals with controversial issues and events. List of suggested readings, sources, and index. Part of the History of the Civil Rights Movement series.

Related Books for Older Readers

McKissack, Patricia, and Fredrick McKissack. *The Civil Rights Movement in America: From 1865 to the Present.* 2nd ed. Illus. Children's Press 1991 (LB 0-516-00579-0) 352pp.

From the years after the Civil War through the early years of the civil rights movement and ending with a discussion of such related issues as the women's movement and children's rights, there is a wealth of information here for students doing research. The organization of the book is inviting: It is divided into chronological eras, each opening with a timeline; there are topic subdivisions and "Cameos" on key people and issues. Bibliography and index.

Patterson, Charles. *The Civil Rights Movement.* Illus. Facts on File 1995 (cloth 0-8160-2968-7) 144pp.

Background information on slavery, the Civil War, and Reconstruction lead to chapters on court cases, school desegregation, freedom rides, marches, voting rights, and militant unrest. Chronology, chapter notes, bibliography, and index. Part of the Social Reform Movements series.

Walter, Mildred Pitts. *Mississippi Challenge.* Illus. Bradbury Press 1992 (LB 0-02-792301-0); Aladdin 1996 (pap. 0-689-80307-9) 224pp.

Before Fannie Lou Hamer led the Congressional Challenge to be recognized at the Democratic National Convention, there was a long history of prejudice and discrimination in Mississippi. Chapters describe this history, from slavery, freedom, and Reconstruction to the politics of the 1960s. Source notes, bibliography, and index.

Hamilton, Alexander (1755?–1804),

the first U.S. secretary of the treasury (1789–1795), is credited with setting up the national bank and the public credit system. He was killed in a duel with Aaron Burr, a political rival whose 1800 bid for the presidency Hamilton had thwarted.

Biographies for Younger Readers

Keller, Mollie. *Alexander Hamilton.* Illus. Franklin Watts 1986 (o.p.) 72pp.

As soldier and statesman, Alexander Hamilton played a leading role in the formation and early growth of the United States. He served as the first secretary of the treasury and founded the *New York Evening Post.* Students who are doing research will appreciate the clearly written, well-organized chapters in this biography. Bibliography and index. Part of the First Book series.

Biographies for Older Readers

O'Brien, Steven. *Alexander Hamilton.* Illus. Chelsea House 1989 (LB 1-55546-810-1) 112pp.

After opening with a chapter on Alexander Hamilton's death following a duel with Aaron Burr, this book looks at the contributions Hamilton made in the Revolutionary War and the early years of the United States. Very informative captions accompany the illustrations and there are quotations (from Hamilton, his contemporaries, and historians) in the margins. Students will get a well-rounded portrait of this key historical figure. Chronology, bibliography, and index. Part of the World Leaders Past & Present series.

Whitelaw, Nancy. *More Perfect Union: The Story of Alexander Hamilton.* Illus. Morgan Reynolds 1997 (LB 1-883846-20-X) 112pp.

Alexander Hamilton was a man of many contrasts. Born in the West Indies, he became a leader in American politics. He promoted unity among his political contemporaries, but he was often in conflict with them and died in a duel with Aaron Burr. This book provides a detailed look at this man. The text includes many quotations (with source notes). Timeline, glossary, bibliography, and index. Part of the Notable Americans series.

Related Books for Younger Readers

Judson, Karen. *The Constitution of the United States.* Illus. Enslow Publishers 1996 (LB 0-89490-586-4) 104pp.

How did the early leaders of our country decide on the laws and procedures? How did they resolve their differences and agree to cooperate? Three appendices supplement the text: one featuring information on the 39 signers of the Constitution, the second giving the text of the Preamble, and the third the text of the Bill of Rights. Alexander Hamilton served on the Committee of Style for the Constitution and at one point proposed having a monarch; this suggestion was ignored. Chapter notes, glossary, bibliography, and index. Part of the American Government in Action series.

Related Books for Older Readers

Hauptly, Denis J. *A Convention of Delegates: The Creation of the Constitution.* Illus. Atheneum 1987 (LB 0-689-31148-6) 160pp.

This is a fascinating book to read. As the process of forming a new government is described, the author gives profiles of key people, including Alexander Hamilton, John Jay, and James Madison, the three authors of the *Federalist Papers.* Their writings provided a foundation for the Constitution. There is also an appendix listing the names of the delegates and one with the text of the Constitution. Bibliography and index.

Wolman, Paul. *The U.S. Mint.* Illus. Chelsea House 1987 (o.p.) 96pp.

A new country needs to establish many agencies and services, including currency and banking. This book examines the historical development of the U.S. Mint, including the role of Alexander Hamilton. There is information about the power of the dollar around the world and the activities of the Mint today. Glossary, bibliography, and index. Part of the Know Your Government series.

Hammarskjöld, Dag (1905–1961), a Swedish diplomat, served as secretary general of the United Nations from 1953 until his death in 1961. In that role, he is credited with significantly extending the influence of the United Nations, particularly in the developing world.

Biographies for Older Readers

Sheldon, Richard N. *Dag Hammarskjöld.* Illus. Chelsea House 1987 (LB 0-87754-529-4) 112pp.

This is a thorough and well-organized presentation, focusing on Hammarskjöld's commitment to service and world peace. The format is very appealing. In addition to the basic text, there are sidebar quotations (from Hammarskjöld and other world leaders) and black-and-white photographs with detailed captions. Chronology, bibliography, and index. Part of the World Leaders Past & Present series.

Related Books for Younger Readers

Brenner, Barbara. *The United Nations 50th Anniversary Book.* Illus. Atheneum 1995 (cloth 0-689-31912-6)

The United Nations brings people from around the world together to work for common goals. There is a fold-out page of "Key Events in UN History." Chapters feature past and present U.N. work for peace, human rights, the environment, health, education, cultural issues, and space exploration. List of addresses of other service organizations and index.

A World in Our Hands: In Honor of the Fiftieth Anniversary of the United Nations. Illus. Tricycle Press 1995 (LB 1-883672-31-7) 96pp.

Following chapters on "A War to End All Wars" and "The League of Nations," this book examines the development of the United Nations, focusing on different aspects of the U.N. mission. Throughout the book, children's prose, poetry, and art tell the story of this world agency. Index.

Related Books for Older Readers

Janello, Amy, and Brennon Jones, eds., with an introduction by Brian Urquhart. *A Global Affair: An Inside Look at the United Nations.* Illus. Jones & Janello 1995 (cloth 0-9646322-0-9) 304pp.

A collection of essays from journalists who have covered the United Nations. Essays include "Keeping the Peace," "The UN Spirit," "Defending Human Rights," and "Nurturing the Children." Wonderful photographs show the work of the United Nations in the past and today. These essays will provide students with different perspectives on the work of the United Nations. List of U.N. agencies.

"The pursuit of peace and progress cannot end in a few years in either victory or defeat. The pursuit of peace and progress, with its trials and its errors, its successes and its setbacks, can never be relaxed and never abandoned."

(Sheldon, p. 59)

Hannibal (247?B.C.–183?B.C.), commander of the Carthaginian army during the second Punic War (218 B.C.–201 B.C.), marched an army of 40,000 men and 40 elephants over the Italian Alps to defeat the Romans. Carthage eventually fell to Rome, but not until after years of resistance and bloodshed.

Biographies for Younger Readers

Green, Robert. *Hannibal.* Illus. Franklin Watts 1996 (LB 0-531-20240-2) 1997 (pap. 0-531-15811-X) 64pp.

This book gives a dramatic account of Hannibal's best-known deed—bringing troops and supplies (on elephants) across the Pyrenees and the Alps. The section "For More Information" includes Internet sites relating to archaeology and the ancient world. Index. Part of the Ancient Biography First Books series.

Rosen, Mike. *The Journeys of Hannibal.* Illus. by Tony Smith. Bookwright Press 1990 (o.p.) 32pp.

Hannibal's father, Hamilcar, was a wealthy leader of Carthage who fought against the Romans and the tribes of Spain. After his death, Hannibal came to power, leading the Carthaginians to some of their greatest victories. Information is presented on double-page spreads with illustrations encompassing the text. Younger researchers will find the format very accessible. Glossary, bibliography, and index. Part of the Great Journeys series.

Related Books for Younger Readers

Corbishley, Mike. *What Do We Know about the Romans?* Illus. Peter Bedrick Books 1991 (LB 0-87226-352-5) 40pp.

At the beginning of this book, there is a timeline that shows events in Rome and links them to events around the world. Double-page spreads then look at aspects of Roman life—food, houses, clothes, holidays, rulers, inventors, and army. Glossary and index. Part of the What Do We Know About? series.

Related Books for Older Readers

Nardo, Don. *The Punic Wars.* Illus. Lucent 1996 (LB 1-56006-417-X) 112pp.

This book begins with a chronology, "Important Dates in the History of the Punic Wars," that places the accomplishments of Hannibal in the context of the Roman republic and empire. The chapters are well organized and there are topic subdivisions that make the text even more convenient for research. There are quotations within the text, many from ancient historians, and sidebars that feature related topics. This is a fine choice to increase understanding of this era. Chapter notes, annotated bibliographies, and index. Part of the World History series.

Henry, Patrick (1736–1799), a political

leader of the Revolutionary period, is perhaps best known as the man who proclaimed "Give me liberty or give me death." He served as governor of Virginia from 1776 to 1779 and later campaigned for inclusion of the Bill of Rights in the Constitution.

"Is life so dear, or peace so sweet, as to be purchased at the price of chains and slavery? Forbid it, Almighty God! I know not what course others may take; but as for me . . . give me liberty or give me death!"

(Reische, p. 59)

Biographies for Younger Readers

Adler, David A. *A Picture Book of Patrick Henry.* Illus. by John Wallner and Alexandra Wallner. Holiday House 1995 (LB 0-8234-1187-7) 32pp.

This is a great book to read aloud and then discuss how the facts are woven into the text. Teachers could use this book to discuss biographies and then have students do their own research. Chronology. Part of the Picture Book Of series.

Fritz, Jean. *Where Was Patrick Henry on the 29th of May?* Illus. by Margot Tomes. Coward-McCann 1975 (cloth 0-698-20307-0); Paperstar 1997 (pap. 0-698-11439-6) 48pp.

Patrick Henry was a lawyer, a farmer, governor of Virginia, and a famous orator. This lively book is filled with interesting vignettes and anecdotes. It is both fun to read and informative. Chapter notes.

Reische, Diana. *Patrick Henry.* Illus. Franklin Watts 1987 (LB 0-531-1-305-6)

When Patrick Henry talked, people listened. This is a more detailed book than those by Adler or Fritz; it is perfect for reports. The focus of this well-organized book is on Henry's skills as an orator and there are many quotations to make the point. Source notes, bibliography, and index. Part of the First Books Biographies series.

Related Books for Younger Readers

Collier, Christopher, and James Lincoln Collier. *The American Revolution, 1763–1783.* Illus. Benchmark Books 1998 (LB 0-7614-0440-6) 96pp.

This very readable book describes the events that led up to the Revolutionary War. One chapter features the Stamp Act and Patrick Henry's outspoken opposition to it; another describes "Taxes and Tea"; and another looks at some of the early battles. Students seeking a well-written overview will appreciate this work. Bibliography and index. Part of the Drama of American History series.

Related Books for Older Readers

Meltzer, Milton. *The American Revolutionaries: A History in Their Own Words 1750–1800.* Illus. HarperCollins 1993 (pap. 0-06-446145-9) 224pp.

Patrick Henry was known as a great orator. His words as well as excerpts from letters, speeches, memoirs, articles, and other documents from the American Revolution are featured here. Included are letters sent between John and Abigail Adams, Patrick Henry's arguments against the Stamp Act, the Bill of Rights, and a letter from George Washington about his troops. Students will find this documentary evidence useful for information and reports. Part of the Trophy Book series.

Henry the Navigator (1394–1460), the son of King John I of Portugal, earned his greatest fame for his support of exploration. In 1416, he set up a base for sea exploration at Sagres, as well as a school for geographers and navigators and an observatory.

Biographies for Younger Readers

Fisher, Leonard Everett. *Prince Henry the Navigator.* Illus. by the author. Macmillan 1990 (cloth 0-02-735231-5) 32pp.

Prince Henry founded a navigational school that refined tools and shipbuilding. From his developments, sailors were able to explore far beyond earlier limits. One of their goals was to accumulate wealth, which they often did by entering the slave trade. This brief biography would be an introduction to the life of this Portuguese prince. The black-and-white paintings add to the drama of the story. Chronology.

Biographies for Older Readers

Simon, Charnan. *Henry the Navigator.* Illus. Children's Press 1993 (o.p.) 128pp.

Students doing research will find useful information in the text and in the maps and reproductions of artworks. These illustrations add to the interest level of this detailed biography. An appendix includes a page from a 15th-century atlas as well as models of Portuguese ships. Timeline, glossary, bibliography, and index. Part of the World's Great Explorers series.

Related Books for Younger Readers

Fritz, Jean. *Around the World in a Hundred Years: From Henry the Navigator to Magellan.* Illus. by Anthony Bacon Venti. Putnam's 1994 (cloth 0-399-22527-7) 128pp.

Follow the exploits of Prince Henry the Navigator, Christopher Columbus, John Cabot, Amerigo Vespucci, Ferdinand Magellan, and more. According to the author, these explorers were "a brave, cruel, ambitious lot." Chapter notes, bibliography, and index.

Related Books for Older Readers

Stefoff, Rebecca. *Vasco da Gama and the Portuguese Explorers.* Illus. Chelsea House 1993 (LB 0-7910-1303-0) 112pp.

The Portuguese explorers were master seamen. Prince Henry the Navigator, Bartolomeu Dias, and Vasco da Gama were daring mariners who expanded Europe's reach to other parts of the world. Chronology, bibliography, and index. Part of the World Explorers series.

"The example and experience of Matthew Henson, who has been a member of each and of all my Arctic expeditions since '91 (my trip in 1886 was taken before I knew Henson), is only another one of the multiplying illustrations of the fact that race, or color, or bringing-up, or environment, count nothing against a determined heart, if it is backed and aided by intelligence."

(Peary's Foreword to Henson, p. xxviii)

Henson, Matthew A. (1866–1955), an African American explorer, was a member of Robert Peary's 1909 expedition to the North Pole. The author of *A Black Explorer at the North Pole* (1912), Henson was honored by the Congress of the United States in 1944 and again by President Truman in 1950. He died in relative obscurity but was reburied at Arlington National Cemetery in 1988 with full honors.

Biographies for Younger Readers

Ferris, Jeri. *Arctic Explorer: The Story of Matthew Henson.* Illus. Carolrhoda Books 1989 (LB 0-87614-370-2); First Avenue Editions (pap. 0-87614-507-1) 80pp.

Matthew Henson was so skilled in arctic exploration that he was the natural choice to accompany Robert Peary on the last, successful section of the journey to the North Pole. This is a great adventure, well told in this biography. Bibliography and index. Part of the Trailblazers Biographies series.

Biographies for Older Readers

Gilman, Michael. *Matthew Henson.* Illus. Chelsea House 1988 (LB 1-55546-590-0) (pap. 0-7910-0207-1) 112pp.

When Admiral Peary reached the North Pole, the accomplishments of Matthew Henson were not widely recognized. Today, the achievements of African Americans are receiving the attention they deserve. This book gives a detailed account of Henson's life emphasizing the specific skills he provided to the expedition. Students will appreciate the honesty with which information about racism is presented. Chronology, suggestions for further readings, and index. Part of the Black Americans of Achievement series.

Henson, Matthew A. Foreword by Robert E. Peary, Rear Admiral, U.S.N. Introduction by Booker T. Washington. *A Black Explorer at the North Pole.* Illus. University of Nebraska Press 1989 (pap. 0-8032-7245-6) 199pp.

What a wonderful opportunity for students to examine a personal account. There is information about the preparations, hardships, and the joy of achieving success. Reading this book is a must for anyone studying Matthew Henson. This edition is reprinted from Henson's 1912 edition.

Related Books for Younger Readers

Hudson, Wade. *Five Brave Explorers.* Illus. by Ron Garnett. Scholastic 1995 (LB 0-590-48032-4)

Jean DuSable, Matthew Henson, Mae Jemison, James Beckwourth, and Esteban Dorantes are profiled in this brief book. With no table of contents or index, students may find it difficult to look for specific facts; however, the easy reading level and variety of illustrations (photographs and color drawings) make it a good choice for beginners. Part of the Great Black Heroes series and of the Hello Reader! series.

Potter, Joan, and Constance Claytor. *African Americans Who Were First.* Illus. Cobblehill Books 1997 (pap. 0-525-65246-9)

The brief biographies in this book are organized by topic from early men and women of achievement such as Benjamin Banneker and Harriet Tubman through scientific and educational contributors such as Matthew Henson and Garrett Morgan, to those in the civil rights movement including Marian Anderson, Thurgood Marshall, and Arthur Ashe, and ending with African Americans today, including Rita Dove and Ronald Brown. While the coverage is brief, this is a great way to introduce students to the variety of accomplishments by African Americans. Index.

Rosen, Mike. *The Journey to the North Pole.* Illus. by Doug Post. Bookwright Press 1990 (o.p.) 32pp.

Robert Peary and Matthew Henson succeeded in reaching the North Pole in 1909. Rosen describes earlier attempts and the hardships faced on their expeditions. This is a dramatic account with many illustrations. Students will find this useful and enjoyable. Glossary, bibliography, and index. Part of the Great Journeys series.

Related Books for Older Readers

Angel, Ann. *America in the 20th Century, 1900–1909.* Marshall Cavendish 1995 (cloth 1-85435-736-0)

Readers will enjoy browsing through this volume on the first decade of the 20th century. It contains such entertaining stories as Rockefeller's meteoric rise to become the richest man in America, Peary and Henson reaching the North Pole, and more. Chronology, list of further readings, and index.

Herod the Great (73 B.C.–4 B.C.), also known as Herod I, is remembered mostly for the slaughter of the male infants of Bethlehem at the time of the birth of Jesus Christ. He ruled as king of Judea, backed by the Roman emperor, from 37 B.C. to 4 B.C.

Biographies for Younger Readers

Green, Robert. *Herod the Great.* Franklin Watts 1996 (LB 0-531-20232-1) (pap. 0-531-15801-2) 64pp.

Herod lived during an era of upheaval. As the Romans invaded Judea and the surrounding areas, Herod and his family balanced their own ambitions against those of their conquerors. This was a very violent time, and Herod was as cruel as any of his contemporaries. Green's biography will inspire students to read further. Timeline, bibliography, and index. Part of the Ancient Biography First Books series.

Related Books for Younger Readers

O'Neill, Amanda. *Biblical Times.* Crescent Books 1992 (cloth 0-517-06560-6)

With many color photographs of architecture, artifacts, and places, this book is visually appealing and informative. Double-page spreads provide information about Eden, Canaan, King David, Herod, Jesus, the Gospels, and more. Index. Part of the Historical Facts series.

Tubb, Jonathan N. *Bible Lands.* Illus. Knopf 1991 (LB 0-679-91457-9) (cloth 0-679-81457-4) 64pp.

The Israelites, the Assyrians, the Babylonians, and the Persians are some of the peoples presented in this book. Information about the Greeks and Romans and King Herod precedes a section on archaeology. The format is attractive—just right for students who like to browse. Index. Part of the Eyewitness Books series.

Hiawatha, the legendary Iroquois chief made famous by Henry Wadsworth Longfellow's epic poem *Song of Hiawatha,* was a brave American Indian married to the maiden Minnehaha. In actuality, Hiawatha was a Mohawk Indian chief who lived in the 1500s and introduced the arts of picture-writing, navigation, and medicine to the members of his tribe. He is credited with bringing about the union of the five separate nations of the Iroquois people.

Biographies for Younger Readers

Fradin, Dennis B. *Hiawatha: Messenger of Peace.* Illus. by Arnold Jacobs. Simon & Schuster 1992 (cloth 0-689-50519-1) 48pp.

After Hiawatha's wife and daughters were killed, he was expected to seek revenge. Instead, Hiawatha spread a message of peace. The text of this brief biography is well organized and the illustrations include reproductions of art works and maps that add information and visual variety. Bibliography and index.

Biographies for Older Readers

McClard, Megan, and George Ypsilantis. *Hiawatha and the Iroquois League.* Illus. by Frank Riccio. Silver Burdett 1989 (LB 0-382-09568-5) (pap. 0-382-09757-2) 138pp.

The work of Hiawatha resulted in the creation of the Iroquois League, a peaceful, cooperative group with a constitution that was memorized and passed down for generations. Part One focuses on

"Hiawatha's Life and Legend" and Part Two tells "The Legacy of Hiawatha." There is no index, but the table of contents is very detailed and will help with access. Bibliography. Part of the Alvin Josephy's Biography of the American Indians series.

Related Books for Younger Readers

Sherrow, Victoria. *The Iroquois Indians.* Illus. Crestwood House 1992 (LB 0-7910-1655-2) 80pp.

Sherrow describes the Great Peace among the Mohawk, Oneida, Onondaga, Seneca, and Cayuga peoples. Hiawatha and Deganawida the Peacemaker helped unite the Iroquois Confederacy. Picture essay of Iroquois masks, chronology, glossary, and index. Part of the Junior Library of American Indians series.

Related Books for Older Readers

Graymont, Barbara. *The Iroquois.* Illus. Chelsea House 1988 (cloth 1-55546-709-1)

According to Graymont, the Hiawatha of Longfellow's poem is most likely based on Hayenwatha, who encouraged his people to participate with other villages in a plan for peace and cooperation. His efforts led to the "Great Peace," but the arrival of European settlers led to the decline of the Iroquois. This is a well-organized book. A section of color pictures in the middle of the book shows masks associated with the Iroquois religion. Glossary, bibliography, and index. Part of the Indians of North America series.

Hillary, Sir Edmund Percival (1919–),

a New Zealand mountaineer and explorer, in 1953 was the first, along with his Nepalese guide Tenzing Norgay, to reach the summit of Mount Everest. In 1958 he led an overland expedition to the South Pole, the first since 1912.

Biographies for Younger Readers

Hacking, Sue Muller. *Mount Everest and Beyond: Sir Edmund Hillary.* Illus. Benchmark Books 1997 (LB 0-7614-0491-0) 48pp.

There are beautiful color photographs in this book, making it a great choice for younger readers, but also a valuable visual image for older students. Addresses are included for the American and Canadian offices of the Hillary Foundation, an organization founded by Sir Edmund Hillary to help his Sherpa friends. Glossary, bibliography, and index. Part of the Benchmark Biographies series.

Biographies for Older Readers

Stewart, Whitney. *Sir Edmund Hillary: To Everest and Beyond.* Illus. with photographs by Anne B. Keiser. Lerner Publications 1996 (LB 0-8225-4927-1)

In addition to being one of the first men (with Tenzing Norgay) to reach the summit of Mount Everest, Sir Edmund Hillary participated in an expedition across Antarctica and has been an activist for environmental concerns. For research projects, this is a well-organized selection, but it is also an exciting story of adventure and accomplishment. Quotations have source notes. Bibliography and index. Part of the Newsmakers Biographies series.

Related Books for Younger Readers

Fraser, Mary Ann. *On Top of the World: The Conquest of Mount Everest.* Illus. by the author. Henry Holt 1991 (o.p.) 40pp.

This book does not provide biographical details about Edmund Hillary or Tenzing Norgay. Instead, it is a dramatic account of their successful climb to the summit of Mount Everest. The picture-book format is perfect for this exciting story, allowing the illustrator to provide breathtaking images. The endpapers include additional information, showing the general route of the expedition and supplies that were needed. Glossary.

Sandak, Cass R. *The Arctic and Antarctic.* Illus. Franklin Watts 1987 (LB 0-531-10137-1)

Double-page spreads provide information about the exploration of these two polar regions. Chapters include "Peary and After," "Racing South," and "An Antarctic Station." Students who use this book will find general information about the conditions in polar regions and brief mention of the accomplishments of explorers. Timeline, glossary, and index. Part of the New Frontiers Exploration in the 20th Century series.

217

"When we climbed Everest, we just heaved all our rubbish outside our camp on the way up the mountain. We never even thought about it because, in those days, conservation simply hadn't become a proper cause. I hope that I wouldn't do the same thing again. . . . I really do look back on it with quite a lot of shame."

(Stewart, p. 108)

Hitler, Adolf (1889–1945), founder and leader of Germany's National Socialist (Nazi) party, gained power in 1933 and led Germany into World War II. He was responsible for the deaths of millions, in concentration camps and on battlefields, before his armies were defeated by Allied forces. Hitler killed himself in April 1945.

Biographies for Older Readers

Heyes, Eileen. *Adolf Hitler.* Illus. Millbrook Press 1994 (LB 1-56294-343-X) 160pp.

This is an excellent selection for students doing research. The author provides a thorough presentation of the horrors of the Holocaust and looks at the role of the political leaders as well as the impact of the defeat of Germany in World War I. The text and photographs are often distressing, chronicling the ordeals of so many people. Chronology, chapter notes for documentation, bibliography, and index.

Marrin, Albert. *Hitler.* Illus. Viking Penguin 1987 (o.p.)

In his childhood and adolescence, Adolf Hitler developed feelings of prejudice, hatred, and cruelty that later were manifested in the Holocaust. This is a thoughtful look at a man who was convinced he was right, and thought torture and destruction were appropriate treatments for those who opposed him. This is a fascinating book to read, focusing on the abuse of power. Thorough bibliography and index.

Rubenstein, Joshua. *Adolf Hitler.* Illus. Franklin Watts 1982 (LB 0-531-04477-7)

Adolf Hitler's rise to power coincided with the need of the German people to recover from their humiliating defeat in World War I and to find scapegoats for their political and economic woes. These needs were met by Hitler's hatred and commitment to destruction of perceived enemies. Many quotations enhance the text and commentary from generals, politicians, and citizens. Annotated bibliography and index. Part of the Impact series.

Related Books for Older Readers

O'Neill, Richard. *World War II: Turning Points in the Global Conflict That Shape Our World.* Illus. Crescent Books 1992 (LB 0-517-06566-5)

Beginning with "Hitler's Rise to Power," O'Neill discusses military landmarks including Pearl Harbor, D-Day, the Battle of the Bulge, and the bombing of Hiroshima and Nagasaki. There are many photographs and additional columns of information called "Fact Files." There is a "Superfacts" section of factoids about the war. Index. Part of the Historical Facts series.

Ross, Stewart. *World War II.* Illus. Raintree Steck-Vaughn 1996 (LB 0-8172-4050-0)

While this is a brief book, it presents complex concepts such as fascism, the iron curtain, superpowers, and the cold war. It would be a very useful book for older students, providing background information. Timeline, list of further readings, glossary, and index. Part of the Causes and Consequences series.

Rossel, Seymour. *The Holocaust: The Fire That Raged.* Illus. Franklin Watts 1989 (o.p.) 128pp.

After providing background information on Hitler and the Nazi party, the author describes the ghettos, concentration camps, and escape efforts. This is a well-documented book that will provide many students with solid background information and analysis about these horrendous events. Chronology of the Holocaust, list of further readings, sources, and index. Part of the New Venture series.

Strahinich, Helen. *The Holocaust: Understanding and Remembering.* Illus. Enslow Publishers 1996 (LB 0-89490-725-5) 112pp.

"Understanding the Holocaust," "The Camps," "Rescuers," and "The Lessons" are among the chapters in this book. The chapters are very well organized with subheadings and boxed sidebars on such topics as anti-Jewish laws and the Resistance. One chapter features non-Jewish groups targeted by Hitler and the Nazis. The author uses quotations and photographs effectively. There is an appendix of Holocaust museums in North America. Chapter notes (documenting sources), glossary, bibliography, and index. Part of the Issues in Focus series.

Hoover, Herbert Clark (1874–1964),
the 31st president of the United States (1929–1933), occupied the White House at the start of the Great Depression. He initiated a major public works program and established the Reconstruction Finance Corporation.

Biographies for Younger Readers

Hilton, Suzanne. *The World of Young Herbert Hoover.* Illus. by Deborah Steins. Walker and Company 1987 (LB 0-8027-6709-5) (cloth 0-8027-6708-7)

Focusing on the childhood of Herbert Hoover, this biography makes him seem very real and approachable. Included are details about his Quaker upbringing, the loss of his parents, his life with different relatives, and experiences that influenced his values, such as his commitment to better treatment of Native Americans. A chronology describes Hoover's adulthood (including his presidency). Bibliography and index.

Biographies for Older Readers

Clinton, Susan. *Herbert Hoover.* Illus. Children's Press 1988 (LB 0-516-01355-6) 100pp.

After covering Hoover's childhood, this biography looks at his accomplishments as an adult. As an engineer, as secretary of commerce, and then as president during the crash of the stock market and the Great Depression, Hoover faced difficult decisions. Chronology and index. Part of the Encyclopedia of Presidents series.

Related Books for Younger Readers

Feinberg, Barbara Silberdick. *Black Tuesday: The Stock Market Crash of 1929.* Illus. Millbrook Press 1995 (LB 1-56294-574-2) 64pp.

October 29, 1929. The "Roaring Twenties" came to a crashing halt. Herbert Hoover spent much of his presidency dealing with the difficulties caused by the depression that followed the stock market crash. This book gives a clear picture of the events that led to the crash and the economic, social, and political impact. Chronology, glossary, bibliography, and index. Part of the Spotlight on American History series.

Related Books for Older Readers

Hakim, Joy. *War, Peace, and All That Jazz.* Illus. Oxford University Press 1995 (LB 0-19-507761-X) (cloth 0-19-509514-6) (pap. 0-19-507762-8) 192pp.

World War I, Prohibition, the Roaring Twenties, jazz, the Depression, and World War II are among the topics presented. The 30 years from 1915 to 1945 were filled with social, political, and economic changes. This book will help students see the interrelationships between people and events of this era. Chronology, bibliography, and index. Part of the History of US series.

Meltzer, Milton. *Brother, Can You Spare a Dime? The Great Depression, 1929–1933.* Illus. Facts on File 1991 (cloth 0-8160-2372-7) 144pp.

The author's text is extended with personal accounts of the impact of the Depression. There are songs and excerpts from interviews, as well as newspaper and magazine articles. There are statements from people we remember, such as Will Rogers and Gordon Parks, and from the forgotten, including a man living in a flophouse. Students will find this a valuable resource for firsthand insights. Bibliography and index. Part of the Library of American History series.

Sherrow, Victoria. *Hardship and Hope: America and the Great Depression.* Twenty-First Century Books 1997 (LB 0-8050-4178-8) 128pp.

Sherrow examines the causes of the stock market crash of 1929 and the ensuing years of economic hardship. Chapters include "A Chain of Disasters," "The Poor Got Poorer: Minorities and Other Special Groups," "From Depression to War," and "The Legacy of the Depression." This is a thorough account, well documented with source notes. Students will appreciate the clarity of the text and sidebars featuring such people as Will Rogers and Frances Perkins and events such as Roosevelt's Fireside Chats. Bibliography and index.

Houston, Samuel (1793–1863), who served Tennessee as both a U.S. congressman and governor, is best known for leading Texas to independence from Mexico. He enjoyed two terms as president of the Republic of Texas, serving the state again as senator and governor after it joined the Union.

Biographies for Younger Readers

Fritz, Jean. *Make Way for Sam Houston.* Illus. by Elise Primavera. Putnam's 1986 (cloth 0-399-21303-1) (pap. 0-399-21304-X) 109pp.

This is a lively biography about a lively character. Jean Fritz has captured the energy of Sam Houston, describing his attack on Santa Anna (following the destruction of the Alamo) and his rule as the first president of the Texas Republic and, later, as governor of the state of Texas. Readers will enjoy the dramatic accounts. Chapter notes, bibliography, and index.

Sanford, William R., and Carl R. Green. *Sam Houston: Texas Hero.* Illus. Enslow Publishers 1996 (LB 0-89490-651-8) 48pp.

Follow Sam Houston's path from soldier to politician, as he leads Texas to statehood. The chapters are brief and would be accessible to younger readers as well as older readers who need simpler resources. Chapter notes, glossary, bibliography, and index. Part of the Legendary Heroes of the Wild West series.

Wade, Mary D. *I Am Houston.* Illus. by Pat Finney. Colophon House 1993 (cloth 1-882539-05-2) (pap. 1-882539-06-0) 64pp.

Sam Houston grew up in the wilderness areas of Tennessee, living for a time with the Cherokee Indians. This early experience made him sensitive to native peoples and their needs. In addition to representing Indian issues, Houston promoted the development of Texas. Index.

Related Books for Younger Readers

Bredeson, Carmen. *The Battle of the Alamo: The Fight for Texas Territory.* Illus. Millbrook Press 1996 (LB 0-7613-0019-8) 64pp.

At the Battle of the Alamo, a small group of defenders (including Jim Bowie and Davy Crockett) lost their lives and were defeated by Santa Anna. The violence of this battle and the loss of these heroic figures became a focal point of efforts to liberate Texas. An Epilogue describes the later accomplishments of key figures. Chronology, source notes, list of further readings, and index. Part of the Spotlight on American History series.

Wills, Charles A. *A Historical Album of Texas.* Illus. Millbrook Press 1995 (LB 1-56294-504-1) (pap. 1-56294-847-4) 64pp.

The history of Texas is full of confrontation: native peoples with conquistadors, American settlers with Mexican soldiers, and Texans in the Confederacy with the Union Army. This brief book gives an overview of the evolution of the state and includes information on the state flower, motto, and bird. Timeline of Texas history is linked to a timeline of American history. List of famous Texans, bibliography, and index. Part of the Historical Album series.

Related Books for Older Readers

Sorrels, Roy. *The Alamo in American History.* Illus. Enslow Publishers 1996 (LB 0-89490-770-0) 128pp.

From "Remember the Alamo" to "Victory or Death" to "The Lone Star State," this is a presentation of dramatic events in the fight for freedom in Texas. One feature will be especially useful to students: boxed "Source Documents" such as an excerpt from William Travis's message for help and a letter from Santa Anna. Timeline, list of further readings, chapter notes (documenting sources), and index. Part of the In American History series.

Hubble, Edwin Powell (1889–1953), an American astronomer who proved that galaxies existed beyond the Milky Way. His research at the University of Chicago and with the Palomar Observatory telescope helped to link a phenomenon called "Red Shift" to the expansion of the universe.

Biographies for Younger Readers

Datnow, Claire. *Edwin Hubble: Discoverer of Galaxies.* Enslow
Publishers 1997 (LB 0-89490-934-7) 128pp.

In recent years, the name "Hubble" has become more familiar
because of the telescope that was sent into space. It was named for
Edwin Hubble, a prominent American astronomer whose research
into the galaxy provided scientific information about the universe
that has influenced many other researchers. A special feature is a
section of activities that extend the understanding of scientific concepts, for example, studying the expansion of a balloon and relating
it to the expansion of a galaxy. Chronology, chapter notes for documentation, glossary, bibliography, and index. Part of the Great Minds
of Science series.

Fox, Mary Virginia. *Edwin Hubble: American Astronomer.*
Franklin Watts 1997 (cloth 0-531-11371-X)

The clear organization of this book makes it a great choice for
students doing research. Chapters feature key events, such as Hubble's education and the development of the giant telescope at the
Palomar Observatory. Chapters are further subdivided, which makes
the book even easier to use. Chronology, source notes, bibliography
(including Internet resources), and index. Part of the Book Report
Biography series.

Related Books for Younger Readers

Vogt, Gregory. *The Hubble Space Telescope.* Illus. Millbrook
Press 1992 (o.p.) 112pp.

This book opens with a description of Galileo's creation of the
first astronomical telescope and then looks at the accomplishments
of other astronomers, including Edwin Hubble. There is a lot of
technical information about telescopes and on the development of
the Hubble space telescope. Glossary, bibliography, and index. Part
of the Missions in Space series.

Related Books for Older Readers

Camp, Carole Ann. *American Astronomers: Searchers and Wonderers.* Illus. Enslow Publishers 1996 (LB 0-89490-631-3) 104pp.

The chronological arrangement of this book allows students to
develop a sense of the history of astronomy. From the early work of
Maria Mitchell to the research of George Ellery Hale and Edwin
Hubble to the studies of Carl Sagan, this book describes the fasci-
nation with observing space. Chapter notes and index. Part of the
Collective Biographies series.

Newton, David E. *1920–1929.* Illus. Twenty-First Century Books 1995 (LB 0-8050-3432-3) 80pp.

Developments in physics, chemistry, life sciences, and earth and space sciences are profiled here. During the 1920s, there were developments in wave-particle duality and quantum mechanics. There were advances in the understanding of vitamins and theoretical biology. King Tut's tomb was discovered and Edwin Hubble researched galaxies. Bibliography and index. Part of the Yearbooks in Science series.

Hughes, Langston (1902–1967), an African American poet and author, is best known for his portraits of urban African American life. In addition to poetry collections, including *The Weary Blues* and *One-Way Ticket,* he wrote a number of novels, plays, and children's books.

Biographies for Younger Readers

Cooper, Floyd. *Coming Home: From the Life of Langston Hughes.* Illus. by the author. Philomel 1994 (cloth 0-399-22682-6) 32pp.

The picture-book format makes this a good choice for pleasure reading or for reading aloud. Cooper's sepia-tone illustrations are just right and show selected moments from Hughes's life. Bibliography.

McKissack, Patricia, and Fredrick McKissack. *Langston Hughes: Great American Poet.* Illus. by Michael David Biegel and with photographs. Enslow Publishers 1992 (LB 0-89490-315-2) 32pp.

Five brief chapters describe the life of Langston Hughes, whose poetry has captured the emotions and experiences of African Americans. Glossary and index. Part of the Great African Americans series.

Biographies for Older Readers

Meltzer, Milton. *Langston Hughes: An Illustrated Edition.* Illus. by Stephen Alcorn. Millbrook Press 1997 (LB 0-7613-0205-0) (pap. 0-7613-0327-8) 240pp.

Chapters describe "Wandering," "Homesick Blues," "I've Known Rivers," "Africa," "A Garret in Paris," "Jim Crow, Southern Style," "Rehearsal," "Poems—and Politics" and "I Used to Wonder." Langston Hughes is shown as a poet, dramatist, and political activist. Thorough bibliography and detailed index.

Osofsky, Audrey. *Free to Dream: The Making of a Poet: Langston Hughes.* Illus. Lothrop, Lee & Shepard 1996 (cloth 0-688-10605-6) 112pp.

Chapter titles in this book are taken from Hughes's own writings. From "Passed Around Child," which describes his own loneliness as a child to the "dream" poems ("I Dream a World," "The Dream Keeper," "Hold Fast to Dreams"), this is a thorough and well-written book. The documentation makes it a fine example of research for students. Quotations are referenced in source notes, so students can continue their work (these sources are also listed in the bibliography). The bibliography includes sound and video recordings. Index.

Rummel, Jack. *Langston Hughes.* Illus. Chelsea House 1989 (LB 1-55546-595-1) (pap. 0-7910-0201-2) 112pp.

What sets this book apart from other biographies is the range of the text and photographs. In addition to describing the life of Langston Hughes, it provides an insight into the experiences of African Americans in the 20th century. Key figures in the Harlem Renaissance are featured and there is information about Hughes's interest in the Soviet Union and Communism and his testimony before the McCarthy Committee. Chronology, bibliography, and index. Part of the Black Americans of Achievement series.

Related Books for Younger Readers

Sullivan, Charles. *Children of Promise: African-American Literature and Art for Young People.* Illus. Abrams 1991 (cloth 0-8109-3170-2) 128pp.

The elegant presentation of this book is sure to attract many readers. Art and artifacts depicting African Americans are presented chronologically. Accompanying these dramatic visual images are poems, excerpts from prose and letters, and songs. For example, there are several poems by Langston Hughes and Gwendolyn Brooks and there are excerpts from the "I Have a Dream" speech and from a book by Walt Whitman. Students will be fascinated by the range of visual images and the historical moments they capture. Biographical notes about the authors and artists and index.

Related Books for Older Readers

Haskins, Jim. *The Harlem Renaissance.* Illus. Millbrook Press 1996 (LB 1-56294-565-3) 192pp.

In the early 1900s, many Southern blacks migrated to the North, settling in urban localities. This Great Migration is considered one of the key factors in the beginning of the Harlem Renaissance, a growth in attention to the creative and artistic talents of African Americans. Chapters in this book look at "Music, Dance, and Musical Theater," "Poetry and Fiction," and "Painters and Sculptors." Source notes, bibliography, and index.

Hughes, Langston, Milton Meltzer, et al. *A Pictorial History of African Americans.* 6th ed. Illus. Crown 1995 (cloth 0-517-59666-0)

The scope of this volume stretches from slavery to the 1990s. Chapters focus on "The Peculiar Institution," "Up From Slavery," "The New Negro," "The Range of Resistance," and "Afro-America Coming Into Its Own." The 1,300 black-and-white illustrations include documents, historical prints, photographs, and drawings. Political leaders, social reformers, educators, scientists, soldiers, entertainers, literary figures, and more are briefly highlighted. This would be an excellent starting point for research on any aspect of African American life.

Hurston, Zora Neale (1901–1960), an African American author and anthropologist, is best known for her collections of folktales, including *Tell My Horse* and *Mules and Men.*

"I have never lived an easy life, but struggled on and on to achieve my ideals."
(Yannuzzi, p. 80)

Biographies for Younger Readers

Calvert, Roz. *Zora Neale Hurston: Storyteller of the South.* Illus. Chelsea House 1993 (LB 0-7910-1766-4) 80pp.

When Zora Neale Hurston wrote stories, she often included personal experiences from her childhood, her life in Harlem, her travels, and elements of folklore from her research. This readable biography is a good choice for students who are working on research projects or just interested in this fascinating woman. Chronology, glossary, bibliography, and index. Part of the Junior World Biographies series.

McKissack, Patricia, and Fredrick McKissack. *Zora Neale Hurston: Writer and Storyteller.* Illus. by Michael Bryant and with photographs. Enslow Publishers 1992 (LB 0-89490-316-0) 32pp.

As an author and a collector of African American stories, Zora Neale Hurston celebrated her heritage. This is a very brief biography that could be used to introduce students to the research process. Glossary and index. Part of the Great African Americans series.

Biographies for Older Readers

Lyons, Mary E. *Sorrow's Kitchen: The Life and Folklore of Zora Neale Hurston.* Illus. with photographs. Collier 1990 (LB 0-684-19198-9); Macmillan 1993 (pap. 0-02-044445-1) 160pp.

This is an excellent biography for middle school and high school students. Well-researched and documented, it is also a wonderful book to read. Hurston left home after her father remarried. She was part of the Harlem Renaissance and the emergence of African American authors and artists. List of suggested readings, bibliography, and index.

Yannuzzi, Della A. *Zora Neale Hurston: Southern Storyteller.* Illus. with photographs. Enslow Publishers 1996 (LB 0-89490-685-2) 104pp.

Chapters focus on Hurston's childhood in Eatonville, Florida, her difficult life after leaving home, her opportunities to attend school, and her life as a writer. Many students will appreciate the inclusion of quotations (documented in chapter notes). Chronology, bibliography, and index. Part of the African American Biographies series.

Related Books for Younger Readers

Cooper, Michael L. *Bound for the Promised Land: The Great Black Migration.* Illus. Lodestar Books 1995 (pap. 0-525-67476-4) 85pp.

After the Civil War and Reconstruction, many blacks left the South to find new lives and work in the North. This migration occurred mainly between 1915 and 1930 and resulted in new black neighborhoods, most notably in Harlem. The concentration of black authors, artists, and musicians called the Harlem Renaissance included Langston Hughes, Zora Neale Hurston, and Duke Ellington. Endnotes, bibliography, and index.

Lawrence, Jacob. ***The Great Migration.*** Illus. with paintings by the author. HarperCollins 1993 (LB 0-06-023038-X) (cloth 0-06-023037-1) 48pp.

After an introduction from the artist about the migration of blacks from the rural areas in the South to the urban, industrialized North, there follows a collection of paintings that capture images of these events. A brief text connects the pictures, which were painted in the early 1940s. These are powerful images showing the difficulties of the journey as well as the strong support of families and friends. Many audiences will want to examine this visual history. A poem, "Migration" by Walter Dean Myers, follows the illustrations.

Related Books for Older Readers

Katz, William L. ***The New Freedom to the New Deal, 1913–1939.*** Illus. Raintree Steck-Vaughn 1993 (LB 0-8114-6279-X) 96pp.

The years covered in this book were filled with opportunities. Blacks migrated to the North and participated in the cultural and artistic celebration signified by the Harlem Renaissance and the successes of Zora Neale Hurston, Countee Cullen, and Langston Hughes. Women received the right to vote. It was also a time of hardship, particularly for native peoples and Mexican-American workers. The Great Depression and the rise of Fascism are also discussed. Sidebars focus on specific people and events. Bibliography and index. Part of the History of Multicultural America series.

Hussein, Saddam (1937–) became the president of Iraq in 1979, having served for the previous 10 years as vice president of the ruling Revolutionary Command Council. He ordered the August 1990 invasion of Kuwait, but Iraqi forces were forced to withdraw in early 1991 by a coalition of Western and Arab forces in Operation Desert Storm.

Biographies for Older Readers

Claypool, Jane. *Saddam Hussein.* Illus. Rourke 1993 (cloth 0-86625-477-3)

This is a very well organized book with clear chapters divided into subtopics that make it easy for students to get a sense of the main ideas. For example, the chapter on Arab Nationalism includes subdivisions on Global Tensions, Israel and the Arab World, Nassar and the Pan-Arab Movement, and the Baath. Appendix on "Sunni and Shiite: The Two Main Branches of Islam," timeline, glossary, annotated bibliography, list of media resources, and index. Part of the World Leaders series.

Stefoff, Rebecca. *Saddam Hussein: Absolute Ruler of Iraq.* Illus. Millbrook Press 1995 (LB 1-56294-475-4) 128pp.

Saddam Hussein is often in the news as he continues to create conflict in the Middle East. This book provides a thorough historical presentation not only of Saddam Hussein, but also of Iraq and the surrounding region. For research projects, students will find information about the complex political and social beliefs that have resulted in hostility and violence. Chronology, chapter notes, bibliography, and index.

Related Books for Older Readers

Hiro, Dilip. *The Middle East.* Illus. Oryx Press 1996 (pap. 0-57356-004-9) 232pp.

In this very detailed book, an overview of the region is followed by information on the individual countries. In each section, there are historical facts as well as information about important issues and people. For example, the author covers the discovery of oil and the important role it has come to play. There is a chapter on the conflict between Arabs and Jews and there is information on the crisis in Kuwait, the Gulf War, and the 1993 Accord. Glossary, bibliography, and index. Part of the International Politics and Government series.

Kent, Zachary. *The Persian Gulf War: "The Mother of All Battles."* Illus. Enslow Publishers 1994 (LB 0-89490-528-7) 128pp.

When Saddam Hussein invaded Kuwait in the summer of 1990, there was a quick, decisive response from the world community. The United Nations forces (led by the United States) organized Operation Desert Shield. This book gives historical information about the region and then focuses on the events of this war. Key figures include George Bush, Saddam Hussein, Norman Schwarzkopf, and Colin Powell. Chronology, chapter notes, bibliography, and index. Part of the American War series.

Messenger, Charles. *The Middle East.* Illus. Franklin Watts 1987 (LB 0-531-10539-3)

Students seeking background information on the Gulf region will find this a useful reference. Chapters examine "The Sources of Conflict," "Arab versus Jew," "The Superpowers Step In," and "Holy War." There is information about the founding of Israel, the Six-Day War of 1967, the Yom Kippur War of 1973, the fall of the Shah, the growth of Islamic fundamentalism, and the activities of the Palestine Liberation Organization. There are several appendices, including one giving biographical information on important figures. Chronology and index. Part of the Conflict in the 20th Century series.

Hutchinson, Anne (1591–1643), a religious liberal, came to Boston from England in 1634. Massachusetts Governor John Winthrop banished her for her religious beliefs. She and her family moved first to Rhode Island and later to New York, where most perished in a raid by Native Americans.

Biographies for Younger Readers

Fradin, Dennis B. *Anne Hutchinson: Fighter for Religious Freedom.* Illus. by Tom Dunnington and with prints. Enslow Publishers 1990 (o.p.) 48pp.

This brief biography will be useful to younger students doing research projects. Chapters feature specific aspects of the life of Anne Hutchinson, from her life in England and her journey to America to her religious beliefs, trial, and expulsion from the Puritan Church. List of important dates, glossary, and index. Part of the Colonial Profiles series.

Nichols, Joan K. *A Matter of Conscience: The Trial of Anne Hutchinson.* Illus. by Dan Krovatin. Raintree Steck-Vaughn 1993 (LB 0-8114-7233-7) 101pp.

Anne Hutchinson's beliefs differed from those of the leaders in Massachusetts. There are eight chapters and there are chapter notes, but there is no index, so some students may find it difficult to access specific facts. Many students, however, will appreciate the drama of this presentation, using it as an exciting reading book, not necessarily for research. Part of the Stories of America series.

Biographies for Older Readers

Ilgenfritz, Elizabeth. *Anne Hutchinson.* Illus. Chelsea House 1991 (LB 1-55546-660-5) 112pp.

The life of Anne Hutchinson is presented within the context of the religious, social, and political beliefs of the era. Students are given information about the religious persecution that resulted in Hutchinson's leaving England, the restricted role of women, and the legal system that allowed her to be persecuted and condemned. Excerpts from the transcripts of her trial provide an additional insight into this time period. Chronology, bibliography, and index. Part of the American Women of Achievement series.

Related Books for Younger Readers

Fradin, Dennis B. *The Massachusetts Colony.* Illus. Children's Press 1987 (LB 0-516-00386-0) 144pp.

After a chapter on "Indians and Early Explorers," this book describes the arrival of the Pilgrims, the settlement of the Puritans, and events surrounding the Revolutionary War. There are biographical sketches of such historical figures as Squanto, Anne Bradstreet, Phillis Wheatley, and Paul Revere. Documents include a page from the records of Governor Bradford and a map of Beacon Hill. Colonial America timeline, bibliography, and index. Part of the Thirteen Colonies series.

Related Books for Older Readers

Kamensky, Jane. *The Colonial Mosaic: American Women, 1600–1760.* Illus. Oxford University Press 1995 (LB 0-19-508015-7) 144pp.

During Colonial times, women were responsible for managing the home and family. This involved working in the fields, preparing food for daily use and for storage, and raising children. Beyond their work responsibilities, women were restricted by laws (both political and religious) and social conventions. Women who broke out of their expected roles were usually punished, sometimes put to death. This book looks at women from different backgrounds and ways of life—immigrants, natives, slaves, and colonists. Chronology, bibliography, and index. Part of the Young Oxford History of Women in the United States series.

Wilbur, C. Keith. *Homebuilding and Woodworking in Colonial America.* Illus. by the author. Chelsea House 1992 (LB 0-7910-4529-3); Globe Pequot Press (pap. 1-56440-019-0) 144pp.

This very detailed book describes the tools, materials, techniques, and designs used to build the basic structures that were common in 17th- and 18th-century America. Students will get a sense of what homes were like and what responsibilities were involved in building and running them. Bibliography and index. Part of the Illustrated Living History series.

Ippisch, Hanneke Eikema (1925–),

participated in the Dutch Resistance during World War II. She was arrested and imprisoned. *Sky*, her autobiography, describes her experiences.

Biographies for Older Readers

Ippisch, Hanneke. *Sky: A True Story of Resistance During WWII.* Simon & Schuster 1996 (cloth 0-689-80508-X) 128pp.

This is an incredible book. Anyone who has read Lois Lowry's fictional account of the Danish Resistance, *Number the Stars*, or Anne Frank's diary will want to read this book. Hanneke Eikema was imprisoned for her efforts to help families being persecuted by the Nazis. This is a personal, first-hand account of the horrors of this time and the inspiring courage of certain individuals. It is enhanced by photographs, documents, and letters from the author's collection. List of suggested readings, chapter notes, and index.

Related Books for Older Readers

Greenfeld, Howard. *The Hidden Children.* Illus. Ticknor & Fields 1993 (LB 0-395-66074-2); Houghton Mifflin 1997 (pap. 0-395-86138-1) 128pp.

One of the events in Hanneke Ippisch's *Sky* is an account of her efforts to hide a young Jewish boy named Martin. In *The Hidden Children*, Greenfeld describes the experiences of several children, including quotations from interviews. Many of the memories focus on fear. Like *Sky*, this is an account of personal tragedy and triumph. It is an excellent documentary of the events of the Holocaust and their impact on individuals.

Meltzer, Milton. *Rescue: The Story of How Gentiles Saved Jews in the Holocaust.* Illus. with maps. HarperCollins 1988 (LB 0-06-024210-8) 1991 (pap. 0-06-446117-3) 224pp.

After examining details of the Holocaust, Meltzer presents accounts of compassion and bravery. Countess Maria von Maltzen (known as Marushka) in Berlin, André Trocmé and the villagers of Le Chambon in France, and Oskar Schindler in Poland are among those featured. There are quotations from documents and interviews and an extensive bibliography. Meltzer has written a related book, *Never to Forget: the Jews of the Holocaust* (Harper & Row, 1976, 0-06-024175-6).

Isabella I (1451–1504), queen of Castile, presided over the unification of Spain with her husband, Ferdinand II of Aragon. She also is credited with launching the Spanish colonization of the New World with her sponsorship of Christopher Columbus's voyages.

Biographies for Younger Readers

Burch, Joann J. *Isabella of Castile: Queen on Horseback.* Franklin Watts (LB 0-531-20033-7)

This is an enjoyable book to read, particularly as a springboard to related topics such as the Spanish Inquisition and the voyages of Columbus. Bibliography and index. Part of the First Book series.

Codye, Corinn. *Queen Isabella.* Illus. by Rick Whipple. Raintree Steck-Vaughn 1990 (LB 0-8172-3380-6) (pap. 0-8114-6758-9) 32pp.

Dramatic illustrations and a narrative text give this biography the look of a picture book. The text appears in English and Spanish. Part of the Raintree Hispanic Stories series.

Related Books for Younger Readers

Brenner, Barbara. *If You Were There in 1492.* Illus. Bradbury
Press 1991 (LB 0-02-712321-9) 112pp.

    As the title suggests, this book looks beyond exploration in
1492 and gives a picture of everyday life. Focusing primarily on life
in Spain, chapters feature "Food and Clothing," "Sickness and
Health," "Education," "Arts and Entertainment," and "Crime and
Punishment." Printing, maps, and ships are additional topics and
there are many details about Ferdinand and Isabella. Chapter notes,
bibliography, and index.

Related Books for Older Readers

Pelta, Kathy. *Discovering Christopher Columbus: How History Is
Invented.* Illus. Lerner Publications 1991 (LB 0-8225-4899-2)
96pp.

    Students will be fascinated by this book, which discusses how
history is developed and often revised. The voyages of Columbus,
the support of the Spanish royalty, the stories Columbus told to keep
their support, and the changing views of explorers are examined.
List of sources and index. Part of the How History Is Invented series.

Ishi (1842–1916), the last living Yahi
tribesman, survived a massacre and stumbled into
the town of Oroville, California, in August 1911. He
was sent to the University of California's
anthropology department to be studied.

Biographies for Younger Readers

Jeffredo-Warden, Louise V. *Ishi.* Illus. by Kim Fujiwara. Raintree
Steck-Vaughn 1993 (o.p.) 32pp.

    Students will find this narrative a compelling story. After Ishi's
family was forced into hiding, they remained hidden for more than
30 years. Readers will get a feeling for the strength and dignity of
Ishi and the values of his people. Chronology. Part of the American
Indian Stories series.

Petersen, David. *Ishi: The Last of His People.* Illus. with photographs. Children's Press 1991 (o.p.) 32pp.

This book is not only a look at the life of Ishi, the last member
of the Yahi people; it is also a description of the settlement of the
West and its tragic impact on native peoples. Photographs (some of
artifacts, several of Ishi) and a map add to the presentation. Chronology and index. Part of the Picture-Story Biographies series.

Related Books for Younger Readers

Stein, R. Conrad. *The California Gold Rush.* Illus. Children's
Press 1995 (LB 0-516-06691-9) 32pp.

In 1849, more than 85,000 people came to California in search
of gold and adventure. Their arrival impacted the environment,
economy, native peoples, and development of this state. Timeline,
glossary and index. Part of the Cornerstones of Freedom series.

Related Books for Older Readers

Griffin-Pierce, Trudy. *The Encyclopedia of Native America.* Illus.
Viking Penguin 1994 (pap. 0-670-85104-3) 192pp.

Each chapter features a region of the United States (for example the Plains, the Great Basin, the Northwest Coast, and the
Northeast) and describes the native peoples who have lived there. In
the chapter on California, there is a boxed section on Ishi as well as
one on arts and crafts. The format of this book is attractive with
numerous illustrations and sidebars. Bibliography and index.

Stanley, Jerry. *Digger: The Tragic Fate of the California Indians
from the Missions to the Gold Rush.* Illus. Crown 1997 (LB 0-
517-70951-1) (cloth 0-517-70951-1)

The diseases brought by Spanish explorers and missionaries
and their violent efforts to acquire land destroyed many of the native
peoples of California. Later, the participants in the gold rush ruined
many of the resources and brought further destruction. The book
ends with a chapter on Ishi. Chronology, glossary of California Indian tribal names, bibliographic notes, and index.

Jackson, Andrew (1767–1845), the 7th president of the United States, earned his early fame as a military hero, defeating the British at New Orleans during the War of 1812. He narrowly lost the presidency to John Quincy Adams in 1824 but mounted a successful campaign for the White House in 1828.

Biographies for Younger Readers

Potts, Steve. *Andrew Jackson.* Illus. Bridgestone Books 1996 (cloth 1-56065-455-4) 24pp.

    Younger students doing research will appreciate this book. There are simple chapters focusing on specific events—"Young Lawyer" and "Running for President." The text is just right for beginning readers and includes a few quotations from Andrew Jackson. List of useful addresses and Internet sites, chronology, glossary, bibliography, and index. Part of the Read and Discover Photo-Illustrated Biographies series.

Biographies for Older Readers

Judson, Karen. *Andrew Jackson.* Illus. Enslow Publishers 1997 (LB 0-89490-831-6) 128pp.

    One special feature of this biography is the inclusion of "Source Documents." These include such items as reproductions of letters from Andrew Jackson and excerpts from his speeches. These documents allow students first-hand access to research materials. Chronology, chapter notes, bibliography, Internet sites, and index. Part of the United States Presidents series.

Meltzer, Milton. *Andrew Jackson and His America.* Illus. Franklin Watts 1993 (LB 0-531-11157-1) 144pp.

    Andrew Jackson was a war hero and president. He was also a slave owner who allowed the relocation of Native Americans, often referred to as the Trail of Tears. This book provides a detailed look at Jackson's strengths and weaknesses. It makes excellent use of quotations (which are documented) and the scholarship is thorough. This is a top choice for older students doing research. Index. Part of the Milton Meltzer Biographies series.

Osinski, Alice. *Andrew Jackson.* Illus. Children's Press 1987 (LB 0-516-01387-4) 100pp.

This is a good choice for middle-school students doing research. It is well organized, presenting information in a straightforward manner. The illustrations add to the appeal by including prints, replicas of cartoons and booklets, and photographs. The Chronology of American History highlights Andrew Jackson's years. Index. Part of the Encyclopedia of Presidents series.

Related Books for Younger Readers

Brill, Marlene Targ. *The Trail of Tears: The Cherokee Journey from Home.* Illus. Millbrook Press 1995 (LB 1-56294-486-X) 64pp.

Although Andrew Jackson fought with and against many native peoples, he supported the removal of the Cherokee people from their homeland. Chapters describe the history of broken treaties and promises leading to the tragic march of the Cherokee from the southern states to Oklahoma. Chronology, bibliography (with addresses of Native American organizations), and index. Part of the Spotlight on American History series.

Carter, Alden R. *The War of 1812: Second Fight for Independence.* Illus. Franklin Watts 1992 (LB 0-531-20080-9) 1993 (pap. 0-531-15659-1) 64pp.

Before he was president, Andrew Jackson was a hero in the War of 1812. This book describes the events leading to that war and Jackson's role in the Battle of New Orleans. Bibliography and index. Part of the First Book series.

Related Books for Older Readers

Goldberg, Michael. *Breaking New Ground: American Women, 1800–1848.* Illus. Oxford University Press 1994 (LB 0-19-508202-8) 144pp.

Chapters describe marriage, home life, education, and politics as they relate to women at this time. One chapter describes Andrew Jackson's policy of Indian relocation and the Cherokee Trail of Tears, focusing on the role of Cherokee women. Chronology, bibliography, and index. Part of the Young Oxford History of Women in the United States series.

Marrin, Albert. *1812: The War Nobody Won.* Illus. Atheneum 1985 (cloth 0-689-31075-7) 192pp.

From the burning of Washington, D.C., to the naval battles of the Great Lakes, the writing of "The Star-Spangled Banner," and, finally, to the Battle of New Orleans, this is a thorough and well-written account. Students will appreciate the analysis of the causes of the war as well as the details about specific battles and people. Bibliography and index.

Jackson, Jesse (1941–), an African American minister active in the civil rights movement of the 1960s, went on to found the National Rainbow Coalition in 1980 (an organization devoted to civil rights) and to seek the Democratic presidential nomination in 1984 and in 1988.

Biographies for Younger Readers

Simon, Charnan. *Jesse Jackson: I Am Somebody!* Illus. Children's Press 1997 (LB 0-516-20291-X)

Jesse Jackson has been an advocate of civil rights and community involvement. Here the focus is on his ability to involve people in projects to help themselves and others. A section called "In Your Community" suggests activities for students. Timeline, bibliography (including addresses and Internet sites), and index. Part of the Community Builders series.

Biographies for Older Readers

Haskins, Jim. *I Am Somebody! A Biography of Jesse Jackson.* Illus. Enslow Publishers 1992 (o.p.) 112pp.

This book, like Jesse Jackson's life, spans the era of the civil rights movement and gives insight into the changing attitudes and efforts of this movement. Thorough bibliography and index. Part of the People to Know series.

Jakoubek, Robert. *Jesse Jackson: Civil Rights Leader and Politician.* Illus. Chelsea House 1991 (LB 0-7910-1130-5) 1992 (pap. 0-7910-1155-0) 112pp.

Jakoubek describes the efforts of Jackson and other key figures in the civil rights movement and includes photographs that help students visualize marches, conventions, and political involvement.

This is a good choice for students doing research. Chronology, bibliography, and index. Part of the Black Americans of Achievement series.

Related Books for Younger Readers

Kosof, Anna. *The Civil Rights Movement and Its Legacy.* Illus. Franklin Watts 1989 (o.p.) 112pp.

Kosof presents key moments in civil rights progress—*Brown* v. *Board of Education,* the Montgomery bus boycott, integration in Little Rock, and protest marches. Excerpts from interviews and speeches add to the understanding of this era. Bibliography and index.

Related Books for Older Readers

Dolan, Sean. *Pursuing the Dream: From the Selma-Montgomery March to the Formation of PUSH (1965–1971).* Illus. Chelsea House 1995 (LB 0-7910-2254-4) (pap. 0-7910-2680-9)

The book ends with the economic and educational programs founded by Jesse Jackson. However, before there were economic opportunities, there were marches and demonstrations. African Americans had more opportunities in entertainment and sports than in other areas. Here is a look at the turbulent era of the late 1960s, focusing on the work of Dr. Martin Luther King, Jr., and other civil rights leaders. Bibliography and index. Part of the Milestones in Black American History series.

Hull, Mary. *Struggle and Love, 1972–1997: From the Gary Convention to the Aftermath of the Million Man March.* Illus. Chelsea House 1997 (LB 0-7910-2262-5) 144pp.

Opening with a chronology, this book examines the more-recent events of the civil rights movement, including Jesse Jackson's presidential campaign in 1988. One chapter features the accomplishments of such black artists as Toni Morrison, Oprah Winfrey, and rappers. Another looks at legislation and criminal justice. Bibliography and index. Part of the Milestones in Black American History series.

Jackson, Thomas Jonathan

"Stonewall" (1824–1863), a brilliant general for the Confederacy in the Civil War, led his troops to victory at the first and second battles of Bull Run. He was fatally wounded by his own troops during the battle for Chancellorsville.

Biographies for Older Readers

Bennett, Barbara J. *Stonewall Jackson: Lee's Greatest Lieutenant.* Illus. Silver Burdett 1990 (pap. 0-382-24048-0) 160pp.

Thomas "Stonewall" Jackson's military career began at West Point. He served in the Mexican War before joining the Confederate Army. The text makes fine use of quotations, many from Jackson's men, that show his skill as a leader and the affection he earned. Students will appreciate the many maps showing the progress of the war. Civil War chronology, timeline of Jackson's life, bibliography and index. Part of the History of the Civil War series.

Fritz, Jean. *Stonewall.* Illus. by Stephen Gammell. Putnam's 1979 (cloth 0-399-20698-1); Paperstar 1997 (pap. 0-698-11552-X) 160pp.

This is a wonderful biography. Jackson comes to life as his accomplishments are woven into a dramatic narrative. Students who enjoy reading well-written history will not be disappointed. Bibliography.

Related Books for Older Readers

Ray, Delia. *A Nation Torn: The Story of How the Civil War Began.* Illus. Puffin 1996 (pap. 0-14-038105-8) 128pp.

Before the Civil War, major issues separated the country. Slavery, of course, was the focal point, but there were other social and economic areas of disagreement. Chapters describe "America, North and South," "Bloody Kansas," and "The Guns Roar." Glossary, bibliography, and index.

"Always mystify, mislead, and surprise the enemy. . . . Never fight against heavy odds if by any possible maneuvering you can hurl your own force on only a part, and that the weakest part, of your enemy and crush it."
(*War Between Brothers,* p. 99)

Reger, James P. *The Battle of Antietam.* Illus. Lucent 1997 (LB 1-56006-454-4) 112pp.

The Battle of Antietam remains the bloodiest day in American history, with more than 23,000 killed or wounded. Reger gives an in-depth account of the issues, people, and events of this horrific day. There are many photographs and sidebars that describe related topics such as medical treatment. An appendix provides brief biographical sketches of the commanding officers. Chronology of the battle, glossary, bibliographies, and index. Part of the Battles of the Civil War series.

War Between Brothers. Illus. Time-Life Books 1996 (cloth 0-7835-6251-9) 192pp.

Chapters feature "The Country at War," "Gibraltar of the West," "High-Water Mark of the Confederacy," and "Showdown." Within each chapter are essays that provide more personal insights, such as one on "The Soldier's Life." The account of the Battle at Chancellorsville (and the death of Stonewall Jackson) is particularly vivid with maps, vignettes, photographs, and quotations. This is an extremely well documented book that will be an excellent choice for research projects. Chronology, bibliography, and index. Part of the American Story series.

Jefferson, Thomas (1743–1826), the 3rd president of the United States, earlier served as secretary of state under George Washington and vice president under John Adams. During his presidency, he accomplished the Louisiana Purchase and launched the Lewis and Clark expedition.

Biographies for Younger Readers

Adler, David A. *Thomas Jefferson: Father of Our Democracy.* Illus. by Jacqueline Garrick. Holiday House 1987 (o.p.) 48pp.

Opening with a list of important dates, this book takes Thomas Jefferson from his birth in Virginia to his years as "The Sage of Monticello." The eight chapters are well organized and would meet the needs of beginning researchers. Index. Part of the First Biographies series. David A. Adler's *A Picture Book of Thomas Jefferson* (Holiday House 1990, 0-8234-0791-8) would be a good introduction to students, who could then move on to this book.

Giblin, James Cross. ***Thomas Jefferson: A Picture Book Biography.*** Illus. by Michael Dooling. Scholastic 1994 (cloth 0-590-44838-2) 48pp.

This is a wonderful introduction to a fascinating man. Giblin captures the contrasts in Jefferson's personality as he describes his love of books, his interest in art and architecture, and the leadership role he took in the formation of the United States. Following the text, there are selections from "The Words of Thomas Jefferson." Timeline, information about "A Visit to Monticello," and index.

Greene, Carol. ***Thomas Jefferson: Author, Inventor, President.*** Illus. Children's Press 1991 (LB 0-516-04224-6) (pap. 0-516-44224-4) 48pp.

A brief biography, with a simple text suitable for beginning readers. The illustrations add information and interest, particularly with the reproductions of Jefferson's writings and inventions. Timeline and index. Part of the Rookie Biographies series.

Morris, Jeffrey. ***The Jefferson Way.*** Illus. Lerner Publications 1994 (LB 0-8225-2926-2) 112pp.

The format encourages readers to look at presidential decisions. After several chapters of background information, the text covers the Louisiana Purchase, exploration, the trial of Aaron Burr, and an embargo against Great Britain. Illustrations and sidebars add information. This is an interesting way to contemplate the decision-making process and could be used by younger and older readers. Part of the Great Presidential Decisions series.

Biographies for Older Readers

Komroff, Manuel. ***Thomas Jefferson.*** Illus. Marshall Cavendish 1991 (o.p.) 160pp.

From "Childhood" to "Penman of Democracy" to "Secretary of State," "Vice-President," and "President," this book focuses on distinct career activities in the life of Thomas Jefferson. Bibliography and index. Part of the American Cavalcade series.

Meltzer, Milton. ***Thomas Jefferson: The Revolutionary Aristocrat.*** Illus. Franklin Watts 1991 (LB 0-531-11069-9) 160pp.

This is a remarkable biography—detailed and readable. Meltzer captures the contrasts of Thomas Jefferson as a politician who sometimes used his power for personal agendas and as a slave-owner who spoke against slavery. Jefferson also influenced architecture, science, and education. Notes on sources and index. Part of the Non-Fiction series.

Related Books for Younger Readers

Egger-Bovet, Howard, and Marlene Smith-Baranzini. *Book of the American Revolution.* Illus. by Bill Sanchez. Little, Brown 1994 (cloth 0-316-96922-2)

History is combined with activities—for example, there are several games (such as British Spy board game) and a project to design a flag. Brief chapters feature such topics as "I Have Rights," "Spy Stories," and "Pirates for Hire." This is an entertaining book that could be used by students or for classroom activities. Part of the USKids History series.

Richards, Norman. *Monticello.* Illus. Children's Press 1995 (LB 0-516-06695-1) 32pp.

After a brief description of Jefferson's early life, this book focuses on the design and construction of his home on the land he inherited from his father. Wonderful color photographs show Monticello, both inside and out, and provide an insight into Jefferson's life away from his political service. Part of the Cornerstones of Freedom series.

Schleifer, Jay. *Our Declaration of Independence.* Illus. Millbrook Press 1992 (LB 1-56294-205-0) (pap. 1-56294-814-8) 48pp.

This entertaining book provides a brief history of the events leading to the Revolutionary War and the writing of the Declaration of Independence. Boxed sidebars add details, such as a glossary of terms in the Declaration, a timeline of what led to the writing, and a discussion of the signers. There is even a humorous dialogue between John Adams and Thomas Jefferson about who should do the actual writing. The text of the Declaration of Independence is included. Bibliography and index. Part of the I Know America series.

Related Books for Older Readers

Jaffe, Steve H. *Who Were the Founding Fathers? Two Hundred Years of Reinventing American History.* Illus. Henry Holt 1996 (cloth 0-8050-3102-2) 160pp.

In answering the title question, the author suggests that, depending on your point of view and your time in history, the founding fathers were traitors, hypocrites, or patriots. This book examines a variety of views of history, showing how it is reshaped to meet different political and social needs. This is a challenging, informative, and thought-provoking look at history and how it is presented. Source notes, bibliography and index. Part of the American History series.

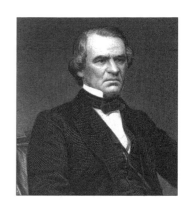

Johnson, Andrew (1808–1875), the 17th president of the United States, succeeded to the presidency after the assassination of Abraham Lincoln, facing one of the most difficult eras in our country's history—rebuilding after the Civil War. He faced impeachment, but was acquitted.

Biographies for Older Readers

Dubowski, Cathy E. *Andrew Johnson: Rebuilding the Union.* Illus. Silver Burdett 1991 (LB 0-382-09945-1) 160pp.

Quotations, maps, and illustrations add to the information about our 17th president, who rose from poverty to a career in politics. Civil War timeline, chronology for Andrew Johnson, bibliography, and index. Part of the History of the Civil War series.

Kent, Zachary. *Andrew Johnson.* Illus. Children's Press 1989 (LB 0-516-01363-7) 100pp.

Students will appreciate this clear, straightforward presentation. The chapters are organized chronologically with numerous illustrations to enhance the text. During his administration, Johnson was criticized for using his veto power, battling with Congress on the enactment of new bills. The result was an impeachment trial, at which Johnson was acquitted. Chronology of American History and index. Part of the Encyclopedia of Presidents series.

Stevens, Rita. *Andrew Johnson: 17th President of the United States.* Illus. Garrett Educational 1989 (LB 0-944483-16-X)

Opening with a chronology, this book then describes the man who became president following the assassination of Abraham Lincoln. Andrew Johnson was a career politician, serving as local alderman and mayor, member of the House of Representatives, governor of Tennessee, senator, vice president, and president. Boxed sidebars focus on related issues—"The Know-Nothing Party" and

"The Polar Bear Garden"—a reference to the purchase of Alaska. Bibliography and index. Part of the Presidents of the United States series.

Related Books for Younger Readers

Cohen, Daniel. *The Alaska Purchase.* Illus. Millbrook Press 1996 (LB 1-56294-528-9) 64pp.

At a price of $7.2 million, the Alaska Purchase was still less than two cents per acre. This book explains the political and economic impact of this land deal. It is a good introduction for students. Chronology, list of further readings, bibliography, and index. Part of the Spotlight on American History series.

Related Books for Older Readers

Gold, Susan Dudley. *Land Pacts.* Illus. Twenty-First Century Books 1997 (LB 0-8050-4810-3) 128pp.

After describing the process of making and ratifying treaties, three chapters describe "The Louisiana Purchase," "Spanish and Mexican Treaties," and the "Alaska Purchase." Students will appreciate the illustrations, which include maps of the areas discussed and photographs, drawings, and cartoons. Source notes, bibliography, and index. Part of the Pacts and Treaties series.

Hakim, Joy. *Reconstruction and Reform.* Illus. Oxford University Press 1994 (LB 0-19-507757-1) (cloth 0-19-509512-X) (pap. 0-19-507758-X) 160pp.

After the Civil War, there was great devastation but also great expansion and accomplishment. The opening chapters of this book look at the many issues faced by Andrew Johnson, including impeachment. Other chapters examine westward exploration and settlement, the experiences of native peoples, immigration, and the ongoing difficulties faced by African Americans. A period of about 30 years is covered. Students will be fascinated by the many events that are presented. Chronology, bibliography, and index. Part of the History of US series.

Johnson, Isaac

ohnson, Isaac (1844–1905), described his life as a slave in a privately published book, *Slavery Days in Old Kentucky* (1904). After the Civil War Johnson worked as a stonecutter in Canada, where his work can still be seen.

Biographies for Younger Readers

Marston, Hope. *Isaac Johnson: From Slave to Stonecutter.* Illus. by Maria Magdalena Brown. Cobblehill Books 1995 (pap. 0-525-65165-9)

Based on Isaac Johnson's own account in *Slavery Days in Old Kentucky,* this book is a personal story of the cruelty and inhumanity experienced by many slaves. Isaac Johnson was sold into slavery by his own father (a white man who fathered several children by Isaac's mother, a slave). After one attempt to run away, Johnson was beaten and saw others being tortured and killed. Later, he did escape and served in the Union Army. After the war, he settled in Canada, working as a stonecutter and mason. This is fascinating reading and will encourage students to look for more information about slavery, the Civil War, and Reconstruction. Chronology, bibliography, and index.

Related Books for Younger Readers

Evitts, William J. *Captive Bodies, Free Spirits: The Story of Southern Slavery.* Illus. Julian Messner 1985 (o.p.) 160pp.

Many of the historical accounts of slavery given here are based on personal experiences and memoirs. From "The Man in the Box," in which Henry Brown endures being shipped in a box from the South to the North, to "A Contest of Wills," which describes violent encounters between slaves and patrols, this is a realistic account of a cruel, tragic time. Bibliography and index.

Related Books for Older Readers

Macht, Norman L., and Mary Hull. *The History of Slavery.* Illus. Lucent 1997 (LB 1-56006-302-5)

How did people come to be enslaved? Often, slaves were taken as captives from wars. In Europe and America, slave trading was an economic venture that later divided America, leading to the Civil War. There are many illustrations that show slavery around the world and sidebars present such issues as "A Greek View of Slavery" and Slave Markets in Zanzibar." List of suggested readings, chapter notes, annotated bibliography, and index. Part of the World History series.

Myers, Walter Dean. *Amistad: A Long Road to Freedom.* Illus. Dutton 1998 (cloth 0-525-45970-7)

On board the *Amistad* were Africans who had been kidnapped. In their homelands, they were leaders and members of families. This is a dramatic account of the efforts of these prisoners to be returned to their homes. John Quincy Adams served on the defense team, which focused on the concept that the Africans had never been slaves and were, therefore, free. Like the biography of Isaac Johnson, this book emphasizes the efforts to escape injustice.

Johnson, James Weldon (1871–1938), an African American attorney, writer, and social activist, in 1897 was the first black to be admitted to the Florida bar. He is the author of "Lift Every Voice and Sing."

Biographies for Younger Readers

McKissack, Patricia, and Fredrick McKissack. *James Weldon Johnson: "Lift Every Voice and Sing."* Illus. Children's Press 1990 (o.p.) 32pp.

Best known for writing the song called "The Negro National Anthem," James Weldon Johnson was also an educator and a lawyer. He was executive secretary of the NAACP and served as U.S. consul to Venezuela and Nicaragua. Timeline and index. Part of the Picture-Story Biographies series.

Biographies for Older Readers

Tolbert-Rouchaleau, Jane. *James Weldon Johnson.* Illus. Chelsea House 1988 (LB 1-55546-596-X) (pap. 0-7910-0211-X) 112pp.

This thorough presentation is a good choice for students doing research. The opening chapter analyzes the impact of "Lift Every Voice and Sing," while later chapters look at Johnson's education, his diplomatic service, and his years with the NAACP. Throughout his life, Johnson influenced the arts, politics, and social issues. Chronology, bibliography, and index. Part of the Black Americans of Achievement series.

Related Books for Younger Readers

Silverman, Jerry. *Just Listen to This Song I'm Singing: African American History Through Song.* Illus. Millbrook Press 1996 (LB 1-56294-673-0) 96pp.

Music has played an important part in the lives of African Americans. During the time of slavery, songs often served as a means of communicating messages and escape routes. Introductory remarks link each song to history. Among those included are "Go Down, Moses," "Follow the Drinking Gourd," "John Henry," and "We Shall Overcome."

Related Books for Older Readers

Haskins, Jim. *The Harlem Renaissance.* Illus. Millbrook Press 1996 (LB 1-56294-565-3) 192pp.

In the early 1900s, many Southern blacks migrated to the North, settling in urban localities. This Great Migration is considered one of the key factors in the beginning of the Harlem Renaissance, a growth in attention to the creative and artistic talents of African Americans. Chapters in this book look at the developments in "Music, Dance, and Musical Theater," "Poetry and Fiction," and "Painters and Sculptors." Source notes, bibliography, and index.

Johnson, Lyndon Baines (1908–1973),

vice president under John F. Kennedy, became the 36th president after Kennedy was assassinated in Dallas in 1963 and won the presidential election of 1964. Facing mounting criticism over his handling of the Vietnam War, he chose not to run for reelection in 1968.

Biographies for Older Readers

Eskow, Dennis. *Lyndon Baines Johnson.* Illus. Franklin Watts 1993 (LB 0-531-13019-3) 112pp.

The focus is on LBJ's strength as a "deal-maker" who succeeded in advancing a strong domestic agenda, yet was politically unable to cope with the issues of the Vietnam War. The text makes good use of quotations to provide insights into personalities and events. Source notes, annotated bibliography, and index. Part of the Impact Biographies series.

Falkof, Lucille. *Lyndon B. Johnson: 36th President of the United States.* Illus. Garrett Educational 1989 (LB 0-944483-20-8)

Chapters include the "Hill Country Boy," "The Whiz Kid of Congress," "The Great Society," "Vietnam," and "The Road Home." Students doing research will find this useful. Chronology, bibliography, and index. Part of the Presidents of the United States series.

Hargrove, Jim. *Lyndon B. Johnson.* Illus. Children's Press 1987 (LB 0-516-01396-3) 100pp.

Beginning with "Three Tragic Hours in Dallas," this book examines the political career of Lyndon Baines Johnson. He capitalized on his wealth and strength in Texas and developed a strong political base in Washington, D.C. This is a solid presentation that will be useful for student reports. It includes a chronology of American history that highlights Johnson's life within the context of other events. Index. Part of the Encyclopedia of Presidents series.

Related Books for Younger Readers

Brown, Gene. *The Nation in Turmoil: Civil Rights and the Vietnam War (1960–1973).* Illus. Twenty-First Century Books 1994 (LB 0-8050-2588-X) 64pp.

Excerpts from primary documents teach students about key figures and issues of this era. The civil rights movement is shown in part of Dr. Martin Luther King, Jr.'s "Letter from a Birmingham Jail" and an excerpt from *The Autobiography of Malcolm X.* Lyndon Baines Johnson writes about the Vietnam War. Chapters focus on the Great Society, the counterculture, and Watergate. Timeline, bibliography, and index. Part of the First Person America series.

Foster, Leila M. *The Story of the Great Society.* Illus. Children's Press 1991 (pap. 0-516-44755-6) 32pp.

Johnson's "Great Society" was designed to extend the federal government's impact in such areas as civil rights, health care, education, and community action. This brief book will be a useful overview for students. Index. Part of the Cornerstones of Freedom series.

Related Books for Older Readers

Bullard, Sara. *Free at Last: A History of the Civil Rights Movement and Those Who Died in the Struggle.* Illus. Oxford University Press 1993 (LB 0-19-508381-4) 1994 (pap. 0-19-509450-6) 112pp.

From "Early Struggles" to "Days of Rage" this book looks at the civil rights movement. Boycotts, freedom riders, marches, voting rights, and riots were a part of this era, as were the deaths of many leaders, workers, and even children. A section profiles "Forty People Who Gave Their Lives," ending with the death of Dr. Martin Luther King, Jr. Timeline, bibliography, and index.

Marrin, Albert. *America and Vietnam: The Elephant and the Tiger.* Illus. Viking Penguin 1992 (pap. 0-670-84063-7) 256pp.

High school students doing research on the history of the Vietnam War and its impact on politics and social change will want to use this comprehensive book. There is information about the roots of the conflict in Vietnam, the impact on political leaders in America (including Kennedy, Johnson, and Nixon), and the growth of the anti-war movement. Bibliography and index.

Wilson, Anna. *African Americans Struggle for Equality.* Illus. Rourke 1992 (LB 0-86593-184-4) 112pp.

Many important events of the civil rights movement occurred during the presidency of Lyndon Johnson, including the Civil Rights Act of 1964, the assassinations of Malcolm X and Dr. Martin Luther King, Jr., and the selection of Thurgood Marshall for the Supreme Court. This book examines education, employment, government, and law enforcement, focusing on the experiences of African Americans. Timeline, lists of addresses of related organizations and media resources, bibliography, and index. Part of the Discrimination series.

Jones, Mary Harris "Mother"

(1830–1930), an American labor leader born in Ireland, worked for the Knights of Labor as an organizer and later became active with the United Mine Workers. At age 89 she was jailed after she took part in a major steel walkout.

Biographies for Younger Readers

Colman, Penny. *Mother Jones and the March of the Mill Children.* Illus. Millbrook Press 1994 (LB 1-56294-402-9) 48pp.

This brief presentation focuses on one main event for union activist Mother Jones. She called herself a "hell-raiser," and in 1903 she led a march to bring the plight of children working in mills to the attention of President Theodore Roosevelt and the citizens of America. Chronology, bibliography, and index.

Biographies for Older Readers

Horton, Madelyn. *The Importance of Mother Jones.* Illus. Lucent 1996 (LB 1-56006-057-3) 112pp.

The descriptions of Mother Jones's activities as an advocate for the rights of workers, women, and children are enhanced by sidebars featuring writings by and about her. Many of the boxed sections include excerpts from her autobiography. This biography provides students with a variety of information and sources. Chronology, chapter notes, annotated bibliographies (one for further readings, one for works consulted), and index. Part of the Importance Of series.

Josephson, Judith Pinkerton. *Mother Jones: Fierce Fighter for Worker's Rights.* Illus. Lerner Publications 1997 (LB 0-8225-4924-7) 144pp.

Mary Harris Jones, a.k.a. "Mother" Jones, had a life filled with tragedy. Her sympathy for workers began in her childhood (her father was part of the Irish resistance and her grandfather had been hanged) and continued in her early adulthood (her husband was an ironworker and a union official). After her husband and children died in a yellow fever epidemic, Jones devoted her energies to helping workers. This is a very readable book that uses many quotations (referenced in source notes). Bibliography and index.

Kraft, Betsy Harvey. *Mother Jones: One Woman's Fight for Labor.* Illus. Clarion 1995 (cloth 0-395-67163-9)

This well-organized book will meet the needs of younger and older students, although the topic is more likely to be studied by students in junior high and high school. Elegantly produced with clear text and excellent illustrations, it includes archival photographs of newspaper accounts, documents, and illustrations. For example, there is a photograph of a company worksheet that shows a worker owing the company instead of being paid. The combination of well-written text and visual support materials will appeal to students. Notes, additional resources, and index.

Related Books for Younger Readers

Colman, Penny. *Strike! The Bitter Struggle of American Workers from Colonial Times to the Present.* Illus. Millbrook Press 1995 (LB 1-56294-459-2) 80pp.

This book will provide students with background information on American labor. Chapters describe the harsh working conditions in mines, textile mills, and factories. Labor organizers provided leadership for workers demanding better conditions. Chronology, list of sources (including addresses of labor organizations), and index.

Related Books for Older Readers

Flagler, John J. *The Labor Movement in the United States.* Illus. Lerner Publications 1990 (o.p.) 96pp.

Workers throughout history have organized to seek improved working hours and conditions along with better pay. Flagler describes the development of unions and collective bargaining in America. Chapters look at child labor, immigration, industrialization, and the role of labor during World War II and after. Glossary and index. Part of the Economics for Today series.

Greene, Laura Ofenhartz. *Child Labor: Then and Now.* Illus. Franklin Watts 1992 (o.p.)

The problem of child labor still exists and students doing research will find this an excellent selection for both a historical perspective and a look at current efforts. It is a very thorough book with detailed documentation of quotations and statistics. The bibliography includes books, articles, government documents, and congressional testimony. Index. Part of the Impact Book series.

Jordan, Barbara Charline (1936–1996),

an African American lawyer and public official, is perhaps best known as a member of the House Judiciary Committee that investigated the Watergate scandal in 1974. She was the first African American woman from a southern state to serve in Congress.

Barbara Jordan received the Presidential Medal of Freedom in 1994. In an interview before the ceremony, she said, "I have spent my career protecting the constitutional and civil rights of Americans. If I were in public office today, my primary task would be one of educating, communication, and pulling in those people who feel so left out."
(Jeffrey, pp. 90–91)

Biographies for Younger Readers

Roberts, Naurice. *Barbara Jordan: The Great Lady from Texas.* Illus. Children's Press 1990 (o.p.) 32pp.

This biography would be a good introduction to Barbara Jordan and the civil rights movement. Segregation, racism, and political upheaval are woven into the experiences of Jordan. Students would need a more recent book to learn about Jordan's later accomplishments and her death. Index. Part of the Picture-Story Biographies series.

Biographies for Older Readers

Blue, Rose, and Corinne J. Naden. *Barbara Jordan: Politician.* Illus. Chelsea House 1992 (LB 1-7910-1131-3) 112pp.

The first chapter reviews key accomplishments of Barbara Jordan, including her tenure on the House Judiciary Committee during the Watergate investigation. Subsequent chapters describe her early life, education, and rise to political success. Quotations and photographs with informative captions add to the presentation. Chronology, bibliography, and index. Part of the Black Americans of Achievement series.

Jeffrey, Laura S. *Barbara Jordan: Congresswoman, Lawyer, Educator.* Illus. Enslow Publishers 1997 (LB 0-89490-692-5) 112pp.

Barbara Jordan, who died in 1996, was a ground-breaker in the civil rights movement. She served as a state senator in Texas and then as a member of the U.S. House of Representatives. This is an accessible book for students doing research. The chapters cover major events and quotations are documented in chapter notes. Chronology, bibliography, and index. Part of the African American Biographies series.

Related Books for Older Readers

Kelley, Robin D. G. *Into the Fire: African Americans Since 1970.* Illus. Oxford University Press 1996 (LB 0-19-508701-1) 144pp.

One chapter, "It's Nation Time! From Black Feminism to Black Caucus," examines the growing political power among blacks, citing the elections of Carl Stokes, Shirley Chisholm, and Barbara Jordan. Other chapters look at urban poverty, the black middle class, and the ongoing efforts of African Americans to be represented and recognized. Chronology, bibliography, and index. Part of the Young Oxford History of African Americans series.

Morin, Isobel V. *Women of the U.S. Congress.* Illus. Oliver Press 1994 (LB 1-881508-12-9) 160pp.

    From Jeannette Rankin, the first woman elected to the U.S. Congress, through Dianne Feinstein, Patty Murray, and Carol Moseley Braun, who were elected in 1993, this book profiles the accomplishments of 11 women. Margaret Chase Smith, Shirley Chisholm, Barbara Jordan, and Nancy Landon Kassebaum are also included. List of women who served in the U.S. Congress, bibliography, and index. Part of the Profiles series.

Joseph, Chief (1840?–1904), chief of a band of Nez Perce, a Native American tribe, led several hundred of his people on a 1,000-mile trek to Canada when fighting broke out over a land cession treaty obtained fraudulently by the United States. They were forced to surrender 30 miles short of the border.

Biographies for Younger Readers

Taylor, Marian W. *Chief Joseph: Nez Perce Leader.* Illus. Chelsea House 1995 (LB 0-7910-1708-7) 112pp.

    Chapters include "Joseph's World," "The War Begins," and "I Will Fight No More Forever." Chief Joseph led his people against the American army and government; he even met with several presidents to plead the cause of his people. Chronology, bibliography, and index. Part of the North American Indians of Achievement series.

Biographies for Older Readers

Fox, Mary Virginia. *Chief Joseph of the Nez Perce Indians: Champion of Liberty.* Illus. Children's Press 1992 (LB 0-516-03275-5) 152pp.

    Chief Joseph tried to prevent violence against his people as white settlers moved onto their lands. After reading this book, students will have a better understanding of the injustices suffered by the native peoples. The thorough timeline features events in the life of Chief Joseph as well as other historical activities of his era. Index. Part of the People of Distinction series.

Warburton, Lois. *The Importance of Chief Joseph.* Illus. Lucent 1992 (LB 1-56006-030-1) 112pp.

The format of this book will meet the needs of students with varying levels of research skills. The text provides basic information about Chief Joseph, leader of the Nez Perce during the era of relocation of native peoples. Quotations and commentaries are woven into the text. Additional insights are presented in boxed sidebars and include newspaper accounts, interviews, and excerpts from other researchers. Chronology, chapter notes, annotated bibliographies, and index. Part of the Importance Of series.

Related Books for Younger Readers

Sneve, Virginia Driving Hawk. *The Nez Perce.* Illus. by Ronald Himler. Holiday House 1994 (LB 0-8234-1090-0) 32pp.

Opening with a creation myth of the Nez Perce, this book describes the customs and everyday activities of these people of the Northwest. The arrival of settlers brought diseases and relocation. The picture-book format will be useful to younger readers, as will the topic divisions, each of which is introduced by a brief quotation. Index. Part of the First Americans series.

Related Books for Older Readers

Freedman, Russell. *Indian Chiefs.* Illus. with photographs by the author. Holiday House 1987 (LB 0-8234-0625-3) 1992 (pap. 0-8234-0971-6) 160pp.

From the haunting photograph of Chief Joseph on the cover to the reproductions of paintings and prints, this book examines the arrival of pioneers in the West and the impact on the native peoples. Six chiefs are profiled: Red Cloud, Satanta, Quanah Parker, Washakie, Joseph, and Sitting Bull. Reading this book will give students insight into the issues related to expansion. Bibliography and index.

Gold, Susan Dudley. *Indian Treaties.* Illus. Twenty-First Century Books 1997 (LB 0-8050-4813-8) 128pp.

In the introduction, "You Cannot Sell a Country," the author describes some of the injustices that have evolved from broken treaties with native peoples. Chapters look at "Land Grabs and Rebellions," "Frontier Treaties," and "Removal West." One vignette describes the movement of the Nez Perce people from their lands in the northwest United States to a reservation in eastern Kansas, an area whose climate and conditions were totally unfamiliar to them.

Students will find that this book provides critical details about the history of the treaties with native peoples. Source notes, bibliography, and index. Part of the Pacts and Treaties series.

Trafzer, Clifford E. *The Nez Perce.* Chelsea House 1992 (cloth 1-55546-720-2) 1994 (pap. 0-7910-0391-4)

Chapters describe "Meeting the Explorers," "The Walla Walla Council," "Good-bye to the Home Land," and "The Nez Perce War." The book is well organized, and there is a color "Picture Essay" that documents many artifacts from the Nez Perce. Glossary, bibliography, and index. Part of the Indians of North America series.

Keller, Helen Adams (1880–1968), blind and deaf from the age of two, managed to overcome her disabilities with the help of teacher Anne Sullivan and graduated in 1904 from Radcliffe College with honors. She lectured and wrote extensively in her later years.

"The world I see with my fingers is alive, ruddy, and satisfying. Touch brings the blind many sweet certainties which our more fortunate fellows miss, because their sense of touch is uncultivated. When they look at things, they put their hands in their pockets."
(Wepman, p. 42)

Biographies for Younger Readers

Adler, David A. *A Picture Book of Helen Keller.* Illus. by John Wallner and Alexandra Wallner. Holiday House 1990 (LB 0-8234-0818-3) 1992 (pap. 0-8234-0950-3) 32pp.

Younger students will find this picture-book presentation just right for them. It could even be used as a read-aloud to introduce Keller. List of important dates. Part of the Picture Book Of series.

Markham, Lois. *Helen Keller.* Illus. Franklin Watts 1993 (LB 0-531-20104-X) 64pp.

This is a well-organized biography for students doing research. Chapters describe Keller's life "At Home," "Into the World," "Earning a Living," and Making a Life." Many photographs add to the presentation. Bibliography and index. Part of the First Books series.

Biographies for Older Readers

Peare, Catherine Owens. *Helen Keller Story.* Illus. HarperCollins 1990 (o.p.) 192pp.

One of the classic tellings of Helen Keller's story, this book is old but not outdated. Her great intelligence and her willingness to use her handicaps to aid others are related. Keller got to know many famous personalities of the time, including Alexander Graham Bell, Eleanor Roosevelt, and Jane Addams. Illustration of the sign language alphabet and index.

Wepman, Dennis. *Helen Keller.* Illus. Chelsea House 1987 (LB 1-55546-662-1)

This detailed book is a great choice for research. Two special sections feature Keller's own words, including a poem "A Chant of Darkness." There are excellent photographs, many showing Keller with famous people such as Eleanor Roosevelt, Winston Churchill, Mark Twain, and Alexander Graham Bell. Chronology, bibliography, and index. Part of the American Women of Achievement series.

Related Books for Older Readers

Mango, Karin N. *Hearing Loss.* Illus. Franklin Watts 1991 (LB 0-531-12519-X) 112pp.

Students studying Helen Keller will want to explore her two handicaps—blindness and deafness. Here is a discussion of different types of hearing loss, and how the hearing-impaired cope in the everyday world, alternative methods of communication, and the use of hearing ear dogs. List of organizations for the hearing impaired, bibliography, and index. Part of the Venture Book series.

Nardo, Don. *The Physically Challenged.* Illus. Chelsea House 1994 (cloth 0-7910-0073-7)

Nardo covers the challenges that disabled people face on a daily basis and how they cope, both physically and psychologically. Therapy, sports and games, and the struggle for legal rights are also addressed. Keller is one of many people with disabilities used as inspiring examples throughout the book. An appendix lists aids available for people with disabilities. Lists of company addresses and organizations and further readings, glossary, and index. Part of the Encyclopedia of Health, Medical Disorders and Their Treatment series.

Walker, Lou Ann. *Hand, Heart, and Mind: The Story of the Education of America's Deaf People.* Illus. Dial 1994 (pap. 0-8037-1225-1)

What a great source of historical information! The first chapter looks at the education and treatment of deaf people from ancient times through the Middle Ages. "The Duel Between Words and Signs" and "Mainstreaming or Residential School?" are presented along with information about educational opportunities including Gallaudet University. List of "Twentieth-Century Deaf People of Achievement," bibliography, and index.

Kennedy, John Fitzgerald

(1917–1963), the 35th president of the United States (1961–1963), established the Peace Corps in 1961 and successfully faced down the Soviet Union during the 1962 Cuban missile crisis. He was assassinated in Dallas in November 1963.

Biographies for Younger Readers

Adler, David A. *A Picture Book of John F. Kennedy.* Illus. by Robert Casilla. Holiday House 1991 (LB 0-8234-0884-1) 1992 (pap. 0-8234-0976-7) 32pp.

Younger readers will find this a good introduction to the life of John F. Kennedy. Information about his childhood, family, political career, and death are presented. List of important dates. Part of the Picture Book Of series.

Potts, Steve. *John F. Kennedy: A Photo-Illustrated Biography.* Illus. Bridgestone Books 1996 (cloth 1-56065-454-6) 24pp.

Here is a well-constructed beginning research book. Each set of facing pages includes a full picture on one side and text on the other, with a one-line description of the facing picture. School years, the presidency, the Soviet Union, and the assassination are covered. At the end of the book are "Words from John F. Kennedy," "Important Dates," "Words to Know," "Read More," and "Useful Addresses and Internet Sites." Words in bold-faced type in the text are defined in the "Words to Know" section. Index.

(To a high-school student who asked how he became a war hero):
"It was absolutely involuntary. They sank my boat."
(Randall, p. 13)

"Now he is a legend
when he would
have preferred to
be a man."
—Jacqueline Kennedy,
former first lady, on
her husband, John F.
Kennedy, 1964
(Randall, p. 29)

Biographies for Older Readers

Harrison, Barbara G., and Daniel Terris. *A Twilight Struggle: The Life of John Fitzgerald Kennedy.* Illus. Lothrop, Lee & Shepard 1992 (cloth 0-688-08830-9) 224pp.

Opening with Robert Frost's poem "Birches," and including many photographs, this is an elegant biography. Students will want to use this book for research and enjoyment. The authors strive to present the complexity of Kennedy, looking at both his strengths and weaknesses. Chronology, source notes, bibliography, and index.

Kent, Zachary. *John F. Kennedy: Thirty-Fifth President of the United States.* Illus. Children's Press 1987 (LB 0-516-01390-4) 100pp.

This is a very readable book with lots of black-and-white photographs. Kennedy's early years, his war years, political events such as the Cuban missile crisis and the civil rights movement, and the Kennedy assassination are all included. The chronology is one of American history, not just of Kennedy's life. Events that took place during Kennedy's lifetime are shaded. This would be especially helpful when trying to tie in world events with his life. Index. Part of the Encyclopedia of Presidents series.

Randall, Marta. *John F. Kennedy.* Illus. Chelsea House 1988 (LB 0-87754-586-3) (pap. 0-7910-0580-1) 112pp.

The text covers Kennedy's life and political career, with such topics as the Bay of Pigs, Cuban missile crisis, Berlin and the Soviet Union, and his assassination. Chronology, list of further readings, and index. Part of the World Leaders Past & Present series.

Related Books for Older Readers

Hakim, Joy. *All the People.* Illus. Oxford University Press 1995 (LB 0-19-507763-6) (cloth 0-19-509515-4) (pap. 0-19-507764-4) 160pp.

This is a wonderful book to browse through, full of historical figures and entertaining slices of information. It covers, among other things, Kennedy's charisma, the Bay of Pigs, his role in the civil rights movement, and the Cuban missile crisis. Chronology and index. Part of the History of US series.

McKissack, Patricia, and Fredrick McKissack. *The Civil Rights Movement in America: From 1865 to the Present.* 2nd ed. Illus. Children's Press 1991 (LB 0-516-00579-0) 352pp.

The text relates the struggle of African Americans to obtain civil rights. Kennedy's presidency is well documented as having one of the strongest positions on civil rights of any 20th-century president. Bibliography and index.

Patterson, Charles. *The Civil Rights Movement.* Illus. Facts on File 1995 (cloth 0-8160-2968-7) 144pp.

Starting with the background of the legacy of slavery, the text covers many aspects of the civil rights movement: school desegregation court cases, the freedom riders, and more. Kennedy's role and reactions to different issues such as civil rights legislation, protection for the freedom riders, and misgivings about the March on Washington are discussed. Chronology, list of further readings, and index. Part of the Social Reform Movements series.

Key, Francis Scott (1779–1843), an American lawyer, wrote a poem inspired by an 1814 attack on Baltimore's Fort McHenry that he witnessed. The words of the poem later were set to the melody of an 18th-century drinking song and named "The Star-Spangled Banner," adopted in 1931 as the U.S. national anthem.

Biographies for Younger Readers

Kent, Deborah. *The Star-Spangled Banner.* Illus. Children's Press 1995 (LB 0-516-06630-7) 32pp.

This is an entertaining account of Key's part in the battle that led to the writing of "The Star-Spangled Banner," and what happened to the poem afterward. It includes the full text of the song. Timeline, glossary, and index. Part of the Cornerstones of Freedom series.

Whitcraft, Melissa. *Francis Scott Key.* Illus. Franklin Watts 1994 (LB 0-531-20163-5) 64pp.

This beginning research book covers Key's early life and education, his working years, the writing of "The Star-Spangled Banner," and his efforts as a lawyer to fight slavery. The complete text of "The Star-Spangled Banner" and a photograph of the flag that inspired him (which now hangs in the Smithsonian) are included. List of further readings and index. Part of the First Book series.

Related Books for Younger Readers

Cohn, Amy, sel. *From Sea to Shining Sea: A Treasury of American Folklore and Folk Songs.* Illus. Scholastic 1993 (cloth 0-590-42868-3) 416pp.

This is a beautiful book illustrated by Caldecott Award-winning artists. It is a compilation of more than 140 folk songs, poems, and stories about America's history and its multicultural society. Students studying Key will enjoy the section on the Revolution with information on Yankee Doodle, Paul Revere's Ride, and Concord Hymn. Each story or song has a short historical note about the time period. Information about the artists, list of further readings, author and title index, and general subject index. A tremendous resource for all time periods in America's history.

Kroll, Steven. *By the Dawn's Early Light: The Story of the Star-Spangled Banner.* Illus. Scholastic 1994 (cloth 0-590-45054-9) 40pp.

This is an account of the writing of the "Star-Spangled Banner," detailing how Key was actually behind enemy lines at the time seeking release of a captured friend from the British, who would not allow their departure until the bombardment of Baltimore was completed. The illustrations are beautiful. The author adds historical notes about the War of 1812 and the battle during which Key wrote his poem. There are maps of the Battle of Baltimore and Washington D.C. in 1814, and the music for our national anthem is included. Index.

King, Coretta Scott (1927–), the widow of assassinated civil rights crusader Martin Luther King, Jr., continued her late husband's work for the Southern Christian Leadership Conference.

"When we achieve equality here in America, we will set an irresistible example of hope for the entire world. We must envision a world free from the ravages of poverty, racism, war and militarism."
(Schraff, p. 107)

Biographies for Younger Readers

Medearis, Angela Shelf. *Dare to Dream: Coretta Scott King and the Civil Rights Movement.* Illus. Lodestar Books 1994 (pap. 0-525-67426-8) 64pp.

Medearis briefly covers her childhood years, her life as Martin Luther King, Jr.'s wife, and her work after her husband's death to promote his causes. List of further readings and index. Part of the Rainbow Biography series.

Schraff, Anne. *Coretta Scott King: Striving for Civil Rights.* Illus. Enslow Publishers 1997 (LB 0-89490-811-1) 128pp.

In addition to describing Coretta Scott King's married life, this book tells of her childhood in Alabama and her efforts to continue her husband's legacy. There are many quotations that capture Mrs. King's commitment to equality and peace. Chronology, chapter notes, bibliography, and index. Part of the African American Biographies series.

Biographies for Older Readers

Henry, Sondra, and Emily Taitz. *Coretta Scott King: Keeper of the Dream.* Illus. Enslow Publishers 1992 (LB 0-89490-334-9) 128pp.

Focusing on her experiences as a black person growing up and as Martin Luther King, Jr.'s wife, this book describes how Coretta Scott King became more active in pursuing his causes after his death. Chronology, list of further readings, and index. Part of the Contemporary Women series.

Patrick, Diane. *Coretta Scott King.* Illus. Franklin Watts 1991 (o.p.) 144pp.

Students doing research will appreciate this thorough and well-organized presentation. Chapters feature Mrs. King as "A Lady with a Commitment" and describe her childhood, education, marriage, life as a wife and mother, and tireless work for civil rights. Source notes, bibliography, and index. Part of the Impact Biographies series.

Related Books for Younger Readers

Dunce, Alice Faye. *The National Civil Rights Museum Celebrates Everyday People.* Illus. by J. Gerald Smith. BridgeWater Books 1995 (pap. 0-8167-3502-6) 64pp.

The Lorraine Motel in Memphis, Tennessee, where Martin Luther King, Jr. was shot, has been turned into a civil rights museum. Color photographs of different parts of the museum are juxtaposed with black-and-white photographs of scenes from the civil rights struggle. Chronology, list of further readings, bibliography, and index.

Kosof, Anna. *The Civil Rights Movement and Its Legacy.* Illus. Franklin Watts 1989 (o.p.) 112pp.

Kosof presents key moments in the civil rights movement— *Brown* v. *Board of Education,* the Montgomery Bus Boycott, integration in Little Rock, and protest marches. Excerpts from interviews and speeches add to the picture of this era of America's history. Bibliography and index.

Related Books for Older Readers

Allen, Zita. *Black Women Leaders of the Civil Rights Movement.* Franklin Watts 1996 (LB 0-531-11271-3) 160pp.

Covering the years 1900–1964, the text tells of the many women who helped shape and lead the civil rights movement. Source notes and index. Part of the African American Experience series.

Dolan, Sean. *Pursuing the Dream: From the Selma-Montgomery March to the Formation of PUSH (1965–1971).* Illus. Chelsea House 1995 (LB 0-7910-2254-4) (pap. 0-7910-2680-9)

This book looks at the turbulent era of the late 1960s, focusing on the work of Dr. Martin Luther King, Jr. and other civil rights leaders. It ends with the economic and educational programs founded by Jesse Jackson. Bibliography and index. Part of the Milestones in Black American History series.

King, Coretta Scott. *My Life with Martin Luther King, Jr.* rev. ed. Illus. Puffin 1993 (pap. 0-14-036805-1) 368pp.

The first edition of this book was written shortly after King's assassination. This second edition contains more historical perspective as it relates Coretta Scott King's personal experiences with the civil rights movement and as the wife of Martin Luther King, Jr. There is a section of photographs in middle of book. Introduction by King's children. Chronology and index.

King, Martin Luther, Jr. (1929–1968), an African American clergyman and civil rights leader, is best known for his campaign of passive resistance to segregation. He first came to national prominence with his leadership of the Montgomery, Alabama, bus boycott. He was assassinated in Memphis in April 1968.

Biographies for Younger Readers

Adler, David A. *A Picture Book of Martin Luther King, Jr.* Illus. by Robert Casilla. Holiday House 1989 (LB 0-8234-0770-5) 1990 (pap. 0-8234-0847-7) 32pp.

This is a brief, illustrated telling of King's philosophy and practice of nonviolent civil disobedience. His marriage, the bus boycott, the march on Washington, winning the Nobel Peace Prize, and his assassination are all covered. Important dates are at end of book. Part of the Picture Book Of series.

Bray, Rosemary L. *Martin Luther King.* Illus. by Malcah Zeldis. Greenwillow 1995 (LB 0-688-13132-8) (cloth 0-688-13131-X); William Morrow & Co. 1997 (pap. 0-688-15219-8) 48pp.

Colorful folk-art paintings add to this dramatic presentation of King's life and accomplishments. Sharing this book aloud would interest students in doing more research about Dr. King and the civil rights movement. Chronology.

Greene, Carol. *Martin Luther King, Jr.: A Man Who Changed Things.* Illus. by Steven Dobson. Children's Press 1989 (LB 0-516-04205-X) (pap. 0-516-44205-8) 48pp.

Illustrated with many photographs, this work briefly tells the story of King's life, focusing on his civil rights struggles. List of important dates and index. Part of the Rookie Biography series.

Lambert, Kathy Kristensen. *Martin Luther King, Jr.* Illus. Chelsea House 1993 (LB 0-7910-1759-1) 1992 (pap. 0-7910-1954-3) 80pp.

From "The Bus Boycott" to "Victories and Defeats" to "I Have Been to the Mountaintop,'" this book will be useful to students learning to do research. This book is well organized with enough details for upper elementary school students. Chronology, glossary, bibliography, and index. Part of the Junior World Biographies series.

Biographies for Older Readers

Darby, Jean. *Martin Luther King, Jr.* Illus. Lerner Publications 1990 (LB 0-8225-4902-6) 1992 (pap. 0-8225-9611-3) 112pp.

Using many black-and-white photographs, this book has an appealing format. The chapters follow Dr. King from his childhood ("Growing Up Black") through his death in Memphis ("Trouble in Memphis") and his legacy ("Free at Last"). Many students will find this an enjoyable book to read. Glossary, bibliography, and index.

Haskins, Jim. *I Have a Dream: The Life and Words of Martin Luther King, Jr.* Illus. Millbrook Press 1992 (LB 1-56294-087-2); Houghton Mifflin (pap. 0-395-64549-2) 112pp.

With an introduction by Rosa Parks, this is a book for all ages. Each chapter title is a quotation from Dr. King and there are longer quotations in boxed sections throughout the book. The text places the words of Dr. King in the context of events. Excellent photographs add to this outstanding presentation. Timeline, chapter notes, bibliography, and index.

Jakoubek, Robert. *Martin Luther King, Jr.: Civil Rights Leader.* Illus. Chelsea House 1989 (LB 1-55546-597-8) 1990 (pap. 0-7910-0243-8)

This book is very well organized for research. After opening with Dr. King's assassination, the author looks back on his life. His commitment to Gandhi's principles of non-violence are described. There are many photographs and quotations. Appendix of Dr. King's writings, chronology, bibliography, and index. Part of the Black Americans of Achievement series.

Shuker, Nancy. *Martin Luther King: Civil Rights Leader.* Illus. Chelsea House 1985 (LB 0-87754-567-7) (pap. 0-7910-0219-5) 112pp.

Shuker tells the story of King's civil rights struggle. It includes quotations, black-and-white photographs, and copies of newspaper clippings illustrating events such as freedom riders, the march on Washington, the Civil Rights Act, and King's assassination. Chronology, list of further readings, and index. Part of the World Leaders Past & Present series.

Related Books for Younger Readers

Andryszewski, Tricia. *The March on Washington 1963: Gathering to Be Heard.* Illus. Millbrook Press 1996 (LB 0-7613-0009-0) 64pp.

One of the defining moments of the civil rights movement was Martin Luther King, Jr.'s "I Have a Dream" speech on August 28, 1963. This book describes the events that led up to the march and features excerpts from some of the other speeches, including those of Whitney Young and A. Philip Randolph. The text of the "I Have a Dream" speech is included. The book ends with a brief look at the Million Man March and the different ideas behind it and the 1963 march. Bibliography and index. Part of the Spotlight on American History series.

King, Dr. Martin Luther, Jr. *I Have a Dream.* Illus. Scholastic 1997 (cloth 0-590-20516-1) 40pp.

This is a beautiful book. The text of the "I Have a Dream" speech is presented with paintings from 15 award-winning artists. Ashley Bryan, Floyd Cooper, Leo and Diane Dillon, Tom Feelings, Brian Pinkney, Jerry Pinkney, and others who have been recognized by the Coretta Scott King Award Committee provide dramatic and moving interpretations to sections of this famous speech, giving students the opportunity to read a historical document and see personal interpretations of outstanding artists. Foreword by Coretta Scott King.

Lucas, Eileen. *Civil Rights: The Long Struggle.* Illus. Enslow Publishers 1996 (LB 0-89490-729-8) 112pp.

Lucas covers not only the civil rights movement but also the history of freedom, government, and the first amendment. She discusses both the nonviolent tactics of Martin Luther King, Jr., and the confrontational efforts of such leaders as Stokely Carmichael. Chronology, chapter notes (documenting quotations), glossary, bibliography, and index. Part of the Issues in Focus series.

Related Books for Older Readers

McKissack, Patricia, and Fredrick McKissack. *The Civil Rights Movement in America: From 1865 to the Present.* 2nd ed. Illus. Children's Press 1991 (LB 0-516-00579-0) 352pp.

This thorough book will be very useful to students doing research. From the years after the Civil War through the early years of the civil rights movement and ending with a discussion of related issues including the women's movement and children's rights, there is a wealth of information here. The organization of the book is inviting: It is divided into chronological eras, each opening with a timeline; there are topic subdivisions; and there are "Cameos" on key people and issues. Bibliography and index.

Myers, Walter Dean. *Now Is Your Time! The African American Struggle for Freedom.* Illus. HarperCollins 1991 (LB 0-06-024371-6) 1992 (pap. 0-06-446120-3) 304pp.

Chapters describe the experiences of Africans kidnapped for slavery, the Dred Scott case, the efforts of abolitionists, Reconstruction, such court decisions as *Brown* v. *Board of Education,* and later events in the civil rights movement. Bibliography (divided by topics, such as Plantation Life and John Brown) and index.

Patterson, Charles. *The Civil Rights Movement.* Illus. Facts on File 1995 (cloth 0-8160-2968-7) 144pp.

Background information on slavery, the Civil War, and Reconstruction leads to chapters on court cases, school desegregation, freedom rides, marches, voting rights, and militant unrest. Chronology, bibliography, and index. Part of the Social Reform Movements series.

Walter, Mildred Pitts. *Mississippi Challenge.* Illus. Bradbury Press 1992 (LB 0-02-792301-0); Aladdin 1996 (pap. 0-689-80307-9) 224pp.

Using the state of Mississippi as the heart of the battle, the text discusses the struggle for civil rights from the time of slavery to the signing of the Voting Rights Act in 1965. A map of Mississippi is included with key cities marked. Source notes, bibliography, and index.

La Salle, René-Robert Cavelier, Sieur de (1643–1687), was a French explorer who in 1682 explored the Mississippi and named the region of Louisiana for Louis XIV, the king of France.

Biographies for Younger Readers

Jacobs, William J. *La Salle: A Life of Boundless Adventure.* Illus. Franklin Watts 1994 (LB 0-531-20141-4) 64pp.

Accounts of La Salle narrowly escaping capture by Spaniards who were lying in wait for him, being entertained by Indians and then watching as they tortured a prisoner, and finally being assassinated by members of his own expedition all make for exciting reading. This explorer was one of the first Europeans to find his way into the interior of the North American continent. Lists of important dates and further readings, and index. Part of the First Book series.

Biographies for Older Readers

Hargrove, Jim. *René-Robert Cavelier, Sieur de La Salle: Explorer of the Mississippi River.* Illus. Children's Press 1990 (o.p.) 128pp.

Full of prints from the past and photographs of the present, this book covers La Salle's journey down the Mississippi River to the Gulf of Mexico. Timeline, glossary, bibliography, and index. Part of the World's Great Explorers series.

Related Books for Younger Readers

Morley, Jacqueline. *Exploring North America.* Illus. Peter Bedrick Books 1996 (cloth 0-87226-488-2) 48pp.

Students will enjoy browsing through this book, which is full of beautiful illustrations and short bits of information. Early explorers, treasure seekers, and conquistadors are just a small part of what is covered. La Salle's enterprising expedition is presented, along with his men's amazement at coming upon Niagara Falls. Timeline, glossary, and index. Part of the Voyages of Discovery series.

Related Books for Older Readers

Coulter, Tony. *La Salle and the Explorers of the Mississippi.* Illus. Chelsea House 1991 (LB 0-7910-1304-9) 112pp.

La Salle's exploration of the Great Lakes and the Mississippi River region is the focus. Two expeditions full of adventure, rediscovering the Mississippi, and La Salle's final assassination by his own men are all part of this absorbing book. Chronology, list of further readings, and index. Part of the World Explorers series.

Lange, Dorothea (1895–1965), an American photographer, earned great fame for her graphic portraits of sharecroppers and migrant workers during the Depression. She also documented the internment of Japanese Americans during World War II.

Biographies for Younger Readers

Meltzer, Milton. *Dorothea Lange: Life through the Camera.* Illus. by Donna Diamond. Photographs by Dorothea Lange. Puffin 1986 (o.p.) 64pp.

A simple but touching account of Lange's life and work, which helped bring about important social reforms for migrant workers. Several of her photographs are included. Part of the Women of Our Time series.

Related Books for Younger Readers

Holland, Gini. *Photography.* Illus. Benchmark Books 1996 (LB 0-7614-0066-4) 64pp.

This is a delightful book to read with attractive "Amazing Facts" that are sure to interest students. Lange's photojournalism is featured. Clear illustrations of the photographic process are also included. A final chapter looks at cameras and computers. Timeline, glossary, bibliography, and index. Part of the Inventors and Inventions series.

Wolf, Sylvia. *Focus: Five Women Photographers.* Illus. Albert Whitman 1994 (LB 0-8075-2531-6) 64pp.

After studying Dorothea Lange's life and career, students may want to take a look at these five women photographers who created art and studied social issues with their cameras: Julia Margaret Cameron, Margaret Bourke-White, Flor Garduño, Sandy Skoglund, and Lorna Simpson. The author gives her own critique of their works. Full of wonderful photographs, from a wide variety of places and periods in time. Selected bibliography and photo credits.

Related Books for Older Readers

Czech, Kenneth P. *Snapshot: America Discovers the Camera.* Illus. Lerner Publications 1996 (cloth 0-8225-1736-1)

A history of the use of the camera in America: to create entertainment, photojournalism, and silent movies. Lange's photos of the Dust Bowl workers are included, along with Civil War photographs of the wounded, and aviators taking pictures of enemy lines from the skies, to name a few. Bibliography and index.

Lavoisier, Antoine Laurent

(1743–1794), born in Paris, is considered the founder of modern chemistry. Among his many achievements were the isolation of the components of air and the development of the naming protocol for chemical compounds.

Biographies for Older Readers

Grey, Vivian. *The Chemist Who Lost His Head: The Story of Antoine Laurent Lavoisier.* Illus. Putnam's 1982 (cloth 0-698-20559-6) 112pp.

Beginning with Lavoisier's execution by guillotine because of his political connections with the reigning monarchy, the book then continues with his countless contributions to the world: showing farmers how to grow better crops, improving conditions in prisons and hospitals, developing a new lighting system for the streets of Paris, and—last but not least—cataloging all the elements and formulating the science known as chemistry. Appendix with a list of the elements and index.

Related Books for Younger Readers

Fitzgerald, Karen. *The Story of Oxygen.* Illus. Franklin Watts 1996 (LB 0-531-20225-9) 64pp.

Fitzgerald explores oxygen: its discovery by Lavoisier, its chemistry, how it works in the body, and its importance in our everyday lives. List of sources, glossary, and index. Part of the First Book series.

Williams, Brian, and Brenda Williams. *The Age of Discovery: From the Renaissance to American Independence.* Illus. by James Field. Peter Bedrick Books 1993 (LB 0-87226-311-8) 64pp.

Readers will enjoy browsing through this book full of illustrations and information on the changing world from 1500 to 1789. Great events in world history, battles, inventions, discoveries, and kings and queens are all included. Lavoisier is one of many scientists named in the amazing evolution of modern society. Timelines, glossary, and index. Part of the Timelink series.

Related Books for Older Readers

Stewart, Gail B. *Life During the French Revolution.* Illus. Lucent 1995 (LB 1-56006-078-6) 112pp.

Thousands of prisoners were put to death by guillotine during the French Revolution, including Antoine Lavoisier. Here is a full description of what life was like in France at the time, both for royalty and for everyday people. One of the strong points of this series is its emphasis on original sources and this volume is full of quotations and passages from historical documents. List of further readings, chapter notes, and index. Part of the Way People Live series.

Lazarus, Emma (1849–1887), an American writer and poet, is remembered best for "The New Colossus," her poem about the Statue of Liberty that is engraved on the base of the statue in New York Harbor. Her poetry collection, *Songs of a Semite,* celebrates Judaism.

Biographies for Older Readers

Lefer, Diane. *Emma Lazarus: Poet.* Illus. Chelsea House 1988 (o.p.) 112pp.

This book tells of Lazarus's development as a writer and also as a supporter of Jewish causes. Included is historical background on the Russian pogroms and Jewish immigration to the United States. Chronology, lists of Lazarus's writings and further readings, and index. Part of the American Women of Achievement series.

Related Books for Younger Readers

Fisher, Leonard Everett. *The Statue of Liberty.* Illus. by the author. Holiday House 1985 (o.p.) 64pp.

With original black-and-white photographs and Leonard Everett Fisher's drawings, this is the story of how the Statue of Liberty came to America. Blueprints, the armature designed by Eiffel, photographs of the people involved, and, of course, Lazarus and her poem, are part of this interesting account. Index.

Maestro, Betsy. *Coming to America: The Story of Immigration.* Illus. by Susannah Ryan. Scholastic 1996 (cloth 0-590-44151-5) 40pp.

This is a picture-book story of immigration to America, starting with the first nomads crossing the landbridge from Asia to Alaska. It describes the Europeans competing with the Indians for land and Africans being brought to America for slavery. The process that people went through at Ellis Island is also covered. Chronology.

Related Books for Older Readers

Press, Petra. *A Multicultural Portrait of Immigration.* Illus. Marshall Cavendish 1995 (LB 0-7614-0055-9) 80pp.

Press covers immigrants from the first Indians to cross the landbridge through colonists, African slaves, Europeans, Mexicans, and Asians. She discusses ethnic groups that came unwillingly (African and Chinese slaves), and how many ethnic groups became prejudiced against the next arrivals. Chronology, list of further readings, glossary, and index. Part of the Perspectives series.

Lee, Robert E. (1807–1870), the leader of Confederate forces in the Civil War, is considered the greatest military strategist in that conflict. Superintendent of West Point from 1852 to 1855, he became general of all Confederate armies in February 1865, only two months before his surrender to Grant.

Biographies for Younger Readers

Adler, David A. *A Picture Book of Robert E. Lee.* Illus. by John Wallner and Alexandra Wallner. Holiday House 1994 (LB 0-8234-1111-7) 32pp.

Reading this book aloud would be a good way to introduce Robert E. Lee and to discuss the elements of a biography. The book describes Lee's childhood, his military training, and his role as commander-in-chief of the Confederate Army. List of important dates. Part of the Picture Book Of series.

" . . . I have not been
able to make up my
mind to raise my hand
against my relatives,
my children, my home.
I have therefore
resigned my
commission in the
army, and, save in
defense of my native
state—with the sincere
hope that my poor
services may never be
needed—I hope I may
never be called upon to
draw my sword. "

(Greene, p. 24)

Greene, Carol. *Robert E. Lee: Leader in War and Peace.* Illus. Children's Press 1989 (o.p.) 48pp.

Simply told, this story of Lee's life and battles includes some moving war stories illustrating why he was loved so deeply by the people of the South. List of important dates and index. Part of the Rookie Biographies series.

Biographies for Older Readers

Aaseng, Nathan. *Robert E. Lee.* Illus. Lerner Publications 1991 (o.p.) 112pp.

Lee's life as a leader loved by people of both the North and the South is described here. Many maps and photographs are included. The list of further readings has books not just about Lee, but also about the Civil War, Civil War leaders, and slavery. Index. Part of the Lerner Biographies series.

Brown, Warren. *Robert E. Lee.* Illus. Chelsea House 1992 (LB 1-55546-814-4) 1982 (pap. 0-7910-0698-0)

This tells the story of a man so well loved that Grant himself threatened to resign if charges were brought against Lee after the war was over. Photographs and quotations line almost every page. Chronology, list of further readings, and index. Part of the World Leaders Past & Present series.

Marrin, Albert. *Virginia's General: Robert E. Lee and the Civil War.* Atheneum 1994 (cloth 0-689-31838-3)

Here is a vivid telling not just of Lee's life, but of the Civil War. It is full of maps and photographs, including one of piles of skulls of men killed during the Battle of Chancellorsville. List of further readings, chapter notes, and index.

Related Books for Younger Readers

Smith, Carter, ed. *Prelude to War.* Illus. Millbrook Press 1993 (LB 1-56294-261-1) 96pp.

Describing the events that led to the Civil War, this book provides students with an understanding of the divided agendas of the North and South. Features include "The Industrial North," "The South: The Cotton Kingdom," "Uncle Tom's Cabin," "Free Blacks," "Abraham Lincoln," "Jefferson Davis," and "The Birth of the Confederacy." Timeline, brief bibliography, and index. Part of the Sourcebook on the Civil War series.

Related Books for Older Readers

Kent, Zachary. *The Civil War: "A House Divided."* Illus. Enslow Publishers 1994 (LB 0-89490-522-8) 128pp.

This book covers many aspects of the Civil War. The impact on families, preparing for battles, and the horrendous conditions for soldiers, the wounded, and prisoners. Key figures include Robert E. Lee, Ulysses S. Grant, Jefferson Davis, and Abraham Lincoln. Chronology, bibliography, chapter notes, and index. Part of the American War series.

Murphy, Jim. *The Long Road to Gettysburg.* Illus. Clarion 1992 (cloth 0-395-55965-0) 128pp.

The Battle of Gettysburg as seen through the eyes of two actual soldiers, one Union and one Confederate, is described here. The affection and respect for Lee come through loud and clear. Bibliography and index.

Ray, Delia. *Behind the Blue and Gray: The Soldier's Life in the Civil War.* Illus. Lodestar Books 1991 (pap. 0-525-67333-4) 112pp.

This book describes the daily life of soldiers for the North and South. What did they eat and how did they get their food? How did they pass the time before or after battles? What medical treatment did they receive? Reading this book, students will get a more personal sense of the experiences during this war. Glossary, bibliography, and index. Part of the Young Readers' History of the Civil War series.

Leeuwenhoek, Antonie van

(1632–1723), born in Delft in the Netherlands, made a number of important discoveries about the human circulatory system using a microscope. Some of his other discoveries increased knowledge about the structure of the musculatory system, hair, and skin.

Biographies for Younger Readers

Kumin, Maxine. *The Microscope.* Illus. by Arnold Lobel. Harper-Collins 1984 (o.p.) 80pp.

A humorous telling, in picture-book format, of Leeuwenhoek's fascination with the microscope and the things he saw with his specially ground lenses that no one had ever seen before. Delightful pictures by Arnold Lobel and Kumin's simple text will entertain the youngest reader. A historical note is added at the end.

Related Books for Younger Readers

Bender, Lionel. *Frontiers of Medicine.* Illus. Gloucester Press 1991 (o.p.) 32pp.

Bender discusses the ways in which microscopes advanced medicine, starting with the study of plants and animals in the 17th century and ending with the discovery of bacteria and viruses two centuries later. Topics covered include cells and microbes, microscopic life, sources of infection, immunization, chemotherapy, infection, blood testing, and embryo research. Leeuwenhoek's microscope is illustrated and there are many wonderful microscopic photographs. Glossary and index. Part of the Through the Microscope series.

Levine, Shar, and Leslie Johnstone. *The Microscope Book.* Illus. Sterling Publishing 1996 (cloth 0-8069-4898-1) 1997 (pap. 0-8069-4899-X) 80pp.

A delightful introduction to microscopes, using light, biology, geology, forensic science, and food and the environment. The book is filled with diagrams, detailed explanations about the scientific process, and photomicrographs. Young scientists are encouraged to keep detailed illustrated journals, as Leeuwenhoek did with his first basic microscope. Glossary and index.

Related Books for Older Readers

Mulcahy, Robert. *Medical Technology: Inventing the Instruments.* Illus. Oliver Press 1997 (LB 1-881508-34-X) 144pp.

In the 17th century, medical treatment included bleeding (to balance the humors) and the use of herbs and medicines from apothecaries. This book describes the development of scientific instruments that improved medical treatment. Included are the thermometer, stethoscope, radiation therapy, and electrocardiograph. The work of Leeuwenhoek, Wilhelm Roentgen, and Marie Curie is described. Medical timeline, glossary, bibliography, and index. Part of the Innovators series.

Parker, Steve. *How the Body Works: 100 Ways Parents and Kids Can Share the Miracle of the Human Body.* Illus. Reader's Digest 1994 (cloth 0-89577-575-1) 192pp.

This book will provide hours of fun. Along with a wealth of information, there are easy-to-follow guidelines for practical, safe experiments on many subjects. The human body is covered in detail—the surface, framework, oxygen supply, fuel, transport and maintenance, nervous system, senses, and life cycle. Leeuwenhoek and his discoveries are mentioned several times. Glossary and index.

Lenin, Vladimir Ilyich (1870–1924), a

Marxist revolutionary and founder of Bolshevism, was a major force in the creation of the Soviet Union. After the Russian Revolution began in 1917, he returned from exile, led the overthrow of the provisional government, and soon became virtual dictator.

Biographies for Older Readers

Rawcliffe, Michael. *Lenin.* Illus. David & Charles (o.p.)

Written while Gorbachev was still in power, this is an excellent work on Russian history during Lenin's lifetime. The book is divided into sections: "Lenin's Reputation," "Interpretations" (of the political movements in Russia), and "Conclusions." Each section has sidebars containing explanations and giving definitions. Timeline of Russian history and Lenin's life, list of Lenin's counterparts, further readings, and index. Part of the Reputations series.

Related Books for Younger Readers

Brewster, Hugh, and Shelley Tanaka. *Anastasia's Album.* Illus. Hyperion 1996 (cloth 0-7868-0292-8) 64pp.

Students of Lenin will be fascinated by this album of Anastasia's short life. (She was shot by Lenin and his followers along with her father, Nicholas II, and the rest of her family.) The question of what happened to Anastasia's bones and whether she really survived is accompanied by beautiful photographs of the palaces where she lived and of her family and childhood. Map of the Russian Empire during Anastasia's lifetime and glossary.

Macdonald, Fiona. *Kings and Queens: Rulers and Despots.* Illus. Franklin Watts 1995 (LB 0-531-14369-4) 48pp.

The author presents an entertaining look at rulers throughout history, both good and bad. Questions posed include "Which king had to have his head sewn back on?" and "Which queen exploded?" Lenin's overthrow of Czar Nicholas II is included in this history of rulers. Timeline, glossary, and index. Part of the Timelines series.

The Making of Modern Russia: Peter the Great, Karl Marx, V. I. Lenin. Illus. Marshall Cavendish 1991 (o.p.) 64pp.

Students learn the impact these three men had on transforming Russia from an unorganized collection of tribal states to one of the most powerful nations in the world. Many pictures illustrate the Russian way of life at that time. Some information is presented in fictional first-person accounts—as when the governess of the czar's children relates the strange influence that Rasputin has on the royal family. Chronology, list of further readings, glossary, and index. Part of the Exploring the Past series.

Related Books for Older Readers

Dunn, John M. *The Russian Revolution.* Illus. Lucent 1994 (LB 1-56006-234-7) 112pp.

An overview of the people and events surrounding the Russian Revolution. Throughout the book there are boxed sidebars on related topics, such as an account of "Bolshevik Violence" excerpted from John Reed's *Ten Days That Shook the World.* The czar and his family, Rasputin, Lenin, Trotsky, and Stalin are featured. List of further readings, chapter notes, bibliography, and index. Part of the World History series.

Lewis, Meriwether (1774–1809) and William Clark (1770–1838), American explorers, led the expedition (1804–1806) bearing their names to explore the newly acquired Louisiana Territory en route to the Pacific Ocean. Lewis later was named governor of the territory; Clark played the role of mapmaker on the journey west.

Biographies for Younger Readers

Kroll, Steven. *Lewis and Clark: Explorers of the American West.* Illus. by Richard Williams. Holiday House 1994 (LB 0-8234-1034-X) 1996 (pap. 0-8234-1273-3) 32pp.

In picture-book format, this book includes many useful maps and illustrations from Lewis and Clark's expedition. There are details about a typical riverman, a keelboat, an air gun, and different tribes of Indians. This would be a useful book to introduce these explorers. Chronology and index.

Biographies for Older Readers

Petersen, David. *Meriwether Lewis and William Clark: Soldiers, Explorers, and Partners in History.* Illus. Children's Press 1988 (o.p.) 152pp.

Starting with a brief biography of both men, the book then concentrates on their journey. Emphasis is put on the safety and the many scientific contributions of their expedition. Chronology, map of the journey, and index. Part of the People of Distinction Biographies series.

Related Books for Younger Readers

Stein, R. Conrad. *Lewis and Clark.* Illus. Children's Press 1997 (cloth 0-516-20461-0)

Full of drawings, photographs, and maps of their journey, this book documents the Lewis and Clark expedition. Timeline, glossary, and index. Part of the Cornerstones of Freedom series.

Twist, Clint. *Lewis and Clark: Exploring the Northwest.* Illus. Raintree Steck-Vaughn 1994 (LB 0-8114-7255-8)

This is an excellent beginning reference book, full of pictures and short pieces of information. It covers Lewis and Clark's expedition with excerpts from journals, an example of a day on the river, and information on getting ready for the trip with the Corps of Discovery. Included are the native American groups they encountered, and what happened later with the exploration of the West. List of further readings, glossary, and index. Part of the Beyond the Horizons series.

Related Books for Older Readers

Stefoff, Rebecca. *Scientific Explorers: Travels in Search of Knowledge.* Illus. Oxford University Press 1992 (LB 0-19-507689-3) 144pp.

This covers the history of scientific exploration from the awakening of Egypt to modern space exploration. It is wonderful browsing. One chapter is devoted to charting the American West, of which Lewis and Clark are a part. Chronology of scientific exploration, further readings, and index. Part of the Extraordinary Explorers series.

Weightman, Gavin. *The Grolier Student Library of Explorers and Exploration: Volume 6, North America.* Illus. Grolier 1998 (cloth 0-7172-9141-3)

With many illustrations and well-organized information, this book presents the exploration of North America. Lewis and Clark's expedition is but one of many entertaining adventures. Index.

Liliuokalani (1838–1917), the last monarch of Hawaii, reigned as queen of the islands from 1891 to 1895, before Hawaii became the 50th state of the Union.

Biographies for Younger Readers

Guzzetti, Paula. *The Last Hawaiian Queen: Liliuokalani.* Illus.
Benchmark Books 1996 (LB 0-7614-0490-2) 48pp.

Guzzetti provides an introduction to Liliuokalani's childhood
as a member of Hawaii's royal family. At that time, Hawaii was its
own country. The changes that occurred as it was developed and
annexed by the United States are described. Contains many color
photographs of present-day Hawaii. Glossary and index. Part of the
Benchmark Biographies series.

Stanley, Fay. *The Last Princess: The Story of Princess Kaiulani.*
Illus. by Diane Stanley. Four Winds Press 1991 (LB 0-02-786785-
4); Aladdin 1994 (pap. 0-689-71829-2) 40pp.

Beautiful illustrations by Diane Stanley illustrate Liliuokalani's royal childhood, her education in England, her marriage,
and her life as her country became a state. Special notes on the
Hawaiian language are included.

Related Books for Younger Readers

Fradin, Dennis B. *Hawaii.* Children's Press 1994 (LB 0-516-
03811-7) (pap. 0-516-26199-1) 64pp.

Young readers learn a lot about Hawaii, its history, geography,
its people, and the kind of work they do. Attractive features include
a gallery of famous Hawaiians, a short "Did you know?" section,
brief facts about Hawaii, and a chronology of Hawaiian history. Glossary and index. Part of the From Sea to Shining Sea series.

Perl, Lila. *It Happened in America: True Stories from the Fifty
States.* Illus. Henry Holt 1992 (cloth 0-8050-1719-4) 1996 (pap.
0-8050-4707-7) 304pp.

Historical anecdotes from each of the 50 states emphasize
women and minorities. The book is arranged alphabetically by state.
Each state has a question-and-answer box featuring a riddle or
entertaining fact. The story for Hawaii tells the tale of Liliuokalani's
nine months imprisoned in her own palace while she wrote music.
Students will enjoy the details in this book and will find it useful for
writing reports.

"As I would not be a slave, so I would not be a master. This expresses my idea of democracy—Whatever differs from this, to the extent of the difference, is no democracy."

(Freedman, p. vii)

Lincoln, Abraham (1809–1865), the 16th president of the United States (1861–1865), led the Union to victory in the Civil War and freed the slaves in the South in 1863. Only days after the end of the war, he was assassinated by John Wilkes Booth.

Biographies for Younger Readers

D'Aulaire, Ingri. *Abraham Lincoln.* Illus. Dell 1987 (pap. 0-440-40690-0) 64pp.

D'Aulaire's lithographs make up a classic and beautiful picture-book rendition of Lincoln's life. His early years, the time spent working on the riverboats, his time in the Indian War, his years in the White House, and the Civil War are all covered.

Kunhardt, Edith. *Honest Abe.* Illus. by Malcah Zeldis. Greenwillow 1993 (LB 0-688-11190-4) (cloth 0-688-11189-0) 32pp.

This oversized book presents dramatic details about Lincoln's life from his boyhood through his assassination. Large folk-art paintings accompany the text. The text of the Gettysburg Address and a chronology of Lincoln's life are appended.

Usel, T. M. *Abraham Lincoln: A Photo-Illustrated Biography.* Illus. Bridgestone Books 1996 (LB 1-56065-341-8) 24pp.

This is a beautiful book. Facing pages consist of one full photograph on one side, and text with a one-sentence description of the picture on the other side. Lists of important dates and useful addresses, glossary, and index. Part of the Read and Discover Photo-Illustrated Biographies series.

Biographies for Older Readers

Freedman, Russell. *Lincoln: A Photobiography.* Illus. Houghton Mifflin 1987 (cloth 0-89919-380-3) 1989 (pap. 0-395-51848-2) 160pp.

Easily read for pleasure or research, this Newbery Award-winning book shares fascinating vignettes about one of our greatest presidents. The last few hours of his life and the funeral procession and train ride back to his resting place are particularly touching. Wonderfully illustrated with archival photographs, prints, and documents. There is an appended list of Lincoln memorials, monuments, and museums that encourages readers to experience historical sites firsthand. Index.

Hargrove, Jim. *Abraham Lincoln: Sixteenth President of the United States.* Illus. Children's Press 1988 (LB 0-516-01359-9) 100pp.

Full of photographs and drawings, this is a nice overview of Lincoln's life and the time period in which he lived. The chronology of American history showing Lincoln's life in perspective is useful. Index. Part of the Encyclopedia of Presidents series.

Meltzer, Milton, ed. *Lincoln: In His Own Words.* Illus. by Stephen Alcorn. Harcourt 1993 (cloth 0-15-245437-3) 224pp.

Illustrated with black-and-white linocuts, this is a beautiful book for browsing. Meltzer has taken quotations from Lincoln's letters, speeches, and public papers and provided background commentary. Brief profiles of Lincoln's contemporaries, chronology, source notes, list of further readings, illustrator's note, and index.

Related Books for Younger Readers

Bial, Raymond. *The Underground Railroad.* Illus. Houghton Mifflin 1995 (cloth 0-395-69937-1) 48pp.

Photographs and documents re-create stations along the Underground Railroad. The author describes the challenges that runaway slaves faced, and depicts the atmosphere of danger, fear, and a longing for freedom.

January, Brendan. *The Emancipation Proclamation.* Illus. Children's Press 1997 (LB 0-516-20394-0)

The text relates the history behind this document and tells of the anger and inspiration that it evoked. Lincoln's role in freeing the slaves is described. Timeline, glossary, and index. Part of the Cornerstones of Freedom series.

Kent, Zachary. *The Story of Ford's Theater and the Death of Lincoln.* Illus. Children's Press 1987 (o.p.) 32pp.

In this detailed account of Lincoln's assassination, there are photographs of Ford's Theater as it now stands, the room where Lincoln died, his funeral processions, and the hanging of four of the conspirators. It also covers the rest of the plot that included the assassination of William Seward and Andrew Johnson. Index. Part of the Cornerstones of Freedom series.

Lincoln, Abraham. *The Gettysburg Address.* Illus. by Michael McCurdy. Houghton Mifflin 1995 (cloth 0-395-69824-3) 32pp.

There is a moving Foreword by Garry Wills that emphasizes the power of this speech. Beautiful illustrations make this a lovely book to look at. The Afterword includes notes by the illustrator about his own interest in this historical period.

Related Books for Older Readers

Feelings, Tom. *The Middle Passage: White Ships/Black Cargo.* Illus. by the author. Dial 1995 (pap. 0-8037-1804-7) 80pp.

Not for younger readers, this important book is about the slave trade. Sixty-four narrative paintings chronicle the journey of a slave ship. It was the winner of the Coretta Scott King award for illustration. A historical introduction traces four centuries of slave trade and includes a map tracing the slave routes.

Henry, Christopher. *Forever Free: From the Emancipation Proclamation to the Civil Rights Bill of 1875 (1863–1875).* Illus. Chelsea House 1995 (LB 0-7910-2253-6) (pap. 0-7910-2679-5)

Opening with a chronology featuring important moments in the Civil War, the author focuses on the impact on African Americans. The formation of the Freedmen's Bureau, the creation of black regiments, and the first election of blacks to the U.S. Senate are all presented. Bibliography and index. Part of the Milestones in Black American History series.

Marrin, Albert. *Commander in Chief: Abraham Lincoln and the Civil War.* Illus. Dutton 1997 (pap. 0-525-45822-0)

Focusing primarily on the Civil War years, this book uses Lincoln's own words and the words of his contemporaries to provide a context for his actions as commander in chief. Accounts of battles, insights from soldiers, and the actions of politicians and other key figures help make this era come to life. Illustrations include photographs, maps, and prints. Chapter notes, bibliography, and index.

Meltzer, Milton, ed. *Voices from the Civil War: A Documentary History of the Great American Conflict.* Illus. Crowell 1989 (cloth 0-690-04800-9) 224pp.

A variety of documents including diaries, newspaper articles, and interviews provide a perspective on northern and southern viewpoints during the Civil War. Bibliography.

Lincoln, Mary Todd (1818–1882),

married Abraham Lincoln—who would become the 16th president of the United States—in 1842. She bore four sons, of whom only one, Robert Todd Lincoln, survived to adulthood.

Biographies for Older Readers

Collins, David R. *Shattered Dreams: The Story of Mary Todd Lincoln.* Morgan Reynolds 1994 (o.p.) 144pp.

This is a story that covers Mary Todd Lincoln's early years, her life as the President's wife, her time in a mental institution, and her final solitary years. Chronology, bibliography, and index. Part of the Notable Americans series.

Related Books for Younger Readers

Blue, Rose, and Corinne J. Naden. *The White House Kids.* Illus. Millbrook Press 1995 (LB 1-56294-447-9) 96pp.

An amusing look at the lives of children in the White House. One story describes Tad Lincoln shooting his toy cannon at the door in the middle of a Cabinet meeting. The loss of one of the Lincolns' sons and Mary Todd Lincoln's failing physical and emotional health are also part of the story. Chronology of presidential families, list of further readings, and index.

Clinton, Susan. *First Ladies.* Illus. Children's Press 1993 (LB 0-516-06673-0) 32pp.

Providing a comparison of several first ladies, both popular and unpopular, this book discusses what a difficult position this can be, both politically and personally. Mary Todd Lincoln is described as one of the most disliked, with strange mood swings and lavish spending habits in the middle of a war. Index. Part of the Cornerstones of Freedom series.

Related Books for Older Readers

Biel, Timothy Levi. *Life in the North During the Civil War.* Illus.
Lucent 1997 (LB 1-56006-334-3) 112pp.

What was it like for the people living during the Civil War?
Those who were not part of the fighting still felt the impact. This
book looks at Army camps, rural life, urban life, and the war's
impact on economics and politics. Chapter notes, two bibliographies
(further reading and works consulted), and index. Part of the Way
People Live series.

Reger, James P. *Life in the South during the Civil War.* Illus.
Lucent 1997 (LB 1-56006-333-5) 112pp.

Students will find useful background information about the
way of life in the South. The lives of plantation owners, slaves, and
"crackers" are described, and two chapters look at the war and its
impact. Chapter notes, annotated bibliographies, and index. Part of
the Way People Live series.

Lindbergh, Charles Augustus

(1902–1974), an American aviator, piloted the first
nonstop solo flight across the Atlantic Ocean in
1927. His sympathy for the Nazi cause in the late
1930s drew criticism. He later served with
distinction as a combat pilot in the Pacific.

Biographies for Younger Readers

Demarest, Chris L. *Lindbergh.* Illus. by the author. Crown 1993
(LB 0-517-58719-X) (pap. 0-517-58718-1) 40pp.

Lovely watercolor illustrations extend the details in this brief
biography of Charles Lindbergh. There are many dramatic events,
ending with his nonstop flight across the Atlantic Ocean. Resource
guide to books, films, and places to visit.

Biographies for Older Readers

Denenberg, Barry. *An American Hero: The True Story of Charles A. Lindbergh.* Illus. Scholastic 1996 (cloth 0-590-46923-1) (pap. 0-590-46955-X) 288pp.

This honest portrayal of the myths and reality of Lindbergh is enhanced with many black-and-white photographs. Lindbergh's connections with the Nazis, his controversial speeches, the transatlantic flight, and the kidnapping of his baby are presented. Chapter notes, bibliography, and index.

Giblin, James Cross. *Charles A. Lindbergh: A Human Hero.* Illus. Clarion 1997 (cloth 0-395-63389-3) 224pp.

This is a beautiful book. The writing is clear and well organized—just right for pleasure reading or for information. Numerous photographs add to the presentation, showing important people and events in Lindbergh's life. An appendix lists "Important Dates in Charles A. Lindbergh's Life." This is a thoroughly researched book. Detailed bibliography, source notes, and index.

Related Books for Younger Readers

Berliner, Don. *Distance Flights.* Illus. Lerner Publications 1990 (LB 0-8225-1589-X) 72pp.

Described are 14 historic great distance flights, of which Lindbergh's is one, with a map of the flights. List of further readings and index. Part of the Space & Aviation series.

Blackman, Steven. *Planes and Flight.* Illus. Franklin Watts 1993 (LB 0-531-14277-9) 32pp.

Full of fascinating facts and experiments for the younger reader to do, this book also covers such major historical flights as Lindbergh's. Glossary and index. Part of the Technology Craft Topics series.

Burleigh, Robert. *Flight: The Journey of Charles Lindbergh.* Illus. by Mike Wimmer. Philomel 1991 (cloth 0-399-22272-3) 32pp.

This is a beautiful picture-book with an introduction by Jean Fritz. It reads like fiction but is full of information about Lindbergh's historic flight with statistics about the flight and the plane.

Related Books for Older Readers

Berliner, Don. *Aviation: Reaching for the Sky.* Illus. Oliver Press 1997 (LB 1-881508-33-1) 144pp.

Reading about the risks people took and the creativity of their efforts to fly is fascinating. In this book students will find information about the dirigible, glider, airplane, seaplane, helicopter, and more. List of "Important Events in Aviation History," glossary, bibliography, and index. Part of the Innovators series.

Low, Juliette Gordon (1860–1927), a member of a socially prominent Savannah, Georgia, family, founded the Girl Scouts of America in 1912. She traveled widely and was inspired by the Girl Guides of Britain to create a similar organization for girls in the United States.

Biographies for Younger Readers

Behrens, June. *Juliette Low: Founder of the Girl Scouts of America.* Illus. Children's Press 1988 (o.p.) 32pp.

The focus here is on Low's creation of the Girl Scouts of America, but the book covers her privileged upbringing and her interest in making a difference in the world. There is a page of quotations about her. Timeline. Part of the Picture-Story Biographies series.

Related Books for Younger Readers

Brower, Pauline York. *Baden-Powell: Founder of the Boy Scouts.* Illus. Children's Press 1989 (LB 0-516-04173-8) 32pp.

Students discovering Juliette Low's story may also be curious about Baden-Powell, who founded the Boy Scouts. His support of Low's program is part of the discussion in this book, which is full of delightful black-and-white photographs and drawings. Chronology and index. Part of the Picture-Story Biographies series.

Related Books for Older Readers

Cadette and Senior Girl Scout Handbook. Illus. Girl Scouts of the United States of America 1987 (pap. 0-88441-342-X) 176pp.

Readers studying Low will want to get a look at the modern-day process that scouts go through. Included in this particular handbook are a history of Low's founding of the scouts, details of ceremonies, badges and ways to earn them, the Girl Scout Promise, and Girl Scout Law. Index.

MacArthur, Douglas (1880–1964), an American soldier, earned his greatest fame for recapturing the Philippine Islands from Japanese forces in World War II. He was named commander of the United Nations forces in Korea when war broke out there in 1950 but was relieved of that post in 1951 when he called for extending the conflict into China.

Biographies for Older Readers

Darby, Jean. *Douglas MacArthur.* Illus. Lerner Publications 1989 (LB 0-8225-4901-8) 112pp.

This biography of MacArthur focuses on his defense of the Philippines during World War II, administration of occupied Japan after the war, and leadership of United Nations troops in the Korean conflict. Appendix with information about the military system and World War II, list of further readings, glossary, and index. Part of the Lerner Biographies series.

Finkelstein, Norman H. *Emperor General: A Biography of Douglas MacArthur.* Illus. Silver Burdett 1989 (LB 0-87518-396-4) 128pp.

An entertaining book about MacArthur, from his refusal to wear a gas mask in World War I, saying it looked undignified, to his many heroic actions during both world wars. Timeline, bibliography, and index. Part of the People in Focus series.

Related Books for Younger Readers

Marx, Trish. *Echoes of World War II.* Illus. Lerner Publications 1994 (LB 0-8225-4898-4) 96pp.

Six stories of people from different parts of the world whose childhoods were affected by World War II are presented here. One relates the experiences of Rupert Wilkinson, whose father was a liaison officer in the Philippines. At age six, while his father was away with MacArthur, Rupert was taken by the Japanese to a prisoner-of-war camp. These are personal stories and there are many photographs of people and locations. Side-by-side chronology of the six people and index.

Related Books for Older Readers

Aaseng, Nathan. *You Are the General.* Illus. Oliver Press 1994 (LB 1-881508-11-0) 160pp.

This would be an excellent book to use in the classroom with older students who are examining great military decisions of the 20th century. Each chapter puts the reader in a military situation, assessing his or her forces and options against those of the opposition, and, finally, the options that a real general took in that situation. MacArthur's decision to invade Korea at Inchon (behind enemy lines) is described. Students will enjoy testing their wits against these real-life situations. Source notes, bibliography, and index. Part of the Great Decisions series.

Oleksy, Walter. *Military Leaders of World War II.* Illus. Facts on File 1994 (cloth 0-8160-3008-1) 160pp.

Students will enjoy reading about the outstanding leadership of these military figures, including MacArthur. The book is divided into the war in the Pacific and the war in Europe. It is nicely organized for research. Each chapter ends with a chronology of that person's life and recommendations for further reading. Index. Part of the American Profiles series.

McAuliffe, Christa (1948–1986) was the first teacher selected by the National Aeronautical and Space Administration to join a space-shuttle mission. She died in 1986 when the *Challenger* exploded minutes after it was launched.

Biographies for Younger Readers

Billings, Charlene W. *Christa McAuliffe: Pioneer Space Teacher.* Illus. Enslow Publishers 1986 (o.p.) 64pp.

Billings presents a short biography of McAuliffe's life and a description of her training to be one of the crew of the *Challenger*. There is also a good description of the space shuttle itself. Index. Part of the Contemporary Women series.

Naden, Corinne J., and Rose Blue. *Christa McAuliffe.* Illus. Millbrook Press 1991 (LB 1-562-94046-5) 48pp.

The *Challenger* space shuttle was to carry six astronauts and one private citizen—Christa McAuliffe—into space. Bibliography and index. Part of the Gateway Biographies series.

Related Books for Younger Readers

Baird, Anne. *The U.S. Space Camp Book of Astronauts.* William Morrow & Co. 1996 (LB 0-688-12227-2) (cloth 0-688-12226-4) 48pp.

Along with fascinating information about the Space Camp program in Huntsville, Alabama, this provides biographies of several astronauts and a history of the space program. McAuliffe is, of course, part of the story. Bibliography and index.

Burch, Jonathan. *Astronauts.* Illus. Garrett Educational 1992 (LB 1-56074-041-8) 32pp.

Burch covers the difficult training that astronauts must go through and the dangers of their job. The experience of lift-off, life in space, landing on the moon, and the space shuttle are all covered. Glossary and index. Part of the Living Dangerously series.

Madison, James (1751–1836), the fourth president of the United States (1809–1817), was a primary participant behind the scenes at the Constitutional Convention of 1787. He was president during the War of 1812, when the British burned much of Washington.

Biographies for Younger Readers

Fritz, Jean. *The Great Little Madison.* Illus. Putnam's 1989 (cloth 0-399-21768-1) 48pp.

Madison's personal relationships are covered as well as his political achievements—clashes with Patrick Henry, romance with Dolley Payne Todd, and friendship with Thomas Jefferson—making this is a very readable commentary on a stirring time in American history. Endnotes, bibliography, and index.

Biographies for Older Readers

Clinton, Susan. *James Madison: Fourth President of the United States.* Illus. Children's Press 1986 (LB 0-516-01382-3) 100pp.

This is a wonderful overview of the period in American history that covers the Louisiana Purchase, the War of 1812, the Continental Congress, Shays' Rebellion, and the signing of the Constitution. Chronology and index. Part of the Encyclopedia of Presidents series.

Leavell, J. Perry. *James Madison.* Illus. Chelsea House 1988 (o.p.) 112pp.

With quotations from both critics and admirers, this is a balanced account of Madison's life as a statesman. His role as "the father of the Constitution" and in the writing of the Bill of Rights is covered, along with his many other political achievements. Chronology, list of further readings, and index. Part of the World Leaders Past & Present series.

Related Books for Younger Readers

Carter, Alden R. *Birth of the Republic.* Franklin Watts 1988 (LB 0-531-10572-5)

Covered are the end of the Revolutionary War and the structuring of the new nation. Madison was a strong proponent of the federal system as being the most effective way for the new government to operate. List of further readings and index. Part of the American Revolution series.

Steins, Richard. *A Nation Is Born: Rebellion and Independence in America (1700–1820).* Illus. Twenty-First Century Books 1993 (LB 0-8050-2582-0) 64pp.

Primary source material illustrates life in the 13 colonies, the problems with England, the Revolution, and the creation of the new government. There are excerpts from Madison's classic work "The Federalist." List of further readings, chronology, and index. Part of the First Person America series.

Related Books for Older Readers

Scott, John A. *The Facts on File History of the American People.*
Illus. Facts on File 1990 (cloth 0-8160-1739-5) 224pp.

This is packed full of historical information about the United States, including songs, maps, and illustrations. Special attention has been given to original sources. Madison's years as president are, of course, a part of this history. List of further readings and index.

Magellan, Ferdinand (1480?–1521), a Portuguese navigator and explorer, led an expedition sponsored by Spain that was the first to completely circle the globe. Magellan was killed by natives in the Philippines, but his ships continued westward to complete the circumnavigation.

Biographies for Older Readers

Hargrove, Jim. *Ferdinand Magellan: First Around the World.*
Illus. Children's Press 1990 (o.p.) 128pp.

With many photographs and illustrations, this book covers Magellan's life and voyage around the world. Included are maps of how the world was perceived at that time. Timeline, glossary, and index. Part of the World's Great Explorers series.

Related Books for Younger Readers

Aylesworth, Thomas G., and Virginia L. Aylesworth. *Territories and Possessions: Guam, Puerto Rico, U.S. Virgin Islands, American Samoa, North Mariana Islands.* Illus. Chelsea House 1988 (o.p.) 64pp.

This is an overview of Puerto Rico, the Virgin Islands, Guam, American Samoa, Wake and Midway Islands, and Micronesia. Magellan discovered Guam and parts of Micronesia. Each section has maps, quick facts, and photographs. Index. Part of the Let's Discover the States series.

Twist, Clint. *Magellan and da Gama: To the Far East and Beyond.* Illus. Raintree Steck-Vaughn 1994 (LB 0-8114-7254-X)

A good research book for enjoyable browsing. Sailing vessels, local cultures, the dangers encountered on the voyages, and later world events are covered. The student is provided with suggestions of other people and places of the time. List of further readings, glossary, and index. Part of the Beyond the Horizons series.

Related Books for Older Readers

Dunnahoo, Terry. *U.S. Territories: And Freely Associated States.* Illus. Franklin Watts 1988 (LB 0-531-10605-5) 128pp.

Dunnahoo presents historical information and pertinent facts about each of the U.S. territories. Magellan is included in the historical section on Guam. Index.

Malcolm X (1925–1965), an African American activist and religious leader, adopted the Black Muslim faith. He became active as a minister and a recruiter for the group. He broke away from the Black Muslims in 1964 and was assassinated in New York City one year later.

Biographies for Younger Readers

Davis, Lucile. *Malcolm X: A Photo-Illustrated Biography.* Illus. Bridgestone Books 1998 (cloth 1-56065-571-2) 24pp.

Black-and-white photographs and a brief text will attract younger students doing research. Additional features include a selection of "Words from Malcolm X" and "Important Dates." Glossary and index. Part of the Read and Discover Photo-Illustrated Biographies series.

Slater, Jack. *Malcolm X.* Illus. with photographs. Children's Press 1993 (LB 0-516-06669-2) (pap. 0-516-46669-0) 32pp.

This is a simply told version of Malcolm X's life, covering his hard childhood years, his involvement with the law as a teenager, and his activities with the Nation of Islam, leading up to his assassination. Index. Part of the Cornerstones of Freedom series.

Biographies for Older Readers

Diamond, Arthur. *Malcolm X: A Voice for Black America.* Illus. Enslow Publishers 1994 (LB 0-89490-435-3) 128pp.

    While describing the hard and violent life Malcolm had even as a young child, the author indicates that some of the information in Malcolm X's autobiography may have been incorrect or exaggerated. This is a very readable version of Malcolm X's life. There is even information about Spike Lee's 1992 movie. Chronology, list of further readings, chapter notes, and index. Part of the People to Know series.

Myers, Walter Dean. *Malcolm X: By Any Means Necessary.* Scholastic 1993 (cloth 0-590-46484-1) 1994 (pap. 0-590-48109-6) 224pp.

    In this well-balanced and thorough biography, Myers presents Malcolm X's violent fight against racism within a historical context. There is a very useful chronology, with Malcolm X's lifetime on one side and events of the era on the other. Bibliography and index.

Rummel, Jack. *Malcolm X: Militant Black Leader.* Illus. Chelsea House 1989 (LB 1-55546-600-1) (pap. 0-7910-0227-6) 112pp.

    This thorough, well-organized book is a fine choice for students doing research. Malcolm X is described within the context of the different attitudes about protest and the civil rights movement. Chronology, bibliography, and index. Part of the Black Americans of Achievement series.

Related Books for Younger Readers

Kallen, Stuart A. *Black History and the Civil Rights Movement.* Abdo & Daughters 1990 (LB 1-56239-020-1)

    Including information on the Black Muslims and Black Power as well as Malcolm X, this is a simple history of the civil rights movement from the Depression years to 1968. Index.

Rediger, Pat. *Great African Americans in Civil Rights.* Illus. Crabtree 1996 (LB 0-86505-798-2) (pap. 0-86505-812-1) 64pp.

    Students will want to take a look at this collection of notable civil rights figures of the 1960s. Each section is full of photographs, quotations, and major accomplishments. Index. Part of the Outstanding African Americans series.

Related Books for Older Readers

Dudley, William, ed. *The Civil Rights Movement: Opposing Viewpoints.* Illus. Greenhaven 1996 (LB 1-56510-369-6) (pap. 1-56510-368-8) 312pp.

Each chapter begins by highlighting a debate on civil rights and then cites several articles written by well-known leaders of the movement. Some of Malcolm X's writings are featured. Appendices list sites of the civil rights movement and acronyms of pertinent organizations. Questions about the issues are raised in each chapter. Chronology, annotated bibliography, and index. Part of the American History series.

Weisbrot, Robert. *Marching Toward Freedom: From the Founding of the Southern Christian Leadership Conference to the Assassination of Malcolm X, 1957–1965.* Illus. Chelsea House 1994 (pap. 0-7910-2256-0)

During the era presented in this book, black political and social activism grew and spread. Activities included sit-ins, boycotts, the formation of organized groups, and the 1963 March on Washington. This book concludes with the Watts riots and the death of Malcolm X. Chronology, bibliography, and index. Part of the Milestones in Black American History series.

Mandela, Nelson (1918–), a South African statesman, led the successful battle to dismantle his country's racist policy of apartheid and became its first black president in 1994. An early member of the African National Congress, he was sentenced to life in prison in 1964 for political crimes and was released in 1990.

Biographies for Younger Readers

Feinberg, Brian. *Nelson Mandela and the Quest for Freedom.* Illus. Chelsea House 1992 (LB 0-7910-1569-6) 80pp.

Apartheid, equality, imprisonment, and justice are some of the issues presented in this biography. Chapters describe "The Man Who Wanted Freedom," "The Blood of Children," and "A Free

Man." This is well-organized for research and makes good use of photographs to extend the text. Chronology, glossary, bibliography, and index. Part of the Junior World Biographies series.

Holland, Gini. *Nelson Mandela.* Illus. Raintree Steck-Vaughn 1997 (LB 0-8172-4454-9)

This book explains the historical culture and political climate of South Africa. Apartheid, his imprisonment, and his presidency are all covered briefly. List of key dates. Part of the First Biographies series.

Roberts, Jack L. *Nelson Mandela: Determined to Be Free.* Illus. Millbrook Press 1995 (LB 1-56294-558-0) 48pp.

Photographs in color and black and white capture important moments in the life of Nelson Mandela. They also provide students with images of the conditions that Mandela worked to change and improve. Chronology, bibliography, and index. Part of the Gateway Biographies series.

Biographies for Older Readers

Denenberg, Barry. *Nelson Mandela: No Easy Walk to Freedom.* Illus. Scholastic 1991 (pap. 0-590-44154-X) 176pp.

Not just a description of Mandela's life, this book is also a good overview of South Africa, its history, and apartheid. It was published shortly after Mandela's release from prison. Chronology, bibliography, and index.

Mandela, Nelson. *Mandela: An Illustrated Autobiography.* Illus. Little, Brown 1994 (cloth 0-316-55038-8)

Definitely for older students, this is a book that should not be overlooked because of its autobiographical details of Mandela's struggle for freedom. It portrays the development of his political consciousness, his pivotal role in the formation of the African National Congress Youth League, his years underground, his 27 years in prison, and his victory in South Africa's first multiracial elections in 1994.

Related Books for Younger Readers

Brickhill, Joan. *South Africa: The End of Apartheid?* Illus. Franklin Watts 1991 (o.p.) 40pp.

Students will enjoy browsing through this book that was published after Mandela's release from prison but before he became president. With informative insets, it covers the history of South African politics: the foundations and establishment of apartheid, resistance to it, repression, and its demise. Chronology, glossary, and index. Part of the Hotspots series.

Meisel, Jacqueline Drobis. *South Africa: A Tapestry of Peoples and Traditions.* Illus. Marshall Cavendish 1997 (LB 0-7614-0335-3) 64pp.

Written after Mandela was freed from prison and elected president, this is up-to-date coverage, well laid out, covering geography and history, the people, family life, festivals, food, school and recreation, and the arts. Lists of further readings, country facts, glossary, and index. Part of the Exploring Cultures of the World series.

Related Books for Older Readers

Pratt, Paula Bryant. *The End of Apartheid in South Africa.* Illus. Lucent 1995 (LB 1-56006-170-7)

Featuring the contributions of Nelson Mandela, this book describes the events leading to the collapse of the political system in South Africa. Bibliography and index. Part of the World in Conflict series.

Mankiller, Wilma (1945–), from 1985 to 1995 served as the first woman tribal chief of the Cherokee Nation, one of the largest American Indian tribes in the United States.

Biographies for Younger Readers

Simon, Charnan. *Wilma P. Mankiller: Chief of the Cherokee.* Illus. Children's Press 1991 (o.p.) 32pp.

A simple telling of Mankiller's life and work to unite the Cherokee Nation. The many black-and-white photographs add details about her life and accomplishments. Timeline and index. Part of the Picture-Story Biographies series.

Biographies for Older Readers

Yannuzzi, Della A. *Wilma Mankiller: Leader of the Cherokee Nation.* Illus. Enslow Publishers 1994 (LB 0-89490-498-1) 104pp.

Yannuzzi covers Mankiller's childhood in Oklahoma to her role as Principal Chief of the Cherokee Nation. Her efforts to create a financially independent nation and re-establish the Cherokee tribal judicial system are related. Chronology, list of further readings, chapter notes, and index. Part of the People to Know series.

Related Books for Younger Readers

Claro, Nicole. *The Cherokee Indians.* Illus. Chelsea House 1991 (LB 0-7910-1652-8) 1994 (pap. 0-7910-2030-4) 80pp.

Here is a description of the life of the Cherokee Indians in the past, the government's attempts to "civilize" them, the Trail of Tears, and Cherokee life today. Chronology, glossary, and index. Part of the Junior Library of American Indians series.

Lund, Bill. *The Cherokee Indians.* Illus. Bridgestone Books 1997 (cloth 1-56065-477-5)

This introductory book describes Cherokee Indians, past and present: villages, food, games, and legends. Lists of further readings and Internet sites, glossary, and index. Part of the Native Peoples series.

Related Books for Older Readers

Kelly, Lawrence C. *Federal Indian Policy.* Chelsea House 1990 (cloth 1-55546-706-7)

Starting with the colonial policy and continuing to the present, this book provides an overview of federal policy toward Indians. How and why policy was formed, Indian removal, the failure of the Dawes Act, the Indian New Deal, and contemporary U.S. policy are all covered. Glossary, bibliography, and index. Part of the Indians of North America series.

Mao Zedong (1893–1976), leader of China's Communist revolution, in 1949 proclaimed the People's Republic of China, which he ruled as president and as chairman of the Communist Party. He began the process of reopening China to the West in the early 1970s.

Biographies for Older Readers

Garza, Hedda. *Mao Zedong.* Illus. Chelsea House 1988 (o.p.) 112pp.

Mao Zedong helped move China toward modernization. This is a thorough presentation with well-organized chapters and numerous illustrations. Quotations from Mao, his contemporaries, historians, and others are presented in the margins surrounding the text and add another perspective to the description of Mao. Chronology, bibliography, and index. Part of the World Leaders Past & Present series.

Stefoff, Rebecca. *Mao Zedong: Founder of the People's Republic of China.* Illus. Millbrook Press 1996 (LB 1-56294-531-9) 128pp.

With a very detailed text, Stefoff presents a clear, well-rounded portrayal of this complex leader. Mao brought many Chinese prosperity and opportunities, yet many others were imprisoned or killed. The final chapter looks at "Mao's Legacy" and gives students an opportunity to review his accomplishments. Chronology, chapter notes, bibliography, and index.

Related Books for Younger Readers

Bradley, John. *China: A New Revolution?* Illus. Gloucester Press 1990 (o.p.)

This book gives a brief overview of China's tumultuous history covering communism, China under Mao, the democracy crisis, and the massacre at Tiananmen Square. Chronology, glossary, and index. Part of the Hotspots series.

Related Books for Older Readers

Ashabranner, Brent. *Land of Yesterday, Land of Tomorrow: Discovering Chinese Central Asia.* Illus. Dutton 1992 (pap. 0-525-65086-5) 96pp.

This is a fascinating essay accompanied by photographs by Paul, David, and Peter Conklin. Ashabranner's text reads like a travelogue, providing a detailed description of his observations of China, including the history and present-day way of life. Bibliography and index.

Ferroa, Peggy. *China.* Illus. Marshall Cavendish 1991 (LB 1-85435-399-3) 128pp.

Using many photographs, this book presents an overview of China's geography, history, government, economy, people, lifestyles, religion, language, and culture. List of facts, glossary, bibliography, and index. Part of the Cultures of the World series.

Pietrusza, David. *The Chinese Cultural Revolution.* Illus. Lucent 1997 (LB 1-56006-305-X)

At the beginning of this book there is a detailed chronology of "Important Dates in the History of the Chinese Cultural Revolution." The chapters expand this chronology, focusing on the leaders, the Red Guard and terrorism, and the deaths of Lin Biao and Mao

Zedong. Boxed sections provide insights from historians and contemporaries. Chapter notes, glossary, bibliography, and index. Part of the World History series.

Marconi, Guglielmo Marchese

(1874–1937), an Italian inventor and physicist, is best known for his development of wireless telegraphy, transmitting the first long-wave signals in 1895. In 1901 he transmitted signals across the Atlantic. He shared the Nobel Prize for physics in 1909.

Biographies for Younger Readers

Tames, Richard. *Guglielmo Marconi.* Illus. Franklin Watts 1990 (o.p.) 32pp.

Not just a biography, this book also contains information about many of the scientific advances (the discovery of electromagnetic waves, the telephone, color photography) on which Marconi based his discovery of "wireless" telegraphy, or radio, and with which he was able to send transatlantic messages. His life as an experimenter, inventor, businessman, soldier, diplomat, and statesman is covered. Lists of important books and dates, glossary, and index. Part of the Lifetimes series.

Related Books for Younger Readers

Bender, Lionel. *Invention.* Illus. Alfred A. Knopf 1991 (LB 0-679-90782-3) (cloth 0-679-80782-9) 64pp.

Marconi's creation of the first radio is just one of many inventions in this entertaining book. Packed with wonderful photographs and illustrations, it covers such inventions as the wheel, gears, levers, clocks, telephones, and rocket engines. Index. Part of the Eyewitness Books series.

Coulter, George, and Shirley Coulter. *Radio.* Illus. Rourke 1996
(LB 0-86625-584-2)

Beginning with a discussion of different kinds of airwaves, the
authors talk about how we get a signal, how a radio station works, the
ways that we use one-way radio, and how we use talk radio. Full of
diagrams, color photographs, and simple explanations. Glossary and
index. Part of the You Make It Work series.

Platt, Richard. *In the Beginning: The Nearly Complete History of
Almost Everything.* Illus. by Brian Delf. Dorling Kindersley 1995
(cloth 0-7894-0206-8) 80pp.

A different topic is presented on each double-page spread,
covering the creation of the world, everyday life, buildings, making
and measuring, and transportation. Hundreds of wonderful illustrations will keep students occupied for hours. Marconi is included in
the section on communications and broadcasting. Indexes.

M arshall, Thurgood (1908–1993), the
first African American justice on the U.S. Supreme
Court, was appointed in 1967. In 1954 as an
attorney active in the civil rights struggle, he
successfully argued before the Court the case of
Brown v. *Board of Education,* which led to the end
of public school segregation.

*"[Thurgood Marshall's]
one of the special
ones—a great rumpled
bear of a man with the
. . . dignity only those
with a true calling
ever achieve."*
—Newsweek
(Hess, p. 42)

Biographies for Younger Readers

Greene, Carol. *Thurgood Marshall: First African American
Supreme Court Justice.* Illus. Children's Press 1991 (LB 0-516-
04225-4) (pap. 0-516-44225-2) 48pp.

Simple text and documentary photographs make for a useful
biography. Marshall's career, with special focus on the civil rights
cases, is covered. Chronology and index. Part of the Rookie Biographies series.

Kent, Deborah. *Thurgood Marshall and the Supreme Court.* Illus. Children's Press 1997 (LB 0-516-20297-9) (pap. 0-516-26139-8)

Written after his death, this is a helpful record of Marshall's life and the civil rights movement for younger readers. Timeline, glossary, and index. Part of the Cornerstones of Freedom series.

Biographies for Older Readers

Hess, Debra. *Thurgood Marshall: The Fight for Equal Justice.* Illus. Silver Burdett 1990 (LB 0-382-09921-4) (pap. 0-382-24058-8) 128pp.

With many black-and-white photographs and a clearly written text, this book puts Marshall's life into the context of the civil rights movement. Each chapter starts out with a well-known quotation by Marshall, about him, or about the civil rights movement. Chronology, list of further readings, sources, and index. Part of the History of the Civil Rights Movement series.

Whitelaw, Nancy. *Mr. Civil Rights: The Story of Thurgood Marshall.* Illus. Morgan Reynolds 1995 (LB 1-883846-10-2) 121pp.

This is a very useful biography for students doing research. The focus throughout the book is on the remarkable achievement of Thurgood Marshall and on his lifetime efforts to provide civil rights for all. Appendix of "Selected Civil Rights Cases," timeline, chapter notes, glossary, bibliography, and index. Part of the Notable Americans series.

Related Books for Younger Readers

Kronenwetter, Michael. *The Supreme Court of the United States.* Illus. Enslow Publishers 1996 (LB 0-89490-536-8) 112pp.

This is a record of the history, powers, and duties of the Supreme Court, containing chapters on how politics affect the Court and on historic decisions. It addresses Marshall's role in *Brown* v. *Board of Education* and his historic place as the first black Supreme Court justice. List of further readings, chapter notes, glossary, and index. Part of the American Government in Action series.

Stein, R. Conrad. *Powers of the Supreme Court.* Illus. Children's Press 1995 (LB 0-516-06697-8) 32pp.

With simple descriptions of the Supreme Court and its role, this book includes both good and disastrous decisions. Marshall's role as a lawyer and as a justice are related. Glossary, timeline, and index. Part of the Cornerstones of Freedom series.

Related Books for Older Readers

Aaseng, Nathan. *You Are the Supreme Court Justice.* Illus. Oliver Press 1994 (LB 1-881508-14-5) 160pp.

Pretending that the reader is one of the Supreme Court justices, this book takes some well-known cases and gives the options available to the Court. Included is the *Brown* v. *Board of Education* case that Thurgood Marshall argued. Part of the Great Decisions series.

Hine, Darlene Clark. *The Path to Equality: From the Scottsboro Case to the Breaking of Baseball's Color Barrier, 1931–1947.* Illus. Chelsea House 1995 (LB 0-7910-2251-X) (pap. 0-7910-2677-9)

The Great Depression of the 1930s had a devastating impact, particularly on blacks who had not had the same opportunities to succeed. It was an era of continued segregation, racial tensions, and violence. Yet, there were moments of great accomplishment, too. Thurgood Marshall began his successful career as a civil rights attorney and Jackie Robinson became the first African American player in the major leagues. Chronology, bibliography, and index. Part of the Milestones in Black American History series.

Patrick, John J. *The Young Oxford Companion to the Supreme Court of the United States.* Oxford University Press 1994 (cloth 0-19-507877-2) 368pp.

Containing entries on each of the justices, well-known court cases, and other information on the court and its proceedings, this is like an encyclopedia of the Supreme Court. Each entry includes cross-references to related information and further reading on the subject. Appendices list the terms of all justices. Map of the Supreme Court Building, list of further readings, and index. Part of the Young Oxford Companion series.

Matzeliger, Jan Ernst (1852–1889) was born in Dutch Guiana to a black mother and a white father. He emigrated to the United States at about the age of 20 and later developed machinery that revolutionized the shoe manufacturing industry.

Biographies for Younger Readers

Mitchell, Barbara. *Shoes for Everyone: A Story about Jan Matzeliger.* Illus. by Hetty Mitchell. Carolrhoda Books 1986 (LB 0-87614-290-0); First Avenue Editions 1987 (pap. 0-87614-473-3) 64pp.

The author begins with a note about the prejudice Matzeliger encountered during his lifetime, covering his early years in Dutch Guiana and his journey as a young man to North America, where he developed his amazing machine that made shoes. Part of the Carolrhoda Creative Minds series.

Related Books for Younger Readers

Hudson, Wade. *Five Notable Inventors.* Illus. by Ron Garnett and with photos. Scholastic 1995 (pap. 0-590-48033-2) 48pp.

Featured are Jan Ernst Matzeliger (shoe last), Elijah McCoy (machine lubricating cup), Granville T. Woods (railway telegraphy, electrical engineering, etc.), Madam C. J. Walker (cosmetics), and Garrett Morgan ("gas inhalator" and traffic signal light). Part of the Great Black Heroes series and of the Hello Reader! series.

McKissack, Patricia, and Fredrick McKissack. *African American Inventors.* Illus. Millbrook Press 1994 (LB 1-56294-468-1) 96pp.

The authors trace the history and accomplishments of African American scientists and inventors, often stressing the obstacles of discrimination and prejudice. The last chapter features "Contemporary Inventors and Their Inventions." Bibliography and index. Part of the Proud Heritage series.

Related Books for Older Readers

Dash, Joan. *We Shall Not Be Moved: The Women's Factory Strike of 1909.* Illus. Scholastic 1996 (LB 0-590-48409-5) 166pp.

Matzeliger would have been interested in the women's factory strike which took place shortly after his death. Black-and-white photographs show the young shirtwaist workers, the strike, women being led to jail, and the well-known and well-to-do women who became involved. Bibliography and index.

Haskins, Jim. *Outward Dreams: Black Inventors and Their Inventions.* Illus. Walker and Company 1991 (LB 0-8027-6994-2) (cloth 0-8027-6993-4) 128pp.

This book highlights the accomplishments of many African American inventors. Because of prejudice and discrimination, their work was often overlooked or credited to others. An appendix lists inventions by blacks from 1834 to 1900 along with patent numbers. Bibliography and index.

Hayden, Robert C. *9 African American Inventors.* Illus. Twenty-First Century Books 1992 (LB 0-8050-2133-7) 171pp.

Matzeliger is one of the nine African Americans featured here whose inventions had an impact on modern life but who achieved little recognition in their time. Appendices of black inventors and index. Part of the Achievers: African Americans in Science and Technology series.

Mayo, Charles Horace (1865–1939), and his brother William James Mayo, (1861–1939), American physicians and surgeons, in 1889 founded with their father a medical facility later named the Mayo Clinic. William was well known for his innovations in stomach, gall bladder, and cancer surgery. Charles's surgical specialties included operations on the thyroid gland, eyes, and the nervous system.

Biographies for Younger Readers

Crofford, Emily. *Frontier Surgeons: A Story About the Mayo Brothers.* Illus. by Karen Ritz. Carolrhoda Books 1989 (LB 0-87614-381-8); First Avenue Editions 1991 (pap. 0-87614-553-5) 64pp.

From a young age, the Mayo brothers watched their father, the county coroner, do autopsies. As teenagers, they assisted him with surgery. This story of the founders of the world-famous clinic is well presented for students just beginning the research process. Part of the Carolrhoda Creative Minds series.

Related Books for Younger Readers

Drotar, David Lee. *The Fire Curse and Other True Medical Mysteries.* Walker and Company 1994 (cloth 0-8027-8327-9)

Students will quickly find that truth is stranger than fiction in this fascinating book. Dogs that can detect the onset of an epileptic seizure, children who age prematurely, children born with hair covering their entire body and face, and spontaneous combustion are just a few of the medical mysteries contained in this book. Extensive bibliography and index.

Miller, Brandon Marie. *Just What the Doctor Ordered: The History of American Medicine.* Illus. Lerner Publications 1997 (LB 0-8225-1737-X)

This is an amazing look at the history of medicine in America, from Native American Indians through the present. Bloodletting with leeches, laxatives for purges, treating headaches with electricity, dissecting cadavers, the development of X-ray machines, pasteurization of milk—all these give some perspective on our medical past and the amazing strides that we have made. Bibliography and index.

Related Books for Older Readers

Nardo, Don. *Medical Diagnosis.* Illus. Chelsea House 1992 (LB 0-7910-0067-2)

Nardo examines methods of medical diagnosis, by early healers and by modern-day physicians. He also looks into topics including AIDS, chronic fatigue syndrome, and Legionnaire's disease. Lists of places to write for more information and further readings, glossary, and index. Part of the Encyclopedia of Health series.

Mead, Margaret (1901–1978), an American anthropologist and author who studied under Franz Boas, is well known for her studies on culture and child rearing. Mead studied extensively in the Pacific, wrote several books, and held a post at the American Museum of Natural History in New York City.

Biographies for Younger Readers

Saunders, Susan. *Margaret Mead: The World Was Her Family.* Illus. by Ted Lewin. Viking Penguin 1987 (pap. 0-14-032063-6)

Margaret Mead's curiosity about people led her to study anthropology and investigate different cultures. The seven brief chapters in this book are easy to read. Students would find this book both enjoyable and informative. Part of the Women of Our Time series.

Related Books for Younger Readers

Jackson, Donna M. *The Bone Detectives: How Forensic Anthropologists Solve Crimes and Uncover Mysteries of the Dead.* Illus. by Charlie Fellenbaum. Little, Brown 1995 (cloth 0-316-82935-8) 48pp.

This fascinating book explores another kind of anthropology. Readers will find out how bones and fingerprints leave us clues. They also learn about the work done by computer specialists, pathologists, and toxicologists. Real-life crimes and their solutions are described. Glossary of forensic terms.

Related Books for Older Readers

Ashby, Ruth, and Deborah Gore Ohrn, eds. *Herstory: Women Who Changed the World.* Illus. Viking Penguin 1995 (pap. 0-670-85434-4) 304pp.

This book contains 120 biographical sketches of women who changed the world, placing them in the context of their times, and taking the viewpoint that women's history has largely been ignored. The section on Mead's anthropological work also includes two lesser-known female anthropologists: Elsie Clews Parsons and Ruth Benedict. Introduction by Gloria Steinem, extensive bibliography, and three indexes: geographical, alphabetical, and occupational.

Meir, Golda (1898–1978), prime minister of Israel from 1969 to 1974, was active in the labor movement. As prime minister she pursued peace initiatives but came under heavy criticism and resigned in 1974 after the Arab-Israeli War.

Biographies for Younger Readers

Adler, David A. *Our Golda: The Story of Golda Meir.* Illus. by
Donna Ruff. Puffin 1986 (pap. 0-14-032104-7) 64pp.

This biography covers Meir's early childhood in Russia where
pogroms threatened her family's safety, her youth in America, and
her move to Jerusalem. Her efforts to make Israel a Jewish homeland
and become its prime minister are described. Part of the Women of
Our Time series.

Davidson, Margaret. *The Golda Meir Story.* rev. ed. Scribner's
1981 (LB 0-684-16877-4)

This readable story was revised in 1981 to include the last
years of Meir's life. It presents her years in the kibbutz and as prime
minister, helping to establish the independent state of Israel. Bibliography and index.

Related Books for Younger Readers

Long, Cathryn J. *The Middle East in Search of Peace.* updated
ed. Illus. Millbrook Press 1996 (LB 0-7613-0105-4) 64pp.

Long focuses on the 1993 signing of the peace pact between
the Palestine Liberation Organization and Israel, and discusses the
origins of the Arab-Israeli conflict. Meir's political career, as well as
her attitude to the plight of the Palestinians and their territorial aspi-
rations are covered. Chronology, list of further readings, and index.
Part of the Headliners series.

Silverman, Maida. *Israel: The Founding of a Modern Nation.*
Illus. by Susan Avishai. Dial 1998 (LB 0-8037-2136-6) (cloth 0-
8037-2135-8) 112pp.

This book provides a historical background to the struggle to
create a Jewish homeland. Chapters focus on ancient times through
British rule, ending with the birth of Israel in 1948. Detailed timeline of Israel's history from 1948 to the present, bibliography, and
index.

Related Books for Older Readers

Altman, Linda Jacobs. *Life on an Israeli Kibbutz.* Illus. Lucent
1996 (LB 1-56006-328-9) 112pp.

Altman describes life on a kibbutz: work, entertainment, children, Arab neighbors, community values, and the kibbutz as a social
model. There are many stories and quotations from people who have
lived on kibbutzim, including Meir. List of further readings, chapter
notes, and index. Part of the Way People Live series.

Mendes, Chico (1944–1988), a Brazilian rubber worker, led an alliance between his fellow rubber workers and Amazonian tribespeople against the deforestation of the Brazilian interior. He was assassinated in late 1988.

Biographies for Younger Readers

Burch, Joann J. *Chico Mendes: Defender of the Rain Forest.* Illus. with photographs. Millbrook Press 1994 (LB 1-56294-413-4) 48pp.

Burch describes the poverty of Mendes's childhood and his fight as an adult to organize the tree tappers and protect the rain forest. Lists of important dates and further readings and index. Part of the Gateway Green Biography series.

DeStefano, Susan. *Chico Mendes: Fight for the Forest.* Illus. by Larry Raymond. Twenty-First Century Books 1992 (cloth 0-941477-41-X)

Chico Mendes's father taught him how to tap rubber trees without damaging the tree or the rainforest ecosystem. Later, Mendes organized rubber tappers and led the fight for better pay as well as for the protection of the rainforest, a commitment that cost him his life. Glossary and index. Part of the Earth Keepers series.

Related Books for Younger Readers

Ganeri, Anita. *Explore the World of Exotic Rainforests.* Illus. by Robert Morton. Golden Book 1992 (cloth 0-308-68606-X) 48pp.

This is a beautifully illustrated book, full of pictures of plants and animals from the rainforest. Chapters are laid out as questions: What is a rainforest? Why do toucans have big beaks? How slowly does a sloth move? Mendes is included in the section on rainforest people, which also includes pygmy tribes, medicine men, and several Indian tribes. Index.

Lewington, Anna. *Rain Forest Amerindians.* Illus. Raintree Steck-Vaughn 1993 (o.p.) 48pp.

The author discusses the Amerindians, their lands, beliefs and values; their response to European contact; and their struggle to preserve their way of life in the modern world. Mendes's union, comprising more than 100,000 rubber tappers, is also discussed. Maps and many attractive photographs enhance the presentation. List of further readings, glossary, and index. Part of the Threatened Cultures series.

Siy, Alexandra. *The Brazilian Rain Forest.* Illus. Dillon Press 1992 (o.p.) 80pp.

Both teachers and students could use this nicely done book on the rainforest and on its importance and its biodiversity. Mendes's efforts to save the rainforests for the rubber workers are included. Activities for each chapter, lists of environmental organizations to contact and 10 ways to help save Brazil's rainforests, glossary, and index. Part of the Circle of Life series.

Michelangelo Buonarroti

(1475–1564), an Italian sculptor and painter, is famous for his magnificent sculptures of the Pietà (in St. Peter's in Rome) and David (in Florence), among others. Pope Julius II commissioned him to paint the ceiling of the Sistine Chapel.

Biographies for Younger Readers

Milande, Veronique. *Michelangelo and His Times.* Illus. Henry Holt 1995 (pap. 0-8050-4660-7) 64pp.

Young readers will enjoy the amusing trivia and historical anecdotes: "How much does David weigh?" and "Garzoni is not a pasta dish" are just two examples. This book is packed full of artistic, personal, and historical information. Part of the W5 (Who, What, Where, When and Why) series.

Venezia, Mike. *Michelangelo.* Illus. by the author. Children's Press 1991 (LB 0-516-02293-8) (pap. 0-516-42293-6) 32pp.

This series will delight children trying to understand art. Pictures of Michelangelo's work and cartoons illustrating moments of his life depict the time and culture of Florence. The different forms of his work, such as fresco painting and sculpture, are explained. List of museums and churches where his works of art can be found. Part of the Getting to Know the World's Greatest Artists series.

Ventura, Piero. *Michelangelo's World.* Illus by the author. Putnam's 1988 (cloth 0-399-21593-X) 48pp.

Told as if by Michelangelo as an old man, this book is delightfully illustrated with scenes of artists working and the cities where Michelangelo lived. Chronology and pictures of Michelangelo's principal works.

Biographies for Older Readers

McLanathan, Richard. *Michelangelo.* Illus. Harry N. Abrams 1993 (cloth 0-8109-3634-8) 92pp.

A historical overview not just of Michelangelo's work but of Europe at the time, this biography describes Florence and Rome and tells why they became the centers of the cultural Renaissance. Maps of contemporary Europe and pictures of many of his works of art—even a pull-out detail of the Sistine Chapel—are included. List of illustrations found in the book and index. Part of the First Impressions series.

Related Books for Younger Readers

Cole, Alison. *The Renaissance.* Illus. Dorling Kindersley 1994 (cloth 1-56458-493-3) 64pp.

Opening with "What is the Renaissance?" this book then looks at different locations and artists including da Vinci, Dürer, Titian, Raphael, and Michelangelo. Like other books in this series, this makes great use of illustrations, which surround the text. Chronology, list of featured works, glossary, and index. Part of the Eyewitness Art series.

Lorenz, Albert, and Joy Schleh. *Metropolis: Ten Cities / Ten Centuries.* Illus. Harry N. Abrams 1996 (cloth 0-8109-4284-4) 64pp.

Students will enjoy browsing through this lavishly illustrated book. Beginning with 11th-century Jerusalem and ending with 20th-century New York, it takes 10 cities and shows their response to change. Michelangelo is featured in the section on 16th-century Florence. Double-page spreads, timelines that border each picture, and detailed illustrations of city life will keep students entertained for a long time.

Related Books for Older Readers

Adams, Simon, et al. *Illustrated Atlas of World History.* Illus. Random House 1992 (LB 0-679-92465-5) (pap. 0-679-82465-0) 160pp.

An overview of world history, covering the ancient world, trade and religion, exploration and empire, and revolution and technology. Full of illustrations, maps, and photographs, there is something here for everybody. Michelangelo is included in the section on the Renaissance, which also covers astronomy, advances in medicine, and the invention of printing. Chronology of world history and index.

Mitchell, Maria (1818–1889), an American astronomer and educator, was the first woman to become a fellow of the Academy of Arts and Sciences. She studied sunspots and nebulae, and in 1847 she discovered a comet, for which she was honored by the king of Denmark.

Biographies for Younger Readers

McPherson, Stephanie S. *Rooftop Astronomer: A Story About Maria Mitchell.* Illus. by Hetty Mitchell. Carolrhoda Books 1990 (LB 0-87614-410-5) 32pp.

This is an entertaining story of Mitchell's life as a champion of women's rights and an ever-questioning scientist. Stories include her fixing a ship captain's chronometer as a 12-year-old and letting her students at Vassar College stay up all night to watch meteors. Part of the Carolrhoda Creative Minds series.

Biographies for Older Readers

Gormley, Beatrice. *Maria Mitchell: The Soul of an Astronomer.* William B. Eerdmans Publishing 1995 (cloth 0-8028-5116-9) (pap. 0-8028-5099-5) 128pp.

In addition to her achievements as an astronomer, this book covers her work in the women's movement and for higher education for women. List of suggestions for further readings, bibliography, and index. Part of the Women of Spirit series.

Related Books for Younger Readers

Camp, Carole Ann. *American Astronomers: Searchers and Wonderers.* Illus. Enslow Publishers 1996 (LB 0-89490-631-3) 104pp.

The chronological arrangement of this book allows students to develop a sense of the history of astronomy. From the early work of Maria Mitchell to the research of George Ellery Hale and Edwin

Hubble to the studies of Carl Sagan, this book describes the fascination with observing space. Chapter notes and index. Part of the Collective Biographies series.

Related Books for Older Readers

Hitzeroth, Deborah. *Telescopes: Searching the Heavens.* Illus. Lucent 1991 (LB 1-56006-209-6) 96pp.

This book provides excellent background information on telescopes and those who study the heavens. Chapters discuss the invention of the telescope, radio telescopes, satellite-borne telescopes, and the Hubble space telescope. Glossary, bibliography, and index. Part of the Encyclopedia of Discovery and Invention series.

Stille, Darlene R. *Extraordinary Women Scientists.* Illus. Children's Press 1995 (LB 0-516-00585-5) (pap. 0-516-40585-3) 208pp.

A beautifully done book, featuring many women scientists who deserve credit for improving our lives. Doctors, mathematicians, inventors, and engineers are all here. Bibliography and index. Part of the Extraordinary People series.

Monroe, James (1758–1831), 5th president of the United States (1817–1825), formulated the Monroe Doctrine, a foreign policy that expresses opposition to European control in the Western Hemisphere.

Biographies for Older Readers

Fitz-Gerald, Christine. *James Monroe: Fifth President of the United States.* Illus. Children's Press 1987 (LB 0-516-01383-1) 100pp.

This book covers Monroe's life and long political career, including his doctrine against increased European encroachment in the Americas. Chronology and index. Part of the Encyclopedia of Presidents series.

Wetzel, Charles. *James Monroe.* Illus. Chelsea House 1989 (o.p.)

Monroe's involvement in the development of the United States included fighting for George Washington in the Revolutionary War at the age of 18 and the formulation of the Monroe Doctrine. Lists of further readings, chronology, and index. Part of the World Leaders Past & Present series.

Related Books for Younger Readers

Kallen, Stuart A. *Days of Slavery: A History of Black People in America 1619–1863.* Illus. Abdo & Daughters 1990 (cloth 1-56239-017-1)

In this introductory book, Kallen presents America from the perspective of African Americans, with many black-and-white illustrations. Monroe's role in the purchase of territory in Africa where blacks could settle is related. Index.

Related Books for Older Readers

Hakim, Joy. *The New Nation.* Illus. Oxford University Press 1993 (LB 0-19-507751-2) (cloth 0-19-509509-X) (pap. 0-19-507752-0) 160pp.

Readers will have fun looking at this book of American history, covering the years from Washington's inauguration to the beginnings of abolitionism. One entire chapter is about "That Good President Monroe," covering the purchase of Florida from Spain and the Monroe Doctrine. Chronology, list of further readings, and index. Part of the History of US series.

Smith, Carter, ed. *The Conquest of the West: A Sourcebook on the American West.* Illus. Millbrook Press 1992 (LB 1-56294-129-1) 1996 (pap. 0-7613-0151-8) 96pp.

The author describes and illustrates the western expansion of the United States, including Monroe's negotiations in obtaining the Louisiana Purchase. Many original documents from the Library of Congress are shown. Index. Part of the American Albums from the Collections of the Library of Congress series.

Morgan, Garrett (1877–1963), an African American inventor, developed a more efficient sewing machine, a substance to help temporarily straighten the hair of African Americans, and an early gas mask. In 1923 he patented an automatic traffic signal and sold it to General Electric.

Biographies for Younger Readers

Jackson, Garnet N. *Garrett Morgan, Inventor.* Illus. by Thomas Hudson. Modern Curriculum Press 1993 (cloth 0-8136-5231-6) (pap. 0-8136-5704-0)

The simple rhyming text of this book makes it accessible to younger readers. It provides a very brief account of Garrett Morgan's invention of a gas mask and the traffic signal light. Part of the Beginning Biographies series.

Sweet, Dovie Davis. *Red Light, Green Light: The Life of Garrett Morgan and His Invention of the Stoplight.* Illus. by Larry Sherman. Exposition Press 1978 (pap. 0-682-49088-1)

The author describes Garrett Morgan's inventions and stresses the importance of his accomplishments.

Related Books for Younger Readers

Hudson, Wade. *Five Notable Inventors.* Illus. by Ron Garnett and with photos. Scholastic 1995 (pap. 0-590-48033-2) 48pp.

Featured are Jan Ernst Matzeliger (shoe last), Elijah McCoy (machine lubricating cup), Granville T. Woods (railway telegraphy, electrical engineering, etc.), Madam C. J. Walker (cosmetics), and Garrett Morgan ("gas inhalator" and traffic signal light). Part of the Great Black Heroes series and of the Hello Reader! series.

McKissack, Patricia, and Fredrick McKissack. *African American Inventors.* Illus. Millbrook Press 1994 (LB 1-56294-468-1) 96pp.

The authors trace the history and accomplishments of African American scientists and inventors, often stressing the obstacles of discrimination and prejudice. The last chapter features "Contemporary Inventors and Their Inventions." Bibliography and index. Part of the Proud Heritage series.

Related Books for Older Readers

Haskins, Jim. *Outward Dreams: Black Inventors and Their Inventions.* Illus. Walker and Company 1991 (LB 0-8027-6994-2) (cloth 0-8027-6993-4) 128pp.

This book highlights the accomplishments of many African American inventors. Because of prejudice and discrimination, their work was often overlooked or credited to others. Among those included are Jan Matzeliger, Lewis Latimer, George Washington Carver, Percy Julian, and Garrett Morgan. An appendix lists the inventions by blacks between 1834 and 1900, along with patent numbers. Bibliography and index.

Muir, John (1838–1914), a Scottish-born American naturalist and explorer, was a key figure in the crusade for national parks. In addition, he was the founder of the Sierra Club and the discoverer of Muir Glacier in Alaska.

Biographies for Younger Readers

Greene, Carol. *John Muir: Man of the Wild Places.* Illus. by Steven Dobson. Children's Press 1991 (LB 0-516-04220-3) (pap. 0-516-44220-1) 48pp.

From "A Boyhood in Scotland" to "The Wild Places," this book introduces John Muir and describes his efforts to preserve nature and the wilderness. The simple text makes this accessible to younger readers. Chronology and index. Part of the Rookie Biographies series.

Talmadge, Katherine S. *John Muir: At Home in the Wild.* Illus.
by Antonio Castro. Twenty-First Century Books 1993 (o.p.)

More than 100 years ago, John Muir helped make people aware
of the importance of protecting the environment. He was a founder
of the Sierra Club and was instrumental in preserving many of the
wilderness areas in the United States. Glossary and index. Part of
the Earth Keepers series.

Biographies for Older Readers

Wadsworth, Ginger. *John Muir: Wilderness Protector.* Illus. Lerner Publications 1992 (LB 0-8225-4912-3) 144pp.

In this detailed biography, students will learn about John
Muir's education as a botanist and geologist, his adventures as an
explorer, and his commitment to conserving the wilderness. His
efforts led to the creation of our national park system and to the
establishment of the Sierra Club. Map of Yosemite National Park,
source notes, bibliography, and index.

Related Books for Younger Readers

Law, Kevin J. *The Environmental Protection Agency.* Illus.
Chelsea House 1988 (o.p.) 96pp.

The Environmental Protection Agency was created in 1970 in
response to the concerns of naturalists, scientists, and other ecology-minded people. This book describes the history of the environmental movement, the responsibilities of the EPA, and the problems
that exist today. Glossary, bibliography, and index. Part of the Know
Your Government series.

Whitman, Sylvia. *This Land Is Your Land: The American Conservation Movement.* Illus. Lerner Publications 1994 (LB
0-8225-1729-9) 88pp.

Many students will be able to use this book to get an overview
of environmental issues. Efforts to preserve wilderness areas, to control pollution, and to establish recycling routines are discussed.
Theodore Roosevelt, Rachel Carson, John Wesley Powell, and John
Muir are included as is information about government agencies and
environmental organization. Bibliography and index.

Related Books for Older Readers

Stefoff, Rebecca. *The American Environmental Movement.* Illus.
Facts on File 1995 (cloth 0-8160-3046-4) 160pp.

After examining the settlement of the American wilderness,
this book looks at efforts to preserve wilderness areas. There are
details about the environmentalists, scientists, and political activists

who have championed the cause of protecting the natural world. Chronology, list of agencies and organizations, bibliography, and index. Part of the Social Reform Movements series.

Murrow, Edward R. (1908–1965)
became famous for his radio broadcasts from Europe during World War II. He went on to be a television newsman and a critic of the investigative tactics of Senator Joseph McCarthy.

Biographies for Older Readers

Finkelstein, Norman H. *With Heroic Truth: The Life of Edward R. Murrow.* Illus. Houghton Mifflin 1997 (cloth 0-395-67891-9)

This is absorbing reading. The famous McCarthy segment that Murrow did at the height of the anticommunist fervor and his coverage of World War II are just two pieces of his amazing career. Bibliography and index.

Vonier, Sprague. *Edward R. Murrow: His Courage and Ideals Set the Standard for Broadcast Journalism.* Illus. Gareth Stevens 1989 (o.p.) 64pp.

With an Afterword by Charles Kuralt, this book chronicles not only Murrow's life but the exciting times that he covered with his news: World War II, McCarthyism, and Kennedy's assassination, to name a few. Chronology, bibliography, and index. Part of the People Who Have Helped the World series.

Related Books for Younger Readers

Finkelstein, Norman H. *Sounds in the Air: The Golden Age of Radio.* Illus. Scribner's 1993 (o.p.) 144pp.

A discussion of radio's influence on American society in the 1930s and 1940s. Music, vaudeville, comedy, and news are all covered. Murrow's journalistic presence in Vienna during Hitler's takeover makes for compelling reading. Bibliography and index.

"The words of Ed Murrow speak for themselves. Spare and lean as the man himself, referred to by many as prose poetry. These words form an anthology of our time."
—CBS News Reporter Robert Trout, April 30, 1965
(Finkelstein, xiii)

Our Century: 1940–1950. Illus. Gareth Stevens 1993 (LB 0-8368-1036-8) 64pp.

The 1940s were full of historical moments: the atrocity of World War II ended with the dropping of the atom bomb, Franklin Roosevelt died during his fourth term, Satchel Paige became the oldest rookie in baseball. Murrow's calm voice was a recognized feature of the coverage of the war. This book is a pleasure to look at, with its many black-and-white photographs, political cartoons, and newspaper articles. Lists of places to write or visit and further readings, glossary, and index. Part of the Our Century series.

Related Books for Older Readers

Calabro, Marian. *Zap! A Brief History of Television.* Illus. Four Winds Press 1992 (cloth 0-02-716242-7) 224pp.

After a brief description of the invention of television, chapters focus on different types of programs. Situation comedies, soap operas, news and politics, sports, children's programs, and advertising are included. Edward R. Murrow's exposé of Senator Joseph McCarthy is mentioned and there is a chapter on the future of television. Appendix of network and cable addresses, bibliography, and index.

Gottfried, Ted. *The American Media.* Illus. Franklin Watts 1997 (LB 0-531-11315-9)

Gottfried covers the history of journalism in America, including yellow journalism, syndicates and chains, war correspondents, opinion makers, women of the press, and radio news. Murrow's coverage during World War II and afterward is included. List of further readings, chapter notes, and index. Part of the Impact Book series.

Newton, Sir Isaac (1642–1727), an English mathematician and physicist, discovered the law of gravity and developed the first reflecting telescope.

Biographies for Younger Readers

Anderson, Margaret J. *Isaac Newton: The Greatest Scientist of All Time.* Illus. Enslow Publishers 1996 (LB 0-89490-681-X) 128pp.

One special feature of this book is a section of experiments that challenge readers' minds and help them understand some of Newton's concepts. The basic biographical information on Newton is well organized for research. Chronology, chapter notes, glossary, bibliography, and index. Part of the Great Minds of Science series.

Parker, Steve. *Isaac Newton and Gravity.* Illus. Chelsea House 1995 (LB 0-7910-3010-5) 32pp.

The pages in this book are filled with information. Well-organized chapters follow Newton from "The Early Years" to "Gravity and Motion" to "Newton in Perspective." Around the text of the chapters there are pictures with detailed captions as well as boxed sidebars on related topics including "The Newtonian Telescope" and "The Falling Apple." This is a good choice for research or browsing. Timeline of "The World in Newton's Time," glossary, and index. Part of the Science Discoveries series.

Biographies for Older Readers

Christianson, Gale E. *Isaac Newton and the Scientific Revolution.* Illus. Oxford University Press 1996 (LB 0-19-509224-4) 160pp.

This is a very thorough biography filled with scientific information that would meet the needs of junior high and high school students. The illustrations include some of Newton's own notes and drawings. Chronology, bibliography, and index. Part of the Oxford Portraits in Science series.

Hitzeroth, Deborah, and Sharon Leon. *The Importance of Sir Isaac Newton.* Illus. Lucent 1994 (LB 1-56006-046-8) 112pp.

This book not only discusses scientific concepts but also depicts Europe in Newton's time. Excerpts from his letters and quotations by and about him enliven the pages. Timeline, list of further readings, chapter notes, bibliography, and index. Part of the Importance Of series.

Related Books for Younger Readers

Schultz, Ron. *Looking Inside Telescopes and the Night Sky.* Illus. by Nick Gadbois and Peter Aschwanden. John Muir Publications 1993 (pap. 1-56261-072-4) 48pp.

From the first telescope to the Hubble space telescope, this book tells how these tools work and describes different kinds of telescopes and basic principles of astronomy. There are color pictures and diagrams. Teachers and students will appreciate the glossarized index. Part of the X-Ray Vision series.

Related Books for Older Readers

Lafferty, Peter. *Space: Revealing the Processes That Shape the Cosmos.* Illus. Crescent Books 1992 (LB 0-517-06555-X)

The color photographs and diagrams make this book a pleasure to browse through. There is a discussion of telescopes, especially comparing Newton's and Galileo's, and of planets, stars, and galaxies. Glossary and index. Part of the Science Facts series.

Nardo, Don. *Gravity: The Universal Force.* Illus. Lucent 1990 (o.p.) 96pp.

Early scientists faced punishment and prison for expressing controversial views. Galileo was found guilty of heresy. Yet scientists continued to challenge convention and to make new discoveries, such as Newton's observations on gravity and Einstein's theories. Glossary, bibliography, and index. Part of the Encyclopedia of Discovery and Invention series.

Nightingale, Florence (1820–1910), an English nurse, dedicated her life to improving health care. Credited with founding the modern nursing movement, she organized nurses in the Crimean War and later formed a school to train nurses at St. Thomas's Hospital in London.

In 1907, at the age of eighty-seven, Florence Nightingale was awarded the Order of Merit *by King Edward VII of England. She was the first woman to win the award.*

(Adler, unpaged)

Biographies for Younger Readers

Adler, David A. *A Picture Book of Florence Nightingale.* Illus. by John Wallner and Alexandra Wallner. Holiday House 1992 (LB 0-8234-0965-1) 1997 (pap. 0-8234-1284-9) 32pp.

Florence Nightingale grew up in a wealthy home, yet she devoted her life to improving health care for all. Important dates. Part of the Picture Book Of series.

Biographies for Older Readers

Brown, Pam. *Florence Nightingale: The Determined English-woman Who Founded Modern Nursing and Reformed Military Medicine.* Illus. Gareth Stevens 1989 (o.p.) 68pp.

More than a biography of Nightingale, this book also describes the poor state of hospitals and nursing in her time and how she set about changing them. It tells about her work during the Crimean War. Chronology, glossary, and index. Part of the People Who Have Helped the World series.

Siegel, Beatrice. *Faithful Friend: The Story of Florence Nightingale.* Scholastic 1991 (o.p.)

This is a readable account of Nightingale's efforts to improve health care, contrasting the life of luxury that Nightingale was born into with the poor conditions around her—child labor, the lack of decent health care for all people, but especially the poor. List of further readings, bibliography, and index. Part of the Scholastic Biography series.

Related Books for Younger Readers

Parker, Steve. *The History of Medicine.* Illus. Gareth Stevens 1991 (LB 0-8368-0024-9)

A historical overview of medicine, covering such topics as ancient medicine, the scientific beginnings of medicine, the era of drugs and X-rays, the medical system today, and medicine in other places. Nightingale is part of a long discussion on medical people who made significant strides in medicine, with her standards for food, hygiene, and health care. Photographs of surgeries and technological advancements, glossary, and index. Part of the Gareth Stevens Information Library series.

Sheafer, Silvia Anne. *Women in America's Wars.* Illus. Enslow Publishers 1996 (LB 0-89490-553-8) 112pp.

Sheafer presents ten biographies of women who have served in the military when America was at war, from the earliest years through the Gulf War. Several served in a medical capacity, and throughout the book the women are compared to Nightingale. Chapter notes and index. Part of the Collective Biographies series.

Related Books for Older Readers

Garza, Hedda. *Women in Medicine.* Illus. Franklin Watts 1994 (LB 0-531-11204-7) 1996 (pap. 0-531-15805-5) 112pp.

Garza maintains that the field of medicine is an indicator of the status of women in society. In the 15th century lay women healers were executed for practicing witchcraft. At one time in the United States, midwives were banned. Three women are noted as being major contributors to the development of nursing: Dorothea Dix, Florence Nightingale, and Margaret Sanger. Chapter notes, bibliography, and index. Part of the Women Then—Women Now series.

Nixon, Richard Milhous (1913–1994), the 37th president of the United States (1969–1974), is recognized for some important foreign policy moves that included improving ties with the former Soviet Union and opening relations with China. The Watergate scandal forced him to resign the presidency.

Biographies for Older Readers

Hargrove, Jim. *Richard M. Nixon: The Thirty-Seventh President.* Illus. Children's Press 1985 (o.p.) 128pp.

Written before his death in 1994, this book covers Nixon's life from his early years up to the day he resigned the presidency. Timeline and index. Part of the People of Distinction Biographies series.

Lillegard, Dee. *Richard Nixon: Thirty-Seventh President of the United States.* Illus. Children's Press 1988 (LB 0-516-01356-4) 100pp.

This book follows the life and career of the first American president to resign from office. Chronology and index. Part of the Encyclopedia of Presidents series.

Randolph, Sallie. *Richard M. Nixon, President.* Walker and Company 1989 (LB 0-8027-6849-0) (cloth 0-8027-6849-0) 128pp.

Randolph capably balances the positive with the negative: Watergate, reestablishment of ties with China, and the end of the Vietnam War. Index. Part of the Presidential Biography series.

Related Books for Younger Readers

Hargrove, Jim. *The Story of Watergate.* Illus. Children's Press 1988 (LB 0-516-04741-8) 32pp.

This is a simple, clear telling of the Watergate break-in and the ensuing political scandal. Part of the Cornerstones of Freedom series.

Related Books for Older Readers

Aaseng, Nathan. *You Are the Senator.* Illus. Oliver Press 1997 (LB 1-881508-36-6) 160pp.

Detailed governmental information is presented in an entertaining fashion. The student is placed in the role of senator and examines eight historic decisions, with background information, a list of the options available, and the final decision. Nixon's role in vetoing the War Powers resolution and his endorsement of the direct election proposal are covered. Bibliography and index. Part of the Great Decisions series.

Herda, D. J. *United States v. Nixon: Watergate and the President.* Illus. Enslow Publishers 1996 (LB 0-89490-753-0) 112pp.

After introducing the political career of Richard Nixon, the author examines the issues involved in the Watergate investigation, including executive privilege and national security. Chapter notes, glossary, bibliography, and index. Part of the Landmark Supreme Court Cases series.

Wright, David. *A Multicultural Portrait of the Vietnam War.* Illus. Marshall Cavendish 1995 (LB 0-7614-0052-4) 80pp.

While covering the Vietnam War from the perspective of minorities and women, this book relates many of the decisions Kissinger and Nixon made about the war. Chronology, list of further readings, glossary, and index. Part of the Perspectives series.

Oakley, Annie (1860–1926), is known for her feats of marksmanship. She was a star attraction of Buffalo Bill's Wild West Show and the subject of Irving Berlin's 1946 musical *Annie Get Your Gun.*

Biographies for Younger Readers

Gleiter, Jan, and Kathleen Thompson. *Annie Oakley.* Illus. by Yoshi Miyake. Raintree Steck-Vaughn 1995 (LB 0-8114-8451-3)

Simply told and nicely illustrated, this book tells about the hard times Annie grew up with and the famous success she became with the Wild West Show and Sitting Bull. Includes key dates in her life at the end. Part of the First Biographies series.

Hamilton, John. *Annie Oakley.* Illus. Abdo & Daughters 1996 (LB 1-56239-563-7)

This biography with simple text covers her childhood, meeting and marrying Frank Butler, joining Buffalo Bill Cody's Wild West Show, becoming friends with Sitting Bull, meeting Queen Victoria, and her retirement. Glossary, bibliography, and index. Part of the Heroes & Villains of the Wild West series.

Wukovits, John. *Annie Oakley.* Illus. Chelsea House 1997 (LB 0-791-03906-4) 64pp.

Annie Oakley was a remarkable woman. In an era where women played a secondary role, she was a star performer. The numerous illustrations in this book, including many historical photographs of Annie Oakley and the Wild West shows, make this a fun book for browsing. Chronology, bibliography, and index. Part of the Legends of the West series.

Related Books for Younger Readers

Alter, Judy. *Wild West Shows: Rough Riders and Sure Shots.* Franklin Watts 1997 (LB 0-531-20274-7) (pap. 0-531-15875-6)

Pure entertainment for younger readers. Each short chapter is introduced as if the reader were at a show, with full-page black-and-white photographs. Annie Oakley is, of course, a part of this. List of further readings, glossary, and index. Part of the First Book series.

Miller, Brandon Marie. *Buffalo Gals: Women of the Old West.* Illus. Lerner Publications 1995 (LB 0-8225-1730-2) 1997 (pap. 0-8225-9772-1) 88pp.

A truly delightful book that includes many photographs of women of the Old West at work and at play. The hardships of everyday life, entertainment, dress, and clashes with Indian culture are all addressed. Bibliography and index.

O'Connor, Sandra Day (1930–), an
American jurist, became the first woman justice on
the U.S. Supreme Court in 1981. She is thought of
as generally conservative but asserts her political
independence.

Biographies for Younger Readers

Holland, Gini. *Sandra Day O'Connor.* Illus. by Mark Roberts.
Raintree Steck-Vaughn 1997 (LB 0-8172-4455-7)

Here is a simple biography for younger readers. It covers her
childhood, college, law school, marriage, and family, and her pro-
gression through positions in the Arizona state senate, as Maricopa
County Superior Court judge, on the Arizona Court of Appeals, and
her U.S. Supreme Court appointment by President Reagan. Chronology. Part of the First Biographies series.

Biographies for Older Readers

Herda, D. J. *Sandra Day O'Connor: Independent Thinker.* Illus.
Enslow Publishers 1995 (LB 0-89490-558-9) 104pp.

When Sandra Day O'Connor became the first woman justice on
the Supreme Court, there were questions about her selection and her
abilities. Early chapters in this book describe her education and
experience. Later chapters look at decisions she has made on the
Supreme Court. Well organized for research, with a chronology,
chapter notes, glossary, bibliography, and index. Part of the Justices
of the Supreme Court series.

Related Books for Younger Readers

Evans, J. Edward. *Freedom of Religion.* Illus. Lerner Publications
1990 (LB 0-8225-1754-X) 88pp.

A historical look at freedom of religion in the United States
and the court cases that defined it, this book covers separation from
state, intolerance versus tolerance, religious freedom according to
the Constitution, and religion in the schools. O'Connor is quoted in
a case involving the use of the illegal drug peyote as a traditional
sacrament in Native American religions. List of further readings,
glossary, and index. Part of the American Politics series.

Sherrow, Victoria. *Freedom of Worship.* Illus. Millbrook Press 1997 (LB 0-7613-0065-1) 48pp.

Sherrow explores freedom of worship as guaranteed by the Bill of Rights and discusses O'Connor's 1985 opinion on silent prayer and its impact on religion in schools. List of further readings, glossary, and index. Part of the Land of the Free series.

Related Books for Older Readers

Aaseng, Nathan. *You Are the Supreme Court Justice.* Illus. Oliver Press 1994 (LB 1-881508-14-5) 160pp.

Pretending that the reader is one of the Supreme Court justices, this book takes well-known cases and gives the options available to the Court. It then gives the reader the background information and asks him or her to make a decision and see whether it is the same one that the Court had handed down. Included is the *Cruzan* v. *Missouri* (Right to Die) case that O'Connor helped to decide. Part of the Great Decisions series.

Kronenwetter, Michael. *The Supreme Court of the United States.* Illus. Enslow Publishers 1996 (LB 0-89490-536-8) 112pp.

Chapters describe "The U.S. Judicial System," "How the Court Works," and "Historic Decisions." One fascinating section looks at "Politics and the Court," describing the nomination process and issues involved in the confirmation hearings. Chapter notes, glossary, bibliography, and index. Part of the American Government in Action series.

Oppenheimer, J. Robert (1904–1967),

an American physicist and teacher, was part of a team that designed the first atom bomb. He headed the advisory committee of the Atomic Energy Commission and later became an advocate for international controls on atomic energy.

Biographies for Older Readers

Driemen, J. E. *Atomic Dawn: A Biography of Robert Oppenheimer.* Illus. Silver Burdett 1988 (o.p.) 160pp.

This entertaining book begins with his bright childhood and continues with the major role Oppenheimer played in the development of the atom bomb. There is fascinating coverage of the construction and detonation of the test bomb. Chronology, bibliography, and index. Part of the People in Focus series.

Related Books for Younger Readers

Holland, Gini. *Nuclear Energy.* Illus. Benchmark Books 1996 (LB 0-7614-0047-8) 64pp.

Students exploring Oppenheimer's work with the atom bomb should also consider nuclear energy as a power source. This book discusses how we use nuclear energy, what nuclear energy is, the making of the bomb, and the dangers and possible future uses of nuclear energy. Timeline, list of further readings, glossary, and index. Part of the Inventors and Inventions series.

Sherrow, Victoria. *Hiroshima.* Illus. New Discovery Books 1994 (LB 0-02-782467-5)

Sherrow relates the events leading up to, including, and following the dropping of the atom bomb on Hiroshima. The reactions of the world and the scientists who developed the bomb are covered. Includes many photographs. List of further readings, chapter notes, and index. Part of the Timestop Book series.

Stein, R. Conrad. *The Manhattan Project.* Illus. with photographs. Children's Press 1993 (LB 0-516-06670-6) (pap. 0-516-46670-4) 32pp.

There were many people involved in the Manhattan Project. Franklin D. Roosevelt supported the development of a nuclear bomb. Enrico Fermi worked on the research project and Robert Oppenheimer was the chief scientist. Albert Einstein expressed his concerns about atomic power. This book provides a brief account of the people and events in this momentous project. Index. Part of the Cornerstones of Freedom series.

Related Books for Older Readers

Saari, Peggy, and Stephen Allison, ed. *Scientists: The Lives and Works of 150 Scientists, Vol. 2.* Illus. UXL 1996 (cloth 0-7876-0961-7)

Students will find Oppenheimer in this volume (covering G–O). Boxed sidebars give information on related people (Joseph Rotblat and Andrei Sakharov). At the front of the book, there is a list of the scientists by their specialization as well as a timeline. List of further readings and glossary.

Owens, Jesse (1913–1981), an African American track star, set world records in the broad jump and 200-meter dash at the 1936 Berlin Olympic Games. He won four gold medals there debunking Hitler's theory of Aryan supremacy.

Biographies for Younger Readers

Adler, David A. *A Picture Book of Jesse Owens.* Illus. by Robert Casilla. Holiday House 1992 (LB 0-8234-0966-X) 1993 (pap. 0-8234-1066-8) 32pp.

The simple picture-book format covers not only Owens's many accomplishments but also the prejudice he encountered abroad at the Olympics and at home in the United States. Chronology. Part of the Picture Book Of series.

Josephson, Judith Pinkerton. *Jesse Owens: Track and Field Legend.* Illus. Enslow Publishers 1997 (LB 0-89490-812-X) 128pp.

Josephson features Jesse Owens's remarkable achievements at the Berlin Olympics. Chapters describe his childhood, education, and training. Later in his life, Owens served as a role model to young people. Chronology, chapter notes, bibliography, and index. Part of the African American Biographies series.

McKissack, Patricia, and Fredrick McKissack. *Jesse Owens: Olympic Star.* Illus. Enslow Publishers 1992 (LB 0-89490-312-8) 32pp.

This is a simple biography of Jesse Owens—growing up as a sharecropper's son, his amazing athletic feats, particularly at the 1936 Olympics, and his struggle after the Olympics to support himself. Glossary and index. Part of the Great African Americans series.

Biographies for Older Readers

Gentry, Tony. *Jesse Owens: Champion Athlete.* Illus. Chelsea House 1990 (LB 1-55546-603-6) (pap. 0-7910-0247-0)

This is a well-organized book that will meet the needs of older students doing research. Numerous photographs show Jesse Owens as a child, a student, an athlete, and a humanitarian. His accomplishments in Berlin are thoroughly described. Chronology, bibliography, and index. Part of the Black Americans of Achievement series.

Related Books for Younger Readers

Jackson, Colin. *The Young Track and Field Athlete: A Young Enthusiast's Guide to Track and Field Athletics.* Illus. Dorling Kindersley 1996 (cloth 0-7894-0855-4) (pap. 0-7894-0470-5) 32pp.

Young athletes will enjoy looking through this book, which covers the basics of track and field, including warming up, sprint drills, training, and the major annual events. There is a short section on the history of track and field, including Owens's amazing performance in the 1936 Olympics. Index.

Kent, Zachary. *U.S. Olympians.* Illus. Children's Press 1992 (LB 0-516-06659-5) 32pp.

Young Olympics and sports fans will enjoy this brief book full of color and black-and-white photographs. No book about the Olympics would be complete without Owens's performance at the 1936 Olympics, and this book is no exception. Index. Part of the Cornerstones of Freedom series.

Related Books for Older Readers

Kristy, Davida. *Coubertin's Olympics: How the Games Began.* Illus. Lerner Publications 1995 (LB 0-8225-3327-8) (pap. 0-8225-9713-6) 128pp.

In the late 1800s, Pierre de Coubertin hoped to organize an event built around athletic internationalism. Bringing people from many countries together in athletic competition would, he hoped, promote friendship, cooperation, and understanding. His efforts led to the establishment of the modern Olympic games. Political issues are discussed briefly, including the treatment of Jesse Owens at the 1936 games in Berlin. Index.

Wright, David. *A Multicultural Portrait of World War II.* Illus. Marshall Cavendish 1994 (LB 1-85435-663-1) 80pp.

Any mention of minorities during World War II has to include Owens's performance during the Berlin Olympics in 1936, when war in Europe was imminent. Juxtaposed against Owens's show of superiority against Hitler's Nazis is the treatment that black enlisted men received while in the service and at home in the United States. Chronology, list of further readings, glossary, and index. Part of the Perspectives series.

Paige, Leroy "Satchel" (1906?–1982), an African American baseball legend, was one of the stars of the early Negro baseball leagues. A gifted pitcher, he was drafted by the Cleveland Indians and later was inducted into the Baseball Hall of Fame.

Biographies for Younger Readers

McKissack, Patricia, and Fredrick McKissack. *Satchel Paige: The Best Arm in Baseball.* Illus. Enslow Publishers 1992 (LB 0-89490-317-9) 32pp.

Here is an entertaining account of Paige's life, the Negro baseball leagues, and the first steps to integrate baseball. Glossary and index. Part of the Great African Americans series.

Biographies for Older Readers

Macht, Norman L. *Satchel Paige.* Illus. Chelsea House 1991 (LB 0-7910-1185-2) 64pp.

Baseball fans will appreciate the focus on Paige's career, from his years in the Negro Leagues to being the oldest rookie in the major leagues to breaking the color barriers. Paige's baseball statistics, list of further readings, chronology, and index. Part of the Baseball Legends series.

Shirley, David. *Satchel Paige: Baseball Great.* Illus. Chelsea House 1993 (LB 0-7910-1880-6) (pap. 0-7910-1983-7) 112pp.

This biography features Satchel Paige as an outstanding pitcher who faced discrimination and prejudice. His career spanned more than 40 years, in which he played for many years in the Negro Leagues before becoming the first black pitcher in the American League. There is an appendix of Paige's statistics. Chronology, bibliography, and index. Part of the Black Americans of Achievement series.

Related Books for Younger Readers

Ritter, Lawrence S. *Leagues Apart: The Men and Times of the Negro Baseball Leagues.* Illus. by Richard Merkin. William Morrow & Co. 1995 (cloth 0-688-13316-9) 40pp.

Young baseball fans will enjoy this book. Prejudice kept many players from professional baseball. Many statistics are included about Satchel Paige, along with the fact that at 59 he was the oldest player ever to have participated in a major league game. List of Hall of Famers from the Negro Leagues.

Related Books for Older Readers

Gilbert, Tom W. *Baseball and the Color Line.* Illus. Franklin Watts 1995 (LB 0-531-11206-3) (pap. 0-531-15747-4) 160pp.

This account is full of excerpts from historical texts and newspaper accounts discussing how attitudes about segregation in baseball have changed. It relates Paige's baseball career and how, in the 1930s and 1940s, he was better known and better paid than most major league players. Appendix with professional baseball leagues chronology, source notes, glossary, bibliography, and index. Part of the African American Experience series.

McKissack, Patricia, and Fredrick McKissack, Jr. *Black Diamond: The Story of the Negro Baseball Leagues.* Illus. Scholastic 1994 (cloth 0-590-45809-4) 1996 (pap. 0-590-45810-8) 192pp.

Baseball fans will enjoy looking through this book. How "Satchel" and his famous "Bee Ball" got their names and other player profiles are just part of the story. Hall of Fame list, timeline of black baseball, and index.

Parker, Quanah (1848–1911), a chief of the Comanche Indians, resisted the efforts of settlers to take over his tribe's land, but was unsuccessful. On the reservation he organized his people to improve their condition through education.

Biographies for Younger Readers

Sanford, William R. *Quanah Parker: Comanche Warrior.* Illus. Enslow Publishers 1994 (LB 0-89490-512-0) 48pp.

This biography covers Parker's childhood, his raids against white settlers from Texas to Colorado, and his later years on the reservation, where he helped his people adjust to their new way of life. It includes many black-and-white photographs and illustrations. List of further readings, chapter notes, glossary, and index. Part of the Native American Leaders of the Wild West series.

Biographies for Older Readers

Marrin, Albert. *Plains Warrior: Chief Quanah Parker and the Comanches.* Illus. Atheneum 1996 (cloth 0-689-80081-9) 208pp.

This is an excellent biography about Quanah Parker with clear writing and informative illustrations. It also explores the Comanche people and the encroachment of the settlers onto their lands. This detailed book will meet the research needs of older students. Chapter notes, bibliography, and index.

Wilson, Claire. *Quanah Parker: Comanche Chief.* Illus. Chelsea House 1992 (LB 0-7910-1702-8) 112pp.

Wilson covers Parker's many raids against the buffalo hunters, depicting him first as a skilled warrior and then as an effective lobbyist for the interests of his people. Chronology, list of further readings, and index. Part of the North American Indians of Achievement series.

Related Books for Younger Readers

Oakley, Ruth. *The Marshall Cavendish Illustrated History of the North American Indians: A Way of Life.* Illus. Marshall Cavendish 1991 (o.p.)

Students are usually fascinated by Indians, and those studying Parker should be no different. This volume deals with the Native American way of life: tribal government, love, marriage, divorce, education, games, war, weapons, hunting trade, travel, and more. Maps of the major linguistic areas and tribal areas, a table of tribes, index of tribes listed in the book, and index.

Related Books for Older Readers

The American West: A Multicultural Encyclopedia, Volume 7, Mormons–Pinchot. Illus. Grolier 1995 (LB 0-7172-7421-7)

This is one in a series of alphabetically arranged books about the American West, emphasizing minorities and women. The section on Parker tells of his famous stand against the buffalo hunters with 700 warriors, his devotion to hallucinogenic drugs, his home that was known as the Comanche White House, and his family of 25 children. Maps, list of further readings, and glossary. Each volume includes a series index.

Marrin, Albert. *Cowboys, Indians, and Gunfighters: The Story of the Cattle Kingdom.* Illus. Atheneum 1993 (LB 0-689-31774-3) 196pp.

Students will have fun browsing through this book. Full of photographs, illustrations, and quotations, including verses of cowboy songs. The section on Parker's fight against the buffalo hunters with 700 braves is especially moving. List of further readings, chapter notes, and index.

Parks, Rosa (1913–), an influential African American figure in the civil rights movement, was arrested in Montgomery, Alabama, in 1955 when she refused to give up her bus seat, thus triggering an African American boycott of the city's public bus system.

"The only tired I was, was tired of giving in."

(Parks)

Biographies for Younger Readers

Adler, David A. *A Picture Book of Rosa Parks.* Illus. by Robert Casilla. Holiday House 1993 (LB 0-8234-1041-2) 1995 (pap. 0-8234-1177-X) 32pp.

When Rosa Parks was growing up, "Jim Crow" laws promoted discrimination. Her decision to stay seated on a public bus helped launch the civil rights movement. This would be a good introduction to Rosa Parks and this era. List of important dates. Part of the Picture Book Of series.

Parks, Rosa, with Jim Haskins. *I Am Rosa Parks.* Illus. by Wil Clay. Dial 1997 (LB 0-8037-1207-3) (pap. 0-8037-1206-5)

Rosa Parks tells her own story for younger students. The four chapters feature "I Get Arrested," "How I Grew Up," "We Stay Off Buses," and "Since the Boycott." Part of the Dial Easy-to-Read series.

Biographies for Older Readers

Hull, Mary. *Rosa Parks: Civil Rights Leader.* Illus. Chelsea House 1994 (LB 0-7910-1881-4) (pap. 0-7910-1910-1) 144pp.

The first chapter of this book is called "The Straw That Broke the Camel's Back." It describes how Rosa Parks decided to defy the law and stay seated on her bus ride home. The bus boycott that resulted helped change the laws and promoted integration. Chronology, bibliography, and index. Part of the Black Americans of Achievement series.

Parks, Rosa, with Jim Haskins. *Rosa Parks: My Story.* Illus. Dial 1992 (pap. 0-8037-0673-1) 200pp.

From "How It All Started" to "We Fight for the Right to Vote" to "Stride Toward Freedom," Rosa Parks gives her personal insights into her own actions and the civil rights movement. This book captures the essence of this courageous woman. Chronology and index.

Related Books for Younger Readers

Siegel, Beatrice. *The Year They Walked: Rosa Parks and the Montgomery Bus Boycott.* Illus. with photographs. Four Winds Press 1992 (cloth 0-02-782631-7) 128pp.

After World War II, many people depended on buses for transportation; yet the arrest of Rosa Parks led to a boycott of buses in Montgomery, Alabama, and eventually to the nonviolent resistance of the civil rights movement that brought political and social change. Bibliography and index.

Stein, R. Conrad. ***The Montgomery Bus Boycott.*** Illus. with photographs. Children's Press 1993 (LB 0-516-06671-4) (pap. 0-516-46671-2) 32pp.

Stein relates the events leading to the boycott that resulted when Rosa Parks refused to give up her seat to a white person. Index. Part of the Cornerstones of Freedom series.

Wade, Linda R. ***Montgomery: Launching the Civil Rights Movement.*** Rourke 1991 (LB 0-86592-465-1) 48pp.

This covers the history of Montgomery, Alabama, portraying it as the heart of the civil rights movement. The bus boycott is just one of many events that took place in Montgomery. Index. Part of the Doors to America's Past series.

Related Books for Older Readers

Dornfeld, Margaret. ***The Turning Tide: From the Desegregation of the Armed Forces to the Montgomery Bus Boycott (1948–1956).*** Illus. Chelsea House 1995 (LB 0-7910-2255-2) (pap. 0-7910-2681-7) 144pp.

After serving in World War II, many African Americans returned home to face discrimination and disillusionment. Efforts to combat Jim Crow laws and attitudes led to the integration of the military, while the first steps of the civil rights movement were taken with the 1956 boycott in Montgomery. Bibliography and index. Part of the Milestones in Black American History series.

Parks, Rosa, with Gregory J. Reed. ***Dear Mrs. Parks: A Dialogue with Today's Youth.*** Illus. Lee & Low Books 1996 (cloth 1-880000-45-8) 1997 (pap. 1-880000-61-X) 112pp.

After a brief biographical opening, this book consists of letters that Rosa Parks received and her responses to them. The letters are grouped according to theme: Courage and Hope, The Power of Knowledge and Education, Living With God, Pathways to Freedom, and Making a Difference. Timeline.

Pasteur, Louis (1822–1895), a French chemist and biologist who won fame for his studies of bacteria and germ theory, developed the process of pasteurization and discovered many vaccines for diseases. He was director of the Pasteur Institute for teaching and research.

Biographies for Younger Readers

Smith, Linda Wasmer. *Louis Pasteur: Disease Fighter.* Illus. Enslow Publishers 1997 (LB 0-89490-790-5) 128pp.

This well-organized biography enables students to go "In Pasteur's Footsteps" and perform some simple experiments using crystals and yeast. It is a very readable book with many illustrations, including some from Pasteur's documents. Chronology, chapter notes, glossary, bibliography, and index. Part of the Great Minds of Science series.

Tames, Richard. *Louis Pasteur.* Illus. Franklin Watts 1989 (o.p.) 32pp.

Filled with information about Pasteur's life, this is an enjoyable book. It also provides scientific information: the development of vaccines against rabies and anthrax and just what those diseases are, and the development of pasteurization. Other scientists who influenced Pasteur's work are also covered. Chronology, list of further readings, glossary, and index. Part of the Lifetimes series.

Biographies for Older Readers

Birch, Beverley. *Louis Pasteur: The Scientist Who Found the Cause of Infectious Disease and Invented Pasteurization.* Illus. Gareth Stevens 1989 (o.p.) 64pp.

Photographs, quotations, and brief explanations help lay the groundwork for discussing Pasteur's great scientific advancements in the developing field of microbiology. Chronology, list of additional readings, glossary, and index. Part of the People Who Have Helped the World series.

Related Books for Younger Readers

Fekete, Irene, and Peter D. Ward. *Disease and Medicine.* Illus. with photographs. Facts on File 1987 (o.p.) 64pp.

This is one volume in a multivolume encyclopedia that deals with scientific subjects. Packed with photographs and text, it covers medicine in the past and today. Glossary and index. Part of the World of Science series.

Related Books for Older Readers

Giblin, James Cross. *When Plague Strikes: The Black Death, Smallpox, AIDS.* Illus. by David Frampton. HarperCollins 1995 (LB 0-06-025864-0) (cloth 0-06-025854-3); Trophy 1997 (pap. 0-06-446195-5) 240pp.

Here are the fascinating stories of three of the most serious and damaging diseases of all time: the Black Death, smallpox, and AIDS. It addresses the difference Pasteur's research made in fighting disease and describes today's work of the Pasteur Institute. Bibliography and index.

Mulcahy, Robert. *Diseases: Finding the Cure.* Illus. Oliver Press 1996 (LB 10881508-28-5) 144pp.

This book examines doctors and scientists who search for medical cures. Their work often spans years and involves careful research. Included is Louis Pasteur. There is an appended list of Nobel Prize winners in physiology and medicine. Glossary, bibliography, and index. Part of the Innovators series.

Peale, Charles Wilson (1741–1827),

painted graceful and dignified portraits of some of the most important figures of the American Revolution, including George and Martha Washington, Thomas Jefferson, and Benjamin Franklin.

Biographies for Older Readers

Wilson, Janet. *The Ingenious Mr. Peale: Painter, Patriot and Man of Science.* Illus. Atheneum 1996 (cloth 0-689-31884-7) 128pp.

This very readable book presents Peale in the context of America in his time. Peale's involvement in the Revolutionary War and also his excavation of a mastodon for his museum are just two of the fascinating parts of this book. The pages are full of wonderful black-and-white prints of Peale's work, including portraits of the many famous people he knew. Bibliography and index.

Related Books for Older Readers

The Revolutionaries. Illus. Time-Life Books 1996 (cloth 0-7835-6256-X) 192pp.

Photographs, prints, maps, and insets give information about people and events in the Revolutionary War. This is a beautiful book that includes many of Peale's paintings. There are biographies, statistics about the country, and notes about lifestyles, politics, science, and the arts. Chronology, bibliography, and index. Part of the American Story series.

Urdang, Laurence, ed. *The Timetables of American History.* updated ed. Illus. Simon & Schuster 1996 (pap. 0-684-81420-X) 512pp.

This is an encyclopedic timeline of American history. It covers history and politics, the arts, science and technology, and miscellaneous information. Many of Peale's works are listed, and readers will see their wider historical context. Extensive index.

Peary, Robert E. (1856–1920), an American explorer and naval officer, has been acknowledged by the U.S. Congress as the first person to reach the North Pole (1909), although this claim continues to be disputed.

Biographies for Younger Readers

Kent, Zachary. *The Story of Admiral Peary at the North Pole.*
Illus. Children's Press 1988 (o.p.) 32pp.

Peary's early attempted expeditions to the North Pole are related in clear text with many photographs. The book also covers the
discussion about whether Cook or Peary (or neither) actually
reached the North Pole. Part of the Cornerstones of Freedom series.

Biographies for Older Readers

Anderson, Madelyn K. *Robert E. Peary and the Fight for the
North Pole.* Illus. Franklin Watts 1992 (LB 0-531-13004-5)
160pp.

This is a very detailed and comprehensive biography that captures the drama of the race to be first to the North Pole, as well as
Peary's personality. There are many quotations, often from Peary's
letters and other publications. Students doing research will want to
use this book. Chapter notes, bibliography, and index.

Dwyer, Christopher. *Robert Peary and the Quest for the North
Pole.* Illus. Chelsea House 1992 (LB 0-7910-1316-2) 112pp.

Life-and-death adventures make this entertaining reading.
Dwyer covers Peary's efforts to reach the North Pole and also discusses in some depth the controversy over whether he really
succeeded. Includes many photographs of the expeditions. Chronology, list of further readings, and index. Part of the World Explorers
series.

Related Books for Younger Readers

Haskins, Jim. *Against All Opposition: Black Explorers in America.* Illus. Walker and Company 1992 (LB 0-8027-8138-1) (cloth
0-8027-8137-3) 128pp.

The accomplishments of African Americans have often
received little attention. This book provides information about the
important contributions of black explorers. Estevanico, James P.
Beckwourth, Matthew Henson, Guion Bluford, and Ronald McNair
are among those included. Bibliography and index.

Steger, Will. *Over the Top of the World: Explorer Will Steger's
Trek Across the Arctic.* Illus. Scholastic 1997 (cloth 0-590-84860-
7)

This is a delightful narration of a contemporary trip across the
North Pole. Taking computers with him, Will Steger communicated
with teachers and students around the world as he went from Russia
to Canada by way of the North Pole. Included are beautiful pho-

tographs, brief sections about each dog, how to keep warm, and how they communicated over the Internet. Mention is made in a Foreword of Peary's attempts to reach the North Pole.

Related Books for Older Readers

Angel, Ann. *America in the 20th Century.* Marshall Cavendish 1995 (cloth 1-85435-736-0)

Readers will enjoy browsing through this series. This volume covers the first decade of the 1900s and includes such inspiring stories as Rockefeller's rise from earning 40 dollars a month to being the richest man in America and Peary and Henson reaching the North Pole. Chronology, list of further readings, and index.

Philip (1639?–1676), chief of the Wampanoag tribe of Native Americans, was given the title "King" by the English. When the settlers continued to appropriate Native American land in New England, he retaliated with a major uprising, called King Philip's War (1675–1676).

Biographies for Older Readers

Cwiklik, Robert. *King Philip and the War with the Colonists.* Illus. Silver Burdett 1989 (LB 0-382-09573-1) (pap. 0-382-09762-9) 144pp.

This absorbing account balances other stories of American colonization, narrating the tensions and confrontations between King Philip and his people and the white colonists. The efforts of the colonists to force the Indians to dress like them, to adopt their god, and to give up their land are told from the Indian point of view. Cwiklik describes the public display of King Philip's head in Plymouth for 25 years and the selling of his people, including his wife and son, into brutal slavery. List of suggested readings. Part of the Alvin Josephy's Biography of the American Indians series.

Related Books for Younger Readers

Oakley, Ruth. ***The Marshall Cavendish Illustrated History of the North American Indians: Conflict of Cultures.*** Illus. Marshall Cavendish 1991 (o.p.)

Students read about Columbus being received hospitably by Arawaks and in return taking several of them captive to show off when he returned to Spain. It continues to the present day with a discussion of political activity and civil rights of Indians in America. Indians who survived King Philip's War were sold as slaves for 30 shillings each. Maps of the major linguistic areas and tribal areas, index of tribes listed in the book, a table of tribes, and index.

Sewall, Marcia. ***Thunder from the Clear Sky.*** Illus. by the author. Atheneum 1995 (cloth 0-689-31775-1) 64pp.

This book does a wonderful job of showing both perspectives of what happened when the colonists came to America and began to take Indian land, resulting in King Philip's War. Each section of the narrative includes "A Pilgrim's Story" and "A Wampanoag's Story." A map shows the Indian nations and the American colonies involved in King Philip's War. List of characters and glossary. *People of the Breaking Day* is a companion book by Sewall (Atheneum, 1990).

Related Books for Older Readers

Hakim, Joy. ***The First Americans.*** Illus. Oxford University Press 1993 (LB 0-19-507745-8) (cloth 0-19-509506-5) (pap. 0-19-507746-6) 160pp.

When the European explorers "discovered" the Americas, native peoples were already established. This book looks at Indian societies from the earliest peoples. In addition to the text, there are features such as a look at the Mound Builders and an excerpt from the journal of a settler in Virginia. Chronology, bibliography, and index. Part of the History of US series.

Pinkerton, Allan (1819–1884), an American detective and author, founded the Pinkerton National Detective Agency in 1850. He organized a secret service in the Civil War and later formed an agency that supplied strike-breakers to businesses.

Biographies for Younger Readers

Green, Carl R., and William R. Sanford. *Allan Pinkerton.* Illus.
Enslow Publishers 1995 (LB 0-89490-590-2) 48pp.

Young readers will enjoy the stories of Pinkerton and the
assassination attempt on Lincoln, of his search for Jesse James, and
of catching spies during the Civil War. List of further readings, chapter notes, glossary, and index. Part of the Outlaws and Lawmen of the
Wild West series.

Biographics for Older Readers

Josephson, Judith Pinkerton. *Allan Pinkerton: The Original Private Eye.* Illus. Lerner Publications 1996 (LB 0-8225-4923-9)

Allan Pinkerton revolutionized the detective business by
establishing procedures for collecting data and documenting
sources. This book describes his methods and gives details of many
of his famous and dramatic cases. This is a well-organized book on
a fascinating man. Source notes, bibliography, and index.

Wormser, Richard. *Pinkerton: America's First Private Eye.* Walker and Company 1990 (cloth 0-8027-6964-0) 119pp.

Older readers will enjoy entertaining tales of Pinkerton's
exploits: foiling one of the assassination attempts on Lincoln, sending his own sons (ages 14 and 16) behind rebel lines as spies,
catching Frank and Jesse James, and publicly raising money to help
John Brown escape imprisonment. His childhood in one of the worst
slums in Scotland, his work with the underground railroad, his first
job catching counterfeiters, and his work with the Chicago police
force in an era of corruption are covered, as well as the development
of his own detective agency. List of further readings and index.

Related Books for Younger Readers

Wormser, Richard. *The Iron Horse: How the Railroads Changed America.* Illus. Walker and Company 1993 (LB 0-8027-8222-1)
(cloth 0-8027-8221-3) 192pp.

Wormser traces the history of railroads in America. The gold
stampede, war, train robbers, and strikes are all part of the story.
Pinkerton's adventures tracking criminals make for entertaining
reading. Index.

Yancey, Diane. *Desperadoes and Dynamite: Train Robbery in the United States.* Illus. Franklin Watts 1991 (o.p.) 64pp.

Pure entertainment. Yancey describes famous train robberies
and such notorious outlaws as Jesse James, Butch Cassidy and the
Sundance Kid, and the Dalton Gang. No book about railroad

holdups would be complete without the Pinkerton Detective Agency and its groundbreaking criminal investigations, and this is no exception. List of further readings, chapter notes, glossary, and index.

Related Books for Older Readers

The American West: A Multicultural Encyclopedia, Volume 8, Pine Ridge Campaign–Shaman. Illus. Grolier 1995 (LB 0-7172-7421-7)

This is one volume in a series featuring alphabetically arranged topics about the American West. Students will enjoy browsing through such topics as "The Sand Creek Massacre" and "Rough Riders." The section on Pinkerton shows a logo of his detective agency and relates his activities protecting the only railroad line out of Washington, D.C., as well as the pursuit of the Jesse James gang, among others. Maps, list of further readings, glossary, and series index.

Pizarro, Francisco (1475?–1541), a Spanish explorer, conquered the wealthy Inca empire in 1532 and founded the city of Lima, Peru.

Biographies for Younger Readers

Jacobs, William J. *Pizarro, Conqueror of Peru.* Illus. Franklin Watts 1994 (LB 0-531-20107-4) (pap. 0-531-15725-3) 64pp.

Jacobs relates Pizarro's devastation of the Inca empire, telling a bloodthirsty tale of greed for gold in the name of Christianity. Lists of important dates and further readings, and index. Part of the First Book series.

Biographies for Older Readers

Marrin, Albert. *Inca and Spaniard: Pizarro and the Conquest of Peru.* Illus. Atheneum 1989 (LB 0-689-31481-7) 224pp.

While describing Pizarro's efforts to find a golden kingdom, the author also explores in great detail the Inca civilization and how Pizarro conquered this proud people. This is an excellent choice for serious researchers. Bibliography and index.

Related Books for Younger Readers

Newman, Shirlee P. *The Incas.* Illus. Franklin Watts 1992 (LB 0-531-20004-3) (pap. 0-531-15637-0) 64pp.

The author describes the Inca empire as it was from the 13th to the 16th century, and what remains today. List of further readings, glossary, and index. Part of the First Book series.

Related Books for Older Readers

Bernhard, Brendan. *Pizarro, Orellana, and the Exploration of the Amazon.* Illus. Chelsea House 1991 (LB 0-7910-1305-7) 112pp.

Read about the journey Pizarro and Orellana made through the Amazon Basin and the conquest of the Inca empire. A picture essay in the middle contains beautiful color photographs of the region and its wildlife. This is a fascinating account of how a small band of Spaniards could overthrow an entire empire. Chronology, list of further readings, and index. Part of the World Explorers series.

Haworth-Maden, Clare. *The Grolier Student Library of Explorers and Exploration: Volume 5, Latin America.* Illus. Grolier 1998 (cloth 0-7172-9140-5)

Full of illustrations and information, this volume details the exploration of Latin America. Pizarro is described as a conquistador who destroyed the Inca empire with fewer than 200 soldiers. Index.

Stefoff, Rebecca. *Accidental Explorers: Surprises and Side Trips in the History of Discovery.* Illus. Oxford University Press 1993 (LB 0-19-507685-0) 152pp.

The author relates the travels of such well-known explorers as Pizarro and the role that chance played in their discoveries. One chapter, "Down the Amazon by Mistake," tells of an expedition planned by Pizarro's half-brother, Gonzalo, into the unexplored jungles of South America. Part of the expedition was sent downstream to look for food and supplies for the starving expedition but the current was so fast they could not return, and instead traveled more than 2,000 miles down the river. Chronology, list of further readings, and index. Part of the Extraordinary Explorers series.

Pocahontas

Pocahontas (1595?–1617), the daughter of Native American Chief Powhatan of Virginia, is credited with rescuing explorer and colonist John Smith from her father's warriors. She was later captured by the English and married a colonist at Jamestown.

At the age of twenty-one Pocahontas died and was buried in the country she had lived in less than a year but had not wanted to leave.

(Fritz, p. 81)

Biographies for Younger Readers

Fritz, Jean. *The Double Life of Pocahontas.* Illus. Putnam's 1983 (cloth 0-399-21016-4); Puffin 1987 (pap. 0-14-032257-4) 48pp.

Told in Fritz's wonderful storytelling style, this book focuses on how Pocahontas was exploited by both the Indians and the white people. There is a map of the Jamestown area in Pocahontas's day. Chapter notes, bibliography, and index.

Biographies for Older Readers

Adams, Patricia. *The Story of Pocahontas, Indian Princess.* Illus. by Tony Capparelli. Gareth Stevens 1996 (LB 0-8368-1471-1) 112pp.

The author stresses that no part of the book has been fictionalized although it is told in a storylike fashion. It relates Pocahontas's efforts, even as a young girl, to be an ambassador for Powhatan and a peacemaker between the Indians. Part of the Famous Lives series.

Related Books for Younger Readers

Asikinack, Bill, and Kate Scarborough. *Exploration into North America.* New Discovery Books 1995 (LB 0-02-718086-7) 1996 (pap. 0-382-39228-0)

Young readers learn about the history of North America from early times to the present day. Native American cultures, the invasion of the explorers, colonization, and the fight for land are discussed. The English portrait of Pocahontas as Lady Rebecca in all her finery is an interesting contrast to the young Indian maiden we usually see. Timeline that shows major events in North America, Europe, and other areas of the world, glossary, and index. Part of the Exploration Into series.

Baker, Susan. *Explorers of North America.* Illus. Raintree Steck-Vaughn 1990 (LB 0-8114-2752-8) 48pp.

This book contains brief descriptions of North American explorers through the time of the gold rush. Pocahontas's bravery in saving John Smith's life is related. Students will enjoy this look at other explorers and their adventures. Timeline, list of peoples and places, and index. Part of the Tales of Courage series.

Oakley, Ruth. *The Marshall Cavendish Illustrated History of the North American Indians: Homes, Food and Clothing.* Illus. Marshall Cavendish 1991 (o.p.)

Students studying Pocahontas will be fascinated by the details on Native American food and clothing, teepees, wigwams, long houses, earth lodges, furniture, cooking, tattooing, face and body painting, jewelry, and more. Map of the major linguistic areas and tribal areas, table of tribes, index of tribes listed in the book, and index.

Related Books for Older Readers

Kamensky, Jane. *The Colonial Mosaic: American Women, 1600–1760.* Illus. Oxford University Press 1995 (LB 0-19-508015-7) 144pp.

During Colonial times women were responsible for managing the home and family. This involved working in the fields, preparing food for daily use and for storage, and raising their children. This takes a look at women from different backgrounds—immigrants, natives, slaves, and colonists. Chronology, bibliography, and index. Part of the Young Oxford History of Women in the United States series.

P

olo, Marco (1254?–1324?), Italian merchant and author, traveled with his father and uncle to China and introduced Chinese products to Europe.

Biographies for Younger Readers

Humble, Richard. *The Travels of Marco Polo.* Illus. Franklin Watts 1990 (o.p.)

Sailing ships, bandit attacks, and 23 years of adventures along with pictures and maps of Polo's journeys make entertaining reading. Timeline, glossary, and index. Part of the Exploration Through the Ages series.

Roth, Susan L. *Marco Polo: His Notebook.* Illus. Doubleday 1990 (cloth 0-385-26495-X) 32pp.

Marco Polo's travels are recorded as a diary and scrapbook that he might have kept. Notes on Polo's travels and a map of his journey.

Biographies for Older Readers

Greene, Carol. *Marco Polo: Voyager to the Orient.* Illus. Children's Press 1987 (o.p.) 112pp.

This account of Polo's travels includes many illustrations and a map of his probable route. Timeline and index. Part of the People of Distinction Biographies series.

Kent, Zachary. *Marco Polo.* Illus. Children's Press 1992 (o.p.) 128pp.

This is a fine overview of the world in the 1200s. In his travels Polo discovered such things as coal to burn for fuel, coconuts, and the unicorn (probably a rhinoceros). There are drawings from the book written about him in the 1200s and modern photographs of the animals and places that Polo visited, as well as a map showing the route of his travels. Timeline of world events during Polo's life, glossary, and index. Part of the World's Great Explorers series.

Related Books for Younger Readers

Major, John S. *The Silk Route: 7,000 Miles of History.* Illus. by Stephen Fieser. HarperCollins 1995 (o.p.) 80pp.

Beginning with a double-page map of the legendary trade route between China and Byzantium, this beautifully illustrated volume follows a load of silk on its dangerous journey through the desert and the mountains of Afghanistan. Students will enjoy this historical overview.

Twist, Clint. *Marco Polo: Overland to Medieval China.* Illus. Raintree Steck-Vaughn 1994 (LB 0-8114-7251-5)

An excellent look at the world that Polo explored. It focuses on the route that Polo took, with illustrations and photographs. Historical background, modes of travel, Oriental civilization, and subsequent events are all covered. There are suggestions throughout the book of places and topics for further research. List of further readings, glossary, and index. Part of the Beyond the Horizons series.

Related Books for Older Readers

Brill, Marlene Targ. *Mongolia.* Illus. Children's Press 1992 (LB 0-516-02605-4) 128pp.

Brill covers the history, geography, culture, industry, and people of Mongolia. Polo is mentioned many times throughout this history. Students will be fascinated by the photographs of the country today. List of "Mini-Facts at a Glance" and index. Part of the Enchantment of the World series.

Lomask, Milton. *Exploration.* Illus. Atheneum 1988 (cloth 0-684-18511-3) 272pp.

Twenty-five explorers are presented in alphabetical order. A chronology allows access by era. Roald Amundsen, Prince Henry the Navigator, Meriwether Lewis, Robert Peary, and Marco Polo are among those included. Bibliography and index. Part of the Great Lives series.

Powell, Colin L. (1937–), a U.S. military leader, was the first African American to be named chairman of the Joint Chiefs of Staff. Powell achieved fame for his leadership in the Gulf War in 1991. His autobiography is entitled *My American Journey.*

Biographies for Younger Readers

Blue, Rose, and Corinne J. Naden. *Colin Powell: Straight to the Top.* Illus. Harcourt 1994 (cloth 0-15-302263-9); Millbrook Press 1997 (LB 0-7613-0256-5); (pap. 0-7613-0242-5) 48pp.

Here is a brief overview of Powell's life, covering his involvement in the Persian Gulf War and his army career. Chronology and index. Part of the Gateway Biographies series.

Biographies for Older Readers

Brown, Warren. *Colin Powell: Military Leader.* Illus. Chelsea House 1992 (LB 0-7910-1647-1) 144pp.

Powell's life and career as the first black chairman of the Joint Chiefs of Staff are examined, with a focus on his role in the Persian Gulf War. Lists of awards and honors and further readings, chronology, and index. Part of the Black Americans of Achievement series.

Hughes, Libby. *Colin Powell: A Man of Quality.* Illus. Silver Burdett 1996 (LB 0-382-39260-4) (pap. 0-382-39261-2) 160pp.

Powell's boyhood years, his career in the army including the Persian Gulf War and his assignment as chairman of the Joint Chiefs of Staff are covered, along with his personal philosophy and speculations about his future. In one section Powell answers some of the author's questions. Timeline, bibliography, and index. Part of the People in Focus series.

Related Books for Younger Readers

Applegate, Katherine. *The Story of Two American Generals: Benjamin O. Davis and Colin L. Powell.* Illus. Gareth Stevens 1991 (LB 0-8368-1380-4) 100pp.

Applegate profiles two men who made a difference in the battle for the rights of blacks in the military. Davis was the first African American to attend West Point and led the first black fighter pilot squadron in American history. Powell was the first African American to become chairman of the Joint Chiefs of Staff, America's highest-ranking military officer. Students will enjoy noting differences and similarities between these two admirable men. Chronology, list of further readings, and index. Part of the Famous Lives series.

Foster, Leila M. *The Persian Gulf War.* Illus. Children's Press 1991 (LB 0-516-04762-0) 32pp.

Readers interested in the Gulf War will enjoy this simple documentation with its many color photographs of the battles, casualties, and ecological damage done. Powell and Schwarzkopf are, of course, part of the story. Index. Part of the Cornerstones of Freedom series.

Related Books for Older Readers

Nardo, Don. *The Persian Gulf War.* Illus. Lucent 1991 (LB 1-56006-411-0) 112pp.

Powell's military leadership is well documented in this book, which begins with Hussein's military buildup and ends with the ceasefire. Full of black-and-white photographs and detailed maps of the military movements. List of further readings, glossary, and index. Part of the America's Wars series.

Powell, John Wesley (1834–1902), an American anthropologist, conservationist, and geologist, explored the Colorado and Creek rivers. He was the first director of the Smithsonian Institution's Bureau of American Ethnology and served as director of the United States Geological Survey from 1881 to 1894.

Biographies for Younger Readers

Fraser, Mary Ann. *In Search of the Grand Canyon: Down the Colorado with John Wesley Powell.* Illus. by the author. Henry Holt 1995 (cloth 0-8050-3495-1) 1997 (pap. 0-8050-5543-6)

An engaging read, each chapter gives a status report on the number of boats, men, and supplies Powell used on a journey down the Colorado River, along with maps of his trip. The book addresses Powell's concern for the Indians living there and the care that must be taken to preserve the water supply. Bibliography and index. Part of the Redfeather Book series.

Biographies for Older Readers

Gaines, Ann. *John Wesley Powell: And the Great Surveys of the American West.* Illus. Chelsea House 1991 (LB 0-7910-1318-9) 112pp.

Photographs document Powell's participation in the four great surveys of the West from 1869 to 1879. Powell, with Clarence King, George Wheeler, and Ferdinand Hayden, explored, mapped, and photographed the West, opening the way to settlement and development. Chronology, list of further readings, and index. Part of the World Explorers series.

Related Books for Younger Readers

Anderson, Peter. *A Grand Canyon Journey: Tracing Time in Stone.* Franklin Watts 1997 (LB 0-531-20259-3)

Students reading about the journeys of Powell will want to take a look at the Grand Canyon. Anderson takes the reader down the Bright Angel Trail and describes the geology and evolution of the canyon. There are beautiful color photographs and a list of Internet resources on the Grand Canyon. List of further readings, glossary, and index. Part of the First Book series.

Whitman, Sylvia. *This Land Is Your Land: The American Conservation Movement.* Illus. Lerner Publications 1994 (LB 0-8225-1729-9) 88pp.

Many students will be able to use this book to get an overview of environmental issues. Efforts to preserve wilderness areas, control pollution, and establish recycling routines are discussed. Theodore Roosevelt, Rachel Carson, John Wesley Powell, and John Muir are included as is information about government agencies and environmental organization. Bibliography and index.

Related Books for Older Readers

Lucas, Eileen. *Naturalists, Conservationists, And Environmentalists.* Illus. Facts on File 1994 (cloth 0-8160-2919-9) 160pp.

Lucas profiles ten Americans who have worked to preserve the natural wilderness of the United States. George Marsh, a diplomat in the 1800s, expressed the same concerns over excessive irrigation in the arid American West that Powell did many years later. Chronology, list of further readings, and index. Part of the American Profiles series.

Randolph, A. Philip (1889–1979), an African American labor leader, was active in the civil rights movement. In 1925 he formed a largely African American union, the Brotherhood of Sleeping Car Porters, and later worked to desegregate the armed forces.

Randolph received the Medal of Freedom from Lyndon B. Johnson in 1964.

(Cwiklik)

Biographies for Younger Readers

Cwiklik, Robert. *A. Philip Randolph and the Labor Movement.*
Illus. Millbrook Press 1993 (LB 1-56294-326-X) (pap. 1-56294-788-5) 32pp.

A. Philip Randolph was a leader in the civil rights movement. He helped organize the Pullman Porters, he used political pressure to help black workers in other industries, and he was one of the organizers of the 1963 march on Washington. Timeline, bibliography, and index. Part of the Gateway Civil Rights series.

Biographies for Older Readers

Hanley, Sally. *A. Philip Randolph: Labor Leader.* Chelsea House 1989 (LB 1-55546-607-9) (pap. 0-7910-0222-5) 112pp.

Randolph made his greatest impact as a civil rights activist. His success in convincing President Franklin D. Roosevelt to issue an order to end discrimination in the defense industries and the organization of the 1963 1963 march on Washington are just two major accomplishments discussed in this book. Chronology, list of further readings, and index. Part of the Black Americans of Achievement series.

Related Books for Older Readers

Candaele, Kerry. *Bound for Glory: From the Great Migration to the Harlem Renaissance, 1910–1930.* Illus. Chelsea House 1995 (LB 0-7910-2261-7) (pap. 0-7910-2687-6) 144pp.

The Civil War left many African Americans in the rural South in poverty and with few opportunities. Many left and settled in urban areas of the North. In an effort to organize and educate blacks, W. E. B. Du Bois co-founded the National Association for the Advancement of Colored People (NAACP) and A. Philip Randolph established the Brotherhood of Sleeping Car Porters. Chronology, bibliography, and index. Part of the Milestones in Black American History series.

McKissack, Patricia, and Fredrick McKissack. *A Long Hard Journey: The Story of the Pullman Porter.* Walker and Company 1989 (LB 0-8027-6885-7) (cloth 0-8027-6885-6) 144pp.

This book is a wonderful addition to the information about Philip A. Randolph. The story of the first black union to win major concessions from a corporate giant is a testament to Randolph's extraordinary leadership. There are many wonderful pictures and stories. Bibliography and index. Part of the American History Series for Young People.

McKissack, Patricia, and Fredrick McKissack. *Red-Tail Angels: The Story of the Tuskegee Airmen of World War II.* Illus. with photographs. Walker and Company 1995 (LB 0-8027-8293-0) (cloth 0-8027-8292-2) 144pp.

Randolph is included here for his efforts to end discrimination in the defense industry, at a time when the nation was preparing for war. Glossary, bibliography, and index.

Reagan, Ronald (1911–), served as the 40th president of the United States for two terms, from 1981 to 1989. Before he was elected president, he was a movie actor and governor of California. He was called "the great communicator" for his skill before the camera.

Biographies for Older Readers

Schwartzberg, Renee. *Ronald Reagan.* Illus. Chelsea House 1991 (o.p.) 136pp.

This is a thorough biography of the first movie star to become president, with numerous photographs, captions, and quotations. Chronology, list of further readings, and index. Part of the World Leaders Past & Present series.

Sullivan, George. *Ronald Reagan.* Illus. Silver Burdett 1985 (o.p.) 128pp.

Written in 1985 while he was still in office, this is an unflinching look at Reagan, by both his critics and admirers. It includes his childhood, film career, and years in state and national politics. Chronology and index.

Related Books for Younger Readers

Jones, Rebecca C. *The President Has Been Shot! True Stories of the Attacks on Ten U.S. Presidents.* Illus. Dutton 1996 (pap. 0-525-45333-4) 144pp.

These stories of attempts on the president's life, some successful, will fascinate the reader. The section on the shooting of President Reagan illustrates why he was so well liked by the public, with his heart-warming comments immediately afterward and during his convalescence. This book might also be of help in the study of gun control laws. Index.

Stein, R. Conrad. *The Iran Hostage Crisis.* Illus. Children's Press 1994 (LB 0-516-06681-1) 32pp.

President Carter and President Reagan are both included in this simple coverage of the 444-day ordeal of the Iran hostages. Index. Part of the Cornerstones of Freedom series.

Related Books for Older Readers

Sadler, A. E., ed. *Affirmative Action.* Greenhaven 1996 (LB 1-56510-387-4) 96pp.

Varying viewpoints on affirmative action are presented, with careful opinions from both sides of the issue. Decisions made during the Reagan years are mentioned. Students must decide whether the impact was positive or negative. List of organizations to contact, bibliography, and index. Part of the At Issue series.

Red Cloud (1822–1909), chief of the Oglala Sioux, fought against white settlement but was defeated in his defense of the Black Hills. He and his tribe were forced to move to reservations.

Biographies for Younger Readers

Sanford, William R. *Red Cloud: Sioux Warrior.* Illus. Enslow Publishers 1994 (LB 0-89490-513-9) 48pp.

Sanford relates moving stories of the ultimately unsuccessful struggles of Red Cloud and his warriors to retain their territory and their freedom. List of further readings, chapter notes, glossary, and index. Part of the Native American Leaders of the Wild West series.

Related Books for Younger Readers

Thomas, David H., and Lorann Pendleton, eds. *Native Americans.* Illus. Time-Life Books 1995 (LB 0-7835-4759-5) 64pp.

Students will spend a lot of time poring over the information on many aspects of Native American Indian life: how they traveled, how they made a living, what their homes were like, their ceremonies and rituals, and how their lives were changed. There are many photographs and illustrations. Glossary and index. Part of the Discoveries Library series.

Dolan, Terrance. *The Teton Sioux Indians.* Chelsea House 1995 (cloth 0-7910-1680-3) (pap. 0-7910-2032-0)

Six chapters describe the circumstances of the Teton Sioux during the settlement of their lands by white pioneers. Led by Red Cloud, Sitting Bull, and Crazy Horse, the Teton Sioux fought the U.S. Army, yet they were still forced onto settlements. A section of color photographs shows their artistry. Chronology, glossary, and index. Part of the Junior Library of American Indians series.

Oakley, Ruth. *The Marshall Cavendish Illustrated History of the North American Indians: Religion and Customs.* Illus. Marshall Cavendish 1991 (o.p.)

This volume gives students background material on Native American Indian religions and customs: shamans, dreams and visions, medicine lodges, dances, potlatch, funerals, the afterlife, and more. Maps of the major linguistic areas and tribal areas, table of tribes, index of tribes listed in the book, and index.

Reiss, Johanna

Reiss, Johanna (1932–), an American author of books for young people, is the prize-winning author of *The Upstairs Room*, the true story of her experience as a young Jewish girl who hid from the Nazis on the second floor of a Dutch farmhouse.

Biographies for Older Readers

Reiss, Johanna. *The Journey Back.* Crowell 1976 (cloth 0-690-01252-7); Trophy 1987 (pap. 0-06-447042-3) 128pp.

In this sequel to *The Upstairs Room,* Reiss describes her efforts to be reunited with her family and rebuild their lives. This is a moving story that is even more emotional because it is true.

Reiss, Johanna. *The Upstairs Room.* HarperCollins 1972 (cloth 0-690-85127-8) 1987 (pap. 0-06-447043-1) 196pp.

This book has become a classic. The author describes her days in hiding as a six-year-old.

Related Books for Older Readers

Friedman, Ina R. *Flying Against The Wind: The Story of a Young Woman Who Defied the Nazis.* Illus. Lodgepole Press 1995 (pap. 1-886721-00-9) 224pp.

This is the true story of Cato Bontjes van Beek, who defied the Nazis and helped countless Jews escape. As a young girl, she refused to join the Hitler Youth and did everything she could to work quietly against them. Eventually, she was imprisoned by the Nazis and put to death. Chronology of events around the world and in van Beek's life, list of further readings, glossary, and index.

Heyes, Eileen. *Children of the Swastika: The Hitler Youth.* Illus. Millbrook Press 1993 (LB 1-56294-237-9) 96pp.

Eileen Heyes looks at both sides of Nazism and its evolution. She became interested in Hitler Youth when she found out a family member had belonged to the organization. There are many interviews with former Hitler Youth members. Black-and-white photographs show Germans being forced to walk past death camp victims, and troops of 15- and 16-year olds surrendering to Allied forces. A chilling epilogue discusses the Neo Nazis, Ku Klux Klan, and other hate groups that exist today. Chronology, list of further readings, chapter notes, and index.

Stewart, Gail B. *Hitler's Reich.* Lucent 1994 (LB 1-56006-235-5) 112pp.

Students researching the Holocaust will want to examine the historical events leading up to the Nazi takeover. Life in Germany after World War II is also discussed. List of further readings, chapter notes, and index. Part of the World History series.

Reno, Janet (1938–), an American attorney and prosecutor, became the first woman attorney general of the United States in 1993.

Biographies for Younger Readers

Simon, Charnan. *Janet Reno: First Woman Attorney General.* Illus. Children's Press 1994 (LB 0-516-04191-6) (pap. 0-516-44191-4) 32pp.

Reno's early years and her time in college and law school are outlined with black-and-white photographs. Timeline and index. Part of the Picture-Story Biographies series.

Biographies for Older Readers

Anderson, Paul. *Janet Reno: Doing the Right Thing.* John Wiley & Sons 1994 (o.p.) 328pp.

Written by a Washington, D.C., reporter, this book covers Reno's hard early life and successful career through her first year in office as attorney general, portraying her as uncompromising and willing to accept responsibility for her decisions. Index.

Meachum, Virginia. *Janet Reno: United States Attorney General.* Illus. Enslow Publishers 1995 (LB 0-89490-549-X) 128pp.

With many quotations from Reno and her contemporaries, this book exposes students to her personality and energy. Reno's experiences and credentials are described. "A Message From Janet Reno to America's Young People" encourages students to achieve their full potential. Chronology, chapter notes, bibliography, and index. Part of the People to Know series.

Related Books for Younger Readers

Hamilton, John. *The Attorney General through Janet Reno.* Illus. Abdo & Daughters 1993 (LB 1-56239-251-4) 32pp.

Here is a simple discussion of the president's Cabinet, the history and organization of the Justice Department, and the bureaus that the attorney general oversees. A short biography of Reno is included. List of further readings, glossary, and index. Part of the All the President's Men and Women series.

Related Books for Older Readers

Holland, Gini. *America in the 20th Century, 1990s.* Illus. Marshall Cavendish 1995 (cloth 1-85435-736-0)

Readers will enjoy browsing through this series. This volume covers the 1990s and describes the crumbling of the Berlin Wall, the end of apartheid, the Tiananmen Square massacre, the Mall of America, Michael Jackson, Jurassic Park, the raid in Waco, Texas, and more. Chronology, list of further readings, and index.

Lindop, Laurie. *Political Leaders.* Illus. Twenty-First Century Books 1996 (LB 0-8050-4164-8) 128pp.

Lindop profiles ten women who have broken through traditional barriers to become leaders in government and politics. Janet Reno is one of the women featured. There is a short biography of each woman and controversial issues are examined. List of further readings, chapter notes, and index. Part of the Dynamic Modern Women series.

Revere, Paul

Revere, Paul (1735–1818), an American silversmith and military leader, was best known for his 1775 ride to Lexington, Massachusetts, to warn colonists of advancing British troops.

Biographies for Younger Readers

Adler, David A. *A Picture Book of Paul Revere.* Illus. by John Wallner and Alexandra Wallner. Holiday House 1995 (LB 0-8234-1144-3) 1997 (pap. 0-8234-1294-6) 32pp.

Paul Revere's historic ride, his military service making gunpowder and cannons, and his work as a silversmith are among the events featured in this introductory book. It could be read aloud to students who are beginning their study of biographies. List of important dates. Part of the Picture Book Of series.

Fritz, Jean. *And Then What Happened, Paul Revere?* Illus. by Margot Tomes. Coward-McCann 1973 (cloth 0-698-20274-0); Paperstar 1996 (pap. 0-698-11351-9) 48pp.

Told with Fritz's usual energy and enthusiasm, this is a book students will enjoy and find useful for research. There is information about his life, his work as a silversmith, and his famous ride.

Sakurai, Gail. *Paul Revere.* Illus. Children's Press 1997 (cloth 0-516-20463-7)

The text is very readable and is supported by many illustrations. Paul Revere's life is presented in the context of the Revolutionary War and his contemporaries. Timeline, glossary, and index. Part of the Cornerstones of Freedom series.

Biographies for Older Readers

Ford, Barbara. *Paul Revere: Rider for the Revolution.* Illus. Enslow Publishers 1997 (LB 0-89490-779-4) 128pp.

Students will appreciate this well-planned presentation. In addition to biographical information about Paul Revere, there are sidebars with interesting, related facts. Information is included about hornbooks, roads, and Revere's children (there were 16 of them). There are many illustrations, including reproductions of paintings and documents. Chronology, chapter notes, glossary, bibliography, and index. Part of the Historical American Biographies series.

Related Books for Younger Readers

O'Neill, Laurie A. *The Boston Tea Party.* Illus. Millbrook Press 1996 (LB 0-7613-0006-6) 64pp.

A very readable account of the Boston Tea Party and of Paul Revere's many activities. Chronology, list of further readings, bibliography, and index. Part of the Spotlight on American History series.

Oleksy, Walter. *The Boston Tea Party.* Illus. Franklin Watts 1993 (LB 0-531-20147-3) 64pp.

This account traces the events that led to the Boston Tea Party and then studies its impact on the American Revolution. Two events related to Revere stand out: his engraving that exaggerated the events of the Boston "Massacre" and his help in publicizing the Boston Tea Party by carrying a written report to New York and Philadelphia. List of further readings and index. Part of the First Book series.

Stein, R. Conrad. *The Boston Tea Party.* Illus. Children's Press 1996 (LB 0-516-20005-4) 32pp.

This book does a nice job of illustrating the Boston Tea Party for the younger student. Timeline, glossary, and index. Part of the Cornerstones of Freedom series.

Related Books for Older Readers

Meltzer, Milton. *The American Revolutionaries: A History in Their Own Words 1750–1800.* Illus. HarperCollins 1993 (pap. 0-06-446145-9) 224pp.

Anecdotes of everyday people during the Revolutionary War, taken from letters, diaries, journals, memoirs, interviews, ballads, newspapers, pamphlets, and speeches make up this work. Index. Part of the Trophy Book series.

Robeson, Paul (1898–1976), an
American actor, singer, and political activist, was
also the first black football player to be named All-
American. Putting aside his law degree, he
performed in many plays, concerts, and movies. His
career was damaged by his support of the Soviet
Union and of the civil rights movement in the
United States.

Biographies for Younger Readers

McKissack, Patricia, and Fredrick McKissack. *Paul Robeson: A
Voice to Remember.* Illus. by Michael David Biegel and with photographs. Enslow Publishers 1992 (LB 0-89490-310-1) 32pp.

The five chapters in this book provide a brief overview of Paul
Robeson's life. Focusing on his accomplishments as a singer, there
is also information about his humanitarian efforts. Glossary and
index. Part of the Great African Americans series.

Biographies for Older Readers

Ehrlich, Scott. *Paul Robeson: Singer and Actor.* Illus. Chelsea
House 1988 (LB 1-55546-608-7) (pap. 0-7910-0206-3) 112pp.

The story of Robeson's life is interspersed with the philosophies of other major black figures including Marcus Garvey and
W. E. B. du Bois, along with their ideas on handling discrimination.
Robeson's troubles during the McCarthy era are also covered. Students will be surprised to see how his freedom was curtailed because
he spoke out about topics that were unpopular at the time. Part of the
Black Americans of Achievement series.

Related Books for Younger Readers

Loxton, Howard. *Theater.* Illus. Raintree Steck-Vaughn 1989 (LB
0-8114-2359-X) 48pp.

Robeson is just one of many actors included in this book of
information and photographs. It covers many aspects of the theater:
playhouses, plays and playwrights, actors and acting, behind the

scenes, Shakespeare, putting on a play, going to the theater, and becoming an actor or working in the theater. List of further readings, glossary, and index. Part of the Arts series.

Related Books for Older Readers

Payton, Shelia. *African Americans.* Illus. Marshall Cavendish 1995 (LB 1-85435-787-5) 80pp.

This is an overview of African American culture that covers history, family and community, religion and celebrations, customs, and the contribution to the overall American culture. There is an especially interesting section on communications and different cultures. Robeson's efforts to change the image of African Americans in film is discussed. Chronology, list of further readings, glossary, and index. Part of the Cultures of America series.

Rensberger, Susan. *A Multicultural Portrait of the Great Depression.* Illus. Marshall Cavendish 1996 (LB 0-7614-0053-2) 80pp.

Rensberger discusses life during the Depression, mostly for minorities and women. Arts and culture, economic difficulties, and growing up in a time of crisis are all covered. Robeson was part of the cincma scene at that time, although he ultimately went abroad where he would experience less racial discrimination. Chronology, list of further readings, glossary, and index. Part of the Perspectives series.

Robinson, Jackie (1919–1972), an American baseball player, was the first African American to play in the major leagues. He played for the Brooklyn Dodgers from 1947 until 1956 and was elected to the Baseball Hall of Fame in 1962.

Being the first black player wasn't easy. Jackie got plenty of hate mail. There were threats that Jackie and his wife would be shot, that their son would be kidnapped.

(Adler, p. 36)

Biographies for Younger Readers

Adler, David A. *Jackie Robinson: He Was the First.* Illus. by Robert Casilla. Holiday House 1989 (LB 0-8234-0734-9) 48pp.

This is a well-organized book, slightly longer than Adler's familiar Picture Book Of series. (Some students may want to read Adler's *A Picture Book of Jackie Robinson.*) Details about baseball and the prejudice faced by Robinson and others are clearly presented. Part of the First Biographies series.

O'Connor, Jim. *Jackie Robinson and the Story of All-Black Baseball.* Illus. by Jim Butcher. Random House 1989 (LB 0-394-92456-8) (pap. 0-394-82456-3) 48pp.

The focus is on Jackie Robinson from the time he joined the Brooklyn Dodgers. The book also traces the history of all-black baseball teams. Part of the Step Into Reading series.

Biographies for Older Readers

Scott, Richard. *Jackie Robinson: Baseball Great.* Illus. Chelsea House 1987 (LB 1-55546-609-5) (pap. 0-7910-0200-4) 112pp.

The statistics and photographs will delight baseball fans. This book documents Robinson's participation in the civil rights movement. Chronology, list of further readings, and index. Part of the Black Americans of Achievement series.

Related Books for Younger Readers

Santella, Andrew. *Jackie Robinson Breaks the Color Line.* Illus. Children's Press 1995 (LB 0-516-06637-4) (pap. 0-516-26031-6) 32pp.

Young baseball fans will enjoy this simple telling of how Robinson broke the color line in baseball. Full of black-and-white photographs. Timeline, glossary, and index. Part of the Cornerstones of Freedom series.

Ward, Geoffrey C., and Ken Burns. *Shadow Ball: The History of the Negro Leagues.* Illus. Knopf 1994 (LB 0-679-96749-4) (cloth 0-679-86749-X) 64pp.

Before Jackie Robinson was the first African American in the major leagues, he was a star of the Negro Leagues. This book is great for browsing and for information. The numerous photographs add to the presentation. Index. This is part of the Baseball, The American Epic series of books, which is excerpted from the longer book *Baseball: An Illustrated History* (from the PBS television series).

Related Books for Older Readers

Brashler, William. *The Story of Negro League Baseball.* Illus. Ticknor & Fields 1994 (cloth 0-395-67169-8) (pap. 0-395-69721-2) 144pp.

    After discussing the Jim Crow laws of this era, Brashler looks at teams and stars, including Roy Campanella, Satchel Paige, and Jackie Robinson. This is a great book for baseball fans and for students doing research. It is enjoyable to read, making good use of quotations and anecdotes. Bibliography and index.

Gilbert, Thomas. *Baseball at War: World War II and the Fall of the Color Line.* Illus. Franklin Watts 1997 (LB 0-531-11330-2)

    Baseball fans will enjoy the discussion of this sport in the 1940s, with the highlights of each year and the effects of the war on the game. Robinson's career and breaking of the color line is covered in one chapter. Source notes, bibliography, and index. Part of the American Game series.

McKissack, Patricia, and Fredrick McKissack, Jr. *Black Diamond: The Story of the Negro Baseball Leagues.* Illus. Scholastic 1994 (cloth 0-590-45809-4) 1996 (pap. 0-590-45810-8) 192pp.

    Students will enjoy browsing through this book. Before Jackie Robinson entered the major league, the Negro Leagues offered black baseball players the opportunity to compete professionally. "Player Profiles," list of players in the Negro Leagues Hall of Fame, timeline of black baseball in the context of other civil rights events, and index.

Rockefeller, John D. (1839–1937), an American industrialist, played a major role in the development of the Standard Oil Company, which by 1878 gained control of 90 percent of the oil-refining capacity in the United States. This virtual monopoly was ended by decision of the U.S. Supreme Court. Rockefeller amassed a large personal fortune and made charitable contributions of millions of dollars.

Biographies for Older Readers

Coffey, Ellen Greenman. *John D. Rockefeller: Empire Builder.*
Illus. Silver Burdett 1989 (o.p.) 112pp.

Rockefeller's early years, his development of the Standard Oil
Company into a powerful monopoly, and his later years as the phil-
anthropist who established the Rockefeller Foundation are covered.
Bibliography and index. Part of the American Dream series.

Related Books for Younger Readers

Aaseng, Nathan. *From Rags to Riches: People Who Started Businesses from Scratch.* Illus. Lerner Publications 1990 (o.p.) 80pp.

Students may want to look at business people who became mil-
lionaires and compare their lives and tactics with Rockefeller's.
Hewlett-Packard (a business that started in a garage), Proctor &
Gamble, and Hershey are just a few of the interesting stories featured. List of further readings and index. Part of the Inside Business
series.

Related Books for Older Readers

Angel, Ann. *America in the 20th Century.* Marshall Cavendish
1995 (cloth 1-85435-736-0)

Readers will enjoy browsing through this series. Among the
inspiring stories in this volume covering the first decade of the
1900s is Rockefeller's rise from a job as bookkeeper to become the
richest man in America. Chronology, list of further readings, and
index.

Hakim, Joy. *An Age of Extremes.* Illus. Oxford University Press
1994 (LB 0-19-507759-8) (cloth 0-19-509513-8) (pap. 0-19-
507760-1) 160pp.

This book focuses on the end of the 19th century and the
beginning decades of the 20th century. Key figures from the early
years include Andrew Carnegie, John D. Rockefeller, and J. P. Morgan, who became very wealthy in industry. Later years feature the
conditions for workers, the rise of organized labor, and Jane
Addams's efforts to reach out to the needy. The many illustrations
and sidebars add to the interest of the presentation. Part of the History of US series.

Levinson, Nancy Smiler. *Turn of the Century: Our Nation One Hundred Years Ago.* Illus. Lodestar Books 1994 (pap. 0-525-67433-0) 144pp.

Levinson relates entertaining stories about life at the turn of the century featuring such icons as the iron horse, inventions, and robber barons (including Rockefeller). List of further readings and index.

Roosevelt, Eleanor (1884–1962), the wife of President Franklin D. Roosevelt, served her country as First Lady from 1933 until 1945. After her husband's death, she was a delegate to the United Nations General Assembly and served as chairwoman of its Human Rights Commission.

Biographies for Younger Readers

Adler, David A. *A Picture Book of Eleanor Roosevelt.* Illus. by Robert Casilla. Holiday House 1991 (LB 0-8234-0856-6) 1995 (pap. 0-8234-1157-5) 32pp.

While Barbara Cooney's picture-book biography (see below) focuses on Eleanor Roosevelt's childhood, this gives a brief overview of her life, including her marriage to Franklin D. Roosevelt, her life as first lady, and her humanitarian efforts. List of important dates. Part of the Picture Book Of series.

Cooney, Barbara. *Eleanor.* Illus. by the author. Viking Penguin 1996 (pap. 0-670-86159-6) 40pp.

In the format of a picture book, this is a lovely biography focusing on the childhood of Eleanor Roosevelt. Barbara Cooney's text and illustrations convey her life of privilege and loneliness. Her father's lessons about caring for the less fortunate (she served food in a lodging house when she was six) helped form her compassionate nature. After reading this book, students will want to know more about this fascinating woman.

[Eleanor] understood that as First Lady, there were limits to what she could say or do. "While I often felt strongly on various subjects, Franklin frequently refrained from supporting causes he believed in because of political realities," she wrote.

(Freedman, p. 116)

Biographies for Older Readers

Freedman, Russell. *Eleanor Roosevelt: A Life of Discovery.* Illus.
Houghton Mifflin 1993 (cloth 0-89919-862-7) 1997 (pap. 0-395-
84520-3) 208pp.

A photobiography of the first wife of a president to have a public life and career of her own, this is a touching testimonial to her
strength and courage. Lists of books by and about Roosevelt and of
historical sites to visit, and index. A Newbery honor book.

Winner, David. *Eleanor Roosevelt: Defender of Human Rights
and Democracy.* Illus. Gareth Stevens 1992 (o.p.) 68pp.

With quotations by and about her, this book examines the
United States of her time as well as Eleanor's own life. Chronology,
list of further readings, glossary, and index. Part of the People Who
Have Helped the World series.

Related Books for Younger Readers

Sinnott, Susan. *Doing Our Part: American Women on the Home
Front during World War II.* Franklin Watts 1995 (LB 0-531-
20198-8) 64pp.

While Eleanor Roosevelt was busy doing her part for the country, the average American woman was working too. Each chapter
starts with words from a woman—letters to loved ones or radio
advertisements, for example. Here are stories of everyday life on the
homefront. List of further readings and index. Part of the First Book
series.

Stein, R. Conrad. *The Great Depression.* Illus. Children's Press
1993 (LB 0-516-06668-4) (pap. 0-516-46668-2) 32pp.

The stock market crash and the economic depression that followed are covered, as is Eleanor Roosevelt's active support of her
husband's New Deal policies. Historical photographs and index.
Part of the Cornerstones of Freedom series.

Related Books for Older Readers

Colman, Penny. *Rosie the Riveter: Women Working on the Home
Front in World War II.* Illus. Crown 1995 (LB 0-517-59791-8)
(cloth 0-517-59790-X) 128pp.

Full of wonderful photographs of women working during the
war years, this is an entertaining overview of life on the homefront,
including conditions when the men finally came home from war.
Mention is made of a film Eleanor Roosevelt helped to create to
encourage women to go to work. There is a list of women's wartime
jobs, with facts and figures about women war workers. Chronology,
bibliography, and index.

Mayo, Edith P., gen. ed. *The Smithsonian Book of the First Ladies: Their Lives, Times and Issues.* Illus. Henry Holt 1996 (cloth 0-8050-1751-8) 352pp.

This lavish presentation describes the lives and eras of the first ladies from Martha Washington through Hillary Rodham Clinton, who wrote the Foreword. Throughout the book are essays about issues that were important for these women: "Did the American Revolution Change Things for Women?" "Why Was It Hard for Women to Get an Education?" and "How Have First Ladies Contributed to Campaigning?" Brief biographical sketches give insight into each woman's personality. We learn that after Woodrow Wilson's stroke, Edith Wilson selected what information he would receive and helped with decisions, thus virtually controlling the presidency, and that Eleanor Roosevelt was so popular that she was sent to the nominating convention to sway the delegates to select her husband to run for a third term as president. There is a brief presentation of "The Smithsonian's First Ladies Collection and the Exhibition." This is a fascinating look at a different perspective on the presidency. Bibliography and index.

Roosevelt, Franklin Delano

(1882–1945), the 32nd president of the United States (1933–1945), is credited with pulling the country out of the depths of depression with his social and economic program called the "New Deal."

Biographies for Younger Readers

Osinski, Alice. *Franklin D. Roosevelt: Thirty-Second President of the United States.* Illus. Children's Press 1987 (LB 0-516-01395-5) 100pp.

This is a record of Roosevelt's life and career, especially his four terms as president. There are many photographs depicting the times. Chronology of American history highlighting events during Roosevelt's lifetime and index. Part of the Encyclopedia of Presidents series.

Potts, Steve. *Franklin D. Roosevelt: A Photo-Illustrated Biography.* Illus. Bridgestone Books 1996 (LB 1-56065-453-8) 24pp.

Double-page spreads describe Franklin Roosevelt's life featuring "School Years," "Surviving Polio," "The Great Depression," "World War II," and "The President Is Dead." This book has an appealing format with black-and-white photographs and a brief text. There are quotations from Roosevelt. Chronology, lists of addresses and Internet sites, glossary, bibliography, and index. Part of the Read and Discover Photo-Illustrated Biographies series.

Biographies for Older Readers

Freedman, Russell. *Franklin Delano Roosevelt.* Illus. Houghton Mifflin 1990 (cloth 0-89919-379-X) 1992 (pap. 0-395-62978-0) 208pp.

This is a very readable record of Roosevelt's life and political career, with many wonderful photographs of the time. List of further readings and index.

Nardo, Don. *Franklin D. Roosevelt: U.S. President.* Illus. Chelsea House 1996 (LB 0-7910-2406-7) 128pp.

Nardo shows how Roosevelt's handicaps from polio did not deter him from winning four terms as president of the United States, from his New Deal for a country in the midst of a depression, and from leadership during World War II. Chronology, list of further readings, and index. Part of the Great Achievers: Lives of the Physically Challenged series.

Schuman, Michael A. *Franklin D. Roosevelt: The Four-Term President.* Illus. Enslow Publishers 1996 (LB 0-89490-696-8) 128pp.

Focusing on Roosevelt's commitment to public service, Schuman describes Roosevelt's political career as governor of New York, president of the United States, and commander in chief during World War II. Chronology, list of places to visit, chapter notes, bibliography, and index. Part of the People to Know series.

Related Books for Younger Readers

Stein, R. Conrad. *The Home Front.* Illus. Children's Press 1982 (o.p.) 48pp.

Full of black-and-white photographs, this is a nice sampling of American life during World War II—collecting scrap metal, victory gardens, air raid drills at school, and the relocation of Japanese Americans, to name but a few. Index. Part of the World at War series.

Tunnell, Michael O., and George W. Chilcoat. *The Children of Topaz: The Story of a Japanese-American Internment Camp:*

Based on a Classroom Diary. Illus. Holiday House 1996 (cloth 0-8234-1239-3) 128pp.

The internment of Japanese Americans during World War II was not one of President Roosevelt's best moments. This book is based on a diary written by one of the relocated Japanese Americans who taught a third-grade class at a camp in Topaz, Utah. Index.

Related Books for Older Readers

Jacobson, Doranne. *The Presidents and First Ladies of the United States.* Illus. Smithmark 1995 (cloth 0-8317-8166-8) 128pp.

From George and Martha Washington to Bill and Hillary Rodham Clinton, this is a wonderful presentation. Each president and wife has a fact box and there are many illustrations that provide insight into the people and their era. Index.

Stewart, Gail B. *The New Deal.* Illus. New Discovery Books 1993 (LB 0-02-788369-8) 112pp.

Stewart makes fascinating reading of Roosevelt's controversial New Deal and how it changed the way people looked at government. Black-and-white photographs extend the text. Part of the Timestop Books series.

Taylor, Theodore. *Air Raid—Pearl Harbor: The Story of December 7, 1941.* Illus. Odyssey Books 1991 (pap. 0-15-201655-4) 190pp.

This is a well-written account of the Japanese attack on Pearl Harbor. The mistakes and the successes of both sides are included, with heroic stories of the people who gave their lives. List of key figures, bibliography, and index.

Roosevelt, Theodore (1858–1919), 26th president of the United States (1901–1908), became a national hero when he led the "Rough Riders," a volunteer calvary unit, into battle in the Spanish-American War. He served as vice president to William McKinley in 1901 and succeeded to the presidency later that year.

Biographies for Younger Readers

Blackwood, Gary L. *Rough Riding Reformer: Theodore Roosevelt.* Illus. Benchmark Books 1998 (LB 0-7614-0520-8) 48pp.

Chapters feature "Teddy, "The Colonel," and "Mr. President" in this brief and appealing biography. List of resources (including books, videos, and museums), glossary, and index. Part of the Benchmark Biographies series.

Potts, Steve. *Theodore Roosevelt: A Photo-Illustrated Biography.* Illus. Bridgestone Books 1996 (LB 1-56065-452-X) 24pp.

This brief biography has features that make it a fine choice for beginning researchers. There are double-page spreads on such topics as "Teddy's Family" and "The Rough Riders." There are quotations from Roosevelt. Chronology, lists of addresses and Internet sites, glossary, bibliography, and index. Part of the Read and Discover Photo-Illustrated Biographies series.

Biographies for Older Readers

Fritz, Jean. *Bully for You, Teddy Roosevelt!* Illus. by Mike Wimmer. Putnam's 1991 (cloth 0-399-21769-X); Paperstar 1997 (pap. 0-698-11609-7) 128pp.

In Fritz's very readable style, here is coverage of Roosevelt's conservation work, hunting expeditions, family life, and political career. Chapter notes, bibliography, and index.

Meltzer, Milton. *Theodore Roosevelt and His America.* Illus. Franklin Watts 1994 (LB 0-531-11192-X) 160pp.

Meltzer uses journal entries, letters, and photographs to document Roosevelt's life and the state of the nation during his lifetime. Index.

Whitelaw, Nancy. *Theodore Roosevelt Takes Charge.* Illus. Albert Whitman 1992 (cloth 0-8075-7849-5) 192pp.

This is a very engaging account of Roosevelt as rancher, author, and politician with many photographs and illustrations. List of books by Roosevelt, chronology, bibliography, and index.

Related Books for Older Readers

Aaseng, Nathan. *You Are the President.* Illus. Oliver Press 1994 (LB 1-881508-10-2) 160pp.

Students examine problems presidents faced: the background, the options, and the solution. One example is Roosevelt's actions in handling the Pennsylvania coal strike. Source notes, bibliography, and index. Part of the Great Decisions series.

Hakim, Joy. *War, Peace, and All That Jazz.* Illus. Oxford University Press 1995 (LB 0-19-507761-X) (cloth 0-19-509514-6) (pap. 0-19-507762-8) 192pp.

World War I, Prohibition, the Roaring Twenties, jazz, the Depression, and World War II are among the topics presented in this book. The 30 years from 1915 to 1945 were filled with many social, political, and economic changes. This book will help students see the interrelationships between people and events of this era. Chronology, bibliography, and index. Part of the History of US series.

Woodburn, Judith. *A Multicultural Portrait of Labor in America.* Illus. Marshall Cavendish 1994 (LB 1-85435-664-X) 80pp.

Students will find information about workers in early America, children and adults working in the Industrial Age, unemployment during the Great Depression, new work opportunities created by World War II, and work in the Space Age. Roosevelt's part in urging Congress to pass legislation that would provide compensation for injured government workers is highlighted. Chronology, list of further readings, glossary, and index. Part of the Perspectives series.

Ross, Betsy (1752–1836), a well-known seamstress in Philadelphia, was the official flagmaker for the Pennsylvania navy. She is widely believed to have made the first flag of the United States, although there is no evidence to support that claim.

Biographies for Younger Readers

St. George, Judith. *Betsy Ross: Patriot of Philadelphia.* Henry Holt 1997 (cloth 0-8050-5440-5)

This biography is entertaining reading. Stories about Ross's Quaker childhood, her marriage outside her faith, her fear for her husband during the Revolutionary War, and meeting with Washington to design the first flag, are all part of the book. It includes a short author's note discussing historical evidence as to whether Ross sewed the first flag. Bibliography.

Wallner, Alexandra. *Betsy Ross.* Illus. by the author. Holiday House 1994 (LB 0-8234-1071-4) 32pp.

Illustrated with vivid folk art painting, this delightful book tells about Betsy's three marriages, the Revolutionary War, sewing the flag for George Washington and his friends, and her upholstery business. An author's note discusses whether Ross really sewed the flag and gives instructions for making a five-pointed star.

Weil, Ann. *Betsy Ross: Designer of Our Flag.* Illus. by Al Fiorentino. Macmillan 1986 (pap. 0-02-042120-6) 192pp.

Weil covers Betsy's life from childhood until meeting her first husband, John, emphasizing her prize-winning sewing skills. The final chapter tells of two modern-day children who visit her house and hear the story of how she made the first flag from Ross's great-great-grandniece. Part of the Childhood of Famous Americans series.

Related Books for Younger Readers

Egger-Bovet, Howard, and Marlene Smith-Baranzini. *USKids History: Book of the American Revolution.* Illus. by Bill Sanchez. Little, Brown 1994 (cloth 0-316-96922-2)

Students browsing or doing research and teachers looking for activities and projects will appreciate this book that highlights the events leading up to the Revolutionary War, life in the colonies during the war, and important people of the time. A game, a play about the Boston Massacre, and suggestions for making your own flag are just a few of the activities included. Index. Part of the Brown Paper School series.

Erdosh, George. *Food and Recipes of the Revolutionary War.* Illus. PowerKids Press 1997 (cloth 0-8239-5113-8)

A very simple description of the foods that were eaten by colonists and soldiers during the Revolutionary War. Several recipes are included among descriptions of daily life and photographs of the kitchens in which they were prepared. Glossary and index. Part of the Cooking Throughout American History series.

Zeinert, Karen. *Those Remarkable Women of the American Revolution.* Illus. Millbrook Press 1996 (LB 1-56294-657-9) 96pp.

This book shows the different contributions women made to the American Revolution: in the army, in the spying business, in the political arena, in the Ladies Association, and on the home front. Whether the Betsy Ross story about the first flag is truth or fiction is discussed. Timeline, list of further readings, chapter notes, bibliography, and index.

Rudolph, Wilma (1940–1994), a track
and field athlete born in Tennessee, wore a leg brace
as a child but in 1960 became the first American
woman to win three gold medals in a single
Olympics, with victories in the 100-meter and 200-
meter dashes and the 4x100-meter relay.

Biographies for Younger Readers

Krull, Kathleen. *Wilma Unlimited: How Wilma Rudolph Became the World's Fastest Woman.* Illus. by David Diaz. Harcourt 1996 (cloth 0-15-201267-2) 40pp.

Beautifully illustrated, this biography of Rudolph relates her struggles from birth as a small and sickly child to her hard work at overcoming the damage that polio left in her leg. Her amazing sports triumphs, especially in light of all she had to overcome, make for inspiring reading.

Biographies for Older Readers

Biracree, Tom. *Wilma Rudolph.* Illus. with photographs. Chelsea House 1987 (cloth 1-55546-675-3)

Starting with her premature birth, this inspiring account covers Rudolph's having to wear leg braces because of polio at an early age, and pregnancy in her senior year of high school. Chronology, list of further readings, and index. Part of the American Women of Achievement series.

Related Books for Younger Readers

Potts, Steve. *Track & Field.* Illus. Creative Education 1993 (LB 0-88682-533-4) 32pp.

This book offers a look at great moments in Olympic track and field, particularly record-breaking events. Rudolph is part of this, with her three Olympic gold medals, and recovery from illness and disability at an early age. Filled with inspiring color and black-and-white photographs. Part of the Great Moments in Sports series.

Rediger, Pat. *Great African Americans in Sports.* Illus. Crabtree 1996 (LB 0-86505-801-6) (pap. 0-86505-815-6) 64pp.

Young sports enthusiasts will enjoy this attractive book that profiles 13 notable African Americans in the field of sports, including both contemporary and historical figures. Rudolph's determination to overcome polio at an early age and her three Olympic gold medals figure among the many inspiring stories. Each sports figure has a photograph, personality profile, list of major accomplishments, and a short story of their career. Index. Part of the Outstanding African Americans series.

Related Books for Older Readers

Woolum, Janet. *Outstanding Women Athletes: Who They Are and How They Influenced Sports in America.* Illus. Oryx Press 1992 (cloth 0-89774-713-5) 296pp.

Here is entertaining coverage of sports in relation to such national issues as segregation and discrimination against women. It is a history of women's sport, with biographies of outstanding women athletes and a directory of sports organizations. Rudolph is portrayed at the crossroads of women's athletics when she excelled at the 1960 Olympics in Rome. Appendices and index.

Ruth, George Herman "Babe"

(1895–1948), is widely considered one of the best professional baseball players ever, with a lifetime batting average of .342.

Biographies for Younger Readers

Macht, Norman L. *Babe Ruth.* Illus. Chelsea House 1991 (LB 0-7910-1189-5) 64pp.

Students who enjoy baseball will find this a fun book. It records Ruth's life and career with many black-and-white photographs. Chronology, statistics, list of further readings, and index. Part of the Baseball Legends series.

Rambeck, Richard. **Babe Ruth.** Illus. Child's World 1992 (LB 0-89565-962-X) 32pp.

A simple, entertaining look at Babe Ruth. Each double-page spread contains a black-and-white photograph with a description of that part of his career. The pictures are full of expression and young fans will delight in this book. Part of the Sports Superstars series.

Biographies for Older Readers

Nicholson, Lois P. **Babe Ruth: Sultan of Swat.** Illus. Goodwood Press 1994 (cloth 0-9625427-1-7) 170pp.

Chapters of this entertaining book are titled "Inning One," "Inning Two," etc., and begin with a quotation from Ruth about baseball. With dozens of photographs, they tell the story of Ruth's life and amazing career. Chronology, statistical record, list of further readings, and index.

Related Books for Younger Readers

Ritter, Lawrence S. **The Story of Baseball.** rev. and expanded. Illus. William Morrow & Co. 1990 (cloth 0-688-09056-7) (pap. 0-688-09057-5) 224pp.

In Part One, read about baseball history, including Ty Cobb, Honus Wagner, Babe Ruth, and Lou Gehrig. There is a chapter on "Jackie Robinson Breaks the Color Barrier." Part Two looks at strategies for playing the game and ends with "Why Is Baseball So Popular?" Index.

Sullivan, George. **Sluggers: Twenty-Seven of Baseball's Greatest.** Illus. Atheneum 1991 (LB 0-689-31566-X) 80pp.

Full of short biographies, colorful photographs, and statistics, this book will please young baseball fans. Some of the names included are better known than others. Ruth, of course, is mentioned as the first great slugger in baseball history. There is a section on all-time records, including home runs, slugging percentages, triples, and runs batted in, doubles, strikeouts, and walks. Index.

Ward, Geoffrey C., and Ken Burns. **25 Great Moments.** Illus. Knopf 1994 (cloth 0-679-86751-1) (pap. 0-679-96751-6) 64pp.

Could you name your 25 great moments of baseball? That is what the authors have done here. Babe Ruth predicting his home run, Lou Gehrig Day at Yankee Stadium, Jackie Robinson breaking the color barrier, Roger Maris getting 61 home runs, and many more wonderful events. Hank Aaron, Joe DiMaggio, the Griffeys, and Bob Feller are some of the great names in this book. Index. Part of the Baseball: The American Epic series of books, which is excerpted from the longer book *Baseball: An Illustrated History* (from the PBS television series), see below.

Related Books for Older Readers

Ward, Geoffrey C., and Ken Burns. *Baseball: An Illustrated History.* Illus. Knopf 1994 (cloth 0-679-40459-7) 1996 (pap. 0-614-20476-3) 512pp.

This is an incredible book for the baseball fan and for anyone interested in the social history of America as reflected in a sport. It is filled with wonderful photographs. Students will want to browse through the memorabilia of baseball and read about the evolution of the game. For the most part, the chapters focus on decades and look at every aspect of the game, including the rules, players, owners, facilities, and fans. This is the companion book to the PBS television series. Bibliography and index.

Sabin, Florence Rena (1871–1953), an American anatomist, is best known for her pioneering studies of the lymphatic system. In 1925 she became the first woman elected to the National Academy of Sciences.

Biographies for Younger Readers

Kaye, Judith. *The Life of Florence Sabin.* Illus. Twenty-First Century Books 1993 (o.p.) 88pp.

As a woman interested in science, Florence Sabin overcame many obstacles to achieve success in medicine. This biography is well organized and features her efforts as a teacher and scientist. Bibliography and index. Part of the Pioneers in Health and Medicine series.

Biographies for Older Readers

Kronstadt, Janet. *Florence Sabin: Medical Researcher.* Illus. Chelsea House 1990 (o.p.) 112pp.

This book chronicles Sabin's amazing scientific work on the lymphatic system from as early as her sophomore year in college. Even after retiring, she contributed to improved health conditions in Colorado through her work on tuberculosis. This record shows how many of her scientific awards and accomplishments were groundbreaking for women. Chronology, lists of her publications and further readings, and index. Part of the American Women of Achievement series.

Related Books for Older Readers

Stille, Darlene R. *Extraordinary Women Scientists.* Illus. Children's Press 1995 (LB 0-516-00585-5) (pap. 0-516-40585-3) 208pp.

Many of the women in this book had to overcome prejudices and deal with restricted opportunities in the sciences. Some of the women featured are Rachel Carson, Marie Curie, Jane Goodall, Mae C. Jemison, Margaret Mead, Maria Mitchell, Sally Ride, and Florence Sabin. There are brief essays throughout this book on the role of women in medicine, inventing, engineering, math, and related topics. Bibliography and index. Part of the Extraordinary People series.

Suplee, Curt. *Everyday Science Explained.* Illus. National Geographic Society 1996 (cloth 0-7922-3410-3)

Readers will enjoy this beautifully illustrated science book from National Geographic. Matter and motion, the forces of nature, and the chemistry of life are all covered. There is something here for everybody! A section on the immune system (Sabin's specialty) includes retroviruses, stress and recovery, lymph nodes, organ transplants, diabetes, and more, all with beautiful color photographs and illustrations. Includes index.

Sacagawea (1784–1884?), a Native American guide and sole female member of the Lewis and Clark expedition, became an important asset when the expedition reached the upper Missouri River area where she had been raised and where, as a girl, she had been captured and traded to Toussaint Charbonneau, who was an interpreter for the expedition.

Biographies for Younger Readers

Sanford, William R., and Carl R. Green. *Sacagawea: Native American Hero.* Illus. Enslow Publishers 1997 (LB 0-89490-675-5) 48pp.

Readers learn not only about the journey Sacagawea made with Lewis and Clark but also what happened to her afterward. List of further readings, chapter notes, glossary, and index. Part of the Legendary Heroes of the Wild West series.

Biographies for Older Readers

Brown, Marion M. *Sacagawea: Indian Interpreter to Lewis and Clark.* Illus. Children's Press 1988 (o.p.) 119pp.

This biography explains what it was like to be an Indian woman at that time. It emphasizes Sacagawea's role in the Lewis and Clark expedition. Timeline and index. Part of the People of Distinction Biographies series.

Rowland, Della. *The Story of Sacagawea, Guide to Lewis and Clark.* Yearling Books 1989 (pap. 0-440-40215-8) 96pp.

Told in story format, this is a chronicle of the Lewis and Clark expedition with Sacajawea. A map of their journey is included.

St. George, Judith. *Sacagawea.* Putnam's 1997 (cloth 0-399-23161-7) 128pp.

In this very readable biography, students will get an insight into the personality of this intrepid woman. Sacagawea accompanied the Lewis and Clark expedition as they explored the wilderness, providing invaluable help that aided their survival. Bibliography and index.

Related Books for Younger Readers

Lake, A. L. *Women of the West.* Illus. Rourke 1990 (LB 0-86625-373-4) 32pp.

Gives several brief biographies of well-known women such as Sacagawea, and describes the life of women homesteaders. Includes chronology and pictures of many of the daily tools of life at that time. Part of the Wild West in American History series.

Related Books for Older Readers

Stefoff, Rebecca. *Women of the World: Women Travelers and Explorers.* Illus. Oxford University Press 1992 (LB 0-19-507687-7) 1994 (pap. 0-19-507688-5) 144pp.

Most books we read about exploration or discovery are books about men. This relates some of the explorations and discoveries made by women. Florence Baker's adventures on the Nile, Marguerite Harrison's exploits as housewife-turned-spy, and Saca-gawea's journey are just three of many wonderful achievements by women. Chronology, list of further readings, and index. Part of the Extraordinary Explorers series.

Sadat, Anwar al- (1918–1981), president of Egypt from 1970 until 1981, was the first Arab leader to recognize Israel. He was killed by Muslim fundamentalists in 1981.

Biographies for Older Readers

Aufderheide, Patricia. *Anwar Sadat.* Illus. Chelsea House 1985 (o.p.) 112pp.

In addition to covering Sadat's tumultuous political career, Aufderheide gives historical background information. Chronology, list of further readings, and index. Part of the World Leaders Past & Present series.

Rosen, Deborah Nodler. *Anwar el-Sadat: A Man of Peace.* Illus. with photographs and maps. Children's Press 1986 (LB 0-516-03214-3)

Rosen details Sadat's political life, starting with his anti-British activities and jail term. Sadat's great peace initiatives after he became president and his eventual repressive measures over the issues of Palestinian autonomy are covered. The book explains the difference in opinions about Sadat: was he peacemaker or traitor? Timeline and index. Part of the People of Distinction Biographies series.

Related Books for Younger Readers

Pimlott, John. *Middle East: A Background to the Conflicts.* Illus. Gloucester Press 1991 (o.p.) 40pp.

Written shortly after the cease-fire was declared by President Bush in the war against Iraq, this book covers the roots of the Middle East conflict, the Arab-Israeli conflict, the Iran-Iraq war, and the Gulf War. Part of the background included is the signing of the Camp David agreement by Sadat and Begin, ending nearly 30 years of hostility between Egypt and Israel. Contains many photographs, maps, and detailed descriptions of each of the Middle Eastern countries. Chronology, glossary, and index. Part of the Hotspots series.

Related Books for Older Readers

Hiro, Dilip. *The Middle East.* Illus. Oryx Press 1996 (pap. 0-57356-004-9) 232pp.

In this very detailed book, an overview of the region is followed by a focus on the individual countries. Each section covers the history and important issues and people. For example, there is information about the discovery of oil and the important role it has come to play. There is a chapter on the conflict between Arabs and Jews. There is information about the crisis in Kuwait, the Gulf War, and the 1993 peace accord. Glossary, bibliography, and index. Part of the International Politics and Government series.

Ross, Stewart. *Arab-Israeli Conflict.* Illus. Raintree Steck-Vaughn 1996 (LB 0-8172-4051-9) 80pp.

Although the format of this book could make it accessible to younger students, the complexity of the issues might be better understood by an older audience. Issues include the formation of Israel, conflicts in the region, the Palestinians, and the peace process. There are many maps, making this a good overview for students who are just beginning to study this area. Timeline, glossary, bibliography, and index. Part of the Causes and Consequences series.

Salk, Jonas (1914–1995), an American epidemiologist, in 1952 developed a vaccine for poliomyelitis (also called polio or infantile paralysis). The vaccine nearly eradicated the disease in the United States.

Biographies for Older Readers

Bredeson, Carmen. *Jonas Salk: Discoverer of the Polio Vaccine.* Illus. Enslow Publishers 1993 (o.p.) 112pp.

Although Jonas Salk is best known for his discovery of the vaccine for polio, he continued to work to protect people from other viruses such as AIDS and influenza. Written before Salk's death, this book describes his education and accomplishments. Chronology, list of further readings, chapter notes, and index. Part of the People to Know series.

Sherrow, Victoria. *Jonas Salk: Research for a Healthier World.* Illus. Facts on File 1993 (cloth 0-8160-2805-2) 144pp.

Here is excellent coverage of the terror of polio epidemics and of Salk's research to develop a vaccine to prevent the disease. There is information about the Salk Institute, the human immune system, epidemics, viruses, vaccines, and AIDS. List of further readings, glossary, bibliography, and index. Part of the Makers of Modern Science series.

Related Books for Younger Readers

Hargrove, Jim. *The Story of Jonas Salk and the Discovery of the Polio Vaccine.* Illus. Children's Press 1990 (o.p.) 32pp.

This book describes the process Salk went through in discovering the polio vaccine. It contains many photographs, including ones of people and microscopic photographs of the polio virus itself. Students will be amazed at the years of research that went into the discovery and the small and large problems Salk encountered. An inspiring story. Index. Part of the Cornerstones of Freedom series.

Turvey, Peter. *Inventions: Inventors and Ingenious Ideas.* Illus. Franklin Watts 1992 (LB 0-531-14308-2) (pap. 0-531-15713-X) 48pp.

A survey of inventions throughout history, from the wheel to virtual-reality games, this is fun to browse through, for young and old alike. Diagrams of the inventions, along with commentary about how they affected life in their time period, are included. Salk's vaccine is part of the chapter covering the 1950s. Timeline, glossary, and index. Part of the Timelines series.

Related Books for Older Readers

Karlen, Arno. *Man and Microbes: Disease and Plagues in History and Modern Times.* Putnam's 1995 (LB 0-87477-759-3) 266pp.

This is a very detailed book for students who are serious about researching diseases through history. Epidemics, plagues, microbes, germs, and infections are described with case studies and well-researched details. One topic is how the arrival of Europeans in the Americas had a devastating effect on the native peoples' health. Extensive bibliography and index.

LeVert, Marianne. *AIDS: A Handbook for the Future.* Illus. Millbrook Press 1996 (LB 1-56294-660-9) 160pp.

At the time of his death, Salk was working on a vaccine to prevent AIDS in individuals who were HIV-infected, and the Salk Institute continues to work with the AIDS virus. LeVert covers how the virus affects the immune system, how it is transmitted, how to reduce the risk of infection, teens and HIV, testing, treatment, and AIDS and society. The information is interspersed with statistics and well-known cases in the news. This is a fairly frank book, but one that should be considered by anyone wanting to know more about the disease. Lists of recommended readings and sources of information including phone numbers, state hotlines, and research foundations. Chapter notes, glossary, and index.

Sasaki, Sadako (1943–1955) died of leukemia at the age of 12, ten years after U.S. forces dropped the atom bomb less than two kilometers from her home in Hiroshima. She folded pieces of paper into the shape of a crane, believing she would get well when she had done this a thousand times.

Biographies for Younger Readers

Coerr, Eleanor. *Sadako.* Illus. by Ed Young. Putnam's 1993 (cloth 0-399-21771-1); Paperstar 1997 (pap. 0-698-11588-0) 48pp.

Ed Young's gorgeous illustrations add to Eleanor Coerr's reworking of the story of Sadako Sasaki. This presentation could be shared as a read-aloud. It will spark students' interest in reading Coerr's other book as well as learning about the human side of war. There is a monument to Sadako in Hiroshima Peace Park.

Coerr, Eleanor. *Sadako and the Thousand Paper Cranes.* Illus. by Ronald Himler. Putnam's 1977 (cloth 0-399-20520-9) (pap. 0-440-47465-5)

Nine chapters describe Sadako's courageous efforts to deal with her leukemia. After her death, her classmates completed the project.

Related Books for Younger Readers

Feinberg, Barbara Silberdick. *Hiroshima and Nagasaki.* Illus. with photographs. Children's Press 1995 (LB 0-516-06627-7) 32pp.

Feinberg takes a short but fascinating look at the missions to drop the atom bombs and describes their terrible effects. Sadako's story is part of the coverage. Timeline, glossary, and index. Part of the Cornerstones of Freedom series.

Kodama, Tatsuharu. *Shin's Tricycle.* Illus. by Norijuki Ando. Trans. by Kazuko Hokumen-Jones. Walker and Company 1992 (LB 0-8027-8376-7) (cloth 0-8027-8375-9) 32pp.

A beautifully illustrated true story of another family's experience of the bombing of Hiroshima. Shin's uncle is able to get him the impossible: the tricycle he desperately wants. He is riding the wonderful, brand-new tricycle when the atom bomb is dropped. Shin is found in the rubble, holding on to his treasure. He dies later that day, ten days before his fourth birthday. The tricycle now sits in the Peace Museum in Hiroshima.

Related Books for Older Readers

Murphy, Wendy, and Jack Murphy. *Nuclear Medicine.* Illus. Chelsea House 1994 (LB 0-7910-0070-2)

The history of nuclear medicine is closely tied to the history of nuclear weapons. At the same time that scientists were beginning to discuss the theories that led to the atom bomb, medical researchers were beginning to experiment with the use of radioactive materials for medical treatment. The effects of the bombing of Hiroshima affected the way the public looked at this treatment in later years. Introduction by former Surgeon General C. Everett Koop. Lists of further readings and places to write for more information, glossary, and index. Part of the Encyclopedia of Health series.

Schindler, Oskar (1908–1974), a German industrialist who, during World War II, saved as many as 1,000 Jews from death in concentration camps.

Biographies for Older Readers

Roberts, Jack L. *The Importance of Oskar Schindler.* Illus.
Lucent 1996 (LB 1-56006-079-4) 112pp.

This covers Schindler's life, focusing on the part he played in
the Holocaust by saving more than 1,000 Jews. It also discusses
whether he saved the Jews for profit or out of true humanitarian concern. List of further readings, chapter notes, and index. Part of the
Importance Of series.

Related Books for Older Readers

Holliday, Laurel. *Children in the Holocaust and World War II:
Their Secret Diaries.* Pocket Books 1995 (cloth 0-671-52054-7)
(pap. 0-671-52055-5) 432pp.

This book marks the 50th anniversary of the end of World War
II. It includes 23 diaries written by young people ages 10 to 18 from
several countries, including Poland, Holland, and Germany. These
touching stories give insight into how people, especially children,
survive horror. Some of the diarists are survivors, some are not. List
of sources and bibliography.

Horn, Joseph. *Mark It with a Stone: A Moving Account of a
Young Boy's Struggle to Survive the Nazi Death Camps.* Barri-
cade Books 1996 (cloth 1-56980-068-5) 224pp.

What happened to the people Schindler was unable to save?
Although every other member of his family perished, Joseph Horn
stayed alive, through slave-labor factories and concentration camps
including Auschwitz and Bergen-Belsen. This is an absorbing story.

Lace, William W. *The Nazis.* Illus. Lucent 1998 (LB 1-56006-091-
3)

Readers studying Schindler's life will find this worthwhile
reading. It covers the birth of the Nazi Party and the party's seizure
of power, the Nazis and the Jews, and the war and its destruction.
Contains many black-and-white photographs. List of further readings, chapter notes, and index. Part of the Holocaust Library series.

Schwarzkopf, H. Norman (1934–), an American general, led U.S. forces in the 1991 Gulf War to drive Iraqi invaders from Kuwait. He earlier served two tours of duty in Vietnam and in 1983 was second in command of the U.S. invasion of Grenada.

Biographies for Younger Readers

Italia, Bob. *General H. Norman Schwarzkopf.* Abdo & Daughters 1992 (LB 1-56239-148-8)

In addition to relating his activities in the Vietnam War, the Persian Gulf War, and the action in Grenada, this book covers his high spirits, his favorite TV shows, and the games he likes to play. Glossary. Part of the War in the Gulf series.

Biographies for Older Readers

Hughes, Libby. *Norman Schwarzkopf: Hero with a Heart.* Illus. Silver Burdett 1992 (LB 0-87518-521-5) 144pp.

Hughes covers his childhood through his adult military career, the story of the general who became a hero. Bibliography and index. Part of the People in Focus series.

Related Books for Younger Readers

King, David. *First Facts about American Heroes.* Illus. Blackbirch Press 1996 (LB 1-56711-165-3) 112pp.

This entertaining book highlights individuals from all walks of life who have contributed to our nation's development over the centuries. It covers figures from the Colonial period such as John Smith and Anne Hutchinson and contemporary figures including Schwarzkopf and Rachel Carson. Schwarzkopf's honors for bravery during the Vietnam War and his leadership of the allied forces during the Gulf War are documented. Lists of further readings and places to visit and index. Part of the First Facts series.

Related Books for Older Readers

Chant, Christopher. *The Military History of the United States: The Gulf War.* Illus. Marshall Cavendish 1992 (o.p.)

Students will find detailed coverage of the events leading up to the Gulf War and of Operation Desert Storm itself. There is some discussion as to whether the operation was halted too soon. Many color photographs. Glossary, bibliography, and index.

Kent, Zachary. *The Persian Gulf War: "The Mother of All Battles."* Illus. Enslow Publishers 1994 (LB 0-89490-528-7) 128pp.

When Saddam Hussein invaded Kuwait in the summer of 1990, there was a quick response from the world community. The United Nations forces (led by the United States) organized Operation Desert Shield and then Operation Desert Storm. This book gives historical information about the region and then focuses on the events of this war. Key figures include George Bush, Saddam Hussein, Schwarzkopf, and Colin Powell. Chronology, chapter notes, bibliography, and index. Part of the American War series.

Sequoyah (1766?–1843), a leader of the Cherokee tribe of Native Americans, put the language of his people into writing, using English, Hebrew, and Greek characters to represent Cherokee sounds. He participated in negotiations to improve relations between Native American tribes who were forcibly relocated to Oklahoma.

Biographies for Younger Readers

Petersen, David. *Sequoyah: Father of the Cherokee Alphabet.* Illus. with photographs and maps. Children's Press 1991 (LB 0-516-04180-0) 32pp.

Petersen relates the trials that Sequoyah endured in developing the Cherokee alphabet, including the burning of his cabin by his own people, with all his papers inside, when they thought he was possessed by evil spirits. The difference between an alphabet and a syllabary is explained, with examples. Historical photographs and maps show the relocation of the Cherokee. Timeline and index. Part of the Picture-Story Biographies series.

Wheeler, Jill C. *The Lame One: The Story of Sequoyah.* Illus.
Abdo & Daughters 1989 (LB 0-939179-70-9) 32pp.

Alongside this story of Sequoyah's invention of the Cherokee
alphabet, or syllabary, is the unpleasant one describing the claiming
of Indian land by the United States government. A map of the Trail
of Tears is included. Part of the Famous American Indian Leaders
series.

Biographies for Older Readers

Klausner, Janet. *Sequoyah's Gift: A Portrait of the Cherokee
Leader.* Illus. HarperCollins 1993 (LB 0-06-021236-5) 128pp.

In the 19th century, many native peoples were displaced from
their lands. They often lost contact with their culture and way of life.
Sequoyah wanted to find a way for the Cherokee people to maintain
their language and history, so he created a system of writing. List of
places to visit, bibliography, and index.

Shumate, Jane. *Sequoyah: Inventor of the Cherokee Alphabet.*
Illus. Chelsea House 1994 (LB 0-7910-1720-6)

Shumate explains Sequoyah's commitment to finding a way for
the Cherokee to communicate and work together for common goals.
This well-organized presentation will be useful for research.
Chronology, bibliography, and index. Part of the North American
Indians of Achievement series.

Related Books for Younger Readers

Bealer, Alex W. *Only the Names Remain: The Cherokees and the
Trail of Tears.* Illus. by Kristina Rodanan. Little, Brown 1996
(cloth 0-316-08518-9) (pap. 0-316-08519-7) 80pp.

This is a simple but dramatic telling of the Cherokees before
the settlers came, their successful adaptation to the presence of the
settlers, and their forceful removal by whites in the action called the
Trail of Tears. Index.

Landau, Elaine. *The Cherokees.* Illus. Franklin Watts 1992 (LB 0-
531-20066-3) (pap. 0-531-15635-4) 64pp.

Landau covers the history and daily life of the Cherokee, the
arrival of the white settlers, the Trail of Tears, and the situation of
Cherokees today. List of further readings, glossary, and index. Part
of the First Book series.

Stein, R. Conrad. *The Trail of Tears.* Illus. Children's Press 1993 (LB 0-516-06666-8) (pap. 0-516-46666-6) 32pp.

In addition to a simple telling of the history of the Cherokee and the Trail of Tears, Stein addresses their status as the most "civilized" tribe. He presents Sequoya's alphabet as an example of the emphasis the tribe placed on education. Part of the Cornerstones of Freedom series.

Related Books for Older Readers

Fremon, David K. *The Trail of Tears.* Illus. Silver Burdett 1994 (LB 0-02-735745-7) 96pp.

Here is a moving account, including political cartoons of the time, of a grim experience. There are quotations from both Indians and settlers. List of further readings, chapter notes, and index. Part of the American Events series.

Serra, Junípero (1713–1784), a Roman Catholic saint, was a Franciscan missionary to North America who founded a number of missions in California which evolved into major cities including San Diego, San Francisco, and Los Angeles.

Biographies for Younger Readers

Thompson, Kathleen. *Junípero Serra.* Illus. Raintree Steck-Vaughn 1989 (LB 0-8172-2909-4) (pap. 0-8114-6765-1) 32pp.

This text in both Spanish and English covers Serra's life, focusing on his development of the missions in California. Glossary in both English and Spanish. Part of the Hispanic Stories series.

Biographies for Older Readers

Genet, Donna. *Father Junípero Serra: Founder of California Missions.* Illus. Enslow Publishers 1996 (LB 0-89490-762-X) 128pp.

Father Junípero Serra was committed to building missions and converting native peoples to Catholicism. Chronology, list of further readings, chapter notes, and index. Part of the Hispanic Biographies series.

Related Books for Younger Readers

Bentley, Judith. *Explorers, Trappers, and Guides.* Illus. Henry Holt 1995 (LB 0-8050-2995-8) 96pp.

These first-person accounts of explorers, trappers, and guides include Serra's 900-mile adventure on foot and horseback. List of further readings, chapter notes, and index. Part of the Settling the West series.

Kalman, Bobbie, and Greg Nickles. *Spanish Missions.* Crabtree 1997 (LB 0-86505-436-3) (pap. 0-86505-466-5) 32pp.

This is an excellent overview of what life was like in a Spanish mission. Housing, meals, crops and livestock, children, festivals, and the problems that were encountered are covered. Color illustrations and photographs of present-day reenactments show the kind of mission in which Father Serra would have worked and lived. Index. Part of the Historic Communities series.

Stone, Lynn M. *Missions.* Illus. Rourke 1993 (cloth 0-86625-445-5)

With pictures of the historic missions built in the Southeast, the Southwest, and California by the Spanish, this book also discusses Serra's work in establishing 18 of the missions in California. Glossary and index. Part of the Old America series.

Related Books for Older Readers

Griffin-Pierce, Trudy. *The Encyclopedia of Native America.* Illus. Viking Penguin 1994 (pap. 0-670-85104-3) 192pp.

Each chapter features a region of the United States and describes the native peoples who have lived there. Among those included are the Plains, the Great Basin, the Northwest Coast, and the Northeast. In the chapter on California, there is information on the missions as well as on arts and crafts. The format of this book is attractive, with numerous illustrations and sidebars. Bibliography and index.

Stanley, Jerry. *Digger: The Tragic Fate of the California Indians from the Missions to the Gold Rush.* Illus. Crown 1997 (LB 0-517-70952-X) (cloth 0-517-70951-1)

This is a very different version of the story of the Spanish missions, and probably should be included in any study of the missions or Father Serra. It tells how the Spanish missionaries brought hunger, disease, and rebellion and how the forty-niners and the gold rush brought war, slavery, and destruction. According to this book, life in a California mission meant "loss of freedom, loss of dignity, loss of humanity, and loss of a culture that was 12,000 years old." One chapter tells of Serra using soldiers to capture Indians for the missions. Chronology, glossary of tribal names, and index.

*"People flocked to the
Globe to see
Shakespeare's plays.
Soon after one o'clock
on fine days, London
bridge would be
crowded with
playgoers."*
(Stanley and Vennema,
unpaged)

Shakespeare, William (1564–1616) is widely considered the greatest playwright in English literature. His plays range from tragedies to comedies to historical dramas, many of which had their debut at London's Globe Theatre.

Biographies for Younger Readers

Stanley, Diane, and Peter Vennema. *Bard of Avon: The Story of William Shakespeare.* Illus. William Morrow & Co. 1992 (LB 0-688-09109-1) (cloth 0-688-09108-3) 48pp.

This is a brief biography of the world's most famous playwright, using only historically accurate information. It gives an overview of life in England at the time, especially of the theater, with beautiful and evocative illustrations.

Turner, Dorothy. *William Shakespeare.* Bookwright Press 1985 (LB 0-531-18018-2) 32pp.

Here is a simple record of Shakespeare's life, education, and plays. Lists of his plays and further readings, glossary, and index. Part of the Great Lives series.

Related Books for Younger Readers

Morley, Jacqueline. *Shakespeare's Theater.* Illus. by John James. Peter Bedrick Books 1994 (LB 0-87226-309-6) 48pp.

Read about theater in Shakespeare's day, the building of the Globe, and what it was like for the people who worked there. Attractive illustrations give readers a good idea of how the theater, the actors, and England at that time looked. Chronology, glossary, and index. Part of the Inside Story series.

Shakespeare's England: Henry VIII, Elizabeth I, William Shakespeare. Illus. Marshall Cavendish 1989 (LB 0-86307-999-7)

Readers will enjoy the many anecdotes and illustrations of England during the times of Henry VIII, Elizabeth I, and William Shakespeare. Chronology, list of further readings, glossary, and index. Part of the Exploring the Past series.

Related Books for Older Readers

Yancey, Diane. *Life in the Elizabethan Theater.* Illus. Lucent 1996 (LB 1-56006-343-2) 112pp.

Although Shakespeare figures largely in this book, it also covers the theater, other playwrights of the time, plays, the audience, and Queen Elizabeth's sponsorship. List of further readings, chapter notes, bibliography, and index. Part of the Way People Live series.

Singer, Isaac Bashevis (1904–1991), a Polish-born author, emigrated in 1935 to New York City. He is best known for his novels and stories of life in the Jewish ghettos of Eastern Europe.

Biographies for Younger Readers

Perl, Lila. *Isaac Bashevis Singer: The Life of a Storyteller.* Illus. by Donna Ruff. Jewish Publication Society 1994 (cloth 0-8276-0512-9) 112pp.

Isaac Bashevis Singer's writing reflected many of his own experiences growing up in Poland and then as an immigrant in America, and this book illustrates the relationship between his writing and his life. Chronology, list of works by Singer, bibliography, and index.

Biographies for Older Readers

Kresh, Paul. *Isaac Bashevis Singer: The Story of a Storyteller.* Illus. by Penrod Scofield. Dutton 1984 (o.p.) 192pp.

Written before his death in 1991, this book reveals the poverty of Singer's early years, his war experience, meeting his son again after 20 years, and, most of all, his writing. Bibliography and index. Part of the Jewish Biography series.

Singer, Isaac Bashevis. *A Day of Pleasure: Stories of a Boy Growing Up in Warsaw.* Illus. Farrar, Straus & Giroux 1986 (pap. 0-374-41696-6); Galahad Books 1992 (cloth 0-88365-798-8) 160pp.

This autobiography won the National Book Award in 1970. It covers Singer's early life in Warsaw, from the age of 3 to 14—a wonderful description both in words and photographs of what life was like for a Jew in Poland at that time.

Related Books for Younger Readers

Drucker, Malka. *The Family Treasury of Jewish Holidays.* Illus. by Nancy Patz. Little, Brown 1994 (LB 0-316-19343-7) 180pp.

A beautiful book for all ages with borders that reflect Hebrew illuminated manuscript pages, this covers ten Jewish holidays and includes stories, games, recipes, and songs. Any student reading about Singer needs to learn about the ethnic heritage that is portrayed so strongly in his books. List of further readings, glossary, and index.

Singer, Isaac Bashevis. *The Power of Light: Eight Stories for Hanukkah.* Farrar, Straus & Giroux 1980 (cloth 0-374-36099-5) 1990 (pap. 0-374-45984-3) 87pp.

In the touching title story, a Hanukkah candle gives a young couple the courage to escape the Warsaw Ghetto.

Related Books for Older Readers

Press, David P., and Elizabeth Kaplan. *Jewish Americans.* Illus. Marshall Cavendish 1995 (LB 0-7614-0153-9) 80pp.

Singer's life and work is closely connected to his heritage. This book is a good overview of Jews in America, their reasons for immigrating, traditions, religion, customs, and their contributions to American culture. Chronology of Jewish people in America, list of further readings, glossary, and index. Part of the Cultures of America series.

Sitting Bull (1831?–1890), a chief of the Sioux tribe of Native Americans, led his people to victory at Little Bighorn against federal forces led by General George Armstrong Custer.

Biographies for Younger Readers

Sanford, William R. *Sitting Bull: Sioux Warrior.* Illus. Enslow Publishers 1994 (LB 0-89490-514-7) 48pp.

Chapters describe "A Boy Named Slow," "The Young Warrior," "The Sioux versus the Railroad," "The Little Bighorn," and "The Final Years." Students doing research can use this brief presentation as an overview of the issues. Chapter notes, glossary, bibliography, and index. Part of the Native American Leaders of the Wild West series.

Wheeler, Jill C. *Dakota Brave: The Story of Sitting Bull.* Illus. Abdo & Daughters 1989 (LB 0-939179-67-9) 32pp.

Many moving stories are shared in this short book, such as being nudged by a grizzly bear as a young boy, facing General Custer at the Battle of the Little Bighorn, joining Buffalo Bill Cody's Wild West Show, and, in the end, being killed by his own people. The text is simple but moving. Part of the Famous American Indian Leaders series.

Biographies for Older Readers

Black, Sheila. *Sitting Bull and the Battle of the Little Big Horn.* Illus. Silver Burdett 1989 (LB 0-382-09572-3) (pap. 0-382-09761-0) 144pp.

Black focuses on the many battles between Sitting Bull and the white man. The Powder River invasion, the battle for the Bozeman Trail, the treaty at Fort Laramie, the Battle of the Little Bighorn, and the ghost dancing when he was killed, are all covered. List of further readings. Part of the Alvin Josephy's Biography of the American Indians series.

St. George, Judith. *To See With the Heart: The Life of Sitting Bull.* Putnam's 1996 (cloth 0-399-22930-2) 192pp.

Students will find this an exciting biography. Written as a narrative, it is a dramatic retelling of Sitting Bull's life and era. There are confrontations with soldiers and settlers, plans for attacks, and broken promises. Detailed bibliography and index.

Schleichert, Elizabeth. *Sitting Bull: Sioux Leader.* Illus. Enslow Publishers 1997 (LB 0-89490-868-5) 112pp.

Featuring key battles including the Battle of the Rosebud and Little Bighorn, this biography is informative and interesting. The many quotations in the text will give students insights into the emotions of Sitting Bull and his contemporaries. One picture shows Sitting Bull with Buffalo Bill Cody, and students may want to read about Cody's Wild West shows for more information. Chronology, chapter notes, glossary, bibliography, and index. Part of the Native American Biographies series.

Related Books for Younger Readers

Ritchie, David. *Frontier Life.* Illus. Chelsea House 1996 (cloth 0-7910-2942-9) 104pp.

The Indian battles are just a part of this book, which covers the hardships that miners, farmers, ranchers, and other frontier people encountered. List of further readings and index. Part of the Life in America 100 Years Ago series.

Related Books for Older Readers

Cox, Clinton. *The Forgotten Heroes: The Story of the Buffalo Soldiers.* Illus. Scholastic 1996 (pap. 0-590-45122-7) 192pp.

After the Civil War, many black men enlisted in the Army and were assigned duty on the frontier, putting them in conflict with native peoples trying to keep their homelands. Encounters with Crazy Horse, Quanah Parker, Sitting Bull, and Geronimo are among those described. Students will find the irony of this situation as compelling as the writing. Very detailed bibliography and index.

Freedman, Russell. *Indian Chiefs.* Illus. with photographs by the author. Holiday House 1987 (LB 0-8234-0625-3) 1992 (pap. 0-8234-0971-6) 160pp.

Freedman examines the arrival of settlers in the West and the impact settlement had on the native peoples. Six chiefs are profiled: Red Cloud, Satanta, Quanah Parker, Washakie, Joseph, and Sitting Bull. Reading this book will give students insights into the many issues related to the nation's westward expansion. Thorough bibliography and index.

Press, Petra. *A Multicultural Portrait of the Move West.* Illus. Marshall Cavendish 1994 (LB 1-85435-658-5) 80pp.

This book describes westward expansion from the perspective of minorities. Sitting Bull's story is just one of many included. Chronology, list of further readings, glossary, and index. Part of the Perspectives series.

Smith, John (1579–1631), an English explorer, joined an early mission to colonize Virginia and was reportedly saved from death by Pocahontas. He served as president of the Jamestown colony from 1608 to 1609.

CAPTAIN JOHN SMITH (1579-1631)
Soldier, explorer, author and maritime expert. President of the Colony of Virginia 1608-9

Biographies for Younger Readers

Graves, Charles P. *John Smith: A World Explorer.* Illus. Chelsea House 1991 (LB 0-7910-1499-1) 96pp.

Smith's life is told as a story, covering his years fighting the Spanish, and with the colonists in Jamestown, and his friendships with Pocahontas and Powhatan. Map of Smith's voyages. Part of the Discovery Biographies series.

Related Books for Younger Readers

Egger-Bovet, Howard, and Marlene Smith-Baranzini. *USKids History: Book of the American Colonies.* Illus. by D. J. Simison. Yolla Bolly Press 1996 (cloth 0-316-96920-6) 96pp.

Full of information and imaginative games and activities, this book covers the reasons for European settlement in America, the growth of the original colonies, and the reaction of the natives to the colonists. Smith is portrayed as a leader disliked by the colonists with whom he had no patience. List of further readings and index. Part of the Brown Paper School series.

Related Books for Older Readers

Hakim, Joy. *Making Thirteen Colonies.* Illus. Oxford University Press 1993 (LB 0-19-507747-4) (cloth 0-19-509507-3) (pap. 0-19-507748-2) 160pp.

Hakim provides entertaining reading about the colonization of the New World through the mid-18th century. John Smith figures prominently in the development of Virginia and New England. Chronology, list of further readings, and index. Part of the History of US series.

Stalin, Joseph (1879–1953), leader of the Soviet Union during World War II, succeeded Lenin as general secretary of the Communist Party in 1922 and served as Soviet premier from 1941 until his death in 1953.

Biographies for Older Readers

Hoobler, Dorothy, and Thomas Hoobler. *Joseph Stalin.* Illus. Chelsea House 1985 (LB 0-87754-576-6) 112pp.

This work details the life of the revolutionary and dictator, with examples of Soviet propaganda of the time. It covers Russian and world history during his life, including his purges both before and after World War II. Chronology, list of further readings, and index. Part of the World Leaders Past & Present series.

Marrin, Albert. *Stalin: Russia's Man of Steel.* Viking Penguin 1988 (o.p.) 256pp.

Marrin examines Stalin's part in Russia's history, chronicling the political terror and millions of deaths he instigated. List of further readings and index.

Otfinoski, Steven. *Joseph Stalin: Russia's Last Czar.* Illus. Millbrook Press 1993 (LB 1-56294-240-9) 128pp.

This well-balanced presentation includes many quotations that give readers insights into the character of a complex leader. The author looks at Stalin's contributions to the Soviet people as well as his ruthless ambition and cruelty. Chronology, chapter notes, bibliography, and index.

Whitelaw, Nancy. *Joseph Stalin: From Peasant to Premier.* Illus. Dillon Press 1992 (o.p.) 160pp.

From "A Georgian Peasant" to "Stalin Takes Over" to "Death of the Premier," this thorough book is a good choice for research projects. In addition to the story of Stalin's life, there is information about the Bolshevik party and the Russian Revolution. Timeline, glossary, bibliography, and index. Part of the People in Focus series.

Related Books for Younger Readers

Gillies, John. *The New Russia.* Illus. Dillon Press 1994 (LB 0-87518-481-2) 128pp.

Gillies provides a social and geographical description of Russia as it is today, with a brief overview of its history. Cities, food, entertainment, education, sports, and more are all covered, with many photographs. Readers will especially enjoy the section on Russian humor. List of Russian embassies and consulates in the United States and Canada, glossary, bibliography, and index. Part of the Discovering Our Heritage series.

Related Books for Older Readers

Dunn, John M. *The Russian Revolution.* Illus. Lucent 1994 (LB 1-56006-234-7) 112pp.

Students will gain an overview of the people and events of the Russian Revolution. Throughout the book there are boxed sidebars on topics including an account of Bolshevik violence excerpted from John Reed's *Ten Days That Shook the World.* The czar and his family, Rasputin, Lenin, Trotsky, and Stalin are featured. List of further readings, chapter notes, bibliography, and index. Part of the World History series.

Smith, Brenda J. *The Collapse of the Soviet Union.* Lucent 1994 (LB 1-56006-142-1)

Step by step, this book takes the reader through the beginning of communism in Russia, the rise of the U.S.S.R. as a world superpower, and the events that led to its collapse. Stalin's part in the Soviet Union's rise is well documented, including the deaths of 50 million people during his years as leader. List of further readings, glossary, and index. Part of the Lucent Overview series.

Stanton, Elizabeth Cady (1815–1902), an

American reformer and pioneering feminist, led the U.S. women's movement jointly with Susan B. Anthony beginning in the middle of the 19th century. In 1848 she helped to organize the Seneca Falls Convention, the first women's rights conference in the United States.

Biographies for Younger Readers

Swain, Gwenyth. *The Road to Seneca Falls: A Story about Elizabeth Cady Stanton.* Illus. by Mary O. Young. Carolrhoda Books 1996 (cloth 0-87614-947-6) (pap. 1-57505-025-0) 64pp.

This biography of Stanton covers her childhood, marriage, the Seneca Falls Convention, and her fight for women's rights. Bibliography and index. Part of the Carolrhoda Creative Minds series.

Biographies for Older Readers

Fritz, Jean. *You Want Women to Vote, Lizzie Stanton?* Illus. by DyAnne DiSalvo-Ryan. Putnam's 1995 (cloth 0-399-22786-5) 88pp.

As usual, Fritz makes an entertaining tale—from Stanton's early years listening to her lawyer father's women clients to wearing bloomers and insisting on the right to vote. Chapter notes, bibliography, and index.

Related Books for Younger Readers

Pascoe, Elaine. *The Right to Vote.* Illus. Millbrook Press 1997 (LB 0-7613-0066-X) 48pp.

Any discussion of the right to vote would be incomplete without mention of the Seneca Falls Convention and Stanton's contributions. Section on "Understanding the Bill of Rights," list of further readings, glossary, and index. Part of the Land of the Free series.

Related Books for Older Readers

Meltzer, Milton. *The Bill of Rights: How We Got It and What It Means.* Crowell 1990 (o.p.) 180pp.

A clear discussion of the Bill of Rights, its history, and contemporary challenges to each of its amendments. Stanton's actions to abolish New York's discriminatory laws against women are related as an example of the need for people to assemble peaceably and to petition the government for redress of grievances. Timeline, bibliography, and index.

Stalcup, Brenda. *The Women's Rights Movement: Opposing Viewpoints.* Illus. Greenhaven 1996 (LB 1-56510-367-X) (pap. 1-56510-366-1) 312pp.

Opposing Viewpoints books are always of great use in the classroom and for student reports. With original articles that present differing viewpoints on such subjects as whether women's suffrage was or was not a radical reform, students are able to examine varied opinions. Discussion notes for each chapter, chronology of women's rights in America, lengthy annotated bibliography, and index. Part of the American History series.

Steinem, Gloria (1934–), feminist writer and political activist, helped found *Ms.* magazine and was a leading figure in the women's rights movement in the 1960s and 1970s.

Biographies for Older Readers

Daffron, Carolyn. *Gloria Steinem: Feminist.* Illus. Chelsea House 1988 (LB 1-55546-679-6) 112pp.

Daffron details Steinem's hard early years growing up with a mentally ill mother and a father who eventually abandoned them. She also covers Steinem's emergence as a writer, especially for feminist causes. Chronology, list of further readings, and index. Part of the American Women of Achievement series.

Related Books for Younger Readers

Brown, Gene. *The Nation in Turmoil: Civil Rights and the Vietnam War (1960–1973).* Illus. Twenty-First Century Books 1994 (LB 0-8050-2588-X) 64pp.

A wonderful collection of short pieces of primary source material, this covers the civil rights movement, the Great Society, the Vietnam War and anti-war sentiment, and the campaign for an Equal Rights Amendment. Excerpts of Steinem's testimony before Congress are included. Chronology, list of further readings, and index. Part of the First Person America series.

Related Books for Older Readers

Chafe, William H. *The Road to Equality: American Women Since 1962.* Illus. Oxford University Press 1994 (LB 0-19-508325-3) 144pp.

During World War II, women took on new roles and many were reluctant to relinquish them at the end of the war. This book describes the frustrations, opportunities, and possibilities that women have faced in the second half of the 20th century. Chronology, bibliography, and index. Part of the Young Oxford History of Women in the United States series.

May, Elaine Tyler. ***Pushing the Limits: American Women, 1940–1961.*** Illus. Oxford University Press 1994 (LB 0-19-508084-X) 144pp.

World War II and the cold war, families in suburbia, and the beginnings of the women's rights and civil rights movements are some of the topics explored in this book. Chronology, bibliography, and index. Part of the Young Oxford History of Women in the United States series.

Stevens, Leonard. ***The Case of Roe v. Wade.*** Putnam's 1996 (cloth 0-399-22812-8) 192pp.

Stevens examines the people, events, and legal questions connected with *Roe* v. *Wade*. It includes a medical and legal glossary, appendices with the Supreme Court justices who were affected by this legislation, and amendments to the Constitution that played roles in this case. Bibliography.

Stowe, Harriet Beecher (1811–1896), wrote *Uncle Tom's Cabin* to reveal to the world the evils of slavery. The powerful novel was translated into more than 20 languages and helped to galvanize the abolitionist movement in the United States.

Biographies for Younger Readers

Ash, Maureen. ***The Story of Harriet Beecher Stowe.*** Illus. Children's Press 1990 (pap. 0-516-44746-7) 32pp.

This account lays the background to Stowe's *Uncle Tom's Cabin*. It describes the uproar that her book caused and mentions the slave's ear that was mailed to her in a hate letter. Index. Part of the Cornerstones of Freedom series.

Biographies for Older Readers

Fritz, Jean. ***Harriet Beecher Stowe and the Beecher Preachers.*** Illus. Putnam's 1994 (cloth 0-399-22666-4) 144pp.

Fritz covers Harriet's childhood, marriage, her six children, and the writing of *Uncle Tom's Cabin* and the fame and notoriety that it brought her. Chapter notes, bibliography, and index.

Jakoubek, Robert. *Harriet Beecher Stowe: Author and Abolitionist.* Illus. Chelsea House 1989 (LB 1-55546-680-X) 112pp.

Students will learn about Stowe's life and the writing of *Uncle Tom's Cabin,* and about slavery in her lifetime, the Civil War, and other literary figures. There are many black-and-white photographs. Chronology, list of further readings, and index. Part of the American Women of Achievement series.

Related Books for Older Readers

Biel, Timothy Levi. *Life in the North During the Civil War.* Illus. Lucent 1997 (LB 1-56006-334-3) 112pp.

What was it like for the people living in the North during the Civil War? Those who were not part of the fighting still felt the impact. This book looks at army camps, rural life, urban life, and the war's impact on economics and politics. Chapter notes, two bibliographies (further reading and works consulted), and index. Part of the Way People Live series.

Chang, Ina. *A Separate Battle: Women and the Civil War.* Illus. Puffin 1996 (pap. 0-14-038106-6) 112pp.

Chang describes women's roles during the Civil War as slaves, abolitionists, advocates of women's rights, northern teachers, and southern refugees. Harriet Beecher Stowe's literary and personal involvement is related (she had a son who fought in the war). Bibliography and index. Part of the Young Readers' History of the Civil War series.

Damon, Duane. *When This Cruel War Is Over: The Civil War Home Front.* Lerner Publications 1996 (LB 0-8225-1731-0)

Personal stories describe life on the homefront during the Civil War. Songs of protest and literary crusades are included. Bibliography and index.

King, Wilma. *Toward the Promised Land: From Uncle Tom's Cabin to the Onset of the Civil War, 1851–1861.* Illus. Chelsea House 1995 (LB 0-7910-2265-X) (pap. 0-7910-2691-4) 144pp.

Sojourner Truth's "Ain't I a Woman" speech and Stowe's *Uncle Tom's Cabin* focused attention on the issues facing women and blacks in the decade prior to the Civil War. Key events covered include the Dred Scott decision and John Brown's raid on Harpers Ferry. The book concludes with the firing on Fort Sumter. Chronology, bibliography, and index. Part of the Milestones in Black American History series.

The company now opened a separate manufacturing plant . . . Sixty women now gathered in one place, a small factory on Fremont Street, and each one completed entire garments. They all stitched both trousers and jackets, then made buttonholes and hammered on rivets. They were paid an average of three dollars a day. By the end of 1873, they had sold over eighteen hundred dozen pants and coats for more than forty-three thousand dollars.

(Van Steenwyk, pp. 60–61)

Strauss, Levi (1829?–1902), a clothing manufacturer, emigrated to the United States from his native Germany in 1847, working first as a peddler in New York City before moving to San Francisco in 1850. The denim work pants he created for miners were reinforced with copper rivets and became known as "Levi's."

Biographies for Younger Readers

Weidt, Maryann N. *Mr. Blue Jeans: A Story about Levi Strauss.* Illus. by Lydia M. Anderson. Carolrhoda Books 1990 (LB 0-87614-421-0); First Avenue Editions 1992 (pap. 0-87614-588-8) 64pp.

This book discusses why Strauss came to America, his move to San Francisco, the gold rush, and the development of his blue jeans. Part of the Carolrhoda Creative Minds series.

Biographies for Older Readers

Van Steenwyk, Elizabeth. *Levi Strauss: The Blue Jeans Man.* Walker and Company 1988 (LB 0-8027-6796-6) (cloth 0-8027-6795-8)

Here is an account of the invention of blue jeans and of that time in American history. The gold rush and the Jewish and Chinese migration to San Francisco are part of this fascinating look at America.

Related Books for Younger Readers

Perl, Lila. *From Top Hats to Baseball Caps, From Bustles to Blue Jeans: Why We Dress the Way We Do.* Illus. by Leslie Evans. Clarion 1990 (o.p.) 118pp.

An entertaining look at the clothes we wear, this book discusses why people dress the way they do and how clothing reflects and even influences history. Blue jeans were invented during the gold rush, and began to show up on college campuses in the 1950s and 1960s. Bibliography and index.

Related Books for Older Readers

The American Frontier: Opposing Viewpoints. Greenhaven 1994
(LB 1-56510-086-7)

   Full of primary source material, this book looks at myths about
the West. "The Indian Cannot be Civilized" and "Billy the Kid Was
a Sociopath" are two of the essays included. Strauss's jeans are discussed as a symbol of the American frontier tradition, along with his
philanthropy to people in need. Chapter notes, extensive annotated
bibliography, and index. Part of the American History series.

Tecumseh (1768?–1813), a chief of the
Shawnee tribe of Native Americans, envisioned a
confederacy of tribes to resist the advance of white
settlers. After a crucial defeat, this plan was
abandoned, although Tecumseh later fought with
the British against the Americans in the War of
1812.

Biographies for Younger Readers

Kent, Zachary. *Tecumseh.* Illus. Children's Press 1992 (LB 0-516-
06660-9) 32pp.

   This tells the story of Tecumseh's life and the many battles he
fought in his hopes to preserve the Indian nations. There are many
maps and illustrations. Index. Part of the Cornerstones of Freedom
series.

Biographies for Older Readers

Cwiklik, Robert. *Tecumseh: Shawnee Rebel.* Illus. Chelsea House
1993 (LB 0-7910-1721-4) 112pp.

   Tecumseh not only led his people in battle; he led them in
diplomatic efforts to negotiate their property rights. This is a
detailed biography with many quotations and historical prints.
Chronology, bibliography, and index. Part of the North American
Indians of Achievement series.

Shorto, Russell. *Tecumseh and the Dream of an American Indian Nation.* Illus. Silver Burdett 1989 (LB 0-382-09569-3) (pap. 0-382-09758-0) 136pp.

Tecumseh is portrayed not just as a bold warrior but also as a statesman. This account covers his early life, his leadership in uniting the Indians, and his death in the War of 1812, fighting alongside the British. There is a map of the continental United States and the American Indian tribes. List of further readings. Part of the Alvin Josephy's Biography of the American Indians series.

Related Books for Older Readers

The American West: A Multicultural Encyclopedia, Volume 9, Shawnee Prophet–Utah War. Illus. Grolier 1995 (LB 0-7172-7421-7)

Tecumseh's leadership and resistance to settlers is portrayed as the "First American Civil War." Maps, list of further readings, and glossary. Each volume of the encyclopedia includes a series index.

Nardo, Don. *The Indian Wars.* Illus. Lucent 1991 (LB 1-56006-403-X) 112pp.

Nardo provides background information about the hostilities that developed between European Americans and native Indians, focusing on Tecumseh and Jefferson. List of further readings and index. Part of the America's Wars series.

Smith, Carter, ed. *The Conquest of the West: A Sourcebook on the American West.* Illus. Millbrook Press 1992 (LB 1-56294-129-1) 1996 (pap. 0-7613-0151-8) 96pp.

This book covers the movement of the frontier westward, the fulfillment of "Manifest Destiny," and the end of the frontier. Fun to browse through, it is full of photos, illustrations, and period advertisements. Tecumseh's role in the Battle of 1812 is a part of this history. Index. Part of the American Albums from the Collections of the Library of Congress series.

Teresa, Mother

Teresa, Mother (1910–1997), a Roman Catholic nun born in Albania, dedicated her life to helping the desperately poor of India. In 1950 she established the Missionaries of Charity, branches of which were stationed throughout the world. She was awarded the Nobel Peace Prize in 1979.

Biographies for Younger Readers

Giff, Patricia Reilly. *Mother Teresa: Sister to the Poor.* Illus. by Ted Lewin. Puffin 1987 (pap. 0-14-032225-6) 64pp.

Giff's very readable account covers Mother Teresa's early years, from her decision to become a missionary to living with and treating the sick and the poor. Part of the Women of Our Time series.

Tames, Richard. *Mother Teresa.* Illus. Franklin Watts 1989 (o.p.) 32pp.

This book has an appealing format. There are large photographs and boxed sections of related facts, such as those describing "The Loreto Order" and discussing "Nobel Prizes." Written before Mother Teresa died, the book closes with a message from her. Glossary, bibliography, and index. Part of the Lifetimes series.

Biographies for Older Readers

Clucas, Joan Graff. *Mother Teresa.* Illus. Chelsea House 1988 (pap. 0-7910-0602-6) 112pp.

Written before Mother Teresa's death in 1997, this gives a very descriptive picture of the poverty and slums of India. It covers Mother Teresa's early years with her family, her calling to religion, and her work as a missionary to alleviate the suffering of the poor and to promote peace. Chronology, list of further readings, and index. Part of the World Leaders Past & Present series.

Gray, Charlotte. *Mother Teresa: Her Mission to Serve God by Caring for the Poor.* Gareth Stevens 1988 (LB 1-55532-816-4)

This story of Mother Teresa's life is interspersed with many wonderful quotations by and about her. It describes her childhood, her work with the Missionaries of Charity, and her acceptance of the Nobel Peace Prize in 1979. There is a map showing where the houses of the Missionaries of Charity are throughout the world and a list of

"At times, I feel rather sad because we do so little. Most people praise us for our actions, but what we do is no more than a drop of water in the ocean. It hardly affects the immensity of human suffering."

(Clucas, p. 97)

organizations associated with Mother Teresa. Timeline, list of further readings, glossary, and index. Part of the People Who Have Helped the World series.

Related Books for Younger Readers

Cifarelli, Megan. *India: One Nation, Many Traditions.* Illus. Marshall Cavendish 1996 (LB 0-7614-0201-2) 64pp.

Students studying Mother Teresa will want to research the country in which she did most of her work. Cifarelli traces the geography and history, people, family life, festivals, food, school, recreations, and the arts of India with many color photographs. Country facts, list of further readings, glossary, and index. Part of the Exploring Cultures of the World series.

Related Books for Older Readers

Ghose, Vijaya. *India.* Illus. Marshall Cavendish 1994 (LB 1-85435-564-3) 128pp.

Any discussion of Mother Teresa needs to examine the condition of women in India. The author explains milestones in the status of Indian women, their place in society, what life is like at different stages in their lifetimes, and profiles several Indian women who devoted their lives to bettering women's conditions. Mother Teresa is included in a short section about Christian missionaries in India. Lists of firsts for India's women and further readings, glossary, and index. Part of the Women in Society series.

Thatcher, Margaret (1925–), a British politician, in 1979 became the first woman prime minister of the United Kingdom, a position she retained until 1990. She led her country into a brief war with Argentina in 1982 over the latter's seizure of the Falkland Islands.

Biographies for Older Readers

Foster, Leila M. *Margaret Thatcher: First Woman Prime Minister of Great Britain.* Illus. Children's Press 1990 (o.p.) 152pp.

Written while she was still in office, this book focuses on Thatcher's amazing political career. Her campaigns are covered, as are such important events as the Falklands War. Timeline and index. Part of the People of Distinction Biographies series.

Garfinkel, Bernard. *Margaret Thatcher.* Illus. Chelsea House 1985 (o.p.) 112pp.

This balanced account of Thatcher's political career includes quotations from both admirers and opponents. Black-and-white photographs are scattered throughout the book. Chronology, list of further readings, and index. Part of the World Leaders Past & Present series.

Hughes, Libby. *Madam Prime Minister: A Biography of Margaret Thatcher.* Illus. Silver Burdett 1989 (LB 0-87518-410-3) 128pp.

Written while she was still prime minister, this book portrays Thatcher as a no-nonsense leader unafraid to be unpopular. It covers her childhood, education, and political career. Index. Part of the People in Focus series.

Related Books for Older Readers

Corbishley, Mike, et al. *The Young Oxford History of Britain & Ireland.* Illus. Oxford University Press, 1996 (cloth 0-19-910035-7) 416 pp.

From the ancient peoples and medieval kingdoms to the British empire and modern Britain, this book gives a great overview of these countries. Thatcher's contributions are discussed in a chapter on "Britain in Doubt." The many illustrations make this a very informative book, both in text and visually. Charts of the Succession and prime ministers and index.

Fuller, Barbara. *Britain.* Illus. Marshall Cavendish, 1994 (LB 1-85435-587-2) 128 pp.

History is woven throughout the text of this book. There are details about early settlers, the Anglo-Saxons, the monarchy, the Victorian age, and the 20th century. Margaret Thatcher is briefly featured. Photographs (many in color) as well as charts and sidebars make this a very pleasant book to use. There is a section of statistics about Britain. Glossary, bibliography, index.

Thoreau, Henry David (1817–1862), an influential American author and philosopher, lived for more than two years at Walden Pond in Massachusetts, recording his thoughts on nature and life. His most famous work *Walden* was distilled from the observations in his journal.

Biographies for Younger Readers

Anderson, Peter. *Henry David Thoreau: American Naturalist.* Illus. Franklin Watts 1996 (LB 0-531-20206-2) (pap. 0-531-15761-X) 64pp.

This is a lovely book with a well-organized text and excellent selection and placement of illustrations. There are photographs of the Walden Pond area and photographs and paintings of Thoreau and his contemporaries. Bibliography and index. Part of the First Book series.

Burleigh, Robert. *A Man Named Thoreau.* Illus. by Lloyd Bloom. Atheneum 1985 (LB 0-689-31122-2) 48pp.

Burleigh explains Thoreau's unique personality, his reasons for living at Walden Pond, his writings, and his sharp criticisms of society. A nice beginning book on Thoreau's life. List of important dates and bibliography.

Related Books for Younger Readers

Herda, D. J. *Environmental America: The Northeastern States.* Illus. Millbrook Press 1991 (LB 1-878841-06-8) 64pp.

Herda explores the environment of the section of the country in which Thoreau lived and what can be done to protect the land, air, and water. List of organizations to contact, chapter notes, glossary, and index. Part of the American Scene series.

Related Books for Older Readers

Amdur, Richard. *Wilderness Preservation.* Chelsea House 1993
(LB 0-7910-1605-6) 112pp.

Thoreau believed that wildlife areas benefit us both physically and spiritually. This book includes those reasons in its list of why we need to preserve wilderness areas. Lists of places to contact for more information and further readings, glossary, and index. Part of the Earth at Risk series.

Hakim, Joy. *Liberty for All?* Illus. Oxford University Press 1994
(LB 0-19-507753-9) (cloth 0-19-509510-3) (pap. 0-19-507754-7)
160pp.

An entertaining look at the period of American history just before the Civil War. Whale hunting, mountain men, and the gold rush are all included. Thoreau's years at Walden and his philosophies about life are also part of the story. Chronology, list of further readings, and index. Part of the History of US series.

Thorpe, Jim (1888–1953), a Native American athlete, first won recognition as an All-American football player while studying at the Carlisle Indian Industrial School in Pennsylvania. He won Olympic gold medals in the pentathlon and decathlon in 1912 but was stripped of his medals when his amateur status was cast into doubt.

Biographies for Younger Readers

Rivinus, Edward F. *Jim Thorpe.* Illus. Raintree Steck-Vaughn
1990 (LB 0-8172-3403-9) 32pp.

This portrays the hard time Thorpe had in school, his amazing sports records, and his professional football and baseball career. Chronology. Part of the American Indian Stories series.

Biographies for Older Readers

Bernotas, Bob. *Jim Thorpe: Sac and Fox Athlete.* Illus. Chelsea House 1993 (LB 0-7910-1722-2) 1992 (pap. 0-7910-1695-1)

Emphasizing his Indian background, this book covers Thorpe's early years on a farm, his time at the Carlisle Indian school, his domination of the 1912 Olympics, and his professional football and baseball careers. It also covers his family's fight for his gold medals. Chronology, list of further readings, and index. Part of the North American Indians of Achievement series.

Lipsyte, Robert. *Jim Thorpe: 20th-Century Jock.* Illus. Harper-Collins 1993 (LB 0-06-022989-6) 1995 (pap. 0-06-446141-6) 112pp.

Each chapter of this biography begins with a quotation, either about Thorpe or illustrating sentiments about Indians at that time. It tells about Thorpe's early years as an Indian in a school meant to educate him in white culture, his amazing sports feats, and his efforts to speak out against the abuses of the Bureau of Indian Affairs. Index. Part of the Superstar Lineup series.

Richards, Gregory B. *Jim Thorpe: World's Greatest Athlete.* Illus. Children's Press 1984 (o.p.) 112pp.

With a Foreword by Thorpe's daughter Grace, this book recounts Thorpe's amazing sports accomplishments along with the tragic story of being stripped of his Olympic medals—they were not returned until after his death. Chronology and index. Part of the People of Distinction Biographies series.

Related Books for Younger Readers

Krull, Kathleen. *Lives of the Athletes: Thrills, Spills (And What the Neighbors Thought).* Illus. by Kathryn Hewitt. Harcourt 1997 (cloth 0-15-200806-3)

Jim Thorpe is just one of the 20 athletes covered here (with colorful stories about each one). Two anecdotes about Thorpe describe him playing against Dwight Eisenhower, future president, and telling the king of Sweden "Thanks, King," when he received his gold medals in the Olympics. Bibliography.

McDaniel, Melissa. *The Sac and Fox Indians.* Chelsea House 1995 (cloth 0-7910-1670-6)

These two tribes, of which Jim Thorpe was a member, have lived and worked together for centuries. This book describes their culture, their lifestyle, and their art. Chronology, glossary, and index. Part of the Junior Library of American Indians series.

Miller, Jay. *American Indian Games.* Children's Press 1996 (LB 0-561-20136-0) 1997 (pap. 0-516-26092-8) 48pp.

A very simple and brief discussion of the toys and games used by Native Americans to teach and amuse their children. Thorpe is mentioned in a discussion of school teams and games, and a picture of the Carlisle Indian school football team in the 1890s is included. The section "To Find Out More" contains books, organizations, and Web sites for students to contact. Short glossary of important words and index. Part of the True Book series.

Related Books for Older Readers

Avery, Susan. *Extraordinary American Indians.* Illus. Children's Press 1992 (LB 0-516-00583-9) (pap. 0-516-40583-7) 260pp.

The author discusses the accomplishments of outstanding Native Americans from the 18th century to the present, emphasizing their activism in supporting Native Americans' rights. Thorpe's sports career and his support of changes to the Sac and Fox tribal constitution are discussed. Extensive list of further readings and index. Part of the Extraordinary People series.

Tombaugh, Clyde (1906–), located the planet Pluto in 1930, ending a 25-year search for the planet known to exist at the edge of the solar system.

Biographies for Younger Readers

Wetterer, Margaret K. *Clyde Tombaugh and the Search for Planet X.* Illus. by Laurie A. Caple. Carolrhoda Books 1996 (LB 0-87614-893-3) (pap. 0-87614-969-7)

This book focuses on Tombaugh's fascination with astronomy and his eventual discovery of Planet X, the planet Pluto, explaining the meticulous process the astronomers followed to find this planet. Chronology. Part of the Carolrhoda On My Own Books series.

Related Books for Younger Readers

Bailey, Donna. *The Far Planets.* Illus. Raintree Steck-Vaughn 1991 (LB 0-8114-2524-X) 48pp.

A simple discussion of the five planets known to lie outside the orbit of Mars, this also considers the possibility of additional planets beyond Pluto. Facts about each planet are given, with a drawing of its orbit and place in the solar system, and color photographs and drawings. Glossary and index. Part of the Facts About series.

Nicholson, Iain. *The Illustrated World of Space.* Simon & Schuster 1991 (o.p.)

Full of information and illustrations, this book covers the first astronomers, modern astronomy, the solar system, and the inner and outer planets. Tombaugh's discovery of Pluto is discussed. Several tables of space facts, glossary, and index.

Vogt, Gregory. *Pluto.* Illus. Millbrook Press 1994 (LB 1-56294-393-6) (cloth 0-7613-0158-5) 32pp.

This book begins with a discussion of Tombaugh's career and discovery of Pluto, including the black-and-white photographs on which he first tracked the planet's movement. Quick facts, list of further readings, glossary, and index. Part of the Gateway Solar System series.

Toussaint L'Ouverture, François Dominique (1743–1803) is remembered as the founder of Haiti. In 1801 he liberated what was then known as Saint-Domingue from French control and was made president for life of the new republic.

Biographies for Younger Readers

Myers, Walter Dean. *Toussaint L'Ouverture: The Fight for Haiti's Freedom.* Illus. with paintings by Jacob Lawrence. Simon & Schuster 1996 (cloth 0-689-80126-2)

In both words and pictures, this is a dramatic retelling of the liberation of Haiti and the efforts of Toussaint L'Ouverture. Jacob Lawrence has created powerful images of the revolution and the establishment of the first black republic. Although the format is that of a picture book, the sophistication of the art and the drama of the events will interest older students, too.

Related Books for Younger Readers

Griffiths, John. *Haiti.* Franklin Watts 1989 (LB 0-531-10735-3)

Griffiths gives a brief description of Haiti, including its history, climate, geography, ethnic composition, language, government, religion, and agriculture. He also discusses the inadequate health and education systems in this very poor nation. Index. Part of the Take a Trip To series.

Rees, Bob. *The Black Experience: In the Caribbean and the USA.* Illus. Peter Bedrick Books 1992 (cloth 0-87226-117-4) 64pp.

In this very browsable book, pieces of information are set beside pictures and quotations. It covers the beginnings of slavery, the history of the Caribbean and the United States before and after slavery, and Toussaint's role in the slave revolt. Index. Part of the Biographical History series.

Related Books for Older Readers

Cheong-Lum, Roseline Ng. *Haiti.* Illus. Marshall Cavendish 1995 (LB 1-85435-693-3) 128pp.

Although only one chapter is distinctly devoted to history, Haiti's past is woven throughout this book. The chapters on religion, the arts, festivals, and food all include details about the people and their culture. Maps, "Quick Notes," glossary, bibliography, and index. Part of the Cultures of the World series.

Truman, Harry S. (1884–1972), the 33rd president of the United States, authorized the use of the atom bomb against Japan, ended segregation in the U.S. military forces, and authorized the Marshall Plan to help rebuild war-torn Europe. In 1950 he dispatched U.S. troops to South Korea when North Korean forces invaded.

Biographies for Older Readers

Greenberg, Morrie. *The Buck Stops Here.* Illus. Silver Burdett 1991 (LB 0-87518-394-8) 128pp.

This biography covers his early years and his time in office as president, examining his decision to drop the atom bomb and his actions during the Berlin blockade and the Korean War. It includes a section on major events in Truman's life. Index. Part of the People in Focus series.

Hargrove, Jim. *Harry S. Truman: Thirty-Third President of the United States.* Illus. Children's Press 1987 (LB 0-516-01388-2) 100pp.

This is an overview of the world during Truman's life, starting with horse-drawn carriages and ending with astronauts walking on the moon. World War II, the atom bomb, and the war in Korea are covered. Chronology of American history highlighting Truman's life and index. Part of the Encyclopedia of Presidents series.

Related Books for Younger Readers

Krull, Kathleen. *V Is for Victory.* Illus. Alfred A. Knopf 1995 (LB 0-679-96198-4) (cloth 0-679-86198-X) 128pp.

This entertaining book was put together to commemorate the 50th anniversary of the Allied victory. It includes advertisements, photographs, cartoons, and statistics. Truman's decision to drop the bomb is, of course, included, as well as photographs from the two-day holiday the president declared when the war was over. Chronology, bibliography, and index.

Related Books for Older Readers

Chant, Christopher. *The Military History of the United States: World War II: The Pacific War.* Illus. Marshall Cavendish 1992 (o.p.)

Truman will always be remembered for his decision to drop atom bombs on Japan. Here, students can look at this controversial decision from a military viewpoint. Many color photographs. Glossary, bibliography, and volume index.

Pious, Richard M. *The Young Oxford Companion to the Presidency of the United States.* Illus. Oxford University Press 1994 (cloth 0-19-507799-7) 368pp.

Students will read this detailed book for research and for enjoyment. The overall arrangement is alphabetical. There are biographical sketches of all the presidents and vice presidents and some First Ladies. There are entries about the powers of the presidency and about presidential advisers, policies, decisions, and perks. Many entries include lists of further readings. Chronology, list of presidential historic sites and libraries, bibliography, and index. Part of the Young Oxford Companion series.

Truth, Sojourner (1797?–1883), freed from slavery in 1827, became a crusader against slavery and for women's rights. In 1843 she said that "voices" had commanded her to devote her life to preaching, and she preached widely throughout northern United States both before and after the Civil War.

Biographies for Younger Readers

Adler, David A. *A Picture Book of Sojourner Truth.* Illus. by Gershom Griffith. Holiday House 1994 (LB 0-8234-1072-2) 1996 (pap. 0-8234-1262-8) 32pp.

The picture-book format of this introduction to Sojourner Truth's life makes it a good selection to read aloud. List of important dates. Part of the Picture Book Of series.

Tolan, Mary, adapt. *Sojourner Truth: The Courageous Former Slave Who Led Others to Freedom.* Illus. Gareth Stevens 1991 (LB 0-8368-0101-6) 64pp.

This book follows the life of Sojourner Truth and her activities as an abolitionist and as an advocate of women's rights. Full of wonderful quotations, it is also a good picture of the times, discussing the various religious groups and their beliefs, and the difference between a northern farm and a southern plantation. Part of the People Who Made a Difference series.

At a speech in Akron, Ohio, after listening to a speaker who called women the weaker sex: "He says women need to be helped into carriages and lifted over ditches and to have the best everywhere. Nobody ever helps me into carriages, over mud puddles, or gets me any best places . . . And ain't I a woman?"

(McKissack, p. 112)

Biographies for Older Readers

Krass, Peter. *Sojourner Truth: Antislavery Activist.* Illus. Chelsea House 1988 (LB 1-55546-611-7) 112pp.

Sojourner Truth's activities as an articulate and outspoken abolitionist and women's rights activist are covered. Photographs of Truth and of life at that time are interspersed throughout. Chronology, list of further readings, and index. Part of the Black Americans of Achievement series.

McKissack, Patricia, and Fredrick McKissack, Jr. *Sojourner Truth: Ain't I a Woman?* Scholastic 1992 (cloth 0-590-44690-8) 1994 (pap. 0-590-44691-6) 192pp.

A useful section at the end of book, "More about the People Sojourner Truth Knew," features short biographies of such figures as Susan B. Anthony, John Brown, Frederick Douglass, William Lloyd Garrison, and Lucretia Mott. Bibliography and index.

Related Books for Younger Readers

Guernsey, Joann Bren. *Voices of Feminism: Past, Present, and Future.* Illus. Lerner Publications 1996 (LB 0-8225-2626-3)

Guernsey covers the feminist movement from the 18th century to the present, discussing fear of feminism, the first 150 years, the backlash, the third wave, voices of dissent, and "power feminism." Excerpts from Sojourner Truth's speech at the Women's Rights Convention in Akron, Ohio, in 1851 are included. List of resources for women, chapter notes, bibliography, and index. Part of the Frontline series.

Related Books for Older Readers

Katz, William L. *Black Legacy: A History of New York's African Americans.* Illus. Atheneum 1997 (cloth 0-689-31913-4)

Sojourner Truth is in good company, as one of a lengthy list of notable African Americans from New York City. Among them are Malcolm X, Marcus Garvey, Colin Powell, Paul Robeson, and Booker T. Washington. Her religious awakening at the African Zion Church at Leonard and Church streets is chronicled, along with her life as a slave, and her fight for the end of slavery and for women's rights. This is an attractive book, with clear writing and black-and-white photographs and drawings. Chapter notes, bibliography, and index.

King, Wilma. *Toward the Promised Land: From Uncle Tom's Cabin to the Onset of the Civil War, 1851–1861.* Illus. Chelsea House 1995 (LB 0-7910-2265-X) (pap. 0-7910-2691-4) 144pp.

Sojourner Truth's "Ain't I a Woman" speech and Harriet Beecher Stowe's *Uncle Tom's Cabin* focused attention on the issues facing women and blacks in the decade before the Civil War. Other key events covered in this book are the Dred Scott decision and John Brown's raid on Harpers Ferry. The book concludes with the firing on Fort Sumter. Chronology, bibliography and index. Part of the Milestones in Black American History series.

Smith, John David. *Black Voices from Reconstruction: 1865–1877.* Illus. Millbrook Press 1996 (LB 1-56294-583-1); University Press of Florida 1997 (pap. 0-8130-1576-6) 176pp.

Reuniting families, the Freedman's Bureau, the right to vote, racial terrorism, education: these are all problems that confronted black people once the Civil War was over and they were free. Here are contemporary illustrations and personal accounts of this time in history. List of further readings, chapter notes, bibliography, and index.

Tubman, Harriet (1820?–1913), an African American abolitionist, is best known for her tireless efforts to lead slaves to freedom via the Underground Railroad. Born a slave in Maryland, she escaped in 1849. During the Civil War she worked as a spy and a nurse for Union forces.

Biographies for Younger Readers

Adler, David A. *A Picture Book of Harriet Tubman.* Illus. by Samuel Byrd. Holiday House 1992 (LB 0-8234-0926-0) 1993 (pap. 0-8234-1065-X) 32pp.

Born into slavery, Harriet Tubman escaped and then returned to the South to help lead other slaves to freedom. Her nickname was "Moses," because, like the biblical figure, she was a leader of her people. List of important dates. Part of the Picture Book Of series.

Lawrence, Jacob. *Harriet and the Promised Land.* Illus. by the author. Simon & Schuster 1993 (pap. 0-671-86673-7)

The rhyming text describes brief moments in the life of Harriet Tubman. Lawrence's insightful paintings show danger, drama, violence, fear, and triumph. This is a special book, ideal to introduce the exploits of Tubman to younger readers.

Schroeder, Alan. *Minty: A Story of Young Harriet Tubman.* Illus. by Jerry Pinkney. Dial 1996 (pap. 0-8037-1888-8) 40pp.

This prize-winning picture-book biography is fictionalized for dramatic effect, but the basic facts are true. It could be used as a read-aloud introduction to Harriet Tubman. Jerry Pinkney's illustrations capture the energy of Tubman's early years.

Biographies for Older Readers

Bentley, Judith. *Harriet Tubman.* Illus. Franklin Watts 1990 (o.p.) 144pp.

Here is coverage of her early years as a slave and as the mother of slaves and of her activities in the Underground Railroad and as a spy and a nurse during the Civil War. It includes "A Note on Research" and many black-and-white photographs. List of further readings, chapter notes, bibliography, and index. Part of the People Who Have Helped the World series.

Carlson, Judy. *Harriet Tubman: Call to Freedom.* Illus. Columbine 1989 (pap. 0-449-90376-1) 118pp.

This book, in narrative style, details Tubman's life and the story of the 18 slaves she helped to escape. List of further readings. Part of the Great Lives series.

Related Books for Younger Readers

Stein, R. Conrad. *The Underground Railroad.* Children's Press 1997 (LB 0-516-20298-7)

Stein provides ample information about Tubman and her trips to the South to help free slaves. Stories of coded songs sung at church services, escaped slaves being shipped in boxes, and false floors in barns make for fascinating reading. Timeline, glossary, and index. Part of the Cornerstones of Freedom series.

Related Books for Older Readers

Feelings, Tom. *The Middle Passage: White Ships/Black Cargo.* Illus. by the author. Dial 1995 (pap. 0-8037-1804-7) 80pp.

This is an important book about the slave trade. Sixty-four narrative paintings chronicle the journey of a slave ship and a historical introduction traces four centuries of slave trade. Map of the slave routes. Winner of the Coretta Scott King award for illustration.

Hakim, Joy. *War, Terrible War.* Illus. Oxford University Press 1994 (LB 0-19-507755-5) (cloth 0-19-509511-1) (pap. 0-19-507756-3) 160pp.

Chapters feature many of the major figures related to the Civil War era, among them Harriet Tubman, Abraham Lincoln, Jefferson Davis, and John Brown. Students will find insights into issues and there are boxed features on topics including slavery and songs of the Civil War. Illustrations surround the text and there are many quotations and observations in the margins. Chronology, bibliography, and index. Part of the History of US series.

Piggins, Carol Ann. *A Multicultural Portrait of the Civil War.* Illus. Marshall Cavendish 1993 (LB 1-85435-660-7) 80pp.

Piggins portrays the Civil War from the perspective of African Americans. Harriet Tubman, the Underground Railroad, and her scouting and spying missions for the Union Army are part of the story. Chronology, list of further readings, glossary, and index. Part of the Perspectives series.

Turner, Nat (1800–1831), a slave, led a revolt in southeastern Virginia in 1831, killing more than 50 whites. Turner's uprising was quickly squashed, and he was captured and subsequently hanged.

Biographies for Younger Readers

Barrett, Tracy. *Nat Turner and the Slave Revolt.* Illus. Millbrook Press 1993 (pap. 1-56294-792-3) 32pp.

This brief book gives a good introduction for students beginning to research this era. The events surrounding Nat Turner's revolt, capture, and death provide a tragic look at the violence of this time. Timeline, bibliography, and index. Part of the Gateway Civil Rights series.

Biographies for Older Readers

Bisson, Terry. *Nat Turner: Slave Revolt Leader.* Illus. Chelsea House 1988 (LB 1-55546-613-3) (pap. 0-7910-0214-4) 112pp.

Focusing on his belief that God meant for him to free the slaves, this book is a wonderful overview of Turner's life and the rebellion. There are copies of newspaper articles and many photographs of events and places. List of further readings and index. Part of the Black Americans of Achievement series.

Related Books for Younger Readers

Kallen, Stuart A. *The Civil War and Reconstruction: A History of Black People in America 1830–1880.* Abdo & Daughters 1990 (cloth 1-56239-018-X)

Entertaining reading. The section on Nat Turner's rebellion is fascinating, with its stories of omens and signs from God (Turner claimed the sun would not shine on the day he was hanged, and it didn't). Index. Part of the Black History and Civil Rights Movement series.

Kalman, Bobbie. *Life on a Plantation.* Illus. Crabtree 1997 (LB 0-86505-435-5) (pap. 0-86505-465-7) 32pp.

Kalman examines what life was like on the southern plantations—the kinds of jobs available, the daily life of children, and the fight for freedom. There are many photographs and color illustrations, including modern-day reenactments. Glossary and index. Part of the Historic Communities series.

Related Books for Older Readers

Ray, Delia. *A Nation Torn: The Story of How the Civil War Began.* Illus. Lodestar Books 1990 (o.p.) 128pp.

Events leading up to the Civil War, of which Turner's bloody revolt was a part, are covered. There are many entertaining anecdotes. Glossary, bibliography, and index. Part of the Young Readers' History of the Civil War series.

White, Deborah Gray. *Let My People Go: African Americans, 1804–1860.* Illus. Oxford University Press 1996 (LB 0-19-508769-0) 144pp.

During this era, the success of the southern agriculture-based economy depended on the inexpensive resource of slavery. This book describes the political, economic, and social issues that led to the Civil War. Escapes and rebellions are presented, along with some graphic illustrations of cruelty. Chronology, bibliography, and index. Part of the Young Oxford History of African Americans series.

Tutankhamen (1343 B.C.–1325 B.C.), was an Egyptian pharaoh who ruled from the age of nine until his death at age 18. Tutankhamen became known in the modern world as "King Tut" following the discovery of his tomb by British archaeologists in 1922.

Biographies for Younger Readers

Sabuda, Robert. *Tutankhamen's Gift.* Illus. by the author. Atheneum 1994 (LB 0-689-31818-9) 1997 (pap. 0-689-81730-4) 32pp.

Robert Sabuda's beautiful pictures help illustrate Tutankhamen's life and reign in ancient Egypt. List of historical notes.

Related Books for Younger Readers

Green, Robert. *Tutankhamun.* Illus. Franklin Watts 1996 (LB 0-531-20233-X) (pap. 0-531-15802-0) 64pp.

Relating the discovery of King Tut's tomb, Green also includes some history of ancient Egypt. Of note is the list of Internet Web sites that cover the ancient world. Timeline, list of further readings, and index. Part of the Ancient Biography First Books series.

Marston, Elsa. *The Ancient Egyptians.* Illus. Benchmark Books 1995 (LB 0-7614-0073-7) 80pp.

Here is a history of ancient Egypt that includes the time of King Tut along with beautiful pictures of many of the artifacts that have been uncovered. Timeline, list of further readings, glossary, and index. Part of the Cultures of the Past series.

Putnam, Jim. *Mummy.* Illus. Alfred A. Knopf 1992 (LB 0-679-93881-8) (cloth 0-679-93881-3) 64pp.

Any student interested in King Tut will be fascinated with this coverage of mummies, both natural and man-made. The pages are filled with photographs and explanatory text; and the treasures of King Tutankhamen are revealed, along with Greek and Roman mummies, and animal mummies. Index. Part of the Eyewitness Books series.

Reeves, Nicholas. *Into the Mummy's Tomb: The Real-Life Discovery of Tutankhamun's Treasures.* Illus. Scholastic 1992 (o.p.) 64pp.

Students will enjoy looking through this account of Howard Carter's discovery of King Tut's tomb and the further discovery, in 1988, of more artifacts. There are amazing photographs of the discovery and uncovering of the three coffins and a detailed explanation of how mummies were made. Glossary.

Tutu, Desmond Mpilo (1931–), a South African leader and Anglican archbishop, was awarded the Nobel Peace Prize in 1984 for his efforts to end apartheid in his native land.

Biographies for Younger Readers

Bentley, Judith. *Archbishop Tutu of South Africa.* Illus. Enslow Publishers 1988 (o.p.) 96pp.

Written in 1988, this remains a useful biography of Tutu and a good account of apartheid. Photographs include images of the Sharpesville shooting, when 67 people were killed. Chronology, list of further readings, glossary, and index.

Biographies for Older Readers

Wepman, Dennis. *Desmond Tutu.* Illus. Franklin Watts 1989 (o.p.) 157pp.

The author makes fine use of quotations from Tutu's speeches, interviews, and writings to capture the essence of this humanitarian and religious leader. Especially moving are his remarks at the funeral of South African civil rights leader Steven Biko. This is a detailed presentation enhanced by black-and-white photographs. Chronology, source notes, bibliography, and index. Part of the Impact series.

Related Books for Younger Readers

Daniel, Jamie, adapt. *South Africa Is My Home.* Illus. with photographs by Stillman Rogers. Gareth Stevens 1992 (o.p.)

Any student studying Desmond Tutu will also want to look at this book full of color photographs. It covers the daily life of a young girl from Soweto. Students will see her eating french fries, going to the supermarket, and playing dodgeball. They will also see the one-room apartment in which she lives and squatters' shacks. Short section of quick facts about South Africa, map, and index. Part of the My Home Country series.

Related Books for Older Readers

Aaseng, Nathan. *The Peace Seekers: The Nobel Peace Prize.* Illus. Lerner Publications 1987 (LB 0-8225-0654-8) 1991 (pap. 0-8225-9604-0) 80pp.

Tutu's stand against apartheid is related among these profiles of nine Nobel Peace Prize winners who fought for peace through words, marches, and protests. Part of the Nobel Prize Winners series.

Peoples of Southern Africa. Illus. Facts on File 1997 (cloth 0-8160-3487-7)

This book covers the region and the people of South Africa, with topics of historical or cultural significance highlighted. The rise and fall of apartheid and Tutu's commitment to nonviolent methods of opposition are discussed. Appendix of South African languages, glossary, and index. Part of the Peoples of Africa series.

Twain, Mark (1835–1910), born Samuel L. Clemens in Hannibal, Missouri, became one of the most influential figures in American literature under his pseudonym. Much of the inspiration for his work came from early experiences as a riverboat pilot, printer, and journalist.

Biographies for Older Readers

De Koster, Katie, ed. *Mark Twain.* Greenhaven 1996 (LB 1-56510-471-4) (pap. 1-56510-470-6)

An in-depth biography of Twain, along with essays by both contemporary and historical contributors that analyze Twain's work. For the serious student of Twain's work, this would prove invaluable. A chronology of Twain's life is tied in with world events. Listing of works by Twain arranged by year, suggestions for further research, and index. Part of the Greenhaven Press Literary Companion to American Authors series.

Hargrove, Jim. *Mark Twain: The Story of Samuel Clemens.* Illus. Children's Press 1984 (o.p.) 128pp.

Hargrove covers Twain's childhood and professional life. Chronology and index. Part of the People of Distinction Biographies series.

Related Books for Younger Readers

Rubel, Donald. *The United States in the 19th Century.* Scholastic 1996 (cloth 0-590-72564-4) 192pp.

Written in timeline fashion, this book explores the era's politics, everyday life, arts and entertainment, and science and technology. Full of entertaining photographs and illustrations. Twain is featured in the section on the Gilded Age. Glossary and index. Part of the Scholastic Timelines series.

Related Books for Older Readers

Barr, Roger. *The American Frontier.* Illus. Lucent 1996 (LB 1-56006-282-7) 112pp.

The people, the country, unifying a nation, taming the frontier, "Manifest Destiny," and the frontier's significance are all covered in this book on westward expansion. Twain's description of mining, from "Roughing It," is part of the section on transforming the West and the mining frontier. List of further readings, chapter notes, and index. Part of the World History series.

Vespucci, Amerigo (1454–1512), an

Italian-born explorer, sailed to the New World seven years after Columbus, exploring the coastal region of Venezuela. Because of an inaccurate account of his voyage published in Europe, his name was given to America.

Biographies for Younger Readers

Alper, Ann Fitzpatrick. *Forgotten Voyager: The Story of Amerigo Vespucci.* Illus. Carolrhoda Books 1991 (LB 0-87614-442-3) 80pp.

Here is a good overview of the Europe of Vespucci's time, including the search for riches on other continents. His early years, his work helping to outfit Columbus's ships, and his voyages are covered. The controversy surrounding who really discovered America is discussed. There are many maps of how the world was perceived by the different explorers of the time. Bibliography and index. Part of the Trailblazers Biographies series.

Related Books for Younger Readers

Krensky, Stephen. *Who Really Discovered America?* Illus. by Steve Sullivan. Hastings 1987 (cloth 0-8038-9306-X); Scholastic (pap. 0-590-40854-2) 64pp.

A simple discussion of ancient America and its discovery, this book examines the possibility that there may have been early exploration that we have not yet been able to prove. Index.

Maestro, Betsy, and Giulio Maestro. *The Discovery and Exploration of the Americas.* Illus. by Giulio Maestro. Lothrop, Lee & Shepard 1991 (LB 0-688-06838-3) (cloth 0-688-06837-5); William Morrow & Co. 1992 (pap. 0-688-11512-8) 48pp.

Both hypothetical and historic voyages to America are discussed, with fascinating comparisons of Old World tools and toys and similar New World objects that support the hypothetical voyages. Vespucci's calculations were amazingly close to the actual dimensions of the earth.

Maestro, Betsy, and Giulio Maestro. *Exploration and Conquest: The Americas after Columbus: 1500–1620.* Illus. by Giulio Maestro. Lothrop, Lee & Shepard 1994 (LB 0-688-09268-3) (cloth 0-688-09267-5)

Students will enjoy the beautifully illustrated facts about exploration between the years 1500 and 1620. Vespucci's voyage to South America and the naming of America are covered. Part of the Discovery of the Americas series.

Related Books for Older Readers

Faber, Harold. *The Discoverers of America.* Illus. Scribner's 1992 (LB 0-684-19217-9) 304pp.

The discovery of America begins with the Indians crossing the Bering Strait. All the major explorers are in this book, with many interesting stories of their exploration. Vespucci's two voyages, along with his part in outfitting Columbus's ships, are covered. Chronology, bibliography, and index.

Villa, Pancho (1877–1923) Francisco Villa, known as Pancho Villa, was a revolutionary leader of rebellious Mexican forces during the revolution of 1910–1911. In 1916, Villa attacked a town in New Mexico. He was assassinated in Mexico in 1923.

Biographies for Older Readers

Carroll, Bob. *The Importance of Pancho Villa.* Illus. Lucent 1996 (LB 1-56006-069-7) 112pp.

Carroll describes Villa's roles as a villain and hero, destroyer and builder of modern Mexico. Chronology, chapter notes, and index.

O'Brien, Steven. *Pancho Villa.* Illus. Chelsea House 1994 (LB 0-7910-1257-3) 144pp.

Young readers will be fascinated by Villa's story of bandit-turned-military-commander. Black-and-white photographs depict his early revolutionary years and end with a picture of his bullet-ridden body. Chronology, list of further readings, and index. Part of the Hispanics of Achievement series.

Related Books for Older Readers

Chant, Christopher. *The Military History of the United States: World War I.* Illus. Marshall Cavendish 1992 (o.p.)

Villa's raids into the United States took place partly during World War I, causing a great number of American forces to be kept in Texas, New Mexico, and Arizona, and prompting the beginning of the National Guard. There are many color photographs. Glossary, bibliography, and index. Part of a series

Schubert, Frank N. *Black Valor: Buffalo Soldiers and the Medal of Honor, 1870–1898.* Illus. SR Books 1997 (cloth 0-8420-2586-3) 184pp.

A collection of remarkable stories about the 23 "buffalo soldiers" who won the Medal of Honor. One of these men was George Wanton, who served part of his tour of duty during the troubles with Pancho Villa. Chapter notes, extensive bibliography, and index.

Walesa, Lech (1943–), a Polish labor leader who helped to bring down his country's communist regime, was elected president and served from 1990 until 1995. Walesa was awarded the Nobel Peace Prize in 1983.

Biographies for Younger Readers

Lazo, Caroline. *Lech Walesa.* Illus. Dillon Press 1993 (LB 0-87518-525-8) 64pp.

This brief book would be a fine choice for students beginning the research process. The chapters are well organized and there are numerous photographs and quotations to add interest. Walesa's commitment to peace through nonviolence brought him worldwide attention. Bibliography and index. Part of the Peacemakers series.

Biographies for Older Readers

Craig, Mary. *Lech Walesa: The Leader of Solidarity and Campaigner for Freedom and Human Rights in Poland.* Illus. Gareth Stevens 1990 (o.p.) 68pp.

Written before Walesa became president, this remains an excellent account of Walesa's life and the development of the Solidarity trade union. Starting before World War II, it explains the extreme hardships that Poland has faced historically. List of places to contact for further information, chronology, glossary, and index. Part of the People Who Have Helped the World series.

Kaye, Tony. *Lech Walesa.* Illus. Chelsea House 1989 (LB 1-55546-856-X) (pap. 0-7910-0689-1) 112pp.

This is a well-documented story of Walesa's life and his part in the formation of Solidarity in Poland. The demonstrations and political upheaval are portrayed. Chronology, list of further readings, and index. Part of the World Leaders Past & Present series.

Vnenchak, Dennis. *Lech Walesa & Poland.* Illus. Franklin Watts 1994 (LB 0-531-11288-8) 112pp.

Vnenchak connects the life of Lech Walesa to the struggle for freedom in Poland. Early chapters look into the past, including the impact of communism. Walesa's leadership of the Solidarity Party is described, and the final chapter features "President Walesa and the Future of Poland." Source notes, glossary, bibliography, and index. Part of the Impact Biographies series.

Related Books for Younger Readers

Bradley, John. *Eastern Europe: The Road to Democracy.* Illus. Gloucester Press 1992 (o.p.) 40pp.

Students will enjoy this book full of pictures and short pieces of information about the transformation of Eastern Europe and the fall of communism. Walesa's role in Solidarity and the collapse of communism in Poland are covered. Chronology, glossary, and index. Part of the Hotspots series.

Related Books for Older Readers

Aaseng, Nathan. *The Peace Seekers: The Nobel Peace Prize.* Illus. Lerner Publications 1987 (LB 0-8225-0654-8) 1991 (pap. 0-8225-9604-0) 80pp.

Walesa's involvement in the Solidarity movement is chronicled among the profiles of nine Nobel Peace Prize winners who fought for peace through words, marches, and protests. Part of the Nobel Prize Winners series.

Kronenwetter, Michael. *Taking a Stand Against Human Rights Abuses.* Franklin Watts 1990 (o.p.)

The author discusses what human rights are, how different governments around the world have abused them, and what people can do about it. Walesa's battle for his fellow workers' rights, his organization of the Solidarity Party, and his winning of the Nobel Peace Prize are featured. Several appendices, list of further readings, and index.

Walker, Madam C. J. (1867–1919),

born Sarah Breedlove, was an entrepreneur who founded companies providing hair-care and other beauty products for black women. She contributed to many organizations, including the NAACP and the Tuskegee Institute.

"Madam Walker made history by becoming America's first female self-made millionaire—white or black!"
(McKissack, p. 20)

Biographies for Younger Readers

McKissack, Patricia, and Fredrick McKissack. *Madam C. J. Walker: Self-Made Millionaire.* Illus. by Bryant Michael and with photographs. Enslow Publishers 1992 (LB 0-89490-311-X) 32pp.

Five short chapters and clearly written sentences make this a good book to introduce the life of this entrepreneur. Born Sarah Breedlove, she married Charles Joseph Walker and used the name Madam C. J. Walker. By creating and selling beauty products for black women, she became a millionaire. Glossary and index. Part of the Great African Americans series.

Biographies for Older Readers

Bundles, A'Lelia Perry. *Madam C. J. Walker: Entrepreneur.* Illus. Chelsea House 1991 (LB 1-55546-615-X) 1992 (pap. 0-7910-0251-9)

Chapters describe "A Hardworking Childhood," "Lady Bountiful," and "The Legacy" of Madam C. J. Walker. As a woman and as an African American, Madam Walker challenged expectations and succeeded in business as well as in promoting opportunities and social change. This is a thorough biography with many quotations and fascinating pictures of the era, including packages and ads for her beauty products. Chronology, bibliography, and index. Part of the Black Americans of Achievement series.

Related Books for Younger Readers

Igus, Toyomi, ed. *Book of Black Heroes, Volume Two: Great Women in the Struggle, An Introduction for Young Readers.* Illus. Just Us Books 1991 (LB 0-940975-27-0) (pap. 0-940975-26-2) 112pp.

"Freedom Fighters," "Educators," "Entrepreneurs," and "Scientists & Healers" are among the topics presented. Mary Bethune, Rosa Parks, Ella Fitzgerald, Madam C. J. Walker, Oprah Winfrey, Barbara Jordan, and Mae C. Jemison are included. Chronology, bibliography, and index.

Related Books for Older Readers

Grossman, James R. *A Chance to Make Good: African Americans, 1900–1929.* Illus. Oxford University Press 1997 (LB 0-19-508770-4)

The early years of the 20th century were full of dramatic changes for many African Americans. In the South, segregation and Jim Crow laws dominated. Many blacks left the rural South, hoping for better opportunities in the North. African Americans were establishing social and political organizations, including the National Association for the Advancement of Colored People. Chronology, bibliography, and index. Part of the Young Oxford History of African Americans series.

Walker, Maggie Lena (1867–1934), a former slave who became the first American woman to found a bank and serve as its president. In 1903, she began what is now known as Consolidated Bank and Trust, the oldest black-owned bank in the United States.

Biographies for Younger Readers

Branch, Muriel Miller. *Pennies to Dollars: The Story of Maggie Lena Walker.* Illus. Linnet Books 1997 (LB 0-208-02453-0) (pap. 0-208-02455-7) 100pp.

Students will find this entertaining reading. It describes Walker's early years, her running of the Independent Order of St. Luke, and her establishment of the first African American-owned bank in the United States. It also relates several personal tragedies, including disability, that Walker had to overcome. Index.

Related Books for Younger Readers

Rediger, Pat. *Great African Americans in Business.* Illus. Crabtree 1996 (LB 0-86505-803-2) (pap. 0-86505-817-3) 64pp.

Thirteen African Americans are featured, including Maggie L. Walker and Oprah Winfrey. Each segment includes pictures, a personality profile, a short biography, and major accomplishments. Students will have fun comparing the achievements of other notable figures. Index. Part of the Outstanding African Americans series.

Spangenburg, Ray, and Diane K. Moser. *The African American Experience.* Facts on File 1997 (cloth 0-8160-3400-1)

Walker's home and library are highlighted, along with many photographs of her and her workers. Each section includes related places and people to discover. Lists of places to visit and further readings, and index. Part of the American Historic Places series.

Wallenberg, Raoul (1912–?), a Swedish diplomat, is credited with saving thousands of Hungarian Jews from deportation to Hitler's concentration camps. When the Soviets invaded Hungary at the end of World War II, Wallenberg was taken to Soviet headquarters and never seen again.

Biographies for Older Readers

Linnéa, Sharon. *Raoul Wallenberg: The Man Who Stopped Death.* Illus. Jewish Publication Society 1993 (cloth 0-8276-0440-8) (pap. 0-8276-0448-3) 168pp.

Including many photographs taken with a camera hidden inside a coat, this book covers Wallenberg's early years, his efforts to save Jews, and his disappearance. Index.

Nicholson, Michael. *Raoul Wallenberg: The Swedish Diplomat Who Saved 100,000 Jews from the Nazi Holocaust before Mysteriously Disappearing.* Gareth Stevens 1989 (o.p.) 68pp.

Wallenberg's privileged early life is covered, as are the spread of Nazi terror in Europe, his efforts to save the Hungarian Jews, and his mysterious disappearance. Chronology, glossary, and index. Part of the People Who Have Helped the World series.

Related Books for Older Readers

Bachrach, Susan D. *Tell Them We Remember: The Story of the Holocaust.* Illus. with images from the United States Holocaust Memorial Museum. Little, Brown 1994 (cloth 0-316-69264-6) (pap. 0-316-07484-5)

This book is full of pictures and personal stories of those who survived persecution by the Nazis, and of many family members who did not. Photographs illustrate the horror that these people lived through. Chronology, list of further readings, glossary, and index.

Friedman, Ina R. *The Other Victims: First-Person Stories of Non-Jews Persecuted by the Nazis.* Houghton Mifflin 1990 (o.p.) 224pp.

Friedman includes personal narratives from 11 survivors of the Holocaust. Among them are gypsies, homosexuals, minorities, and dissenters. Part Five relates the stories of people who were used as slaves by the Nazi regime. Each chapter begins with a chilling quote from Hitler or another Nazi leader. List of further readings and index.

Perel, Solomon. *Europa, Europa.* John Wiley & Sons 1997 (cloth 0-471-17218-9)

Another inspiring story of Jewish survival during World War II. Solomon Perel fled across Nazi-occupied Poland hoping to find safety in Russia. Once he got to Russia, he was placed in an orphanage. When the Nazis invaded Russia, he fled and was captured by German forces. He pretended to be an ethnic German, and survived by taking part in an elite Hitler Youth boarding school, all the while fearing he would be found out. Exciting reading.

Washington, Booker T. (1856–1915),

an African American educator born into slavery, attended Virginia's Hampton Institute and later became principal of Tuskegee Institute. He developed Tuskegee into an influential center for the education of African Americans.

"More and more, we must learn to think not in terms of race or color or language or religion or political boundaries, but in terms of humanity."
(McLoone, p. 22)

Biographies for Younger Readers

Gleiter, Jan, and Kathleen Thompson. *Booker T. Washington.* Raintree Steck-Vaughn 1995 (LB 0-8114-8454-8)

Booker T. Washington's struggles and accomplishments, his determination to get an education, and the beginning of the Tuskegee Institute are related here. List of key dates. Part of the First Biographies series.

McKissack, Patricia, and Fredrick McKissack. *The Story of Booker T. Washington.* Illus. with photographs. Enslow Publishers 1991 (o.p.) 32pp.

The authors recount Booker T. Washington's life, focusing on his stewardship of Tuskegee Institute. He was nine years old when slavery ended, and his constant search for education is chronicled. Index. Part of the Cornerstones of Freedom series.

McLoone, Margo. *Booker T. Washington: A Photo-Illustrated Biography.* Illus. Bridgestone Books 1997 (cloth 1-56065-520-8)

The format of this book is great for beginning researchers. Double-page spreads provide information about such topics as "Work and School," "Ideas on Education," and "Spokesperson for African Americans." There are selections from Washington's words and writings. Chronology, lists of useful addresses and Internet sites, glossary, bibliography, and index. Part of the Read and Discover Photo-Illustrated Biographies series.

Roberts, Jack L. *Booker T. Washington, Educator and Leader.* Illus. Millbrook Press 1995 (LB 1-56294-487-8) 32pp.

This book would be a good choice for students beginning the research process. The brief text provides an overview of Washington's life and serves as a springboard to more detailed presentations.

The focus is on Washington's recognition of the value of education. Chronology, bibliography, and index. Part of the Gateway Civil Rights series.

Biographies for Older Readers

Schroeder, Alan. *Booker T. Washington: Educator and Racial Spokesman.* Illus. Chelsea House 1992 (LB 1-55546-616-8) (pap. 0-7910-0252-7) 144pp.

From "A Child of Slavery" to "Tuskegee" to "A New Frankness," this book gives a thorough portrait of Booker T. Washington. His role of spokesperson is described, including the criticism he received for his ideas about compromise. Many photographs with detailed captions add information and provide an image of Washington and his contemporaries. Chronology, bibliography, and index. Part of the Black Americans of Achievement series.

Related Books for Younger Readers

Farrar, Hayward. *Leaders and Movements.* Rourke 1995 (LB 1-57103-030-1) 48pp.

A history of African American politics. Farrar discusses Washington's influence and how he used his power to shape the education of African Americans and build up black businesses and farms. Lists of notable African American politicians and further readings, glossary, and index. Part of the African American Life series.

Taylor, Kimberly Hayes. *Black Abolitionists and Freedom Fighters.* Illus. Oliver Press 1996 (LB 1-881508-30-7) 160pp.

Read about the lives of eight African Americans who helped blacks gain either freedom or citizenship, including Sojourner Truth, Nat Turner, Frederick Douglass, Harriet Tubman, and Booker T. Washington. Washington's leadership in getting education for blacks is discussed, along with his controversial refusal to confront racism head-on. Bibliography and index. Part of the Profiles series.

Related Books for Older Readers

Dudley, William, ed. *African Americans: Opposing Viewpoints.* Illus. Greenhaven 1996 (LB 1-56510-522-2) (pap. 1-56510-521-4)

Original essays discuss many aspects of the African American experience in the United States, from the founding fathers to the present. One entire chapter discusses Booker T. Washington's views on whether blacks should agitate for political equality and higher education. A thought-provoking book. Discussion notes for each chapter, chronology, annotated bibliography, and index. Part of the Opposing Viewpoints Series.

Hauser, Pierre. *Great Ambitions: From the "Separate But Equal" Doctrine to the Birth of the NAACP (1896–1909).* Illus. Chelsea House 1995 (cloth 0-7910-2264-1) (pap. 0-7910-2690-6)

In the late 1800s, opportunities for blacks were often separate and unequal. Through the early years of the new century, many people spoke out for equality. This book looks at Jim Crow laws, the Niagara Movement, and the founding of the NAACP. Key figures in this era include W. E. B. Du Bois, Paul Laurence Dunbar, Booker T. Washington, Ida Wells-Barnett, and William Monroe Trotter. Bibliography and index. Part of the Milestones in Black American History series.

Washington, George (1732–1799), the first president of the United States, led American forces to victory over the British in the Revolutionary War as commander in chief of the Continental Army. He was chairman of the Constitutional Convention of 1787 and was elected president two years later, serving two terms.

Biographies for Younger Readers

Adler, David A. *A Picture Book of George Washington.* Illus. by John Wallner and Alexandra Wallner. Holiday House 1989 (LB 0-8234-0732-2) 1990 (pap. 0-8234-0800-0) 32pp.

This biography is a good choice for reading aloud to introduce students to biographies and to Washington. Basic facts are included in the simple narrative and students could be encouraged to look in other books to expand their information. List of important dates. Part of the Picture Book Of series.

Giblin, James Cross. *George Washington: A Picture Book Biography.* Illus. by Michael Dooling. Scholastic 1992 (o.p.) 48pp.

The biographical information in this introductory book is very well written and would encourage students to look for more. The narrative is followed by additional information that makes this fine book even more useful. Map of the United States in 1797, chronology,

Besides our national capital, 121 other American towns and villages have been named for George Washington. So have 1 American state, 7 mountains, 10 lakes, 33 countries, and 9 colleges and universities.

(Giblin, Appendix on Monuments to George Washington)

essays about "George and the Cherry Tree," "George Washington's Rules of Good Behavior," "Monuments to George Washington," and "Mount Vernon," and index.

Jacobs, William J. *Washington.* Illus. Simon & Schuster 1991 (o.p.) 48pp.

This is a brief biography of Washington with coverage of the basic causes and events of the American Revolution. Jacobs discusses Washington's violent temper and his need to get along with people at this difficult time. Illustrated with engravings and photographs.

Usel, T. M. *George Washington: A Photo-Illustrated Biography.* Illus. Bridgestone Books 1996 (LB 1-56065-340-X) 24pp.

Facing pages consisting of a picture on one side and text on the other make this a well-constructed research book for beginners. Among the topics included are Washington's early years, first careers, family, the Revolutionary War, the Continental Army, Valley Forge, and the presidency. At the end of the book are "Words from George Washington," "Important Dates," and "Useful Addresses." List of further readings, glossary, and index. Part of the Read and Discover Photo-Illustrated Biographies series.

Biographies for Older Readers

Kent, Zachary. *George Washington.* Illus. Children's Press 1986 (LB 0-516-01381-5) 100pp.

Washington's life as a Virginia surveyor, soldier, plantation owner, and president are covered. Chronology of American history highlighting events at Washington's time and index. Part of the Encyclopedia of Presidents series.

Osborne, Mary Pope. *George Washington: Leader of a New Nation.* Illus. Dial 1991 (LB 0-8037-0949-8) 96pp.

This especially well-written book gives a very well-rounded portrayal of Washington, describing not only his years in politics but also his service as a soldier and his life as a farmer in Virginia. This would be a good choice for both research and pleasure reading. Chronology, bibliography, and index.

Related Books for Younger Readers

Collier, Christopher, and James Lincoln Collier. *The American Revolution, 1763–1783.* Illus. Benchmark Books 1998 (LB 0-7614-0440-6) 96pp.

This is a very readable book that clearly describes the events that led to the Revolutionary War. One chapter features the Stamp Act, another describes "Taxes and Tea," and another looks at some of the early battles. Students looking for a well-written overview will appreciate this book. Bibliography and index. Part of the Drama of American History series.

Stein, R. Conrad. *Valley Forge.* Illus. Children's Press 1994 (LB 0-516-06683-8) 32pp.

Illustrations of the terrible conditions that surrounded the fighting at Valley Forge are contrasted with photographs of the site today as it has been historically preserved. Index. Part of the Cornerstones of Freedom series.

Related Books for Older Readers

Dolan, Edward F. *The American Revolution: How We Fought the War of Independence.* Illus. Millbrook Press 1995 (LB 1-56294-521-1) 112pp.

How could the upstart American army defeat the highly trained forces of the British? What strategies were used by George Washington and other military leaders to bring independence to the United States? This book emphasizes the people, decisions, and battles that brought success to the colonists. Bibliography and index.

Jaffe, Steve H. *Who Were the Founding Fathers? Two Hundred Years of Reinventing American History.* Illus. Henry Holt 1996 (cloth 0-8050-3102-2) 160pp.

This book debunks many of our favorite myths about American history and even includes a section titled "Countries Have No Fathers." Chapter notes, bibliography and index. Part of the American History series.

Lukes, Bonnie. *The American Revolution.* Illus. Lucent 1996 (LB 1-56006-287-8) 112pp.

After opening with a chronology of the American Revolution, chapters present events from the years of British control and unpopular measures such as the Stamp Act through the uniting of the colonies and the Revolutionary War. There are boxed sidebars—among them one featuring verses from Emerson's "Concord Hymn" and another an excerpt from George Washington's diary during the war. Source notes, annotated bibliography of further readings and works consulted, and index. Part of the World History series.

Murphy, Jim. *A Young Patriot: The American Revolution as Experienced by One Boy.* Illus. Clarion 1995 (cloth 0-395-60523-7) 49pp.

An eyewitness account of the American Revolution. From 1776 when he was 15, until 1783, Joseph Plumb Martin fought in the war. Historical background details are included, but most of this record is taken from Joseph's memoirs. Chronology, bibliography, and index.

Washington, Martha (1732–1802),

born Martha Dandridge, was the wife of George Washington, the first president of the United States. As the nation's first First Lady, she set an example as a gracious hostess.

Biographies for Younger Readers

Anderson, LaVere. *Martha Washington: First Lady of the Land.* Chelsea House 1991 (cloth 0-7910-1452-5)

In story-book format, this account relates Martha Washington's life as a young girl, during the Revolutionary War, as the president's wife, and her later years. Part of the Discovery Biography series.

Marsh, Joan F. *Martha Washington.* Illus. Franklin Watts 1993 (o.p.) 64pp.

This attractive biography for younger readers covers her early years in Virginia, the running of Mount Vernon, the years at war, and her life as First Lady. It is full of portraits and photographs of some of the items on display at the Mount Vernon museum. List of further readings and index. Part of the First Book series.

Related Books for Younger Readers

Brenner, Barbara. *If You Were There in 1776.* Illus. Bradbury Press 1994 (LB 0-02-712322-7) 144pp.

The North, the South, and the frontier are all looked at through the eyes of a child in 1776. What people wore, what they ate, how they played, and how they worshiped are all covered. Chapter notes, bibliography, and index. Part of the If You Were There series.

Related Books for Older Readers

Kent, Deborah. *The American Revolution: "Give Me Liberty, or Give Me Death!"* Illus. Enslow Publishers 1994 (LB 0-89490-521-X) 128pp.

Kent provides an overview of the events leading to the American Revolution and the state of the country after the war in chapters including "The Shot Heard Round the World," "Taxation without Representation," "Beyond the Battlefield," "Shifting the Balance," "The Final Act," and "Shaping the Peace." Included are some of Washington's letters to Martha. Chronology, chapter notes, and index. Part of the American War series.

Siegel, Beatrice. *George and Martha Washington at Home in New York.* Illus. by Frank Aloise. Four Winds Press 1989 (o.p.) 80pp.

Siegel looks at the 16 months when New York City was the nation's capital. Martha Washington is portrayed as a woman full of energy and good cheer, who served her country and her husband well. A list of places to visit also describes what has happened to many of the landmarks. List of further readings and index.

Wells-Barnett, Ida B. (1862–1931), an African American crusader for civil rights, helped to establish the National Association for the Advancement of Colored People. She also fought for women's right to vote.

Biographies for Younger Readers

Freedman, Suzanne. *Ida B. Wells-Barnett and the Anti-Lynching Crusade.* Illus. Millbrook Press 1994 (LB 1-56294-377-4) (pap. 1-56294-859-8) 32pp.

Full of black-and-white photographs, this biography covers Wells-Barnett's life, emphasizing her efforts as a journalist to expose the lynchings that were occurring in America. It also covers her efforts for woman's suffrage. Chronology, list of further readings, and index. Part of the Gateway Civil Rights series.

Medearis, Angela Shelf. *Princess of the Press: The Story of Ida B. Wells-Barnett.* Lodestar Books 1997 (cloth 0-525-67493-4)

This simple biography relates Wells-Barnett's activities as a journalist, newspaper owner, and suffragette. It also discusses her role in the creation of the National Association for the Advancement of Colored People. Chronology, list of further readings, chapter notes, and index. Part of the Rainbow Biography series.

Related Books for Younger Readers

Kallen, Stuart A. *The Twentieth Century and the Harlem Renaissance: A History of Black People in America 1880–1930.* Abdo & Daughters 1990 (cloth 1-56239-019-8)

Starting with the end of slavery, this book covers African American voices of hope, African American inventors, African Americans in World War II, and African American artists. Full of black-and-white photographs. Index.

Rennert, Richard, ed. *Female Leaders.* Illus. Chelsea House 1994 (LB 0-7910-2057-6) (pap. 0-7910-2058-4)

Wells-Barnett's activities as a journalist and her crusade against lynching are covered in just one section of this fascinating book full of inspirational African American women. Introduction by Coretta Scott King. List of further readings and index. Part of the Profiles of Great Black Americans series.

Related Books for Older Readers

Hauser, Pierre. *Great Ambitions: From the "Separate But Equal" Doctrine to the Birth of the NAACP (1896–1909).* Illus. Chelsea House 1995 (cloth 0-7910-2264-1) (pap. 0-7910-2690-6)

In the late 1800s, opportunities for blacks were often separate and unequal. Through the early years of the new century, many people spoke out for equality. This book looks at Jim Crow laws, the Niagara Movement, and the founding of the NAACP. Bibliography and index. Part of the Milestones in Black American History series.

Wheatley, Phillis (1753?–1784), an
African-born American poet, was educated by John Wheatley, a merchant who bought her as a slave. Her poems were important in that they reflected what blacks could attain with a proper education.

Biographies for Older Readers

Richmond, Merle. *Phillis Wheatley: Poet.* Chelsea House 1987 (cloth 1-55546-683-4)

Recorded here is Wheatley's amazing fame as a teenager for her literary work—this at a time when women were best admired for their charm and not their intelligence. There are good descriptions of life in America. Richmond also covers Wheatley's later years and her death at the age of 31, penniless. Chronology, list of further readings, and index. Part of the American Women of Achievement series.

Related Books for Younger Readers

Kalman, Bobbie. *Colonial Life.* Illus. Crabtree 1992 (LB 0-86505-491-6) (pap. 0-806505-511-4) 32pp.

This is a good overview of what settled colonial life was like for men, women, children, and slaves. Present-day reenactments show clothing, games, and travel at that time. One section discusses prejudice in the past and the present. Glossary and index. Part of the Historic Communities series.

Related Books for Older Readers

Feelings, Tom. *The Middle Passage: White Ships/Black Cargo.* Illus. by the author. Dial 1995 (pap. 0-8037-1804-7) 80pp.

This is an important book about the slave trade, including a map tracing the slave routes. Sixty-four narrative paintings chronicle the journey of a slave ship and a historical introduction traces four centuries of slave trade. Winner of the Coretta Scott King award for illustration.

Katz, William L. *Exploration to the War of 1812, 1492–1814.* Illus. Raintree Steck-Vaughn 1993 (LB 0-8114-6275-7) 1995 (pap. 0-8114-2912-1) 96pp.

Chapters feature "Discovering America," "To Come to America," "To Stand Against Slavery," and "The War of 1812." One chapter describes "Women Poets," featuring Phillis Wheatley, while another looks at "American Cultural Figures" such as Benjamin Bannaker and Philip Freneau. This series is designed to feature the accomplishments of diverse races and cultures and many students will appreciate the opportunity to find out about these contributions. Bibliography and index. Part of the History of Multicultural America series.

Zell, Fran. *A Multicultural Portrait of the American Revolution.* rev. ed. Illus. Marshall Cavendish 1996 (LB 0-7614-0051-6) 80pp.

This book describes the history of the American Revolution from the perspective of African Americans, Native Americans, and women. Phillis Wheatley's identification with the patriotic cause and her expression of it in her writing is a part of this engaging book. Chronology, list of further readings, glossary, and index. Part of the Perspectives series.

White, Elywn Brooks (1899–1985), an American editor and writer, wrote for *New Yorker* magazine and was well known for his witty observations of society. He also created books for children and wrote a column for *Harper's Bazaar*.

Biographies for Younger Readers

Collins, David R. *To the Point: A Story about E. B. White.* Illus. by Amy Johnson. Carolrhoda Books 1989 (LB 0-87614-345-1) (pap. 0-87614-508-X) 56pp.

This simple version of White's life portrays his privileged childhood, college years, work during the Great Depression, and his children's books. It includes an Afterword about the writing of *Charlotte's Web*. Bibliography. Part of the Carolrhoda Creative Minds series.

Biographies for Older Readers

Gherman, Beverly. *E. B. White: Some Writer!* Illus. Atheneum 1992 (LB 0-689-31672-0); William Morrow & Co. 1994 (pap. 0-688-12826-2) 144pp.

This is a wonderful account of E. B. White's relationship with his writing and his concern for the world around him. The Depression years and the growing totalitarianism in Europe concerned him greatly. The description of his funeral service is deeply touching. Notes and index.

Related Books for Younger Readers

Rylant, Cynthia. *Margaret, Frank, and Andy: Three Writers' Stories.* Harcourt 1996 (cloth 0-15-201083-1) 56pp.

Three simple stories about three well-known children's writers: Margaret Wise Brown, Frank Baum, and E. B. White. Each story is brief and touching, with faded black-and-white photographs of the authors and where they lived.

Related Books for Older Readers

Bredeson, Carmen. *American Writers of the 20th Century.* Illus.
Enslow Publishers 1996 (LB 0-89490-704-2) 104pp.

Besides writing the children's books that he is so well-known
for, E. B. White also wrote adult essays. Here is a collection of information about other adult writers of the 20th century. It is interesting
to compare the lives and times of these authors, who wrote very different kinds of works. Chapter notes and index. Part of the
Collective Biographies series.

Whitman, Walt (1819–1892), one of the
great American poets, spent much of his early career
as a teacher and newspaper editor. The volume of
poems entitled *Leaves of Grass* launched his new
career.

Biographies for Older Readers

Reef, Catherine. *Walt Whitman.* Illus. Clarion 1995 (cloth 0-395-
68705-5) 148pp.

Whitman's work is placed in the context of his life and the
United States of his time. Photographed and illustrations extend the
text. Index.

Related Books for Younger Readers

Panzer, Mora, ed. *Celebrate America in Poetry and Art.* Illus.
Hyperion Books for Children; published in association with the
National Museum of American Art, Smithsonian Institution 1994
(LB 1-56282-665-4) 96pp.

A collection of works by American poets, celebrating more
than 200 years of American history, and illustrated with fine art from
the collection of the National Museum of American Art. Whitman's
"I Hear America Singing" is just one work among many in this beautiful book. It is noted that the National Museum of American Art was
used as a makeshift hospital during the Civil War, and Whitman
came there to help with the wounded and to read his poetry. Short
biographical notes on all artists and poets whose works appear in the
book and index.

Related Books for Older Readers

Blum, Joshua, et al. *The United States of Poetry.* Illus. Harry N. Abrams 1996 (cloth 0-8109-3927-4) 176pp.

Based on the public television series, this is a selection of works describing America by a wide range of poets, from Nobel Laureates to rappers. The book claims to be a collection of the "varied carols" that Whitman heard America singing. Readers of Whitman's work will enjoy this modern collection. Beautiful photographs surround each poem. Selected bibliography and index of poets.

Reynolds, Clark G. *The Civil War.* CLB International 1991 (cloth 1-85833-703-8)

Whitman spent a lot of time in hospitals filled with wounded soldiers from the Civil War. Here is another compendium of the war, filled with photographs and illustrations chronicling battles, maps, hospitals, and sea and river operations.

Whitney, Eli (1765–1825), an American inventor, is best known for his invention of the cotton gin—a machine that removes the seed from cotton. It revolutionized the industry but earned little for him because of patent difficulties. He later built a machine that standardized parts for firearms, an endeavor that proved more lucrative.

Biographies for Younger Readers

Alter, Judy. *Eli Whitney.* Illus. Franklin Watts 1990 (o.p.) 64pp.

Whitney's talent and creativity became evident early: at the age of 12 he made his own violin. Photographs compare the procesing of cotton in Whitney's time and today. List of further readings, glossary, and index. Part of the First Book series.

Latham, Jean Lee. *Eli Whitney: Great Inventor.* Illus. Chelsea House 1991 (LB 0-7910-1453-3) 80pp.

Whitney's early years as a curious child, his work making nails during the Revolutionary War, his education at Yale, and the invention of the cotton gin are all discussed. Part of the Discovery Biography series.

Related Books for Younger Readers

Meltzer, Milton. *Weapons & Warfare: From the Stone Age to the Space Age.* Illus. by Sergio Martinez. HarperCollins 1996 (LB 0-06-024876-9) (cloth 0-06-024875-0) 96pp.

Although remembered mainly for the cotton gin, Whitney also made great strides in developing mass manufacturing of rifles, which led to the production of such power tools as the drill press. This in turn led to all kinds of mass production worldwide. In this book, Meltzer highlights weapons throughout history, how they were used, and the impact they had on society. Bibliography and index.

Related Books for Older Readers

Littlefield, Daniel C. *Revolutionary Citizens: African Americans 1776–1804.* Illus. Oxford University Press 1997 (LB 0-19-508715-1) 144pp.

A look at African Americans in the United States in the years immediately after the Revolutionary War. Colonists gaining freedom from the King of England made slaves look differently at their own lack of freedom. Whitney's invention and its impact on helping slavery to thrive are discussed. Chronology, list of further readings, and index. Part of the Young Oxford History of African Americans series.

Nardo, Don. *The War of 1812.* Illus. Lucent 1991 (o.p.) 112pp.

An account of the strategies, personalities, and outcomes of the War of 1812, emphasizing its uselessness. Whitney, usually remembered for his invention of the cotton gin, is included here for his advances in musket design, enabling him to produce thousands for the military. Further readings, glossary, and index. Part of the America's Wars series.

Williams, Daniel Hale (1858–1931), surgeon and educator, in 1883 became one of the first African Americans to graduate from medical school. He later established a medical training program for blacks.

Biographies for Younger Readers

Patterson, Lillie. *Sure Hands, Strong Heart: The Life of Daniel Hale Williams.* Illus. Abingdon 1981 (LB 0-687-40700-1) 159pp.

Told as a story, this biography covers Williams's early years, his education as a barber and a surgeon, and his part in helping to found one of America's first truly interracial hospitals. The first open-heart surgery (performed by Williams) makes for exciting reading.

Related Books for Younger Readers

Gold, John Coppersmith. *Heart Disease.* Crestwood House 1996 (o.p.) 64pp.

Full of color diagrams and photographs, this book covers heart attacks, how the heart works, types and causes of heart disease, and diagnosis and treatment. Readers will be even more amazed at William's attempt at open-heart surgery in 1893 when they look at the medical procedures and equipment used now. List of places to write for more information, glossary, and index. Part of the Health Watch series.

McKissack, Patricia, and Fredrick McKissack. *African American Scientists.* Illus. Millbrook Press 1994 (LB 1-56294-372-3) 96pp.

Read about the lives and achievements of African American scientists from colonial times to the present. Notable figures in medicine, life science, chemistry, and physics are all covered. Long list of important work, including Williams's work as the first open-heart surgeon, bibliography and index. Part of the Proud Heritage series.

Related Books for Older Readers

Hayden, Robert C. *11 African American Doctors.* rev. and expanded. Illus. Twenty-First Century Books 1992 (LB 0-8050-2135-3) 208pp.

Hayden describes the work of 11 African Americans who raised our health standards through their medical practice, research, or teaching. Daniel Hale Williams's land-breaking open-heart surgery, Solomon Carter Fuller's work with Alzheimer's and other degenerative diseases of the brain, and Jane Wright's pioneering work with chemotherapy make up just a small part of the motivating reading. Index. Part of the Achievers: African Americans in Science and Technology series.

Wilson, Woodrow (1856–1924), the 28th president of the United States (1913–1921), pursued a reformist program that included an eight-hour workday and child-labor laws. Although he pledged to keep the country out of World War I, he was forced to declare war on Germany in April 1917, at the same time proposing a peace plan that eventually brought Germany to the bargaining table.

Biographies for Older Readers

Leavell, J. Perry. *Woodrow Wilson.* Illus. Chelsea House 1987 (o.p.) 112pp.

Discussed here is much of the history of Wilson's political life: trust-busting, the sinking of the *Lusitania,* women's suffrage, World War I, and the League of Nations. Chronology, list of further readings, and index. Part of the World Leaders Past & Present series.

Osinski, Alice. *Woodrow Wilson: Twenty-Eighth President of the United States.* Illus. Children's Press 1989 (LB 0-516-01367-X) 100pp.

His early years, life at Princeton, the presidency, World War I, and the League of Nations are covered. Chronology of American history highlighting Wilson's lifetime and index. Part of the Encyclopedia of Presidents series.

Rogers, James T. *Woodrow Wilson: Visionary for Peace.* Illus. Facts on File 1997 (cloth 0-8160-3396-X) 112pp.

Students will learn about Wilson's childhood and his life as educator, governor, and pre- and postwar president, emphasizing his efforts for worldwide peace. Many black-and white-photographs. Chronology, list of further readings, and index. Part of the Makers of America series.

Related Books for Younger Readers

Giblin, James Cross. *Edith Wilson.* Illus. by Michele Laporte. Viking Penguin 1992 (pap. 0-670-83005-4) 64pp.

Six brief chapters and a lively style of writing bring this fascinating woman to life—and tell about her husband, too. When Woodrow Wilson suffered a stroke, Edith Wilson was invaluable to him, helping him continue his duties as president. Giblin describes how her efforts were both supported and undermined by political participants. Part of the Women of Our Time series.

McGowen, Tom. *World War I.* Illus. Franklin Watts (LB 0-531-20149-X) (pap. 0-531-15660-5) 64pp.

Here is a discussion of the strategies, battles, and equipment used in each year of World War I. Maps show the changing outline of European countries before and after the war. List of further readings and index. Part of the First Book series.

Related Books for Older Readers

Kent, Zachary. *World War I: "The War to End Wars."* Illus. Enslow Publishers 1994 (LB 0-89490-523-6) 128pp.

An overview of the war, focusing on the horrors of modern warfare and the many men who died from disease and poor fighting conditions. Woodrow Wilson is just one of many colorful American figures mentioned. Chronology, list of further readings, chapter notes, and index. Part of the American War series.

Uschan, Michael V. *A Multicultural Portrait of World War I.* Illus. Marshall Cavendish 1995 (LB 0-7614-0054-0) 80pp.

Uschan portrays this time period from the perspective of ethnic minorities and women. At a time when the United States was emerging as a world power, Wilson is portrayed as a brilliant speaker, peacemaker, and visionary. Chronology, list of further readings, glossary, and index. Part of the Perspectives series.

Winfrey, Oprah (1954–), talk-show host whose program is one of the most popular shows on television. Winfrey also appeared in the movies *The Color Purple* (1985) and *Native Son* (1986).

Biographies for Younger Readers

Buffalo, Audreen. *Oprah Winfrey: A Self-Made Woman of Many Talents.* Illus. Random House 1993 (pap. 0-679-85425-8) 112pp.

A very readable biography, full of photographs relates Oprah's life from childhood to her success on television and Buffalo accompanies her on the production of a show. Part of the Bullseye Biography series.

Woods, Geraldine. *The Oprah Winfrey Story: Speaking Her Mind.* Illus. Dillon Press 1991 (LB 0-87518-463-4) 80pp.

Woods covers Oprah's life, emphasizing that she was the first woman to own her own talk show and the first black woman to own her own production company. Index. Part of the Taking Part series.

Biographies for Older Readers

Beaton, Margaret. *Oprah Winfrey: TV Talk Show Host.* Illus. Children's Press 1990 (o.p.)

Winfrey's life, from her childhood in Mississippi to her achievements in broadcasting and film, is covered. Chronology, chapter notes, and index. Part of the People of Distinction Biographies series.

Nicholson, Lois P. *Oprah Winfrey: Entertainer.* Illus. Chelsea House (LB 0-7910-1886-5) (pap. 0-7910-1915-2) 144pp.

This detailed biography gives a well-rounded portrait of Oprah Winfrey. Her incredible success as a talk-show host is linked to her interest in people and her efforts to help others. Numerous black-and-white photographs add interest and information. Chronology, list of further readings, and index. Part of the Black Americans of Achievement series.

Related Books for Younger Readers

Cooper, Alison. *Media Power?* Illus. Franklin Watts 1997 (cloth 0-531-14452-6)

How much influence should the media have on the way people think? Students will learn about subliminal messages, the level of violence that we observe on television, and the invasion of the media in legal cases. Facts to think about, list of useful addresses, glossary, and index. Part of the Viewpoints series.

Related Books for Older Readers

Williams, Mary, ed. *Discrimination.* Illus. Greenhaven 1997 (LB 1-56510-657-1) (pap. 1-56510-656-3)

Winfrey often makes a point of talking about racism and discrimination in America: in her movies, on her television shows, and in her interviews. Essays in this book take opposing views on whether discrimination is a serious problem, what causes it, whether reverse discrimination is valid, and how society can put an end to it. Students will find much to debate in this thought-provoking book. Notes for further discussion for each chapter. List of organizations to contact, bibliography, and index. Part of the Opposing Viewpoints series.

Winters, Paul A., ed. *The Media and Politics.* Greenhaven 1996 (pap. 1-56510-382-3)

A thoughtful collection of original articles about the changing face of the media and whether it remains a positive or negative force in our society. Winfrey is mentioned in an article on tabloid culture and confessional programs. List of organizations to contact, bibliography, and index. Part of the At Issue series.

Wright, Frank Lloyd (1867–1959), an American architect, introduced open concepts and the use of natural, regional materials. He had a major influence on the industry both at home and abroad. He also designed and built interiors, including furniture.

Biographies for Younger Readers

Thorne-Thomsen, Kathleen. *Frank Lloyd Wright for Kids.* Illus. Chicago Review 1994 (pap. 1-55652-207-X)

Photographs and drawings appear throughout this account of Wright's life and work. Projects following the text include making an edible model of Fallingwater.

Biographies for Older Readers

Davis, Frances A. *Frank Lloyd Wright: Maverick Architect.* Illus. Lerner Publications 1996 (cloth 0-8225-4953-0)

This detailed biography examines the personal and professional experiences of this innovative architect. His challenge to conventional style and his creative spirit influenced American architecture. List of Frank Lloyd Wright buildings open to the public, source notes, bibliography, and index.

Richards, Kenneth C. *Frank Lloyd Wright.* Illus. Children's Press 1968 (LB)

Richard tells the story of Wright's tumultuous professional and personal life. Black-and-white photographs show many of Wright's architectural structures. Bibliography and index. Part of the People of Destiny series.

Rubin, Susan Goldman. *Frank Lloyd Wright.* Illus. Harry N. Abrams 1994 (cloth 0-8109-3974-6)

The emphasis here is on the uniqueness of Wright's life and work. There are many photographs of his structures. List of illustrations and index. Part of the First Impressions series.

Related Books for Younger Readers

Adam, Robert. *Buildings: How They Work.* Illus. Sterling Publishing 1995 (cloth 0-8069-0958-7) 48pp.

Readers will enjoy looking at this nicely illustrated overview of buildings from all stages of history and all around the world. How different kinds of buildings support themselves, how roofs stay up, and how buildings stay warm or cool are just a few of the topics discussed. Index.

Brown, David J. *The Random House Book of How Things Were Built.* Illus. Random House 1991 (LB 0-679-92044-7) (pap. 0-679-82044-2) 144pp.

Detailed diagrams and illustrations show many notable structures throughout history. Students will enjoy looking at the Tower of London, the Pantheon, the Colosseum, the Great Pyramid, and the Hoover Dam. Glossary and index.

Lynch, Anne. *Great Buildings.* Illus. Time-Life Books 1996 (cloth 0-8094-9371-3)

Fallingwater is, of course, one of the buildings in this beautiful collection of monuments, cathedrals, palaces, stadiums, and more. Young and old readers alike will enjoy browsing through this book. Glossary and index. Part of the Discoveries Library series.

Related Books for Older Readers

Giblin, James Cross. *The Skyscraper Book.* Illus. by Anthony Kramer. Photographs by David Anderson. HarperCollins 1981 (LB 0-690-04155-1) (cloth 0-690-04154-3) 96pp.

The skyscraper evolved in Chicago from the necessity of replacing structures lost in the great Chicago fire. Louis Sullivan became one of the leading architects of skyscrapers, and his vision influenced many of his colleagues, including Frank Lloyd Wright. This is a fascinating book with wonderful details about design and construction. Facts about well-known skyscrapers, glossary of architectural terms, bibliography, and index.

Wright, Orville (1871–1948), and his brother **Wilbur** (1867–1912), American aviation pioneers, in 1903 flew sustained flights at Kitty Hawk, North Carolina, in a plane powered by an engine they had built. The brothers later formed an aircraft manufacturing plant.

In one of the most famous photographs ever taken, the Wright Flyer *takes off on the world's first successful airplane flight at 10:35* A.M. *on December 17, 1903. Orville is at the controls, while Wilbur runs alongside. Estimated distance and time: 120 feet in 12 seconds.*
(Photo caption, Freedman, p. 79)

Biographies for Younger Readers

Tames, Richard. *Wright Brothers.* Illus. Franklin Watts 1990 (LB 0-531-14002-4) 32pp.

An entertaining look at the development of flying with many explanatory drawings and photographs. Section on where to find further information, list of important dates, glossary, and index. Part of the Lifetimes series.

Biographies for Older Readers

Freedman, Russell. *Wright Brothers: How They Invented the Airplane.* Illus. Holiday House 1991 (cloth 0-8234-0875-2) 1994 (pap. 0-8234-1082-X) 132pp.

This book, a Newbery Award winner, gives a very readable account of how two self-taught bicycle mechanics solved problems that had baffled scientists and engineers for generations. Almost 100 photographs by the Wright brothers and their comtemporaries are included, along with many drawings explaining the mechanics of flight. Index.

Reynolds, Quentin. ***Wright Brothers: Pioneers of American Aviation.*** Illus. Random House 1981 (pap. 0-394-84700-8) 160pp.

Written in story format, here is a book on the Wright brothers with information about kite making, the bicycle business, typhoid fever, making a glider, Kitty Hawk and the Wrights' flying machines. Part of the Landmark series.

Related Books for Younger Readers

Berliner, Don. ***Before the Wright Brothers.*** Illus. Lerner Publications 1990 (LB 0-8225-1588-1) 72pp.

Berliner describes the concepts and experiments that led to the first powered flight, mentioning such key figures as William Henson, Otto Lilienthal, Samuel Langley, and Orville and Wilbur Wright. List of further readings and index. Part of the Space & Aviation series.

Taylor, Richard L. ***The First Solo Flight Around the World: The Story of Wiley Post and His Airplane, the "Winnie Mae."*** Illus. Franklin Watts 1993 (LB 0-531-20160-0) 64pp.

Wiley Post's record-setting solo flight around the world in 1933 is described. List of further readings and index. Part of the First Book series.

Related Books for Older Readers

Berliner, Don. ***Aviation: Reaching for the Sky.*** Illus. Oliver Press 1997 (LB 1-881508-33-1) 144pp.

Reading about the risks people took and the creativity of their efforts to fly is fascinating. In this book students will find information about the dirigible, glider, airplane, seaplane, helicopter, and more. List of "Important Events in Aviation History," glossary, bibliography, and index. Part of the Innovators series.

Stacey, Tom. ***Airplanes: The Lure of Flight.*** Illus. Lucent 1990 (LB 1-56006-203-7) 96pp.

Many people have dreamed of flying. The ancient Greek myth of Daedalus focuses on flight as do drawings by Leonardo da Vinci. Balloons and gliders led to experiments with powered flight, including the efforts of the Wright brothers. The chapters in this book provide a chronological look at aircraft, including the rockets of the space age. Glossary, bibliography, and index. Part of the Encyclopedia of Discovery and Invention series.

Yeager, Charles E. "Chuck" (1923–), a U.S. Air Force test pilot, in 1947 became the first man to break the sound barrier when he piloted the Bell X-1 airplane at a speed of 670 miles per hour in level flight. Tom Wolfe's book *The Right Stuff* featured Yeager as its main character.

Biographies for Older Readers

Levinson, Nancy Smiler. *Chuck Yeager: The Man Who Broke the Sound Barrier.* Walker and Company 1988 (o.p.) 133pp.

Breaking the sound barrier for the first time and amputating a companion's leg in World War II are just two examples of Yeager's bravery and persistence. Glossary and index. Part of the Science Biography series.

Related Books for Younger Readers

Johnstone, Michael. *Planes.* Illus. Dorling Kindersley 1994 (pap. 1-56458-520-4) 32pp.

Listed as a book for younger readers, this is actually full of technical flight information that would fascinate any person interested in flight—with cross-sections of many planes, both historic and modern, including the Concorde. Timeline with drawings of historic, glossary, and index. Part of the Look Inside Cross-Sections series.

Kerrod, Robin. *Amazing Flying Machines.* Illus. Alfred A. Knopf 1992 (LB 0-679-92765-4) (pap. 0-679-82765-X) 32pp.

Young students will enjoy browsing through this collection of short pieces of text and pictures of flying machines throughout history. Index. Part of the Eyewitness Juniors series.

Taylor, Richard L. *The First Supersonic Flight: Captain Charles E. Yeager Breaks the Sound Barrier.* Illus. Franklin Watts 1994 (LB 0-531-20177-5) 64pp.

A good beginning point for research, this book covers the problems of high-speed flight and also Yeager's historic flight. Section on facts and statistics, lists of important dates and further readings, and index. Part of the First Book series.

Yeltsin, Boris Nikolayevich (1931–),

president of Russia since 1990, played a key role in the formation of the Russian Commonwealth of Independent States following the collapse of the Soviet Union. He initiated many internal economic and social reforms and forged closer ties with the West.

Biographies for Older Readers

Ayer, Eleanor H. *Boris Yeltsin: Man of the People.* Illus. Dillon Press 1992 (o.p.) 144pp.

This detailed biography describes not only Yeltsin's life but also the political upheaval in the recent history of the former Soviet Union. This is a great choice for research. It is thorough and well-organized, making fine use of quotations. Timeline, chapter notes, glossary, bibliography, and index. Part of the People in Focus series.

Lambroza, Shlomo. *Boris Yeltsin.* Illus. Rourke 1993 (cloth 0-86625-482-X)

Lambroza places Yeltsin in historical context, with details of Russian history and a comparison of the past and present structure of Russian government. Along with color and black-and-white photographs, there is a list of key figures in Russian and Soviet history. Timeline, glossary, bibliography, media resources, and index. Part of the World Leaders series.

Miller, Calvin Craig. *Boris Yeltsin: First President of Russia.* Illus. Morgan Reynolds 1994 (LB 1-883846-08-0) 144pp.

Chapters feature Yeltsin's many roles: "Farm Boy," "Factory Boss," "People's Champion," and "President Yeltsin." Miller describes Yeltsin's childhood during the reign of Stalin and his adult political career, including his relationship with Mikhail Gorbachev. Chronology, chapter notes, glossary, bibliography, and index. Part of the Champions of Freedom series.

Related Books for Younger Readers

Cumming, David. *Russia.* Illus. Thomson Learning 1995 (LB 1-56847-240-4) 48pp.

Boris Yeltsin's Russia is well illustrated in this attractive book. Color photographs and maps, along with short pieces of information and newspaper quotes, give a bleak picture of food shortages, the Mafia, the homeless, and drug use. List of further information, glossary, and index. Part of the Modern Industrial World series.

Kallen, Stuart A. *Gorbachev/Yeltsin: The Fall of Communism.* Illus. Abdo & Daughters 1992 (LB 1-56239-105-4)

The format of this book makes the information accessible to students in upper elementary and middle school. The issues of the collapse of the Soviet Union are briefly presented. Glossary and index. Part of the Rise & Fall of the Soviet Union series.

Our Century: 1980–1990. Illus. Gareth Stevens 1993 (LB 0-8368-1040-6) 64pp.

The 1980s were full of historical events: the Berlin Wall was torn down, the Chernobyl disaster occurred in Russia, and Yeltsin became a member of the National Congress in the Soviet Union's first free elections since 1917. This book is a pleasure to look at, with its many black-and-white photographs, political cartoons, and newspaper articles. Lists of places to write or visit and further readings, glossary, and index. Part of the Our Century series.

Related Books for Older Readers

Warren, James A. *Cold War: The American Crusade Against World Communism, 1945–1991.* Illus. Lothrop, Lee & Shepard 1996 (cloth 0-688-10596-3)

After World War II, the United States and the Soviet Union were locked in an antagonistic relationship that influenced world politics and policies. This book profiles the rivalry between these two countries and includes information about Berlin, Korea, and Vietnam. This is a detailed analysis of a complex era. Chronology, notes, bibliography, and index. Two appendices look at budgetary issues, including defense spending during these years.

Zaharias, Mildred ("Babe") Didrikson

(1914–1956), an American athlete, won two gold medals in the javelin and hurdles at the 1932 Olympic Games. She also excelled at golf and won the U.S. Open three times.

Biographies for Younger Readers

Sanford, William R., and Carl R. Green. *Babe Didrikson Zaharias.* Illus. Crestwood House 1993 (LB 0-89686-736-6) 48pp.

This brief book provides a quick overview of the life of "Babe" Didrikson Zaharias. Many of the black-and-white photographs show Zaharias in action—shooting baskets, golfing, playing tennis, and receiving a gold medal. One fun feature is a trivia quiz. There are questions placed in boxed sections throughout the book; the answers appear in the back of the book. Glossary, bibliography, and index. Part of the Sports Immortals series.

Biographies for Older Readers

Lynn, Elizabeth A. *Babe Didrikson Zaharias.* Illus. Chelsea House 1989 (LB 1-55546-684-2) 112pp.

The opening chapter describes how Zaharias was "The Best at Everything." Subsequent chapters look at her training, her career, and her battle with cancer, which ultimately took her life in 1956. This is a well-organized book that will be a good choice for students doing research. Chronology, bibliography, and index. Part of the American Women of Achievement series.

Related Books for Younger Readers

Jennings, Jay. *Comebacks: Heroic Returns.* Illus. Silver Burdett 1991 (o.p.) 64pp.

Young sports fans will find great pleasure in these stories of five athletes who made courageous comebacks in their careers. Zaharias's amazing golf statistics, even after a bout with cancer, are inspirational. Along with detailing her sports triumphs, the chapter explains some simple golf terms, includes her sports statistics, and shows several photographs that demonstrate her wonderful spirit. Other athletes in the book include cyclist Greg LeMond, football player Rocky Bleier, gymnast Olga Korbut, and pitcher Dave Dravecky. Index. Part of the Sports Triumphs series.

Krull, Kathleen. *Lives of the Athletes: Thrills, Spills (And What the Neighbors Thought)*. Illus. by Kathryn Hewitt. Harcourt 1997 (cloth 0-15-200806-3)

Both humorous and informative, this book profiles 20 very different athletes. Each athlete is introduced with one line: Zaharias's is "getting goosebumps." Zaharias is described as a "team of one." Bibliography.

Our Century: 1930–1940. Illus. Gareth Stevens 1993 (LB 0-8368-1035-X) 64pp.

The 1930s encompassed much turmoil: the Nazis rose to power in Germany, the king of England abdicated his throne for the woman he loved, America was deep in an economic depression, and Babe Didrikson starred in the 1932 Olympics. This book is a pleasure to look at, with its many black-and white-photographs, political cartoons, and newspaper articles. Lists of further readings and places to write or visit, glossary, and index. Part of the Our Century series.

Related Books for Older Readers

Macy, Sue. *Winning Ways: A Photohistory of American Women in Sports.* Illus. with photographs. Henry Holt 1996 (cloth 0-8050-4147-8) 160pp.

From bicycle riding in the 1800s to the women's hockey teams competing in the 1998 Olympics, this is a record of women's sports history. Zaharias is but one of the many amazing female athletes covered. Noteworthy events since the 1800s are included, along with such issues as gender, homophobia, African Americans, and sports reporting. Chronology, list of further readings, and index.

Author Index

T

Title Index

G

Subject Index

The Subject Index groups biographees by broad category, offering connections between individuals of different backgrounds and different eras. The book is organized alphabetically by biographee.

Abolitionists

Brown, John
Douglass, Frederick
Stowe, Harriet Beecher
Truth, Sojourner
Tubman, Harriet

Activists

Addams, Jane
Angelou, Maya
Anthony, Susan B.
Ashe, Arthur
Blackwell, Elizabeth
Bly, Nellie
Carmichael, Stokely
Chavez, Cesar
Edelman, Marian Wright
Farrakhan, Louis
Gandhi, Mohandas
Hutchinson, Anne
Jackson, Jesse
Johnson, James Weldon
Jones, Mother
King, Coretta Scott
King, Martin Luther, Jr.
Malcolm X
Mendes, Chico
Randolph, A. Philip
Robeson, Paul
Stanton, Elizabeth Cady
Steinem, Gloria
Walesa, Lech

African Americans

Ali, Muhammad
Anderson, Marian
Angelou, Maya
Armstrong, Louis "Satchmo"
Ashe, Arthur
Banneker, Benjamin
Beckwourth, James
Bethune, Mary McLeod
Bluford, Guion
Bunche, Ralph J.
Campanella, Roy
Carmichael, Stokely
Carver, George Washington
Chisholm, Shirley
Coleman, Bessie
Douglass, Frederick
Drew, Charles
Du Bois, W. E. B.
Dunbar, Paul Laurence
Edelman, Marian Wright
Ellington, Duke
Ellison, Ralph
Farrakhan, Louis
Forten, Charlotte
Hamer, Fannie Lou
Henson, Matthew
Hughes, Langston
Hurston, Zora Neale
Jackson, Jesse
Johnson, Isaac
Johnson, James Weldon

Jordan, Barbara
King, Coretta Scott
King, Martin Luther, Jr.
Malcolm X
Marshall, Thurgood
Matzeliger, Jan
Morgan, Garrett
Owens, Jesse
Paige, Leroy "Satchel"
Parks, Rosa
Powell, Colin
Randolph, A. Philip
Robeson, Paul
Robinson, Jackie
Rudolph, Wilma
Truth, Sojourner
Tubman, Harriet
Turner, Nat
Walker, Madam C. J.
Walker, Maggie Lena
Washington, Booker T.
Wells-Barnett, Ida B.
Wheatley, Phillis
Williams, Daniel Hale
Winfrey, Oprah

American Revolution

Adams, Abigail
Adams, John
Franklin, Benjamin
Hamilton, Alexander
Henry, Patrick

Jefferson, Thomas
Madison, James
Revere, Paul
Ross, Betsy
Washington, George

Ancient Egypt
Cleopatra
Tutankhamen

Ancient Rome
Caesar, Augustus
Caesar, Julius
Hannibal

Arts and photography
Audubon, John James
Bourke-White, Margaret
Cassatt, Mary
Da Vinci, Leonardo
Lange, Dorothea
Michelangelo
Peale, Charles Wilson
Wright, Frank Lloyd

Authors
Alcott, Louisa May
Angelou, Maya
Brontë family
Cather, Willa
Churchill, Sir Winston
Dickens, Charles
Douglass, Frederick
Du Bois, W. E. B.
Dunbar, Paul Laurence
Edmonds, Emma
Ellison, Ralph
Forten, Charlotte
Hughes, Langston
Hurston, Zora Neale
Lazarus, Emma
Reiss, Johanna
Shakespeare, William
Singer, Isaac Bashevis
Thoreau, Henry David
Twain, Mark
Wheatley, Phillis
White, E. B.
Whitman, Walt

Aviation and space
Armstrong, Neil
Blériot, Louis
Bluford, Guion
Coleman, Bessie
Earhart, Amelia
Lindbergh, Charles
McAuliffe, Christa
Wright, Orville and Wright, Wilbur
Yeager, Chuck

Business and industry
Carnegie, Andrew
Eastman, George
Ford, Henry
Gates, Bill
Matzeliger, Jan
Rockefeller, John D.
Strauss, Levi
Walker, Madam C. J.
Walker, Maggie Lena

Civil rights *see also* **Human Rights**
Carmichael, Stokely
Du Bois, W. E. B.
Hamer, Fannie Lou
Jackson, Jesse
King, Coretta Scott
King, Martin Luther, Jr.
Parks, Rosa
Randolph, A. Philip
Wells-Barnett, Ida B.

Civil War
Barton, Clara
Davis, Jefferson
Edmonds, Emma
Farragut, David Glasgow
Grant, Ulysses Simpson
Jackson, Thomas "Stonewall"
Johnson, Andrew
Lee, Robert E.
Lincoln, Abraham
Pinkerton, Allan
Tubman, Harriet

Disabled persons
Braille, Louis
Gallaudet, Thomas H.

Keller, Helen
Rudolph, Wilma

Educators
Bethune, Mary McLeod
Blackwell, Elizabeth
Forten, Charlotte
Gallaudet, Thomas H.
Washington, Booker T.
Williams, Daniel Hale

Environmentalists
Carson, Rachel
Carver, George Washington
Cousteau, Jacques
Mendes, Chico
Muir, John
Powell, John Wesley

Exploration and conquest
Alexander the Great
Amundsen, Roald
Columbus, Christopher
Cook, James
Cortés, Hernán
De Soto, Hernando
Drake, Sir Francis
Eriksson, Leif
Frémont, John Charles
Hall, Daniel Weston
Henry the Navigator
Henson, Matthew
Hillary, Sir Edmund
Isabella I
La Salle, René-Robert
Lewis, Meriwether and Clark, William
Magellan, Ferdinand
Muir, John
Peary, Robert
Pizarro, Francisco
Polo, Marco
Powell, John Wesley
Smith, John
Vespucci, Amerigo

Film and entertainment
Disney, Walt
Robeson, Paul

Chronology

1400 B.C.– 0

Tutankhamen **1343 B.C.–1325 B.C.**
Alexander the Great **356 B.C.–323 B.C.**
Archimedes **287 B.C.–212 B.C.**
Hannibal **247? B.C.–183? B.C.**
Caesar, Julius (Gaius Julius Caesar) **100 B.C.–44 B.C.**
Herod the Great **73 B.C.–4 B.C.**
Cleopatra **69 B.C.–30 B.C.**
Caesar, Augustus **63 B.C.–A.D. 14**

A.D. 0– 1700

Eriksson, Leif **975–1020**
Polo, Marco **1254?–1324?**
Henry the Navigator **1394–1460**
Gutenberg, Johann **1397?–1468**
Isabella I **1451–1504**
Columbus, Christopher **1451–1506**
Leonardo da Vinci **1452–1519**
Vespucci, Amerigo **1454–1512**
Pizarro, Francisco **1475?–1541**
Michelangelo Buonarroti **1475–1564**
Magellan, Ferdinand **1480?–1521**
Cortés, Hernán **1485–1547**
De Soto, Hernando **1500?–1542**
Elizabeth I **1533–1603**
Drake, Sir Francis **1540–1596**
Shakespeare, William **1564–1616**
Galileo **1564–1642**
Smith, John **1579–1631**
Hutchinson, Anne **1591–1643**
Pocahontas **1595?–1617**
Leeuwenhoek, Antonie van **1632–1723**
Philip **1639?–1676**
Newton, Sir Isaac **1642–1727**

La Salle, René-Robert Cavelier, Sleur de **1643–1687**
Halley, Edmund, or Edmond **1656–1742**

A.D. 1701– 1800

Franklin, Benjamin **1706–1790**
Serra, Junípero **1713–1784**
Cook, James **1728–1779**
Banneker, Benjamin **1731–1806**
Washington, George **1732–1799**
Washington, Martha **1732–1802**
Boone, Daniel **1734–1820**
Revere, Paul **1735–1818**
Adams, John **1735–1826**
Henry, Patrick **1736–1799**
Peale, Charles Wilson **1741–1827**
Lavoisier, Antoine Laurent **1743–1794**
Toussaint L'Ouverture, François Dominique **1743–1803**
Jefferson, Thomas **1743–1826**
Adams, Abigail Smith **1744–1818**
Madison, James **1751–1836**
Ross, Betsy **1752–1836**
Wheatley, Phillis **1753?–1784**
Hamilton, Alexander **1755?–1804**
Monroe, James **1758–1831**
Fulton, Robert **1765–1815**
Whitney, Eli **1765–1825**
Sequoyah **1766?–1843**
Jackson, Andrew **1767–1845**
Adams, John Quincy **1767–1848**
Tecumseh **1768?–1813**
Bonaparte, Napoleon **1769–1821**
Clarke, William **1770–1838**
Lewis, Meriwether **1774–1809**
Appleseed, Johnny **1774–1845**
Key, Francis Scott **1779–1843**

Bolívar, Simón **1783–1830**
Sacagawea **1784–1884?**
Audubon, John James **1785–1851**
Crockett, Davy **1786–1836**
Gallaudet, Thomas H. **1787–1851**
Faraday, Michael **1791–1867**
Houston, Samuel **1793–1863**
Truth, Sojourner **1797?–1883**
Beckwourth, James **1798–1867**
Turner, Nat **1800–1831**
Brown, John **1800–1859**

A.D. 1801–1850

Farragut, David Glasgow **1801–1870**
Lee, Robert E. **1807–1870**
Johnson, Andrew **1808–1875**
Davis, Jefferson **1808–1889**
Braille, Louis **1809–1852**
Lincoln, Abraham **1809–1865**
Darwin, Charles Robert **1809–1882**
Stowe, Harriet Beecher **1811–1896**
Dickens, Charles **1812–1870**
Frémont, John Charles **1813–1890**
Stanton, Elizabeth Cady **1815–1902**
Brontë, Charlotte **1816–1855**
Thoreau, Henry David **1817–1862**
Douglass, Frederick **1817?–1895**
Brontë, Emily **1818–1848**
Lincoln, Mary Todd **1818–1882**
Mitchell, Maria **1818–1889**
Pinkerton, Allan **1819–1884**
Whitman, Walt **1819–1892**
Anthony, Susan B. **1820–1906**
Brontë, Anne **1820–1849**
Nightingale, Florence **1820–1910**
Tubman, Harriet **1820?–1913**
Blackwell, Elizabeth **1821–1910**
Barton, Clara **1821–1912**
Grant, Ulysses Simpson **1822–1885**
Pasteur, Louis **1822–1895**
Red Cloud **1822–1909**
Jackson, Thomas Jonathan "Stonewall"
   1824–1863
Strauss, Levi **1829?–1902**
Geronimo **1829?–1909**

Jones, Mary Harris "Mother" **1830–1930**
Sitting Bull **1831?–1890**
Alcott, Louisa May **1832–1888**
Powell, John Wesley **1834–1902**
Twain, Mark **1835–1910**
Carnegie, Andrew **1835–1919**
Cleveland, Stephen Grover **1837–1908**
Forten, Charlotte L. **1837–1914**
Muir, John **1838–1914**
Liliuokalani **1838–1917**
Rockefeller, John D. **1839–1937**
Joseph, Chief **1840?–1904**
Hall, Daniel Weston **1841–?**
Edmonds, Emma **1841–1898**
Crazy Horse **1842–1877**
Ishi **1842–1916**
Johnson, Isaac **1844–1905**
Cassatt, Mary **1844–1926**

Cody, William F. "Buffalo Bill" **1846–1917**
Bell, Alexander Graham **1847–1922**
Edison, Thomas Alva **1847–1931**
Parker, Quanah **1848–1911**
Lazarus, Emma **1849–1887**

A.D. 1851–1900

Matzeliger, Jan Ernst **1852–1889**
Eastman, George **1854–1932**
Washington, Booker T. **1856–1915**

Peary, Robert E. **1856–1920**
Wilson, Woodrow **1856–1924**
Roosevelt, Theodore **1858–1919**
Williams, Daniel Hale **1858–1931**
Eastman, Charles **1858–1939**
Oakley, Annie **1860–1926**
Low, Juliette Gordon **1860–1927**
Addams, Jane **1860–1935**
Wells-Barnett, Ida B. **1862–1931**
Ford, Henry **1863–1947**
Carver, George Washington
    1864?–1943
Mayo, Charles Horace **1865–1939**
Henson, Matthew A. **1866–1955**
Wright, Wilbur **1867–1912**
Walker, Madam C. J. **1867–1919**
Bly, Nellie **1867–1922**
Walker, Maggie Lena **1867–1934**
Curie, Marie **1867–1934**
Wright, Frank Lloyd **1867–1959**
Du Bois, W. E. B. **1868–1963**
Gandhi, Mohandas Karamchand
    1869–1948
Lenin, Vladimir Ilyich **1870–1924**
Johnson, James Weldon **1871–1938**
Wright, Orville **1871–1948**
Sabin, Florence Rena **1871–1953**
Dunbar, Paul Laurence **1872–1906**
Amundsen, Roald **1872–1928**
Blériot, Louis **1872–1936**
Cather, Willa Sibert **1873–1947**
Marconi, Guglielmo Marchese
    1874–1937
Hoover, Herbert Clark **1874–1964**
Churchill, Sir Winston Leonard Spencer
    1874–1965
Bethune, Mary McLeod **1875–1955**
Villa, Pancho **1877–1923**

Morgan, Garrett **1877–1963**
Stalin, Joseph **1879–1953**
Einstein, Albert **1879–1955**
MacArthur, Douglas **1880–1964**
Keller, Helen Adams **1880–1968**
Fleming, Sir Alexander **1881–1955**
Goddard, Robert Hastings **1882–1945**
Roosevelt, Franklin Delano **1882–1945**
Roosevelt, Eleanor **1884–1962**
Truman, Harry S. **1884–1972**
Ben-Gurion, David **1886–1973**
Thorpe, Jim **1888–1953**
Hitler, Adolf **1889–1945**
Hubble, Edwin Powell **1889–1953**
Randolph, A. Philip **1889–1979**
Eisenhower, Dwight David **1890–1969**
Coleman, Bessie **1893–1926**
Mao Zedong **1893–1976**
Ruth, George Herman "Babe"
    1895–1948
Lange, Dorothea **1895–1965**
Earhart, Amelia **1897–1937**
Anderson, Marian **1897–1993**
Robeson, Paul **1898–1976**
Meir, Golda **1898–1978**
Ellington, Duke **1899–1974**
White, Elwyn Brooks **1899–1985**
Armstrong, (Daniel) Louis "Satchmo"
    1900–1971

A.D. 1901–1925

Hurston, Zora Neale **1901–1960**
Disney, Walt **1901–1966**
Mead, Margaret **1901–1978**
Hughes, Langston **1902–1967**
Lindbergh, Charles Augustus **1902–1974**
Gehrig, Lou **1903–1941**
Drew, Charles Richard **1904–1950**
Oppenheimer, J. Robert **1904–1967**

Bourke-White, Margaret **1904–1971**
Bunche, Ralph J. **1904–1971**
Singer, Isaac Bashevis **1904–1991**
Hammarskjöld, Dag **1905–1961**
Tombaugh, Clyde **1906–**
Farnsworth, Philo Taylor **1906–1971**
Paige, Leroy "Satchel" **1906?–1982**
Carson, Rachel Louise **1907–1964**
Murrow, Edward R. **1908–1965**
Johnson, Lyndon Baines **1908–1973**
Schindler, Oskar **1908–1974**
Marshall, Thurgood **1908–1993**
Cousteau, Jacques Yves **1910–1997**
Teresa, Mother **1910–1997**
Reagan, Ronald **1911–**
Wallenberg, Raoul **1912–?**
Parks, Rosa **1913–**
Owens, Jesse **1913–1981**
Begin, Menachem **1913–1992**
Nixon, Richard Milhous **1913–1994**
Zaharias, Mildred **1914–1956**
Ellison, Ralph **1914–1994**
Salk, Jonas **1914–1995**
Kennedy, John Fitzgerald **1917–1963**
Hamer, Fannie Lou **1917–1977**
Mandela, Nelson **1918–**
Sadat, Anwar al- **1918–1981**
Hillary, Sir Edmund Percival **1919–**
Robinson, Jackie **1919–1972**
Friedan, Betty Naomi **1921–**
Campanella, Roy **1921–1993**
Yeager, Chuck **1923–**
Bush, George Herbert Walker **1924–**
Carter, James Earl, Jr. **1924–**
Chisholm, Shirley **1924–**
Thatcher, Margaret **1925–**
Ippisch, Hanneke Eikema **1925–**
Malcolm X **1925–1965**

A.D. **1926– Present**

Castro, Fidel **1926–**
King, Coretta Scott **1927–**
Chavez, Cesar **1927–1993**
Angelou, Maya **1928–**
Frank, Anne **1929–1945**

King, Martin Luther, Jr. **1929–1968**
O'Connor, Sandra Day **1930–**
Armstrong, Neil Alden **1930–**
Gorbachev, Mikhail Sergeyevich **1931–**
Tutu, Desmond Mpilo **1931–**
Yeltsin, Boris Nikolayevich **1931–**
Reiss, Johanna **1932–**
Ginsburg, Ruth Bader **1933–**
Farrakhan, Louis **1933–**
Goodall, Jane **1934–**
Schwarzkopf, H. Norman **1934–**
Steinem, Gloria **1934–**
Clemente, Roberto Walker **1934–1972**
Dalai Lama **1935–**

Jordan, Barbara Charline **1936–1996**
Powell, Colin L. **1937–**
Hussein, Saddam **1937–**
Reno, Janet **1938–**
Edelman, Marian Wright **1939–**
Rudolph, Wilma **1940–1994**
Jackson, Jesse **1941–**
Carmichael, Stokely **1941–**
Ali, Muhammad **1942–**
Bluford, Guion **1942–**
Walesa, Lech **1943–**
Sasaki, Sadako **1943–1955**
Ashe, Arthur R. **1943–1993**
Mendes, Chico **1944–1988**
Mankiller, Wilma **1945–**
Clinton, William Jefferson **1946–**
McAuliffe, Christa **1948–1986**
Bhutto, Benazir **1953–**
Winfrey, Oprah **1954–**
Gates, William **1955–**

Photo Credits